C. P. E. Bach Studies

# C. P. E. BACH STUDIES

Edited by

## Stephen L. Clark

Clarendon Press · Oxford

1988

Oxford University Press, Walton Street, Oxford OX2 6DP

Oxford New York Toronto
Delhi Bombay Calcutta Madras Karachi
Petaling Jaya Singapore Hong Kong Tokyo
Nairobi Dar es Salaam Cape Town
Melbourne Auckland
and associated companies in
Berlin Ibadan

Oxford is a trade mark of Oxford University Press

British Library Cataloguing in Publication Data
Clark, Stephen L.
C.P.E. Bach studies
1. Composers—Germany—Biography
I. Title
780'.92'4   ML410.B16
ISBN 0-19-316412-4

Library of Congress Cataloging in Publication Data
C.P.E. Bach studies/edited by Stephen L. Clark.
"C.P.E. Bach in literature": p.
Includes indexes.
1. Bach, Carl Philipp Emanuel, 1714–1788. 2. Bach, Carl Philipp
Emanuel, 1714–1788—Criticism and interpretation. I. Clark,
Stephen L. II. title: Carl Philipp Emanuel Bach studies.
ML410.B16C2   1988   780'.92'4—dc19   87-30786

Set by the Alden Press, Oxford.
Printed in Great Britain
at the University Printing House, Oxford
by David Stanford
Printer to the University

To

E. Eugene Helm

# Preface

RACHEL WADE and I came up with the idea for this volume of essays about C. P. E. Bach over a dinner at the 1984 annual meeting of the American Musicological Society in Philadelphia. We decided that the coincidence of the two-hundredth anniversary of the death of Bach on 14 December 1988 and E. Eugene Helm's sixtieth birthday on 23 January 1988, together with the burgeoning state of C. P. E. Bach research in the 1970s and 1980s, provided the appropriate circumstances for a book of articles by scholars active in the field to be published in 1988. Although I assumed the editorial responsibilities myself, I want to acknowledge Rachel's support and advice throughout the project.

There are two particular hallmarks of C. P. E. Bach scholarship over the last decade: Helm's thematic catalogue of Bach's works, and the inception of the edition of the composer's collected works under the direction of Helm and Wade at the University of Maryland. The latter project has been supported since 1983 by a grant from the National Endowment for the Humanities, and Oxford University Press will be publishing the first volumes in the near future. Virtually every article in this book depends on Helm's scholarship and, more importantly, on his generosity in sharing information from his catalogue before its publication. We, the authors, dedicate these essays to him.

The general guideline provided for contributors was simply that submissions were to relate to the life and works of C. P. E. Bach. The broad range of topics that resulted from this solicitation fall into some general categories. Two of the essays are thorough genre studies: Darrell Berg treats Bach's character pieces and Michelle Fillion his trios. Both studies consider questions of authenticity, chronology, and terminology as well as style.

The contributions of Pamela Fox and David Schulenberg continue the approach taken in their recent dissertations, which shed new light on the originality of C. P. E. Bach's style, considered on its own terms. Susan Wollenberg adopts a similar analytic viewpoint in her look at humour in some of Bach's works.

Concertos provide the focus for the articles by Shelley Davis and Jane Stevens; Davis examines recapitulatory tuttis and Stevens the 'piano climax'. Both studies place Bach's concertos in relation to those by his contemporaries.

The essays by Howard Serwer and myself are related by their use of Bach's correspondence to capture aspects of his personality and his dealings with publishers. We both relied on Ernst Suchalla's recent edition of Bach's letters to Breitkopf and Forkel, another significant contribution to the field.

Hans-Günter Ottenberg takes a close look at the relationship between Bach and Carl Friedrich Zelter, calling attention to a draft of a C. P. E. Bach biography that Zelter had planned. His article is complemented by Elias Kulukundis's survey of the sources of Bach's music formerly in the Berlin Singakademie, which Zelter directed from 1800 until 1832.

Etienne Darbellay uses Bach's treatise, *Versuch über die wahre Art das Clavier zu spielen*, for some new insights into the composer's aesthetic. He identifies a paradox between the composer's precise notation and the role of the performer in interpreting Bach's works. Christopher Hogwood provides a translation of a treatise by Ernst Wilhelm Wolf that is in the tradition of Bach's *Versuch*. Wolf's debt to 'Vater Bach in Hamburg', as he phrases it, is obvious.

Douglas Lee makes a convincing case, using primarily calligraphic evidence, for Bach's authorship of a fantasia previously attributed to Christoph Nichelmann. Rachel Wade considers a number of editing problems stemming from the filiation of sources of Bach's works; her article grapples with issues that all critical editors must confront.

In addition to the contributors, several individuals and institutions were essential to the success of the book. Philip Whitmore translated the article by Ottenberg, and Richard Strawn was an enormous help with the translation of the Darbellay essay. Maxine Dreyer spent numerous patient hours photocopying various versions of the submissions, and Debbie Wagers assisted with the voluminous correspondence. A number of libraries were helpful in providing facsimiles and permission for their publication: the Deutsche Staatsbibliothek, Berlin/DDR, Musikabteilung, for Facsimiles 1 and 2 in Berg's article and for both facsimiles in Lee's article; the Goethe- und Schiller Archiv, Weimar, for the facsimiles in Ottenberg's article; the Staatsbibliothek Preussischer Kulturbesitz, Berlin, Musikabteilung, for the facsimiles in Fillion's article and for Facsimile 2a in Wade's article; the British Library, London, for the facsimile in Serwer's article; the Library of Congress, Washington, DC, for the facsimile in Hogwood's article; Music Library, University of Michigan for Facsimiles 3–6 in Berg's article. Miami University, Mills College, the board of the Music Faculty, Oxford University, the Hilles Publication Fund of Yale University, and others were generous with subventions for the engraving of musical examples. Finally, Bruce Phillips, music books editor at Oxford University Press, encouraged the project from the beginning. He and his capable colleagues made the book a reality.

*June, 1987* Stephen L. Clark

# Contents

# Notes on Contributors

*Darrell Berg* is on the faculty of the St Louis Conservatory of Music. She received her Ph.D. in musicology from the State University of New York at Buffalo. She is the editor of *The Collected Works for Solo Keyboard by Carl Philipp Emanuel Bach* (New York, 1985).

*Stephen Clark* received his Ph.D. in musicology from Princeton University. He has done research on C. P. E. Bach's choral works and correspondence.

*Etienne Darbellay* is on the faculty of Geneva University. He received his Ph.D. in musicology from Fribourg University in Switzerland.

*Shelley Davis* is on the faculty of the University of Maryland. He received his Ph.D. in musicology from New York University.

*Michelle Fillion* is on the faculty of Mills College. She received her Ph.D. in musicology from Cornell University.

*Pamela Fox* is on the faculty of Miami University. She received her Ph.D. in musicology from the University of Cincinnati.

*Christopher Hogwood* is director of the Academy of Ancient Music.

*Elias N. Kulukundis* is an editor of concertos for the C. P. E. Bach Edition. He is also a collector of archival materials relating to C. P. E. Bach.

*Douglas Lee* is on the faculty of the Blair School of Music at Vanderbilt University. He received his Ph.D. in musicology from the University of Michigan. He has produced many writings on eighteenth-century composers, including thematic catalogues of the works of Franz Benda and Christoph Nichelmann.

*Hans-Günter Ottenberg* is on the faculty of the Technische Universität, Dresden. He received his Ph.D. in musicology from Humboldt University, Berlin. He has recently written a biography of C. P. E. Bach (Leipzig, 1982; English trans. Oxford, 1987).

*David Schulenberg* is on the faculty of Columbia University. He received his Ph.D. in musicology from the State University of New York at Stony Brook.

*Howard Serwer* is on the faculty of the University of Maryland, where he directs an annual Handel festival. He received his Ph.D in musicology from Yale University.

*Jane Stevens* is on the faculty of Yale University, where she received her Ph.D. in music history.

*Rachel Wade* is General Editor of the C. P. E. Bach Edition at the University of Maryland. She received her Ph.D. in musicology from New York University. She is the editor of *The Catalog of Carl Philipp Emanuel Bach's Estate* (New York, 1981).

*Susan Wollenberg* is a lecturer on the Faculty of Music at Oxford University, where she received her D.Phil. in music.

# Abbreviations

| | |
|---|---|
| *AfMw* | *Archiv für Musikwissenschaft* |
| *AlMz* | *Allgemeine Musik-Zeitung* |
| *AM* | *Acta Musicologica* |
| *AMZ* | *Allgemeine Musikalische Zeitung* |
| *BJ* | *Bach-Jahrbuch* |
| *BWV* | Wolfgang Schmieder, *Thematisch-systematisches Verzeichnis der Werke Joh. Seb. Bachs* (Leipzig, 1950) |
| *CJ* | *The Choral Journal* |
| *CM* | *Current Musicology* |
| *CMS* | *College Music Symposium* |
| *Essay* | C. P. E. Bach, *Essay on the True Art of Playing Keyboard Instruments*, trans. and ed. William J. Mitchell [see item 7 in bibliography] |
| *Geiringer Festschrift* | *Studies in Eighteenth-Century Music. A Tribute to Karl Geiringer on His Seventieth Birthday*, ed. H. C. Robbins Landon and Roger E. Chapman (New York, 1970) |
| H. | E. Eugene Helm, *Thematic Catalogue of the Works of C. P. E. Bach* [see item 151 in bibliography] |
| *Helm/Grove* | E. Eugene Helm, 'Bach ,Carl Philipp Emanuel', *New Grove*, vol. 1, 844–63 |
| *JAMS* | *Journal of the American Musicological Society* |
| *JM* | *Journal of Musicology* |
| *JMT* | *Journal of Music Theory* |
| *Mf* | *Die Musikforschung* |
| *MG* | *Musik und Gesellschaft* |
| *MGG* | *Die Musik in Geschichte und Gegenwart* (Kassel and Basel, 1949–68) |
| *MJ* | *Mozart-Jahrbuch* |
| *ML* | *Music and Letters* |
| *MM* | *Mens en Melodie* |
| *MMR* | *The Monthly Musical Record* |
| *MO* | *Musical Opinion* |
| *MQ* | *The Musical Quarterly* |
| *MR* | *The Music Review* |
| *MT* | *The Musical Times* |
| *MU* | *Musik im Unterricht* |

| | |
|---|---|
| NBA | *J. S. Bach: Neue Ausgabe sämtlicher Werke* (*Neue Bach-Ausgabe*) (Kassel and Basel, 1954– ) |
| New Grove | *The New Grove Dictionary of Music and Musicians* (London, 1980) |
| NMA | *W. A. Mozart: Neue Ausgabe sämtlicher Werke* (Kassel, 1955– ) |
| Notes | *Music Library Association: Notes* |
| NRMI | *Nuova rivista musicale italiana* |
| NV | *Nachlass-Verzeichniß* [see item 345 in bibliography] |
| NZfM | *Neue Zeitschrift für Musik* |
| PQ | *Piano Quarterly* |
| PRMA | *Proceedings of the Royal Musical Association* |
| RBM | *Revue Belge de Musicologie* |
| RdM | *Revue de musicologie* |
| RISM | *Répertoire international des sources musicales* |
| RMI | *Rivista musicale italiana* |
| SIMG | *Sammelbände der Internationalen Musik-Gesellschaft* |
| Suchalla/Briefe | Ernst Suchalla, ed., *Briefe von Carl Philipp Emanuel Bach an Johann Gottlob Immanuel Breitkopf und Johann Nikolaus Forkel* (Tutzing, 1985) [see item 334 in bibliography] |
| Versuch | C. P. E. Bach, *Versuch über die wahre Art das Clavier zu spielen* (Berlin, 1753, 1762) [see item 7 in bibliography] |
| W. | Alfred Wotquenne, *Catalogue thématique des oeuvres de Charles Philippe Emmanuel Bach (1714–1788)* (Leipzig, 1905) [see item 372 in bibliography] |
| ZfM | *Zeitschrift für Musik* |
| ZfMw | *Zeitschrift für Musikwissenschaft* |
| ZH | *Zeitschrift für Hausmusik* |
| ZIMG | *Zeitschrift der Internationalen Musikgesellschaft* |

## Library Abbreviations
## (following RISM)

| | |
|---|---|
| A Wgm | Vienna, Gesellschaft der Musikfreunde in Wien |
| A Wn | Vienna, Österreichische Nationalbibliothek |
| B Bc | Brussels, Conservatoire Royal de Musique, Bibliothèque |
| D-brd B | Berlin, Staatsbibliothek Preussischer Kulturbesitz |
| D-brd Hs | Hamburg, Staats- und Universitätsbibliothek |
| D-brd Kll | Kiel, Schleswig-Holsteinische Landesbibliothek |
| D-ddr Bds | Berlin/DDR, Deutsche Staatsbibliothek |
| D-ddr Dlb | Dresden, Sächsische Landesbibliothek |
| D-ddr LEm | Leipzig, Musikbibliothek der Stadt Leipzig |
| D-ddr WRgs | Weimar, Goethe- und Schiller-Archiv |
| DK Kmm | Copenhagen, Musikhistorisk Museum |

| | |
|---|---|
| DK Kv | Copenhagen, Københavus Universitets Musikvidenskabelige Institut |
| F Pn | Paris, Bibliothèque Nationale |
| GB Lbm | London, The British Library |
| US Wc | Washington, DC, The Library of Congress |

# C. P. E. Bach's Character Pieces and his Friendship Circle

## Darrell M. Berg

ACCORDING to his *Nachlass-Verzeichniß* (NV), Carl Philipp Emanuel Bach composed twenty-four character pieces for solo keyboard between the years 1754 and 1757:[1]

| 1754 | La Gause | H. 82/W. 117, 37 |
|------|----------|------------------|
|      | La Pott | H. 80/W. 117, 18 |
|      | La Borchward | H. 79/W. 117, 17 |
|      | La Boehmer | H. 81/W. 117, 26 |
| 1755 | La Philippine | H. 96/W. 117, 34 |
|      | La Gabriel | H. 97/W. 117, 35 |
|      | La Caroline | H. 98/W. 117, 39 |
|      | La Prinzette | H. 91/W. 117, 21 |
|      | L'Aly Rupalich | H. 95/W. 117, 27 |
|      | La Gleim | H. 89/W. 117, 19 |
|      | La Stahl | H. 94/W. 117, 25 |
|      | La Bergius | H. 90/W. 117, 20 |
|      | La Buchholtz | H. 93/W. 117, 24 |
|      | L'Herrmann | H. 92/W. 117, 23 |
| 1756 | La Capricieuse | H. 113/W. 117, 33 |
|      | La Complaisante | H. 109/W. 117, 28 |
|      | Les Langueurs tendres | H. 110/W. 117, 30 |
|      | La Journaliere | H. 112/W. 117, 32 |
|      | L'Irresolüe | H. 111/W. 117, 31 |
|      | La Louise | H. 114/W. 117, 36 |
| 1757 | La Xenophon et la Sybille | H. 123/W. 117, 29 |
|      | La Sophie | H. 125/W. 117, 40 |
|      | L'Ernestine | H. 124/W. 117, 38 |
|      | L'Auguste | H. 122/W. 117, 22 |

[1] The *Nachlass-Verzeichniß* (NV) was published by his widow a year and a half after his death. It is probable that Bach prepared this catalogue himself in his last years; see Ernst Suchalla, *Die Orchestersinfonien Carl Philipp Emanuel Bachs* (Augsburg, 1968), 153, and Darrell M. Berg, 'Towards a Catalogue of the Keyboard Sonatas of C. P. E. Bach', *JAMS*, 32 (1979), 280–5.

If the *NV* catalogue is correct, Bach's interest in character pieces, like his engagement with several other genres, was short-lived;[2] no character pieces are listed after 1757.[3] The pieces in this little repertory, playful, on the whole, and of slight difficulty, signal Bach's involvement with keyboard miniatures. It might be argued that Bach had been writing miniatures for keyboard from the start of his career—the character pieces may not at first glance seem very different in form and substance from some of the short whimsical movements in Bach's early sonatas—and that his reason for writing character pieces was much the same as his purpose in composing easy sonatas: to provide amateur keyboard players with lesson material. Yet between the character pieces and the light movements of earlier sonatas there are significant differences in style. The character pieces, moreover, mark the beginning of the spate of single-movement keyboard pieces that Bach composed between 1754 and 1767.[4] Doubtless the publication in 1753 of the first part of the *Versuch*, itself a didactic work, generated more didactic activity on Bach's part in the years that followed.

Why did Bach devote himself so intensely to composing character pieces in the mid-1750s? It is perhaps more than coincidence that a reference to French

[2] The seven fugues for keyboard H. 75.5, 76, 99–102/W. 119, 1–7, are dated 1754–5; the prelude and six sonatas for organ H. 84–7, 107, 133–5/W. 70, 1–7, 1755–8; the ensemble sonatinas with obbligato harpsichord H. 449–53, 455–64/W. 96–110, 1762–4. Several movements in the group of sonatinas are arrangements of character pieces, some of them transposed: in H. 451/W. 98, *L'Auguste* (to G major); in H. 453/W. 109, *La Gause, La Pott* (to D major); in H. 455/W. 100, *La Xenophon, L'Ernestine* (to E major); in H. 456/W. 102, *La Complaisante* (to D major), *La Louise*; in H. 457/W. 103, *La Philippine* (to C major); in H. 459/W. 110, *La Bergius*.

[3] Eugene Helm's *Thematic Catalogue of the Works of Carl Philipp Emanuel Bach*, soon to be published by Yale University Press, lists a character piece titled *La Juliane*, H. 333, not found in *NV* or in the catalogue by Alfred Wotquenne, *Thematisches Verziechnis der Werke von Carl Philipp Emanuel Bach* (Leipzig, 1905). Whether or not this piece is genuinely by C. P. E. Bach, no date can be assigned to it.

Two sonatas, H. 129/W. 52, 6, and H. 143/W. 65, 33, dated 1758 and 1759 respectively, have movements with titles in the style of character pieces. The second movement of H. 129 has the title *L'Einschnitt*, and there is no reason to doubt that Bach assigned this title. *Einschnitt* ('incision') describes the music itself: each phrase begins with the same three notes that end the preceding one. In the autograph of H. 143 in D-ddr WRgm, C. P. E. Bach assigns the title *La Guillelmine* to the second movement and *La Coorl* to the third movement (see the article by Hans-Günter Ottenberg in this volume). Two other sources of H. 143 assign titles to the second movement, *La Guillelmine* (found in both D-brd Kll, Mb 50:10 and D-ddr Bds, Mus. ms. 30385) and to the third movement, *La Caroline* (Mb 50:10) and *La Coorl* (Mus. ms. 30385). According to Carl Friedrich Zelter, *Carl Friedrich Christian Fasch* (Berlin, 1801), 8, the title *La Coorl* refers to the nickname that the Austrian-born composer Karl Höckh (1707–73) gave to Fasch when the latter was a child: 'Monsieur Coorl'. Fasch (1736–1800) was C. P. E. Bach's colleague in Berlin, and it was with Fasch's family in Zerbst (where Höckh also lived) that Bach stayed when he and his family fled Berlin in 1758.

[4] These include the miniatures of the collections listed by Wotquenne as nos. 113 and 114, and the single pieces of W. 116 and W. 117. *NV* assigns to 59 of these miniatures (not including the 24 character pieces) dates between 1754 and 1767; to 7, the year 1775. 30 pieces in the W. 116 group (nos. 15, 29–57) are undated; the style of these (four of which have a length and structure similar to sonata movements, and hardly qualify as miniatures) suggests that they were composed in the 1750s or later.

character pieces appeared in an article in Friedrich Wilhelm Marpurg's *Historisch-kritische Beyträge zur Aufnahme der Musik* in 1754, the year that *NV* assigns to Bach's first compositions in the genre:

Words have exercised more power over the singer and his performance than people believe.... With instrumental pieces, however, this Ariadnian guideline drops away, and players lose their way in the labyrinth of a more or less extravagant performance, according to whether they have many embellishments in their heads, their throats, or their hands, and according to whether they possess less or greater capability of comprehending the true sense of the piece. French character pieces largely preclude such [extravagant performance], and one would wish that it weren't considered sufficient, in all compositions in the new style, to set nothing more than the words 'allegro' or 'adagio' at the head of a piece without giving the player more explicit information about the inner nature and distinctiveness of this particular Adagio.... When, some years ago, a certain Wit among us made fun of the characters in French pieces, he surely had no other reason for it than that he wanted to sneer. And if some French composers have not always conveyed the character in the caption of a piece in all of its ramifications, we must ask whether other composers among them, and elsewhere, might not portray it more felicitously. But is it actually necessary that precisely everything belonging to this character always, and in all circumstances, be treated exhaustively? Wouldn't one thus fall into pedantry? And can't one, further-more, name a piece a posteriori after something or other if [the piece] has only *some* resemblance to this or that thing? It is better to become aware of this Something than not to take note of it, and this Something can indeed, in such circumstances, be sufficient to guide the hand of the player. Let no one tell me that many of the characters in French pieces are quite absurd, or, at least, seem so....

Whence do vocal pieces derive the advantage that they charm and move more than instrumental pieces? In truth, the text, the content, and the variety contribute perhaps most to this advantage. I do not believe that the mere empty sound of the human voice ... satisfies the ear if not accompanied by words. Now if instrumental pieces do not have this advantage that vocal music has, is it not unfair to want deliberately to take away from them another advantage by means of which they might be able to compensate somewhat for their shortcoming? What could result then but, frequently, an empty harmonic-melodic noise? Why not make such a sound more effective? Why not give the listener the opportunity to think of something on hearing this sound, rather than of nothing? It must certainly give him more pleasure to recognize what has been done to engage his understanding than not to be acquainted with it in the least. If instrumental music that represents nothing, that means nothing, is in fact lacking in soul, why are people reluctant to prefix a character to that music which is intended to represent and mean something? An orator always takes pains to announce the content of his speech, and if, on one occasion, a certain Wag has held the speech in disdain, he too has served to advertise its intention. It seems to me that as long as one doesn't want to think about an instrumental piece, the purpose for which music is composed is not realized. The listener will never retain a full measure of satisfaction in his soul. He will go home and not know what he has heard.[5]

[5] *Historisch-kritische Beyträge zur Aufrahme der Musik* (Berlin, 1754–7), vol. 1, 'Anmerkungen über vorhergehendes Schreiben', 32 ff.: 'Die Worte haben über den Sänger und seinen Vortrag

With this commentary on Christian Gottfried Krause's 'Lettre à Mr. le Marquis de B\*\*\* sur la différence entre la musique italienne et françois' (1748), Marpurg fired another salvo in the battle he was waging with Johann Friedrich Agricola over the relative merits of French and Italian music.[6] It was Agricola (the 'Wit' and 'Wag' of Marpurg's article) who wrote disparagingly of the

mehr Gewalt, als man glaubt, gesetzt . . . Bey den Instrumentalsachen aber fällt dieser Ariadnische Leitfaden weg, und die Spieler verirren sich im Labyrinth eines ausschweifenden Vortrages mehr oder weniger, nachdem sie viel Manieren im Kopfe, in der Kehle und in der Faust haben, und nachdem sie weniger oder mehr Fähigkeit besitzen, sich in den wahren Sinn des Stückes zu versetzen. Die französischen charakterisierten Stücke bewahren sehr davor, und es wäre zu wünschen, daß man es auch nicht allezeit in allen Sachen nach dem neuen Geschmack bei uns genug sein liesse weiter nichts als die Wörter Allegro oder Adagio ec. über ein Stück zu setzen, ohne den Spieler von der inneren Beschaffenheit und dem Unterschiede dieses Adagio nähere Nachricht zu geben. . . . Wenn ein gewisser witziger Kopf bey uns sich vor einigen Jahren über die Characters in der französischen Musik etwas lustig machte: so hattte er wohl keinen andern Grund dazu, als daß er sich nur lustig machen wollte. Haben einige französische Tonkünstler nicht allezeit den über ein Stück gesetzten Character nach allen Prädicamenten durchgeführt, so ist die Frage, ob ihn andere Tonkünstler unter ihnen und anderswo nicht glücklicher durchführen können. Ist es aber nötig, daß just alles was nur zu diesem Character gehören kann, allezeit und bey aller Gelegenheit erschöpft werde? würde man es nicht in etwas Pedantisches verfallen? und kann man ferner nicht ein Stück a potiori [sic], wenn es nur einige Aehnlichkeit mit der oder jener Sache hat, darnach benennen? Es ist besser etwas, als nichts wahrzunehmen, und dieses Etwas kann ja in diesen Umständen genug seyn, die Hand des Spielers zu leiten. Man sage mir nicht, daß viele Characters in den französischen Sachen sehr lächerlich sind, oder wenigstens so scheinen. . . .

Woher erhalten die Singsachen den Vortheil, daß sie mehr gefallen und rühren als Spielstücke? In Wahrheit, so viele Gewalt die menschliche Stimme über uns hat, so tragen vielleicht der Text, der Inhalt und die Verschiedenheit desselben das meiste zu diesem Beyfalle bey. Ich glaube nicht, daß dem Ohr durch blosse leere Klänge der menschlichen Stimme, die nicht mit Worten begleitet werden . . . alleine diese Genugthuung geschehen wird. Haben die Spielstücke nun diesen Vortheil der Vocalmusik nicht, ist es da nicht unbillig, einen andern Vortheil, wodurch sie diesen Mangel einigermassen ersetzen können ausdrücklich von ihnen entfernen zu wollen. Was kann daher anders als ein leeres harmonisch–melodisches Gethöse öfters entstehen? Warum will man aber solches Gethöse nicht tätiger machen? Warum will man dem Zuhörer nicht Gelegenheit geben, vielmehr etwas als nichts bey diesem Gethöse zu gedenken? Es muß ja diesem mehr Vergnügen geben, dasjenige zu kennen, was man zur Beschäftigung seines Verstandes unternimmt, als davon im geringsten nicht unterrichtet zu seyn. Fehlet in der That derjenigen Spielmusik die Seele, die nichts vorstellet, die nichts bedeutet: warum will man derjenigen, die etwas vorstellen und bedeuten soll den Charakter vorzusetzen, sich scheuen? Ein Redner trägt allezeit Sorge, den Inhalt seiner Rede anzukündigen, und wenn einstens ein gewisser muntrer Kopf eine Rede von Nichts gehalten, so hat er auch dieses Vorhaben zuförderst angezeiget. Mich deucht, daß so lange man nicht bey einem Instrumentalstücke denken will, so lange auch der Endzweck, wozu die Musik eingesetzet ist, nicht erreichet werden wird. Dem Zuhörer wird niemahls eine Art völliger Beruhigung in seinem Gemüthe zurückbleiben. Er gehet nach Hause, und weiß nicht, was er gehört hat. Der Spieler hat etwas vorgetragen und weiß nicht was es gewesen.'

[6] This controversy had flared up periodically since the seventeenth century. Krause's 'Lettre', translated by Marpurg in the *Historisch-Kritische Beyträge*, vol. 1, 1–23, as 'Schreiben an den Herrn Marquis von B. über den Unterschied zwischen der italiänischen und französischen Musik', seems to have reintroduced the subject to music aestheticians in Berlin. Friedrich Wilhelm Marpurg and Johann Friedrich Agricola became embroiled in the controversy in 1749, the latter under the pseudonym Flavio Anicio Olibrio. The documents in this exchange, too numerous to itemize here, are listed most recently in Hans-Günter Ottenberg, *Der Critische Musicus an der Spree: Berliner Musikschrifttum von 1748 bis 1799* (Leipzig, 1984), 55–9.

French character piece, singling out Marpurg's collection published in Paris in 1741 for particular jibes.[7] Embedded in this windy controversy were issues that would spread beyond the confines of French–Italian rivalry and continue to nag theories of aesthetics to the present day: the problem of music's capacity to represent non-musical ideas, and the question of whether purely musical relationships could, by themselves, possess aesthetic value.[8] To Marpurg, instrumental music was clearly in need of the verbal assistance that the French titled character piece could give. Whether Marpurg's remarks served as a catalyst to Bach's compositional efforts, or whether these remarks simply expressed thoughts that were already on Bach's mind and in his discourse, he accepted the challenge implicit in Marpurg's article: to compose effective character pieces.

Precedents for C. P. E. Bach's character pieces may be found among seventeenth-century lute and harpsichord pieces and movements of French ballets of the late seventeenth and eighteenth centuries, and in even earlier instrumental repertories.[9] But, in fact, one need not look back beyond the *pièces de caractère* of François Couperin and his contemporaries for Bach's models.[10] David Fuller has described Couperin's engagement with the *pièce de*

[7] 'Schreiben an Herrn *** in welchem Flavio Anicio Olibrio, sein Schreiben an den critischen Musikus an der Spree vertheidiget, und auf dessen Wiederlegung antwortet' (Berlin, 1749), 16–17, 23–7. Agricola examines Marpurg's collection of pieces in considerable detail, enumerating syntactical mistakes, disparaging Marpurg for his prosaic musical ideas, and ridiculing him for attempts to portray subjects that are unfit for musical treatment.

[8] Theories of aesthetics in the 18th century were generally concerned with the moral, as well as the entertaining, effects of art. See, for example, the beginning of the article 'Aesthetik' in Johann Georg Sulzer's *Allgemeine Theorie der schönen Künste*, 2nd edn. (1792; fac. repr., Hildesheim, 1967), i. 47, where the author asserts that 'The main object of the fine arts is the awakening of a keen sense of the True and the Good . . .' ('Die Hauptabsicht der schönen Künste geht auf die Erwekung eines lebhaften Gefühls des Wahren und des Guten . . .')

[9] Martha Vidor, *Zur Begriffs-Bestimmung des musikalischen Charakterstück für Klavier*, (diss., Leipzig, 1924), 41–2, observes that in the ballet music of the 17th century, there are movements that resemble character pieces while retaining an 'independent' musical aspect.

[10] In his article 'Charakterstück' in *MGG*, vol. 2, cols. 1094–1100, Willi Kahl objects to the use of the term *Charakterstück* to refer to these pieces, primarily, it would appear, because their composers were too diffident to entrust the keyboard instrument with the expression of individual feelings. Thus Kahl's distinction between these pieces and the *Charakterstücke* of Schumann and his contemporaries seems to be one of sensibility, rather than of genre. Yet there is little reason *not* to accept the term 'character piece' as a designation for Couperin's *Pièces de clavecin*; his contemporaries referred to them as *pièces de caractère* and *pièces caracterisées* (see n. 11). Nor can distinctions of genre be made between French character pieces of the 18th century and their German counterparts on the basis of nationality. Not only does Marpurg (who might be discounted as a Francophile) refer to such pieces as *characterisierte Stücke* (see n. 5), but the same term appears in Daniel Gottlob Türk's *Klavierschule* (1789), repr., ed. Erwin Jacobi, Documenta Musicologica, Series 1, vol. 23 (Kassel and Basel, 1962), 395, and the term *Charakterstück* occurs in Johann Friedrich Reichardt's *Musikalisches Kunstmagazin* (Berlin, 1782–96), no. 1, 25; no. 5, 38–9). The designation *Charakteristische Tonstücke* is used less approbatively in Heinrich Koch's *Versuch einer Anleitung zur Composition* (Leipzig, 1782–93, repr. Hildesheim, 1969), ii. 41–2; Koch, like Kahl after him, finds these pieces often lacking in the proper sensibility ('nicht Empfindung, sondern Spielwerk für den Verstand'). The article 'Mahlerey (Redende Künste; Musik)' in Sulzer's *Allgemeine Theorie der schönen Künste*, iii. 356–7, discusses Couperin's and C. P. E. Bach's character pieces as examples of the same genre. The entries in Bach's *NV* (11–14) that refer to these works as 'Petites Pieces' indicate that to him, also, they were character pieces.

*caractère* as a 'revolution' that transformed the Baroque keyboard suite into a flexible vehicle for expression, and created a standard of excellence for his contemporaries. Like most revolutions, this one does not seem to have taken place overnight. Towards the end of the seventeenth century, the kinds of mythological and pastoral titles that had been attached to lute pieces of the mid-century began to give way to titles borrowed from the seventeenth-century literary pieces known as *portraits*. It was Couperin, however, who realized the potential of the character piece, not only with the impressive number of his *Pièces de clavecin*, but also with the elegance of their style.[11]

Several passages in C. P. E. Bach's *Versuch* indicate that he had a broad acquaintance with the keyboard music of eighteenth-century French composers.[12] Very likely, his conversance with Couperin's music began in the years when Bach was a student of his father; two of Couperin's works are found in sources that derive from J. S. Bach's circle.[13] Whatever the nature of C. P. E. Bach's access to the works of the *clavecinistes*, the presence of the French feminine article in the title of each of his character pieces (except for the one plural title) leaves no doubt that he took the *pièces caracterisées* of Couperin and other French composers as models. Titles of Bach's pieces that refer to attributes of character or to states of mind have French substantives as well as articles (e.g., *L'Irresoluë*, *La Journaliere*). Several of Bach's titles—*L'Auguste, La Sophie, Les Langueurs tendres, La Capricieuse*, and *La Complaisante*—are identical to titles of keyboard pieces by French composers.[14]

The significance of the feminine article in the French character piece was sometimes misunderstood in the eighteenth century as it is, frequently, today. *La* referred not to the gender of the person or trait portrayed, but to the word *pièce*, implied in each title. Undoubtedly Carl Philipp Emanuel Bach was acquainted with this convention whether he learned it in his childhood or among Francophiles in the Prussian capital. It seems clear that most of the

---

[11] Professor Fuller has kindly allowed me to read a typescript of the chapter titled 'François Couperin', to be published in his study of French harpsichord music of the 18th century. In this excellent account of Couperin's character pieces, the author mentions a number of designations by which works in this genre were known: *pièces caractérisées* (Marin Marais, in the preface to his collection of viol pieces of 1717), *pièces de caractère* (Marais, in the preface to a collection of 1725, and Dupuits, in the title of a collection of pieces published in the 1740s), and *airs caractérisées* (Rameau, in 1727).

[12] *Essay*, pp. 31, 79, 83, 85, 419.

[13] The rondeau *Les Moissoneurs* from the second book of *Pièces de clavecin* (1716–17), copied by Anna Magdalena Bach into the second *Clavier-Büchlein* that bears her name (BWV Anh. 183, begun after 1725); an arrangement by J. S. Bach of a *Minuet en rondeau* from the trio sonata *L'Impériale* as an *Aria* for organ, BWV 587. According to Wilfrid Mellers, *François Couperin and the French Classical Tradition* (New York, 1968), 103, the part of *L'Impériale* to which this movement belongs probably originated around 1715. The entire work was first published in 1726. *BWV*, p. 436, gives 1723–30 as the period within which this arrangement was probably made.

[14] There are pieces entitled *L'Allemande L'Auguste, Les Langueurs tendres*, and *La Sophie* by Couperin, and *La Capricieuse* and *La Complaisante* by Dandrieu. Several pieces by Dandrieu have titles similar to Bach's *Langueurs: La Languissante, Les Tendres accens, Les Tendres reproches*.

surnames in his character pieces refer to men with whom he was acquainted in Berlin, rather than to ladies of his circle.[15] Bach seems to have reserved French forms of given names (e.g., Philippine, Caroline) to designate ladies of his acquaintance, and on one occasion, to have coined a feminine form from a surname: from von Printzen, *la Prinzette* (see the discussion at the end of this paper).

C. P. E. Bach's emulation of the French character piece was not merely nominal; it included the cultivation of forms preferred by French composers for such pieces. He was, in fact, more intensely concerned with formal structures within the group of character pieces, notwithstanding the brevity of some of them, than in his previous works for solo keyboard. In compositions written before 1754, most of them sonatas, his attention seems to have focused more upon details—texture, embellishment, and thematic elaboration—than upon the development of large structures. Within the group of character pieces, on the other hand, Bach rapidly developed a variety of rondo conformations.

There are no rondos among the four pieces assigned to 1754.[16] The first and last of these, *La Gause* and *La Boehmer*, are in binary form, and there is nothing in the structure of either to suggest a drift towards the rondo. But the second and third pieces do have two formal aspects in common with the traditional eighteenth-century French *rondeau*: recurrence and symmetry. *La Pott*, a minuet, conforms to the periodic specifications of Bach's time: each part consists of two eight-measure phrases.[17] In the first strain, which is marked with repeat signs, the two phrases are almost alike, the first ending on the dominant, the second, an embellished version of it, ending in the tonic. After the second strain, for which no repeat is indicated, a da capo of the first strain is

---

[15] The following passage in an article, 'Ueber die Gemeinnützigkeit der Musik', *Ephemeriden der Menschheit* (June 1784), no. 6, 648 may have been one source of the widespread misconstruction of the meaning of the titles of character pieces, at least in Germany: 'While he was still in Berlin, Carl Philipp Emanuel Bach characterized several ladies that he knew with appropriate keyboard pieces; and several persons that knew each individual in those days assured me their temperament and manner in company were felicitously expressed in [these pieces]; one simply had to hear them played by Bach himself.' ('Karl Philipp Emanuel Bach charakterisirte, wie er noch in Berlin war, mehrere Frauenzimmer, die er kannte, durch angemessene Clavierstücke; und mehere Personen, die jedes Individuum damals kannten, versicherten mich, ihr Humor und Benehmen im Umgange sei glücklich in denselben ausgedrückt gewesen; nur habe man sie von Bach selbst spielen hören müssen.') If this description of the 'ladies' in Berlin had been an eyewitness account, it would, of course, constitute impressive evidence. But the account is, after all, hearsay. It should be noted here that whatever the source of the information about the originals of the character pieces, the titles of some of Bach's character pieces *cannot* refer to ladies—there was no Frau Gleim, and Aly Rupalich was surely a masculine appellation.

[16] The present discussion of stylistic development in Bach's character pieces is based on the chronology given in *NV*. Although parts of the *NV* chronology have been challenged from time to time, and occasionally shown to be inaccurate, the *NV* account is nevertheless the most reliable existing record of the origin and revision of Bach's works. It seems proper therefore to accept the *NV* chronology of Bach's character pieces unless firm evidence of its inaccuracy can be adduced.

[17] See, for example, Johann Mattheson, *Der vollkommene Capellmeister* (Hamburg, 1739), repr., ed. Margarethe Reimann (Kassel, 1954), 224–5.

prescribed.[18] Whether or not Bach regarded the da capo form as the most rudimentary of rondo structures, this return of the first strain, itself containing a reiterated phrase, bears considerable resemblance to the recurrence of a refrain.

*La Borchward*, a polonaise, has, like many dances of the eighteenth century, a binary repetition scheme superimposed on a ternary tonal scheme (in which the first strain closes in the tonic, and the second modulates, then returns to the tonic). The symmetry of the ternary scheme, shown in Figure 1, would be perfect, if it were not for the repetition of the little b melody (measures 25–6) as a *petite reprise*.

### Figure 1. Structural Scheme of *La Borchward*, H. 79/W. 117, 17

| Key      | G        |          |          | G to D   |          |          | G        |          |          |          |
|----------|----------|----------|----------|----------|----------|----------|----------|----------|----------|----------|
| Binary   | mm. 1–6  |          |          | mm. 7–26 |          |          |          |          |          |          |
| Ternary  | A (6 mm.)|          |          | B (12 mm.)|         |          | A (6 + 2 mm.) |      |          |          |
| Measures | 1–2      | 3–4      | 5–6      | 7–10     | 11–14    | 15–18    | 19–20    | 21–2     | 23–4     | 25–6     |
| Melody   | a        | a        | b        | c        | d        | e        | a        | a        | b        | b        |

In 1755, his most productive year for the genre, C. P. E. Bach composed ten character pieces and launched new variants of the rondo form. Of the ten, only four can be considered to be rondos, even of an experimental sort. The first four and the seventh listed for the year (*La Philippine, La Gabriel, La Caroline, La Prinzette*, and *La Stahl*) are in binary form. *La Bergius*, the eighth, has, like *La Borchward* of the previous year, a binary frame enclosing a ternary tonal plan and, like *La Pott*, a first strain with two similar phrases (here they are identical, in fact). Symmetry, once more, is almost complete, but is offset by the addition of a coda after the final repeat.

Bach's first character piece in which refrain sections alternate more than once with episodes (*couplets*) as in French *rondeaux* is *L'Aly Rupalich*. Comprising 194 measures in a rapid tempo, this piece displays several levels of recurrence. If it is viewed as a rondo with a non-modulating refrain, it appears to have four such refrains in C major enclosing three large structural sections. These refrains are not neatly distinguished from *couplets* as in most French *rondeaux*, and sections that are not in the tonic are constantly invaded by refrain material. Some of this material, moreover, is as clearly profiled in related keys as it is in the tonic, and there is nothing that prevents it from being construed as a refrain except the convention that prescribes the tonic for all refrains. If this piece is viewed as a modulating rondo, the recurrence of refrain material is more easily accounted for. It is obvious, however, that the structural parts of *L'Aly Rupalich* do not have the symmetry that a

---

[18] It is not clear whether the da capo requires repetition of the first strain.

conventional French *rondeau* has, but are irregular, as in a ritornello form. The refrain, for example, is followed in its initial appearance, a (Facsimile 1, measures 1–7), by an accompanying transitional segment, b (measures 13–19). In their recurrences, the refrain and its accompanying segment are not always in their original sequence; for example, when it appears in G major (measure 41), the a material is framed by the b material.

The ritornello principle, in fact, had considerable influence on Bach's development of rondo forms.[19] It is evident in certain slow middle movements (none of them in the usual binary or rounded binary form) of his sonatas of the 1740s.[20] Each of these movements is interspersed with recurrences of opening material, at least one of which is not in the tonic. As in most ritornellos, this material has different lengths in some of its appearances and often leads without close to episodes. It might be difficult to argue that these ritornello forms of the 1740s have much significance for the evolution of the rondo in Bach's character pieces, were it not for the existence of certain other slow movements in his sonatas with a closely related structure.[21] In these movements, Bach has repeated portions of the opening material with the same freedom and irregularity as in the group of ritornello movements described above. This material does not modulate, however, as in the ritornello forms, but always appears in the tonic, as in a conventional rondo.

In 1748, Bach essayed a further combination of ritornello and rondo forms, this time in the final movement of a sonata in G major. H. 56/W. 65, 22. This movement has a ternary tonal scheme enclosed in a binary frame. After the close of the first section in the tonic and an eight-measure phrase in the dominant that opens the second section, the ritornello-rondo element is added to this hybrid: Bach states the opening phrase in the dominant. Bach would return to this structure repeatedly throughout his career, not only in his character pieces, but also in the final movements of sonatas.

The only regular recurrence in *L'Aly Rupalich* is to be found on the smallest level: the oscillating Murky bass that is present in all but nine measures of the piece.[22] Like the bass in Couperin's two *Musétes* in the third book of *Pièces de clavecin*, this bass functions mostly as a pedal. Despite the propulsive quality of

---

[19] Witold Chrzanowski, *Das instrumentale Rondeau und die Rondoformen im XVIII. Jahrhundert* (Leipzig, 1911), 39 ff., recognizes the influence of the ritornello in C. P. E. Bach's rondos, but mentions only works written after 1758.

[20] H. 28/W. 48, 5, from the Prussian collection; H. 30/W. 49, 1 and H. 33/W. 49, 3, from the Württemberg collection; H. 37/W. 52,4 and H. 46/W. 65, 16.

[21] H. 32.5/W. 65, 13; H. 36/W. 49, 6, from the Württemberg collection; H. 47/W. 65, 17; H. 53/W. 69.

[22] It is curious that Bach chose this bass. In the *Versuch*, 3, he views it with a jaundiced eye: 'People torment beginning students with tasteless Murkys and Gassenhauers in which the left hand is used merely for drumming and rendered permanently unfit for its true use . . .' ('Man martert im Anfange die Scholaren mit abgeschmackten Murkys und andern Gassen-Hauern, wobey die lincke Hand bloß zum Poltern gebraucht, und dadurch zu ihrem wahren Gebrauche auf immer untüchtig gemachet wird . . .)'

*Darrell M. Berg*

Facsimile 1. *L'Aly Rupalich*, H. 95/W. 117, 27. *Musikalisches Mancherley* (Berlin, 1762–3), 130

*L'Aly Rupalich* and its numerous modulations (the tonalities established are
C–G–Am–F–C–G–Cm–C), its monotonous bass accompaniment and the
harmonic ambiguity incurred by frequent passages of pedal point give it a
curiously non-directional, modern aspect. In the beginning, the pedal serves to
define tonality. The B flat introduced in the third measure does not in the least
call the main key, C major, into question; as a fleeting reference to the
subdominant, it has a stabilizing effect. Yet this B flat, and the F natural that
functions as its upper parallel in the key of G major, ultimately prove to be more
dissonant than they appear at first. During the section in A minor (measures
59–75), B flat is for a moment part of a Neapolitan chord participating in the
peculiar descent of parallel first inversions (measures 66–70) that barely
avoids hidden fifths (the ear supplies parallel fifths to some extent, despite the
notated rests). Although B flat plays a comfortable role in the F major section
that follows (measures 85–97), its dissonant aspect emerges in measures
122–9 (see Example 1). Here there is no mistake about the importance of B flat.
It is repeatedly emphasized, demanding harmonic change with each reiteration, showing, each time it is heard, a different facet of its personality, and
inhabiting a harmonic progression that adumbrates the style of some of Bach's
works composed in Hamburg. As in many of the Hamburg compositions, the
harmonic destination of this passage is deliberately concealed until the last
moment. When Bach returns to the refrain in G major (measure 131), it seems
reasonable, despite the progression that has just been heard, to expect that the

Example 1. *L'Aly Rupalich*, H. 95/W. 117, 27, mm. 119–33

upper parallel, F natural, will have a stabilizing effect as in other appearances
of the refrain. Yet the F natural becomes an agent of subversion, leading to C
major. It might be argued that since C major is the tonic key, F natural has,
after all, performed a stabilizing role on a larger level. But it has also revealed its
ambiguity. By the end of the piece, the ear is convinced that any modulation
may take place and that the tonic pedal may have almost any harmony above
it. This pedal combines with the transitional segment b (see Facsimile 1,
measures 13–19) in the last four measures to produce an inconclusive ending.
The ear is left with the impression that *L'Aly Rupalich* has no beginning or end
(see Example 2).

There is no doubt of the form of *La Gleim*, which follows *L'Aly Rupalich* in the
*NV* chronology, or of its derivation from French models. Bach has labelled this
piece *Rondeau* and divided it into two large sections, each titled *Partie*. The first
*partie*, in A minor, has the structure of a conventional French *rondeau*: the
*couplets* are clearly defined, and recurrence of the full refrain is indicated by a
da capo at the end of each *couplet*. The second *partie* begins in the major mode
as if independent of the first. But this independence proves to be a visual
illusion like the avoidance of fifths in *L'Aly Rupalich*; after what proves to be a
long *couplet*, the A minor refrain from the first part returns. The designation
*partie* thus seems to be merely an expedient for calling attention to the change
of mode.

This deceptively gentle piece has a piquant harmonic style unlike that of any
of Bach's other works. The reiterated phrase of the refrain has an underlying
harmonic framework that is clear and simple: a series of descending thirds in
the bass and, in the upper voice, a similar descent with each note a third above
its bass (see Example 3). Bach has displaced the consonant notes in the upper
voice, however; every beat in the first two and half measures contains a non-
harmonic tone (see Example 4). Even if the non-harmonic tones in the upper
voice were shifted to weaker parts of each measure, these two phrases of the
refrain would retain their harmonic cloudiness, for the harmony would still be
blurred by the pedal on A in the middle voice. The harmonic style of the first
four *couplets* is similar: simple underlying harmony garnished with a surface
containing many pungent unresolved dissonances. Only in the second part
does the pedal on A have a tranquilizing influence and support harmonies that
are mostly consonant.

Example 2. *L'Aly Rupalich*, H. 95/W. 117, 27, mm. 191–4

Example 3. *La Gleim*, H. 89/W. 117, 19, mm. 1-4, harmonic framework

Example 4. *La Gleim*, H. 89/W. 117, 19, mm. 1-4

Two other pieces of 1755, *La Buchholtz* and *L'Herrmann*, display variants of the rondo principle. *L'Herrmann*, with a refrain that does not modulate and a single *couplet* that appears twice, has the structure A B A B A. Both the A and the B sections are embellished in each of their recurrences.

*La Buchholtz* has the same structure as the final movement of the sonata in G major H. 56/W. 65, 22—an amalgam of binary, ternary, and rondo forms— and, like the sonata movement, tiny dimensions. Much of this short character piece (23 of its 37 measures) is occupied by material belonging to the refrain. The refrain, like that of *L'Aly Rupalich*, is divisible into two segments, a (measures 1-2) and b (measures 3-4), each segment beginning on the upbeat to a measure (see Facsimile 2 and Figure 2). Bach's subtle variation of these two diminutive building-blocks results in a rich series of events; the frequent recurrence of a and b material produces a formidable unity. The a segment is presented alone, transposed to F major in measures 13-14. At the return to D minor (measures 17-19), this segment is extended from two to three measures. The b section undergoes motivic development in measures 24-7, the b′ segment in measures 32-3. Although Bach did not exploit this kind of development in subsequent character pieces, he did not abandon it permanently. He returned to it as a means of expansion in the rondos of the 'Kenner und Liebhaber' collections, written after his move to Hamburg.

It might be objected that *L'Aly Rupalich* and *La Buchholtz* should not be called rondos because their refrains modulate as in a traditional ritornello form. Certainly the ritornello element is one of the formal components of these pieces. But the fact that Bach designated his Hamburg compositions with modulating refrains as 'rondos' indicates that he also perceived in them a relation to the *rondeau*. It seems likely that he had a similar perception of the

Facsimile 2. *La Buchholtz*, H. 93/W. 117, 24. *Musikalisches Mancherley*, (Berlin, 1762–3), 82

Figure 2. Combined structural schemes of *La Buchholtz*, H. 93/W. 117, 24

| Key | D minor | | | | F major | | | D minor | | | | | | | | |
|---|---|---|---|---|---|---|---|---|---|---|---|---|---|---|---|---|
| Binary | I | | | | II | | | | | | | | | | | |
| Ternary | A | | | | B | A | C | A | | | | | | | | |
| Rondo | A | | | | B | A | | A | | | | | | | | |
| Measures | 1–2 | 3–4 | 5–6 | 7–8 | 9–12 | 13–14 | 15–16 | 17–19 | 20–1 | 22–3 | 24–7 | 28–9 | 30–1 | 32–3 | 34–5 | 36–7 |
| Melody | a | b | a | b' | c | a | d | a' | a | b | devel. | a | b' | devel. | a | b' |

character pieces written in 1754–7, years during which he was adapting the forms of French character pieces to his own purpose.

Of the six pieces composed in 1756, two are in binary form, and one, *La Louise*, is a long rondo with a modulating refrain. For three pieces, *La Complaisante, Les Langueurs tendres*, and *La Journaliere*, all modulating rondos, Bach employed a structure that is explicitly ternary: all three are marked 'da capo'. By 1757, Bach was committed to the modulating rondo as a compositional principle for his character pieces. In three of the four pieces listed for that year, there is some sort of recurrent refrain. *La Xenophon et la Sybille* has a compound structure with many symmetries. On the largest level, it is a da capo form, requiring the repetition of *La Xenophon*, itself a modulating rondo in da capo form, after *La Sybille*, a *partie* in rounded binary form. *L'Auguste* and *L'Ernestine* have the binary-ternary-rondo structure of the finale of the G major sonata H. 56/W. 65, 22, of 1748 (see the discussion above).[23]

*La Sophie*, the fourth composition listed for 1757 and the most anomalous of the twenty-four miniatures listed as character pieces, has, in all of its surviving sources, a text beginning 'O holde Zeit'. It can be argued that Bach did not conceive this work as a character piece, and there is some evidence, beyond the designation 'Aria', to support this argument. In the seventeenth and eighteenth centuries, a texted work was not, conventionally, called *pièce*, the term being reserved for instrumental compositions. And the fact that *La Sophie* does not appear in D-ddr Dlb, Ms. 3029.17, a source prepared by Bach's copyist known as 'An 303', containing the other twenty-three character pieces, might seem to indicate that this piece does not belong with the others.[24]

But there are strong indications that Bach did intend this work, its anomalous aspect notwithstanding, to be part of the repertory of character pieces. First, it is listed in two authoritative catalogues of his works with pieces belonging to this repertory. *La Sophie* appears in the section of *NV* containing solo keyboard works as one of four 'Petites Pieces' of 1757, the others being *La Xenophon et la Sybille, L'Ernestine*, and *L'Auguste*. This piece is listed with the other twenty-three in the catalogue of the collection of Bach's works assembled by the Schwerin organist Johann Jacob Heinrich Westphal in consultation with C. P. E. Bach and two members of Bach's family who survived him.[25] Secondly, the contexts in which sources of *La Sophie* survive indicate that in Bach's time, this work was considered to be one of the

---

[23] If the *NV* chronology is correct, *L'Ernestine* originated in 1755 as the last movement of the sonata in E major for solo keyboard H. 83/W. 65, 29, and was transposed to D major as a character piece in 1757.

[24] See Paul Kast, *Die Bach-Handschriften der Berliner Staatsbibliothek*, Tübinger Bach-Studien, vols. 2/3, ed. Walter Gerstenberg (Trossingen, 1958), and 139, where anonymous scribes identifiable as C. P. E. Bach's copyists are given '300' numbers.

[25] Berg, 'Towards a Catalogue', pp. 285–6, 292; Rachel W. Wade, *'The Keyboard Concertos of Carl Philipp Emanuel Bach* (Ann Arbor, 1981), 9–12. An explicit basis for the classification in Westphal's catalogue is Bach's own assurance, in a letter of 8 May 1787, that 'you have all of the character pieces'. See Erwin Jacobi, 'Three Additional Letters from C. P. E. Bach to J. J. H. Westphal', *JAMS*, 37 (1974), 122.

character pieces. One of these sources, D-brd B, P 997, a manuscript in the hand of An 303, contains, besides the 'Sophie' aria, *only* character pieces. *La Sophie* is found in three additional sources, followed by a texted minuet in G major titled *L'Ernestine*:[26] B Bc, 5897, in Westphal's script, at the end of a section containing the other twenty-three pieces; D-brd B, Ms. 38050,[27] in the middle of a section in the script of An 301 containing all but three of the character pieces; and D-brd B, P 743, C. P. E. Bach's autograph, containing *La Xenophon et la Sybille* and *L'Auguste*. Thirdly, *La Sophie* and its companion, the 'Ernestine' minuet, despite their German texts, are provided with titles in the style of French *pièces de caractère*.

From this evidence, it would appear that Bach's contribution to the character piece consisted not only in the creation of rich and novel structural combinations, but also in the extension of the genre to include texted pieces. The inclusion of *La Sophie* with the other twenty-three character pieces does not seem so illogical, therefore, as the omission of the texted *L'Ernestine* from the group of twenty-four in the two early catalogues. It would doubtless be enlightening to learn how this texted *L'Ernestine* is related to the four character pieces listed for 1757 and whether the Ernestine of the texted minuet is the same person as the Ernestine of the Allegretto, H. 124/W. 117, 38. Until further information is uncovered, we can only offer the following conjecture: perhaps the texted minuet was composed in honour of an Ernestine of Bach's acquaintance around the same time as *La Sophie*—1757. The *NV* chronology indicates that the Allegretto, which originally served as the finale of the sonata of 1755 (see n. 23), assumed its D major version in 1757; at that time, it may have received the title *La Frederique*, which it has in D-brd B, Ms. 38050. Around 1761, Bach may have removed the texted *L'Ernestine* from the repertory of character pieces in order to publish it as 'Am Namenstag der Mademoiselle S.' in his 1762 collection of odes, and renamed the Allegretto *L'Ernestine*. Thus the little minuet that was once situated in the shadow of *La Sophie* was handed down to posterity as a song.

Whatever its aberrant features, *La Sophie* displays structural kinship with the other three character pieces of 1757. Because it is an aria, the sections that enclose its texted parts must properly be designated ritornellos. But its voice part contains keyboard ornaments and can, except for one or two long notes, be played as the right-hand part of a keyboard piece. In that case, *La Sophie*'s ritornellos would be indistinguishable from the modulating refrains in Bach's rondos.

---

[26] The texted *L'Ernestine*, H. 685.5/W. 199, 16, is not the same composition as the piece *L'Ernestine*, H. 124/W. 117, 38 (see n. 23). This texted minuet, with its title changed to 'Am Namenstag der Mademoiselle S.', was published in C. P. E. Bach's *Oden mit Melodien* (Berlin, 1762). Gudrun Busch, *C. Ph. E. Bach und seine Lieder*, Kölner Beiträge zur Musikforschung, vol. 12 (Regensburg, 1957), 72, surmises that the initial 'S.' may stand for 'Sack' or 'Stahl'.

[27] I am grateful to Pamela Fox and Rachel Wade for bringing this manuscript to my attention.

There has been much disagreement over the significance of the titles of seventeenth- and eighteenth-century instrumental pieces. Captions on seventeenth-century lute pieces, C. F. Weitzmann notes, were merely theatrical labels and bore no relation to musical content.[28] But Martha Vidor argues, in her study of the character piece, that it is difficult to account for unity between titles and music in the eighteenth century unless the evolution of such unity throughout the seventeenth century is assumed.[29] Nor were eighteenth-century authors in accord on this issue. Ernst Gottlieb Baron declared that titles were more or less arbitrarily assigned to pieces to honour friends and patrons, or named after elegant ladies whom they had pleased.[30] The point of Heinrich Koch's reference to character pieces that purport to depict hypochondriacs, musical clocks, thunderstorms, or lovers' quarrels was that these pieces were better appreciated if heard without their titles.[31] The well-known passage in Couperin's preface to the *Pièces de clavecin* is at variance with such assertions:

I have always had a purpose in composing all of these pieces. Various occasions have furnished them. Thus the titles correspond to the ideas I have had . . . however, because, among these titles, there are some that seem to flatter me, it is well to announce that the pieces that carry them are portraits of a sort that people have sometimes found to be tolerable likenesses under my fingers, and that most of these flattering titles apply to the lovable originals that I wanted to represent, rather than to the copies that I have made of them.[32]

The controversy over whether or not titles were related to musical content is a particularly myopic one. Clearly, they were conferred in a variety of ways.[33]

---

[28] Carl Friedrich Weitzmann, Max Seiffert, and Oskar Fleischer, *Geschichte der Klaviermusik* (Leipzig, 1899), ii. 159.

[29] See Vidor, 'Charakterstück', p. 41.

[30] *Untersuchung des Instruments der Lauten* . . . (Nuremberg, 1727), 86.

[31] *Versuch einer Anleitung zur Composition*, ii 41–2: 'Auf diese Art malt man in der Tonkunst Hypochondristen und Singuhren, Donnerwetter und verliebte Zänkereyen u. d. gl. Anstatt also mit der Kunst auf das Herz zu würken, sucht man den Verstand der Zuhörer mit Witz zu beschäftigen. Das Lustigste bey der ganzen Sache ist noch dieses, daß viele solcher charakteristischer Tonstücke als bloßes Ideal des Componisten, das ist, so lange man nicht weiß, daß sie charakteristisch seyn sollen, gefallen, und nur alsdenn erst mißfallen, wenn man sie aus der Absicht hört, aus welcher sie eigentlich gehört werden sollen.'

[32] François Couperin, *Pièces de clavecin*, Book I (Paris, 1713), preface: 'J'ay toujours eu un objet en composant toutes ces piéces: des occasions différentes me l'ont fourni. Ainsi les Titres répondent aux idées que j'ay eues . . . cependant, comme, parmi ces Titres, il y en a qui semblent me flater, il est bon d'avertir que les pièces qui les portent sont des espèces de portraits qu'on a trouvé quelques fois assés ressemblans sous mes doigts, et que la plûpart de ces Titres avantageux sont plûtot donnés aux aimables originaux que j'ay voulu representer, qu'aux copies que j'en ay tirées.'

[33] One of the liveliest and most informative discussions of the titled instrumental piece, unfortunately not yet published, is the lecture, 'Titles', delivered by David Fuller at the Second Aston Magna Academy in 1979. Professor Fuller, who has examined the role of titles as signifiers at length, offers a resolution to the controversy: it is foolish to expect consistency in the application of titles. Referring primarily to titled French instrumental pieces of the late seventeenth and early eighteenth centuries, he describes the many facets that titles have had. He cites, as an example of a

They might, as Couperin announced, denote a source of inspiration for a musical portrait, or, as Baron and Marpurg pointed out, be assigned a posteriori. They might celebrate dynastic figures, the theatre, or fashions, or be given simply because a title was needed.

It would be sanguine to expect to establish connections between the titles using given names, e.g. *La Louise, La Sophie, La Gabriel*, and the music to which they belong. Whether these were nicknames, names of characters in a play, or actual names of Bach's aquaintances, their identity has disappeared. The chances of discovering the significance of *L'Aly Rupalich* and *La Xenophon et la Sybille* are also slim; the topical aspects of these titles have long been forgotten. But a title may, as Marpurg indicates, be an intimation of the 'inner nature' of a piece and serve to guide the hand of the player.[34] Titles that refer to abstract character traits or states of mind often serve as an index to the music that they designate or, at least, to the manner in which it should be performed. Indeed, for many character pieces in which the illustrative aspects of the music are restrained, subtle, or ambiguous, the title bears the main responsibility for indicating a style of performance.

Such is the case with two pieces titled *La Complaisante*, one by Dandrieu, the second (influenced, perhaps, by the earlier) by C. P. E. Bach. Each piece, Dandrieu's in 6/4 metre, Bach's in 3/4, has an underlying rhythm that flows consistently in half-notes and quarter-notes. Each contains passages of greater rhythmic animation—the diminutions of Bach's *La Complaisante* displaying considerably more variety—but such passages occur within a rhythmic framework that is affably regular. Yet the musical features that convey complaisance are so general that without its title (and the tempo designation 'Allegretto grazioso' in Bach's *La Complaisante*), each piece could plausibly be supposed to portray other ideas.

The same might be said of C. P. E. Bach's piece *L'Auguste*, which seems to owe nothing but its name to Couperin's *L'Auguste*. The title of Couperin's piece, the first in his collection of 1713, is preceded by the designation *L'Allemande*. In Bach's piece, written almost half a century later, the title is followed by the designation *Polonaise*. Which of these two dance styles is more inherently august must remain a matter of taste; both have a stately character. The music

---

title that cannot be expected to have reference to a musical feature of the composition, *La Raporte*, assigned to a piece by Sainte-Colombe's copyist because he had transcribed part of it from tablature to staff notation. As an example of the opposite circumstance, he mentions the titles of pieces published by Dandrieu in 1724, intended as designations of style and tempo of the music.

[34] Marpurg may have arrived at this rather self-evident conclusion by his own reasoning, or he may have been influenced by the following passage in Jean-François Dandrieu's preface to his book of pieces of 1724: 'For the names that I have chosen I have intended to delineate the very character of the pieces that they designate in order that they may determine the style and tempo . . .' ('Pour les noms que j'ai choisi, j'ai prétendu les tirer du caractère même des Piéces qu'ils désignent, afin qu'ils puissent en déterminer le goût et le mouvement . . .'), *Trois liveres de clavecin*, ed. Pauline Aubert and Brigitte François-Sappey (Paris, 1973).

of Couperin's piece reinforces its title, however: he has cast his *L'Auguste* in the dotted rhythm of the French overture, a style with connotations of majesty and divinity. Bach's *L'Auguste* depends upon its title (and, possibly, upon some topical connotations that are irretrievably lost) for the indication that it must be played in a regal manner.

In Bach's four remaining pieces with abstract titles, affective and pictorial devices are manipulated so inventively that the music of each becomes an explication of the title. His modulating rondo, *Les Langueurs tendres*, shares not only a title with Couperin's *Les Langueurs tendres*, but also a pining character. In Couperin's piece, every phrase begins with a three-note upbeat figure. Bach's *Langueurs* employs a three-note upbeat with a languishing contour (an upward leap of a third followed by an appoggiatura that descends stepwise) to begin all phrases except one; this one phrase, a passage of *Fortspinnung* in measures 32–42 (see Facsimile 3) might also be construed as beginning with a three-note upbeat. Both pieces begin with a general descent in the melody. Bach's *Les Langueurs tendres* exploits the melancholy implications of the title further than does Couperin's. His melodic descent is longer, extending over eight measures and proceeding in chromatic motion, outlining the traditional Baroque *Schmerzfigur*. In his second phrase, measures 9–16, Bach brings into play two additional pathetic intervals redolent of a later era: a leap of a seventh followed soon afterwards by a leap of a sixth in the opposite direction.

A somewhat different aesthetic informs Bach's other three pieces with abstract titles. Instead of borrowing from the stock of Baroque rhetorical figures, he has carved out of musical materials new metaphors appropriate to each portrayal. The illustrative aspects of *La Journaliere* ('The Fickle One') are somewhat less conspicuous than those of the other two pieces. Yet its musical elements are deftly arranged to give it a quality of inconstancy. Most of its phrases consist of several groups of gyrating eighth-notes that dovetail into each other, producing kaleidoscopic formations (see Facsimile 4). These eighth-note figures appear at the beginning of every phrase; but in each *couplet* their shapes vary: in measures 9–10 they are presented in inversion; from the second eighth-note of measure 17 through the first eighth-note of measure 18, they are in retrograde. By starting the first of these groups on the second eighth-note of the measure, Bach gives it the character of an upbeat and appears to be following Couperin's practice (noted by Fuller) of beginning a piece in a part of the measure that allows the motion to proceed smoothly through cadences and connect seamlessly with phrases and strains that follow.[35] The last *couplet* of *La Journaliere* does proceed in this way, slipping easily into the da capo. But this piece displays no real fidelity to any method of locomotion, not even one of such lubricity. The first phrase, instead of flowing into the second, is brought up short on the third beat of the fourth measure, a

[35]  Fuller, 'François Couperin'.

Facsimile 3. *Les Langueurs tendres*, H. 110/W. 117, 30. *Musikalisches Allerley*, (Berlin, 1761), 39

termination in the style of a polonaise. The absence of a downbeat in the next measure contributes to the effect of cessation and resumption, and the purpose of the upbeat figure proves, in the second phrase, to be entirely different from what it first appeared to be.

Bach's musical portrayal is more vivid in *La Capricieuse*, the name of which may have been suggested by Dandrieu's gigue with the same title. Dandrieu achieves capriciousness with sections of hemiola in the melody that occur rather regularly, and with a few other syncopations. Bach also employs rhythmic shifts to convey capriciousness, but there are many more of them, and their waywardness is reinforced by dynamic changes, large melodic leaps, and sudden reversals in the direction of the melody (see Facsimile 5). Bach's

Facsimile 4. *La Journaliere*, H. 112/W. 117, 32. *Musikalisches Allerley*, (Berlin, 1761), 44

piece does not have the underlying regularity of pulse, moreover, that gives Dandrieu's *La Capricieuse* a rational aspect at variance with its title. In Bach's *La Capricieuse*, the quarter-note pulse that is established in the beginning ceases at the ends of several phrases (measures 4, 6, 11, 15, 23, 27, 31, 33), and, even more disturbingly, fails to appear on two downbeats.

In *L'Irresoluë*, Bach has made ingenious use of syncopation to portray hesitation (see Facsimile 6). The most conspicuous device for conveying indecisiveness is the hemiola that constitutes measures 2, 10, 18, and 22 (obviously measures of 3/4, even though no new time signatures are inserted). The first phrase illustrates other kinds of syncopation in addition to the notated hemiola (measure 2). Although the 3/8 metre is apparently restored in

Facsimile 5. *La Capricieuse*, H. 113/W. 117, 3. *Musikalisches Allerley*, (Berlin, 1761), 22–3

Facsimile 6. *L'Irresoluë*, H. 111/W. 117, 31. *Musikalisches Allerley*, (Berlin, 1761), 43

measure 3 for the remainder of the phrase, Bach disrupts this motion once again in measures 4–7. In these measures, the rhythm in the melody, and the duple grouping of eighth-notes in the left hand indicate movement in quarter-notes. Here Bach has created another layer of uncertainty. Measures 4–7 can be heard either as a hemiola—two measures of 3/4—or as another kind of dislocation—three measures of 2/4. Measures 12–15, in the reiteration of the first phrase, are less easily construed as three 2/4 measures because the changes of configuration in the melody and left-hand part at measure 14 constitute a barely perceptible articulation that implies the separation of two measures of 3/4. Measures 20–1 are still less ambiguous; they can be heard only in 3/4. Thus the entire piece is dominated by a hemiola that saps its resolution at every turn. Only briefly, in measures 25–9, is 3/8 comfortably established.[36]

It is tempting, in view of these vivid musical portrayals of abstract characters and moods, to assume equally felicitous portrayals of the persons whose surnames provide nine other titles of Bach's character pieces, and to entertain conjectures about the personalities who bore these names. Was Prof. Dr Pott, the subject of the little minuet in C major, H. 80/W. 117, 18, as artless and uncomplicated as this piece suggests? Was Herr Bergius as warm-hearted and affable as the vibrant dissonances and comfortable resolutions in his piece imply? Was Herr Borchward as dignified and gracious as the polonaise with his name? Did Herr Gleim have the urbane and slightly hypochondriacal air that his *rondeau* projects? One of C. P. E. Bach's early biographers, Carl Herrmann Bitter, could not resist indulging in such speculations about Bach's character pieces, and allowed his fantasy to range in supple dialectic waves over the music and its subjects:

If one were to analyse these pieces, even along very general lines, one might say that *L'Herrmann* represents a woman of gentle, sensitive character with a wistful elegance, not without passionate impulse; that in *La Buchholtz*, a somewhat melancholy, sentimental mood prevails, in which an easily stimulated imagination induces choleric outbursts, but in which a fine sense of humour is not lacking; *La Boehmer* depicts a fiery, vigorous, and spirited nature that forges tirelessly ahead full of vehement outbursts, flying into a passion, but without expression of deeper feeling; *La Stahl* portrays a serious temperament, an elegiac mood. A certain romanticism and a feeling that wells up from the innermost depths are unmistakable. In *L'Aly Rupalich*, on the other hand, a restless, outgoing nature full of changing passions and affections is depicted—proud, but without nobility, and without inwardness or profundity, hardly capable of grief, which, when it appears, disappears again quickly.[37]

Such perceptions of Bach's musical portraiture are of limited value because there is no way of assessing their accuracy. A perception of the musical vagaries of *La Capricieuse*, however subjective, can be measured against a general concept of capriciousness. But since little is known about the characters of the people after whom nine of the pieces seem to have been named, the illustrative features of these pieces must probably remain for ever unverified. Yet the very names of these people are valuable to us for the entry they provide into the ambience in which Bach's career developed. Even though we are not permitted a close look at Bach's acquaintances with all of the subtleties of their characters, we can consider their world from the broader perspective that a remoter vantage-point affords. These character pieces, like

[36] Johann Nikolaus Forkel, *Allgemeine Geschichte der Musik* (Leipzig, 1788), 58, cites the 'elongation' (*Verlängerung*) of the rhythm in this piece as one example of a rhetorical figure which he designates as *dubitatio* or *Zweifel*.

[37] *Carl Philipp Emanuel und Wilhelm Friedemann Bach und deren Brüder*, 2 vols. (Berlin, 1868), i. 85–6.

their French models, can be compared with certain literary expressions of the time. For Bach's pieces, it is difficult to find such precise counterparts as the French literary *portraits* upon which Couperin seems to have modelled his pieces. The portraits in Gellert's *Moralische Charaktere*, for example, are homiletic in tone, and do not have the playfulness of Bach's character pieces. The analogy between the German musical and literary creations in question is a looser one. C. P. E. Bach's character pieces, as tokens of his regard for a circle of friends, are related to the gestures of the literary cult of friendship that flourished during Bach's tenure in Berlin.

There are precedents for the friendship vogue in some of the pastoral verses of the Hamburg poet Friedrich von Hagedorn (1708–54). In the poem *Anacreon*, Hagedorn, speaking through the mouth of the Greek poet, declares wine and love, roses and spring, friendship and dancing to be the themes of his poetry.[38] Many exponents of the friendship cult were nurtured in the Pietistic atmosphere of the University of Halle. Samuel Gotthold Lange (1711–81) and Jakob Immanuel Pyra (1715–44), who met in Halle as students, celebrated friendship in an exalted vein, and in blank verse.[39] In their poetry, Pietistic ideals are mixed with Anacreontic elements and pastoral allusions—Pyra was designated as Thirsis, Lange as Damon, Lange's wife as Doris.[40] Titles of their writings reflect their preoccupation with friendship: Lange and Pyra, *Thirsis und Damons freundschaftliche Lieder* (1745); Lange, *Freundschaftliche Briefe* (Berlin, 1746); Lange, *Sammlung gelehrter und freundschaftlicher Briefe* (Halle, 1769, 1770).

In 1742, two years before his death, Pyra accepted a position in Berlin, where he met the poet Johann Wilhelm Ludwig Gleim (1719–1803), a leading German proponent of Anacreontic poetry and a central figure in the friendship cult. Gleim, with three fellow students at the University of Halle, Johann Peter Uz (1720–96), Johann Nikolaus Götz (1721–81), and Paul Jacob Rudnick (1718–4?) had founded the group of poets known as the Anakreontik during the winter of 1739–40. In his first published book of poetry, a collection of

[38] The acquaintance of 18th-century authors with Anacreon of Teos, a Greek poet of the 6th century BC, was based on an edition of 60 poems, allegedly by Anacreon, published by Henri Estienne in 1556. Joseph Addison published an English translation of these poems: *The Works of Anacreon* (London, 1735); Johann Nikolaus Götz published a German translation: *Die Oden Anacreons in reimlosen Versen* (Frankfurt am Main, 1746).

[39] Lange was the son of the theologian Joachim Lange (1670–1744), a noted exponent of Pietism. In 1738, S. G. Lange and his wife took Pyra into their home at Laublingen bei Halle, where the two poets devoted themselves intensively to writing poetry for more than three years.

[40] Although these names came originally from classical sources, they travelled to Germany, as did so many 18th-century cultural phenomena, by way of England. The names Damon, Daphnis, Strephon, Alexis, Hylas, Daphne, Lycidas, and Thyrsis, which appear in Lange's and Pyras's poems, in Gellert's *Fabeln und Erzählungen*, and in the Gleim–Ramler and Gleim–Uz correspondences, are found in the *Pastorals* (1709) of Alexander Pope, *Complete Works*, vol. 1 (1871; repr. New York, 1967).

light, sentimental, and satirical poems titled *Versuch in scherzhaften Liedern* [1744], Gleim named Anacreon as his teacher.

It seems likely that there was another circumstance, in addition to the fascination with the playful geniality of pastoral poetry and the Pietistic absorption in close personal relationships, that contributed to the preoccupation with friendship in eighteenth-century Germany. In Germany's political structure, there were many centres of government of various sizes, rather than a single large capital that inevitably became a centre of fashion and culture. Since the proportion of people with cultivated literary tastes was small, it must have been difficult or impossible for those living in small centres to find congenial spirits. The theme of *Einsamkeit* is found in much German poetry of the eighteenth century and in the *moralische Wochenschriften* that were published sporadically in Germany as imitations of the *Spectator* and other English moral weeklies.[41] As 'solitude', one of the words by which it was rendered in English, *Einsamkeit* was beneficial, inasmuch as it afforded precious opportunities for the contemplation of life's highest priorities. *Einsamkeit* in another sense, rendered by 'loneliness', does not play such an explicit role in eighteenth-century German literature; yet it gazes out from between the lines of much discourse, including the writings of Gleim. Loneliness was a blight on the quality of life, to be mitigated by whatever means were available.

Gleim's dedication to friendship is reflected in the copious correspondence that he conducted throughout his life. His letters to fellow poets not only promulgate the Anacreontic style, but also retail information about a variety of subjects and eagerly solicit news. During his intermittent residence in Berlin, he gathered about him a circle of friends:[42] Wilhelm Hempel (d. 1758), a portrait painter;[43] Lucas Friedrich Langemack (d. 1761), a police registrar and councilman; Johann Georg Sulzer (1720–79), successively professor of mathematics and professor of philosophy at the Joachimsthal Gymnasium;[44]

---

[41] Lange, together with his teacher at Halle, G. F. Meier, was the editor of several *moralische Wochenschriften: Der Gesellige* (1748–50), *Der Mensch* (1751–6), *Das Reich der Natur und der Sitten* (1757–62), *Der Glückselige* (1763–8). See *Neue deutsche Biographie*, vol. 13 (Berlin, 1982), 549–50.

[42] In 1740, Gleim left Halle for Berlin, where he held positions simultaneously as tutor in the service of Colonel von Schulz in Potsdam and secretary to Prince Wilhelm of Brandenburg-Schwedt in Berlin. In 1744 he accompanied Prince Wilhelm to the second Silesian War. After the prince had fallen, Gleim returned to Berlin to become secretary to Prince Leopold von Dessau and lived in Berlin until his departure for Halberstadt in 1747. See *Allgemeine deutsche Biographie*, Vol. 9 (Leipzig, 1879), 228–9.

[43] Information about Hempel and several other members of Gleim's circle (Sulzer, Sucro, Bergius, and Krause) is found in the list of members in the *Kalender auf das Jahr des Montagsklubs 1849*, (Berlin), 2–5, which gives birth and death dates (if known), dates of membership in the *Club*, and professional positions held. Their names also appear frequently in Gleim's correspondence with Ramler (see n. 45).

[44] Sulzer's most important and lasting accomplishment was his encyclopaedia of the fine arts, *Allgemeine Theorie der schönen Künste* (see n. 8).

Karl Wilhelm Ramler (1725–98) and Ewald von Kleist (1715–59), poets;
Johann Georg Sucro (1722–86), a pastor;[45] Ernst Samuel Jakob Borchward
(1717–76), Prussian court councillor and Ansbach-Bayreuth resident;
Johann Wilhelm Bergius (1713–63), a court councillor; Samuel Buchholtz
(1717–74), a pastor; Christian Gottfried Krause, (1719–70), civil court
counsel.[46] The names of these men, many of whom owed their livelihood to
positions in the bureaucracy of the Prussian government, appear in Gleim's
correspondence, and we are often permitted small glimpses of their personalities. That several of these colleagues perceived themselves as a close group is
suggested by a remark in one of Ramler's letters to Gleim: 'Here is a whole
streetful of friends . . . Langemack, Sulzer, Bergius, Ramler, Krause, all live in a
row.'[47]

Towards the end of 1747, Gleim left Berlin to become secretary of the
cathedral chapter in Halberstadt, a small town about a hundred miles south-
west of Berlin.[48] He made occasional trips to Berlin and was visited in
Halberstadt by friends from all parts of Germany, but his life was far more
solitary than in Berlin. Gleim's letters from Halberstadt to Ramler in Berlin are
sprinkled with requests for news about the circle of friends and hints to Ramler
that the circle must be preserved.[49]

Ironically, it was not until Gleim had left Berlin that his circle coalesced into
an institution. In the autumn of 1749, Johann Georg Schultheß (1724–
1804), a young Swiss candidate for the pastorate, arrived in Berlin for a visit of
a few months. He stayed long enough to persuade six members of the Gleim
circle—Sulzer, Langemack, Hempel, Sucro, Ramler, and Bergius—to form an
organization that took the English club as its model.[50] In its early years, the

[45] Sucro was editor of the *moralische Wochenschrift* titled *Der Druide* (Berlin, 1748–50). See
*Briefwechsel zwischen Gleim und Ramler*, vol. 1, ed. Carl Schüddekopf, Bibliothek des Litteratur
Vereins in Stuttgart, vol. 242 (Tübingen, 1906/7), 142.

[46] Krause's passion for music seems to have equalled his allegiance to the legal profession. As
an accomplished amateur, whom his father may have originally intended for a musical career, he
was a keyboardist and violinist, an accomplished timpanist, a composer, and the author of a noted
monograph on music aesthetics: *Von der musikalischen Poesie* (Berlin, 1752). See Joseph Beaujean,
*Christian Gottfried Krause: Sein Leben und seine Persönlichkeit im Verhältnis zu den musikalischen
Problemen des 18. Jahrhunderts als Ästhetiker und Musiker* (Dillingen am Donau, 1930), 8–9 and
*passim*.

[47] *Gleim–Ramler Briefwechsel*, i. 227 (letter of May 1750): 'Hier ist eine gantze Straße voll
Freunde . . . Langemack, Sulzer, Bergius, Ramler, Krause wohnen alle in geraden Linie.'

[48] See *Briefwechsel zwischen Gleim und Uz*, ed. Carl Schüddekopf, Bibliothek des Litteratur
Vereins in Stuttgart, vol. 218 (Tübingen, 1899), 198, for Gleim's letter of 31 Jan. 1748, in which
he writes that he has taken the post in Halberstadt, breaking his vow never to let himself be
persuaded to leave Berlin: 'Mich soll kein Fürst, aus deinen Mauren bringen / Wenn mich ein Gott
in sie Zurück gebracht.'

[49] *Gleim–Ramler Briefwechsel*, i. 94–189: Gleim's letters of 1748–9 are full of solicitous inquiries
about the group in Berlin and gentle reproaches to Ramler for neglecting certain members of the
group.

[50] Gleim was informed of the founding of the Berlin *Club* in a letter dated December 1749. See
*Briefe der Schweizer Bodmer, Sulzer, Geßner aus Gleims litterarischem Nachlasse*, ed. Wilhelm Körte

*Club,* to be known eventually as the Berliner Montags-Klub, seems to have met on Thursday evenings for fellowship, supper, and conversation. The organization admitted Christian Gottfried Krause (see n. 47) in 1750 and, during the decade that followed, accepted Gotthold Ephraim Lessing (1729–81) and the publishers Christian Friedrich Voß (1725–95) and Christoph Friedrich Nicolai (1733–1811) as members. In this decade, its rolls also included Johann Friedrich Ernst Schlichting (d. 1775), possibly the Schlichting whose name appears as copyist of a number of C. P. E. Bach's keyboard works.[51]

Although literature and the arts seem to have been important topics of conversation, the organization did not limit its membership to professional writers and artists. Meetings of the *Club* were not devoted entirely to intellectual exchange, or, on the other hand, simply to social activities, but to a mixture of the two. The organization was highly selective, requiring affirmative votes of all but one member for acceptance into the group.[52] Only four professional musicians—Quantz, Agricola, Reichardt, and Zelter—were admitted during the eighteenth century, and although it is sometimes assumed that C. P. E. Bach, Carl Heinrich and Johann Gottlieb Graun, Christoph Nichelmann, and Franz Benda were members, their names do not appear on the membership rolls.[53]

The *Club,* despite its exclusiveness, did contribute in some measure to the cause of friendship. It was a means of furthering the collaboration between Krause and Ramler for the collection of musical settings of Anacreontic poems published in 1753.[54] It appears that the *Club* was not so exclusive that

(Zurich, 1804), 116–17. One of the most entertaining discussions of the English clubs of the early eighteenth century is Joseph Addison's satirical description in *The Spectator* (no. 9, 10 Mar. 1711). See *The Spectator*, ed. Henry Morley (London, 1891), 337–41.

[51] Gleim–Ramler: 4 Mar., 24 May, 27 July 1748; 13 Mar. 1749; all of the manuscripts for which Schlichting can be identified as copyist contain either solo keyboard works or works with a leading keyboard part (by C. P. E. Bach: D-brd B, P 772 (H. 5/W. 65, 3 and H. 52/W. 65, 21); P 776 (H. 64/W. 65, 26); P 786 (H. 23/W. 65, 12); St 197 (H. 407/W. 5); St 524 (H. 441/W. 31); St 534 (H. 442/W. 32); St 544 (H. 420/W. 17); and by J. S. Bach: D-brd B, St 463–St 468 (BWV 1014–1019).

[52] *Kalender*, 31, rule VIII.

[53] See *Gleim–Ramler Briefwechsel*, ii. 394, in which Ramler names Quantz, Agricola, Nichelmann, and Krause as members of the *Club*; Bernhard Engelke, 'Neues zur Geschichte der Berliner Liederschule', *Riemann-Festschrift* (1909; repr. Tutzing, 1965), 463, mentions Nichelmann, Carl Heinrich Graun, and Bach as members; Beaujean, *Krause*, p. 11, also calls Nichelmann a member and asserts that during Krause's time, Bach, Franz Benda, and the Graun brothers frequented ('verkehrten') the *Club*; Paul F. Marks, in 'The Rhetorical Element in Musical "Sturm und Drang": Christian Gottfried Krause's "Von der musikalischen Poesie"', *MR*, 33 (1972), 100, implies that Bach, Nichelmann, and two of the Benda brothers, Franz and Georg, were members.

[54] *Oden mit Melodien* (Berlin, 1753), published anonymously by Krause and Ramler. A number of similar anthologies, containing settings of secular and spiritual poems appeared in Berlin in the 1750s: *Oden mit Melodien*, Pt. 2 (1755); [F. W. Marpurg,] *Neue Lieder zum Singen beym Claviere* (1756); [Marpurg], *Geistliche, moralische und weltliche Oden . . .* (1758); [Marpurg,] *Geistliche Oden in Melodien gesetzt von einigen Tonkünstlern in Berlin* (1758). Although these collections were by no means an official function of the *Club*, they included music and poetry by some of its members and surely were of interest to the organization.

membership in it precluded fraternization with non-members. Gleim, in one of his letters, mentions a visit to Berlin during which he met 'daily' with a group that included C. P. E. Bach and one of the Graun brothers as well as those whose names are on the rolls of the *Club*:

> Ramler, Lessing, Sulzer, Agricola, Krause (the musician, not the stupid journalist), Bach, Graun—in short, all that belong to the muses and the liberal arts—joined each other daily, sometimes on land, sometimes on the water; what fun it was in such society to vie with the swans swimming in the Spree! What a pleasure to lose oneself in the Tiergarten, along with the entire group, among a thousand girls![55]

C. P. E. Bach was probably acquainted with members of Gleim's circle during the 1740s, but he appears to have become more deeply involved with the group around 1750. In 1751, Bach stopped in Halberstadt en route to Brunswick and Hamburg.[56] His name appears from time to time during the 1750s in Gleim's correspondence with Uz and Ramler.[57] Several of Bach's character pieces are named after members of the Gleim circle: after Gleim himself and, surely, after Krause (*La Gause*), after Bergius, Borchward, and Buchholtz. Although Bach's circle of friends and Gleim's obviously intersected, the titles of the character pieces indicate that it also included 'originals' who were outside the group that Gleim mentions with affection and concern.[58]

*La Pott.* The name of Johann Heinrich Pott (1692–1777), professor of chemistry at the Medicinisch-Chirurgische Bildungsanstalt in Berlin and member of the Academy, does appear in a letter from Ramler to Gleim where Pott is discussed, in a rather detached manner, as the author of a controversial publication.[59]

*La Stahl.* Georg Ernst Stahl (1713–72), son of a more famous father with the same name (1660–1734), was the court councillor and physician in whose home J. S. Bach stayed during his visit to Berlin in 1741; two members of the Stahl family were godparents to C. P. E. Bach's children.[60]

---

[55] *Gleim–Uz Briefwechsel*, 291 (16 Aug. 1758): 'Ramler, Lessing, Sulzer, Agricola, Krause (der Musicus, nicht der dumme Zeitungsschreiber, für den behüte der Himmel), Bach, Graun, kurz alles, was zu den Musen und freyen Künsten gehört, gesellte sich täglich zu einander, bald zu Lande, bald zu Wasser; was für Vergnügen war es in solcher Gesellschaft auf der Spree mit den Schwänen um die Wette zu schwimmen! Was für Lust, in dem Thier-Garten sich mit der gantzen Gesellschaft unter tausend Mädchen zu verirren!' Agricola had joined the *Club* in 1750; Lessing, in 1752.

[56] *Gleim–Uz Briefwechsel*, p. 231.

[57] See *Gleim–Uz Briefwechsel*, pp. 105, 231, 248, 291, 313, and *Gleim–Ramler Briefwechsel*, vol. 2, pp 18, 38, 75, 225, 245, 259, 307, 345, 350–1.

[58] In the famous preface to the *Pièces de clavecin*, Couperin speaks of the persons to whom his titles refer as 'their lovable originals'.

[59] *Gleim–Ramler Briefwechsel*, i. 114 (9 Apr. 1748); see also *Allgemeine deutsche Biographie*, vol. 26 (Leipzig, 1888), 486 f.

[60] Heinrich Miesner, 'Beziehungen zwischen den Familien Stahl und Bach', *BJ*, 30 (1933), 71–6; Frau Hofrätin Stahl was godmother to Johann August in 1745, and Herr Hofrat Stahl was godfather to Anna Carolina Philippina in 1747.

*La Boehmer.* The 'original' of this piece may have been one of the sons of a famous jurist, Just Henning Böhmer (1674–1749): probably Johann Samuel Friedrich (1704–73), jurist and author of reforms of the penal code, and after 1750 professor of law at the University in Frankfurt an der Oder. Böhmer married Luise Charlotte, daughter of the elder Georg Ernst Stahl.[61]

*L'Herrmann.* The subject of this piece may have been Friedrich Gottfried Herrmann, privy councillor and clerk, who is mentioned in a letter from Sucro to Ramler.[62]

*La Prinzette.* This title may refer to Johanna Benedicte von Printzen, wife of Baron Friedrich Wilhelm von Printzen. Baroness von Printzen and her mother were listed among those present at the christening of C. P. E. Bach's son Johann Sebastian on 26 September 1748.[63]

Curiously, two prominent members of Gleim's circle in Berlin, Ramler and Sulzer, do not seem to be represented among the character pieces (unless by cryptic titles whose topicality is now lost).[64] It would be interesting, in fact, and possibly even enlightening, to know why Bach chose the particular 'originals' whom he distinguished with his vignettes of 1754–7. Stahl and the putative 'original' of *La Prinzette* were friends of Bach's family. Gleim and Krause were connected with Bach professionally through the publication of collections of *Lieder*. Borchward, like Krause, was an amateur composer, and Bach may have advised him formally or informally.[65] A letter from Ramler to Gleim indicates that Bergius may also have been an amateur composer. 'Bergius wrote to me yesterday,' says the poet, 'to [ask me to] make him a cantata. It doesn't have to be beautiful because it will be sung beautifully. And if a beauty sings it, how can it fail to be successful?'[66]

Is there a rationale behind Bach's choice of the other 'originals'? Perhaps some were the keyboard students for whom he composed lessons and wrote embellishments. His performance of the character pieces must surely have inspired his students, for by at least one eighteenth-century account (see n. 15) these pieces, like Couperin's *pièces de caractère*, came alive under the composer's fingers. It is possible that *all* of the 'originals' that Bach honoured

---

[61] See *Allgemeine deutsche Biographie*, vol. 3 (Leipzig, 1876), 76.

[62] See Friedrich Wilhelm, 'Briefe an Karl Wilhelm Ramler', *Vierteljahrschrift für Litteraturgeschichte*, 4 (1891), 77.

[63] Heinrich Miesner, 'Aus der Umwelt Philipp Emanuel Bachs', *BJ*, 34 (1937), 133–5.

[64] It is possible that the title *L'Aly Rupalich* referred to Ramler, who, in his letters to Gleim, sometimes signed himself with the pastoral name 'Alexis'. The initials of the title would thus have correspond to Ramler's initials. Ramler seems to have had the rather intense, energetic character that this piece conveys.

[65] See *Allgemeine deutsche Biographie*, 3 (1876), 156. Robert Eitner, *Biographisches-Bibliographisches Quellen-Lexikon*, 2nd rev. edn. (Graz, 1959), ii. 130, lists a sonata by Borchward as part of the Thulemeier collection in the Joachimsthal Gymnasium.

[66] *Gleim–Ramler Briefwechsel*, i. 120 (7 May 1748): 'Bergius schrieb mir gestern ihm eine Cantate zu machen. Sie darf nicht schön seyn, denn sie wird schön gesungen werden. Und wenn sie eine Schöne singt, wie kann es ihr an Beyfall fehlen.'

with character pieces were connected in some way with the composition or performance of the songs of the First Berlin *Lieder* School, a repertory that consisted in large part of settings of odes and other anacreontic poems. Bach's character pieces, like the writings of Gleim and his contemporaries, may have been composed to flatter and entertain his friends and to assure them of his regard for them. These twenty-four miniatures of 1754–7, like the *Kleinig-keiten* of Gleim, Uz, and Ramler, are light-hearted and playful, but they are more than mere bagatelles. They reflect a significant stage in Bach's development as a composer. In them, he examined the rondo principle purposefully and combined it with several other formal methods, preparing the way for the great expansive rondos of the 'Kenner und Liebhaber' collections.

# The Letters from C. P. E. Bach to K. W. Ramler

## Stephen L. Clark

WHEN C. P. E. Bach left Berlin in 1768 to assume the responsibilities of music director of the five main churches in Hamburg, he did not lose touch with his former home. In fact, upon his departure from Berlin, Frederick the Great's sister Princess Anna Amalia named Bach her honorary Kapellmeister. Bach also maintained a lively correspondence with a number of Berlin residents while he was in Hamburg. This correspondence includes four letters from Bach to the Berlin poet Karl Wilhelm Ramler, which are presented here with translations[1] and commentary.

Two of the letters, dated 5 May 1778 and 20 November 1780, have been published previously.[2] The other two, dated 5 December 1781 and 21 January 1785, are part of the collection of the National Forschungs- und Gedenkstätten der klassischen deutschen Literatur in Weimar and are given here for the first time. Ramler was the author of the libretto for Bach's cantata *Die Auferstehung und Himmelfahrt Jesu* H. 777/W. 240 (hereinafter *Auferstehung*), and the letters concern revisions and publication plans for the cantata. Bach composed the work in 1774, made extensive revisions at least until 1784, and finally, after several change of heart, published the work with Breitkopf in 1787.[3] The letters to Ramler reveal a close collaboration between the poet and the composer on the subject of revisions, and they help to clarify why it took so long for Bach to have the cantata printed.

The 1778 letter was written less than two months after the first public performance of *Auferstehung* on 18 March,[4] and Bach refers to a positive reception.

---

[1] I am grateful to Ute Brandes for assistance with the translations.

[2] Friedrich Wilhelm, 'Briefe an Karl Wilhelm Ramler nebst einem Briefe an Lessing', *Vierteljahrschrift für Litteraturgeschichte*, 4 (1891), 254, 256–7. The autograph of the first letter is in the Bachhaus, Eisenach, the second is in GB Lbm, Add. MS. 47843. I would like to thank Rachel Wade for providing me with a photograph of the second letter.

[3] Richard Kramer has summarized documents pertaining to the composition and revision of *Auferstehung* in 'The New Modulation of the 1770s: C. P. E. Bach in Theory, Criticism, and Practice', *JAMS*, 38 (1985), 578–81.

[4] A review of 17 Mar. 1778 in the *Hamburgische unparteiische Correspondent* (hereinafter, *HCorr*) publicizes a performance of *Auferstehung* to take place the following day. A notice of 4 Apr. 1778 in *HCorr* refers to a performance on 6 Apr.

Hamburg, d. 5 May 78.

Liebster Herr Professor, und alter Freund,

Die Composition Ihrer sehr schönen Cantate hat mir viel Vergnügen gemacht. Sie hat das Glück gehabt zu gefallen. Ob sie es verdient, laße ich dahin gestellt seyn. Ihre Veränderungen haben Grund. Vielleicht kan ich davon einen Gebrauch machen. So leicht aber, wie Sie, liebster Freund, glauben, wird es nicht angehen. Vielleicht denke ich vorher, ehe ich schreibe, mehr, als gewöhnlich. Indeßen bin ich Ihnen dafür, besonders für das geneigte Andenken meiner Person sehr verbunden. Ich werde nicht leicht Berlin wieder zu sehen kriegen; aber wie groß wurde meine Freude seyn, Sie, alter Freund, noch in meinem Leben einmahl hier zu umhalsen!

Thun Sie dies. Ich bin mit der vollkommensten Hochachtung jederzeit

Ihr ergebenster<br>
Freund und Diener<br>
Bach.

An den Herrn Professor Ramler, in Berlin.

Hamburg, the 5th of May 1778.

Dearest Professor, and old friend,

The composition of your very beautiful cantata has given me much pleasure. It has succeeded in pleasing others; whether deservedly or not, who can say? Your changes are justified. Perhaps I can make use of them. They cannot be realized as easily as you believe, though, dearest friend. Perhaps I will ponder more than usual, before I write. Meanwhile, I am greatly obliged to you for these, especially for favouring me with remembrances. I will not get to see Berlin again very easily, but how great would my joy be, old friend, to embrace you here once more in my life.

It is up to you. I am always with the fullest respect

Your most devoted<br>
friend and servant<br>
Bach.

To Professor Ramler, in Berlin.

From this letter it would appear that Ramler initiated some of the revisions in the cantata. The process of revision was clearly a collaborative one, but it may have been Ramler's interest in tinkering with the text as much as Bach's desire for musical improvements that was the source of some changes. Bach's intention to give special care to the revisions reflects his high regard for the cantata, an opinion he reiterated over the years.

The next letter is more specific about revisions to *Auferstehung.*

Hamburg, d. 20. Nov. 80

Bester Freund

So schön Ihre eingesandte Arie ist, so wünschte ich doch, daß sie im ersten Theile gleich mit einem zärtlichen Adagio anfinge, bey dem ich mich, wie bey allen ersten Theilen einer Arie, ausdehnen könnte. Der andere und kürzere Theil kan aus den 3 letzten Zeilen bestehen, und damit wird die Arie, <u>ohne da Capo</u> geschloßen. Wenn ich Ihr fiat! bekommen kan, so bin ich sehr zufrieden; Z. B. wenn die Arie mit den Worten: <u>Wie bang</u>—bis <u>Lied geweint</u> den ersten Theil ausmacht, und die 3 letzten Zeilen mit den Worten: <u>Heil mir!</u> bis <u>Gram sich auf</u>, die Arie ohne da Capo schließen. Von dieser Art Arie haben wir in der ganzen Cantate noch keine: hingegen sind 4 Arien in diesem Stücke, wovon der erste Theil munter, und der 2te Theil langsamer ist. Die Aenderungen im Recitative sind bereits geschehen und ich erwarte von Ihrer Güte ein baldiges fiat! oder was dem ähnlich ist. Ich umarme Sie und bin

> Ihr alter treuer Fr. und Dr.
> Bach.

NB nicht zûgĕbĕn,[5] bleibt

[in margin:] Weil ich nicht weiß, ob Sie Ihren Aufsatz noch haben, so schicke ich ihn wieder mit: erbitte mir ihn aber wieder. Beykommenden Brief werden Sie gütigst bald dem Herrn Wever[6] zustellen lassen.

Hamburg, the 20th of November 1780

Dearest friend,

Beautiful as the aria that you sent is, I would prefer that it begin directly in the first section with a <u>tender</u> Adagio, which I could expand as in all initial sections of an aria. The other and <u>shorter</u> part can consist of the last three lines and with that the aria is being closed <u>without da capo</u>. If I can receive your approval, then I shall be very satisfied. For example, if the first part of the aria consists of the words: <u>Wie bang</u> until <u>Lied geweint</u> and the last three lines with the words: <u>Heil mir</u> until <u>Gram sich auf</u> close the aria without da capo. We still have no arias of this type in the whole cantata, whereas there are 4 arias in this piece in which the first part is lively and the second part slower. The changes in the recitatives have already taken place and I await from your kindness a speedy approval or something similar. I embrace you and am

> Your old true friend and servant
> Bach.

NB nicht zûgĕbĕn, stays.

[in margin:] Since I don't know whether you still have your essay, I am sending it along again, but please send it back again. Will you be so good as to arrange soon the delivery of the enclosed letter to Mr Wever.

Bach inserted the aria discussed in this letter, 'Wie bang', in place of an aria beginning with the text, 'Sey gegrüßet'. The autograph score of *Auferstehung* has only the new aria. Bach used 'Sey gegrüßet' later in his 1784 Easter Cantata (H. 807/W. 243), and the aria survives in the autograph score of that work.[7] The physical structure of these two manuscripts suggests that Bach

---

[5] The words 'nicht zugeben' occur in the first chorus of the cantata.

[6] Wever was a book-dealer in Berlin (Wilhelm, 'Briefe', p. 257).

[7] The autograph score of *Auferstehung* and a set of parts marked by Bach are in D-brd B, Mus. ms. Bach P 336 and St 178 respectively. The autograph score of the 1784 Easter Cantata is in D-ddr Bds, Mus. ms. Bach P 339.

removed three bifolios with the 'Sey gegrüßet' aria from the *Auferstehung* score and then inserted three new ones with the 'Wie bang' aria.[8]

The texts of both arias relate well to the preceding recitative in *Auferstehung* discussing the empty grave and the fulfillment of the prophesy of Christ's ascension. The earlier text is joyful throughout, while the new text begins in a mournful tone before turning to an expression of joy.

> Sey gegrüßet, Fürst des Lebens!
> Jauchzet, die sein Tod betrübte!
> Er, den dieser Hügel deckte,
> Jesus lebt; ihr klagt vergebens!
> Sehet da sein leeres Grab!
>
> Der die Todten auferweckte,
> Sollte der im Grabe bleiben?
> Himmel! soll der Gottgeliebte,
> Soll der Gottheit Sohn zerstäuben?
> Todesengel, lasset ab!
>
> Wie bang hat dich mein Lied beweint;
> Ach! unser Trost, der Menschenfreund
> Sieht keinen Tröster, steht verlassen,
> Der blutet, der sein Volk geheilt,
> Der Tote weckte, muß erblassen:
> So hat mein banges Lied geweint.
>
> Heil mir! Du steigst vom Grab herauf,
> Mein Herz zerfließt in Freudenzähren.
> In Wonne löst mein Gram sich auf.

Bach carried out the musical plan for the 'Wie bang' aria described in his letter to Ramler. The first six lines of the poem are set in the manner of a standard first section of a da capo aria, with an 'adagio' tempo. An 'allegro' second section sets the final three lines of the poem and there is no da capo.[9] It is curious that Bach was seeking Ramler's approval for these musical decisions. Their relationship clearly went beyond that of composer and mere supplier of texts.

In the letter Bach hints that the new aria was intended to add some variety to the cantata: 'We still have no arias of this type in the whole cantata, whereas there are 4 arias in this piece in which the first part is lively and the

---

[8]  A more detailed discussion of the manuscripts is in Stephen L. Clark, 'The Occasional Choral Works of C. P. E. Bach', Ph.D. diss., Princeton University, 1984, 168–70.

Early textbooks of *Auferstehung* contain the 'Sey gegrüßet' text (there is a copy attached to the autograph score and another in D-brd Hs, 70001/19). Also, the 1772 edition of Ramler's poetry has the 'Sey gegrüßet' aria, while the 1801 edition has 'Wie bang' with 'Sey gegrüßet' included in a 'Lesearten der Ausgabe vom Jahre 1772' section.

[9]  'Sey gegrüßet' is allegro throughout and has a written out da capo. The two arias do share the same key (B flat major), voice part (soprano) and instrumentation (strings and continuo).

second part slower.' In fact, 'Wie bang' is the only aria in Bach's surviving choral works that has a slow first section, a fast second section, and no da capo. The fact that 'Sey gegrüßet' is a parody of an aria from a 1763 wedding cantata also may have had something to do with its replacement.[10]

The next letter from Bach to Ramler is dated more than a year after the letter discussing the 'Wie bang' aria.

Hamburg, d. 5 Dec. 81

Ich bedaure Sie herzlich, liebster Herr Profeßor, wegen des Verlußtes Ihres braven Generals.

Herr Lehmann hat abermahl durch Herr Chodowieki um unsere Cantate angesuchet. Ich werde sie nicht leicht wieder aufführen. Zum Druck ist sie etwas kostbar. Sie ist unter allen meinen Singstücken im Ausdruck und in der Arbeit vorzüglich. Es wäre Schade, wenn sie bey Ihrer sehr schönen Poesie beständig bey mir verschloßen bleiben und nicht gehört werden sollte.

Herr Lehmann kan damit machen, was er gut findet, wenn er mir 100 Dukaten dafür giebt. Durch Ihre Veränderungen in den Worten ist meine Partitur etwas unleserlicher geworden, als sie vorher war. Folglich will ich, wenn wir eins werden, eine saubere und ganz correkte Copie der Partitur besorgen, und zwar unter meinen Augen in meinem Hause. Diese Partitur ist 44 ziemlich voller Bogen stark und es ist nicht unbillig, wenn Herr Lehmann wegen meiner Durchsicht und Mühe, über obige 100 Dukaten, noch 2 zulegt. Ich erwarte Ihre gütige Antwort hierüber bald. Die Bezahlung geschieht bey meiner Auslieferung hier. Ich beharre, wie allezeit,

Ihr wahrer Freund u. ergebenster Diener     Bach.

[in margin:] Ich bin gar nicht in Verlegenheit, wenn aus unsrem Handel nichts wird; folglich erwarte ich von Ihrer Güte eine ungeschminkte Antwort

Hamburg, the 5th of December 1781

I pity you from the heart, dearest professor, because of the loss of your brave general.

Mr Lehmann has once again made a request through Mr Chodowieki about our cantata. I will not perform it again easily. It is somewhat expensive to print. It is pre-eminent among all my vocal works in expression and in the composition. It would be a shame, considering your very beautiful poetry, should it remain locked up with me and not be heard.

Mr Lehmann can do with it what he pleases (he considers it good), if he gives me 100 ducats. My score has become somewhat more unreadable than it was before because of your changes in the words. Accordingly, I intend to procure a clean and quite correct copy of the score, if we reach an agreement, and indeed under my supervision in my house. This score is 44 rather full sheets large and it is not unreasonable for Mr Lehmann to add another 2 ducats to the above mentioned, on account of my revision and trouble. I expect your gracious answer about this matter soon. The payment takes place here with my delivery. I remain, as always,

your true friend and most sincere servant     Bach.

[10] For information on the wedding cantata see Heinrich Miesner, *Philipp Emanuel Bach in Hamburg* (Leipzig, 1929; repr. Wiesbaden, 1969), 76, 90–1 and Clark, Occasional Choral Works', pp. 189–90.

[in margin:] I am not at all in difficulty even if nothing comes out of our deal. As a result I expect from your kindness a plain answer.

Bach makes clear his own high opinion of the cantata in this letter, and we also learn of his unwillingness to have the piece printed, at least when the letter was written. He had broached the subject of printing the cantata earlier in three letters to his Leipzig publisher, Breitkopf.[11] In the correspondence with Breitkopf Bach discusses specific details about the project and suggests that the procedures to be followed should be similar to those Breitkopf used in printing Bach's oratorio *Die Israeliten in der Wüste* in 1775.

By the end of 1781, as he relates in the letter to Ramler, Bach had abandoned publication plans. His main reason for not printing the cantata at this time was clearly that he did not think it would be profitable.[12] This reasoning is entirely consistent with Bach's characteristic good sense when it came to money matters.

Since Bach did not pursue publication of the cantata in 1781, anyone who was interested in performing the piece had to obtain a copy from Bach himself. Most of the 1781 letter to Ramler concerns just such a request for a copy, apparently made more than once by Herr Lehmann. The request was delivered to Bach through the Berlin painter, Chodowiecki.[13] Bach tells Ramler of his intention to supervise the copying of the score for Lehmann, should the proper financial arrangements be agreed upon.[14] He refers specifically to the autograph score, and his description of the condition of the manuscript ('somewhat more unreadable') reflects the many revisions that had been made.[15]

Bach's request for Ramler's approval to have the cantata copied and for the amount of the fee to be collected from Lehmann again shows the closeness of the relationship between them. The poet and composer must have had some sort of agreement about the distribution of the cantata, and Ramler was

[11] Two of the letters are dated (27 Oct. 1780 and 14 Feb. 1781), and a third is postmarked 31 Jan. 1781. The letters are published in *Suchalla/Briefe*, pp. 135–9. Dr Suchalla was kind enough to provide me with a typescript of relevant letters to Breitkopf before the publication of his book.

[12] I am grateful to Richard Kramer and Rachel Wade for sharing their thoughts on this subject.

[13] Daniel Chodowiecki (1726–1801). See Hans-Günter Ottenberg, *Carl Philipp Emanuel Bach* (Leipzig, 1982), 203, 392. David Schulenberg has suggested to me that Lehmann is probably Johann Philipp Lehmann or his son Georg Gottlieb (1745–1816), both of whom served as organist at the Nikolaikirche in Berlin.

[14] Bach also followed this procedure with his 1769 Passion Cantata. There are at least 20 surviving manuscript scores of this piece, many of which were prepared under Bach's supervision (see Clark, 'Occasional Choral Works', p. 52). Other than the autograph, I know of only one surviving manuscript score of *Auferstehung*, in A Wgm, Q 678. This is the score used and marked by Mozart for performances of *Auferstehung* in 1788 (see Andreas Holschneider, 'C. Ph. E. Bachs Kantate "Auferstehung und Himmelfahrt Jesu" und Mozarts Aufführungen des Jahres 1788', *MJ* (1968/70), 264–80). Given the length of time it took for Bach to publish *Auferstehung*, it would not be surprising if other manuscript scores are discovered in the future.

[15] The autograph score, D-brd B, Mus. ms. Bach P 336, consists of 44 bifolios, corresponding to the reference in Bach's letter.

apparently supposed to receive royalties for his poetry, just as Bach was for his music.

Bach pursued publication of the cantata again in 1784. Evidence of this renewed interest is found in two notices in *HCorr* dated 9 July and 17 December 1784, and in the correspondence with Breitkopf. Bach's decision to publish the cantata is announced in the first notice (a reprint, with slight changes, of the 17 March 1778 review in *HCorr*): '. . . however, he [Bach] has finally decided to publish this excellent Ramler cantata (it is no oratorio) in a full score, just as the *Israeliten*, with [the] music printer, Breitkopf'.[16] The 17 December advertisement lists the subscription price for the score ('3 Thaler 8 Groschen') and mentions that it is scheduled to appear at Easter.

Then, in a long letter dated 23 December 1784, Bach asks Breitkopf to stop printing the cantata immediately because of the small number of subscribers. He offers to cover any expenses Breitkopf has incurred, explaining that a small loss would be better than proceeding with the print and suffering greater losses. Bach asks for the return of the *Auferstehung* manuscript and mentions plans to prepare a keyboard edition, for which he anticipates a greater demand (possibly because of the success of the keyboard edition of his cantata *Morgengesang am Schöpfungsfeste*, published by Breitkopf in 1784). He also refers to extensive revisions in the manuscript.

Bach announced the cancellation of the printing of the score and the possibility of a keyboard edition in a notice of 12 January 1785 in *HCorr*. The last letter from Bach to Ramler is dated nine days after this notice.

Hamburg, d. 21 Jan. 85.

Liebster alter Freund,

Was denken Sie! Unsere Cantate wird nicht gedruckt. Ich kriege die Kosten bey weitem nicht heraus. Sagen Sie mir doch offenherzig, aus gewißen Ursachen: hat der Herzog von Curland,[17] bey dem Sie oft gegeßen haben, nie etwas gegen Sie von mir gesprochen? u. wenn es geschehen ist, was? Herr Hering[18] wird Ihnen die gütigst übersandten 3 Rt. 8 Gr. wieder geben. Gratias! Bedauern Sie mich! Lieben Sie ferner

Ihren Verehrer
Bach.

H. Prof. Ramler

[16] '. . . endlich aber hat er sich entschlossen, diese vortreffliche Ramlersche Cantate (sie ist kein Oratorium) in einer vollständigen Partitur, so wie die Israeliten, mit Breitkopfschen Notendruck herauszugeben.' Bach refers to the timing of the announcement in a letter to Breitkopf of 23 June 1784, in which he discusses details about printing the cantata (see *Suchalla/Briefe*, p. 167).

[17] Bach had dedicated a set of six concertos to Peter III, the last duke of Curland (1724–1800) in 1772 (see Rachel Wade, *The Keyboard Concertos of Carl Philipp Emanuel Bach* (Ann Arbor, 1981) 57). The duke presented Bach with a gold medallion in 1782 (see *Suchalla/Briefe*, p. 562). Bach's music was available in Curland through his friend and agent, Baron Dietrich Ewald von Grotthus (1751–86), a resident of Gieddutz.

[18] Johann Friedrich Hering was an agent for Bach in Berlin (see Wade, *Keyboard Concertos*, p. 40; *Suchalla/Briefe*, pp. 305, 542).

Hamburg, the 21st of January 1785

Dearest old friend,

What do you think! Our cantata is not being printed. I will not retrieve the cost any more, by far. Tell me <u>openly</u>, for certain reasons: has the Duke of Curland, with whom you have often dined, ever said something to you about me? And if so, what? Mr Hering will return to you the most kindly sent 3 Thaler 8 Groschen. Thank you! Sympathize with me! Continue to love

your devotee
<u>Bach.</u>
To Prof. Ramler

Once again the reason given to Ramler for abandoning the publication plans is that Bach was not anticipating a return on his investment. Ramler himself had apparently subscribed, since Bach returned the amount of the subscription price announced in the *HCorr* notice of 17 December 1784.

Breitkopf finally printed a full score of the cantata in 1787 after two more years of extensive negotiations. In fourteen letters to Breitkopf, written between April 1785 and February 1787, Bach works out the details of the size, appearance, price, and marketing of the print, and he also manages to persuade Breitkopf to assume the financial risk—an unusual arrangement.[19] Bach once again solicits subscriptions at the price of 3 Thaler 8 Groschen in a notice in *HCorr* dated 2 August 1786. A notice of 10 March 1787 attests to the appearance of the print and a rise in the price to 4 Thalers. The notice continues with high praise of the cantata, and the wording suggests that Bach may have helped write the advertisement: 'We must only repeat a certain amount [from previous reviews][20] out of conviction that we consider this work [to be] one of the greatest masterpieces that our celebrated Kapellmeister has ever composed.'[21] It is likely that there was further correspondence with Ramler at this point that has not survived.

Sales of the cantata print were not what Bach and Breitkopf had hoped for, and Bach manages an interesting rationalization for the slow business in a letter to Breitkopf dated 21 September 1787:

This Ramler cantata is, to be sure, by me. However, I can claim, without ridiculous egotism, that it will wear well for many years, because it is among my masterpieces an important one, from which young composers can learn something. In time it will also

---

[19] Excerpts from two of these letters (dated 30 Nov. 1785 and 28 Feb. 1786) and a facsimile of a third (dated 25 Nov. 1786) are printed in Hermann von Hase, 'Carl Philipp Emanuel Bach und Joh. Gottl. Im. Breitkopf', *BJ*, 8 (1911), 102–3. All the letters are in *Suchalla/Briefe*.

[20] The previous reviews appeared in *HCorr*, 17 Mar. 1778 and 9 July 1784 (see nn. 4, 16.).

[21] 'Nur so viel müssen wir aus Ueberzeugen wiederholen, daß wir diese Musik für eins der größten Meisterstücke halten, welche unser berühmter Herr Kapellmeister je componirt hat.'

sell as well as Graun's *Tod Jesu*. Initially, there is a hitch with all such things that are written for teaching and not for women and musical windbags.[22]

Bach's categorization of *Auferstehung* as a piece intended for the connoisseur rather than the amateur recalls a 1784 letter to Johann Kühnau in which Bach distinguishes between published works that cater to the general public's taste and unpublished ones that allow a composer more freedom of expression.[23] Although he finally published *Auferstehung*, Bach clearly felt that he had not made any compromises as a composer in order to appeal to a broader audience.

The letters from Bach to Ramler are, then, an integral part of the lengthy history of Bach's revision and publication of his favourite vocal work. The letters betray Bach's typical preoccupation with financial considerations as well as his great care with small details pertaining to the text and music of the cantata. This mixing of practical and aesthetic matters characterizes much of Bach's correspondence. He was a smart businessman,[24] but he always maintained his artistic integrity, especially when dealing with works such as *Auferstehung* for which he had a special fondness.

[22] Hase, 'Carl Philipp Emanuel Bach', p. 104; *Suchalla/Briefe*, p. 221: 'Diese Ramlersche Cantate ist zwar von mir, doch kann ich ohne närrische Eigenliebe behaupten, daß sie sich viele Jahren erhalten wird, weil sie von meinen Meisterstücken ein beträchtliches mit ist, woraus junge Componisten etwas lernen können. Mit der Zeit wird sie auch so vergriffen werden, wie Grauns Tod Jesu. Anfänglich haperts mit allen solchen Sachen, die zur Lehre und nicht für Damen und musikalische Windbeutel geschrieben sind.'

[23] The letter is printed in Friedrich Chrysander, 'Briefe von Karl Philipp Emanuel Bach und G. M. Telemann', *AMZ*, 4 (1869), 186–7 and in La Mara, *Musikerbriefe aus Fünf Jahrhunderten* (Leipzig, 1886), 208–9: 'Bey Sachen, die zum Druck, also für Jedermann, bestimmt sind, seyn Sie weniger künstlich und geben mehr Zucker. . . . In Sachen, die nicht sollen gedruckt werden, lassen Sie Ihrem Fleisse den vollkommenen Lauf.' A translation of part of the letter is in Wade, *Keyboard Concertos*, p. 56. See the article by Pamela Fox in this volume for a discussion of the published vs. unpublished issue.

[24] I am grateful to Dr Ernst Suchalla for sharing his thoughts about Bach's motivations in his business dealings.

# C. P. E. Bach's Aesthetic as Reflected in his Notation

## Etienne Darbellay

THE emergence, at the height of the Enlightenment, of a style such as the *Empfindsamkeit* of C. P. E. Bach is not the least of the paradoxes surrounding the ideas of the Berlin School. At a time when the European *Zeitgeist* is imbued with empiricism and reason, there is an effort to find in the aesthetic of *Affekt* that which cannot be expressed, an effort which, on the level of the compositional process, looks so much like the antithesis of an organized plan that this school is often termed 'pre-Romantic'. Once C. P. E. Bach's procedure has been completely examined, however, what finally emerges is a confirmation of the ideas of the eighteenth century in a form that was not foreseeable from an initial approach to this para-Romantic aesthetic. I shall now explore that paradox from the perspective of notation and the creative conscience that it conveys, both through the famous *Versuch* and through the application of its precepts to music.

A central key to eighteenth-century thinking about the aesthetics of music is the notion of musical expression, as opposed to a parallel domain of musical creation, a domain in which we may characterize music as formal. This notion, though extremely difficult to define systematically, can be easily grasped intuitively. Applied to an isorhythmic *ars nova* motet, the modifier 'expressive' was generally considered inappropriate, whereas it did not occur to anyone to challenge its pertinence in connection with a fantasia for clavier by C. P. E. Bach, however the term was defined philosophically.[1] In most cases, the eighteenth-century aestheticians approached this notion through the mechanism of analogical metaphors which centred basically around metaphors of the human manifestations of expression suitable for a dynamic interpretation that can be related to movement as a visible token of their existence. Thus music (notably in the French and German aesthetics of the second half of the century) comes into its own in the depiction of feelings, through the dynamic devices peculiar to it.

From a sociological point of view, art (and music in particular) for the eighteenth century is primarily an embellishment. Thought of as part of refined sensibility, the art of music is even called *galant*: the feminine sensibility

---

[1] See Willi Apel, *Harvard Dictionary of Music* (Cambridge, Massachusetts, 1973), S. V. 'Expression'.

is viewed as the ideal to which this art must turn. Lacépède revises his 'Poétique de la musique' in the *Bibliothèque universelle des dames* in 1787, carefully noting in his preface that his latest version is purged of any technical discussion in order to preserve its ideas only in their 'most interesting aspect', that which will not only appeal to the technical-minded and the practitioners but may also serve as a standard by which the larger public for whom this art is intended can judge it.[2] This perspective consists in applying, through the dramatic (short scenes setting the circumstances), a systematic typology of those feelings and passions capable of being given musical form. The horrible and the sublime go arm in arm, the more to delight the ladies.

## A Systematic Inventory of Expressive Devices

The central categories in the century (from about 1750) are expression, sensibility, feeling, sense of proportion, *galanterie*, and the natural. The nature that is to be imitated is in fact circumscribed, controlled by the artist by means of a network of formal and expressive devices that he insatiably seeks to define with Utopian preciseness. To teach, for instance, the workings of music, he proceeds by way of metaphors that repeatedly set up parallels between imaginary dramatic situations and expressive embodiments of their musical equivalents, broadening the span so as to cover practically every possible situation (cf. Lacépède's technique). Addressing the technically trained, he will proceed likewise but also list the set of known procedures that fit whatever one is aiming to accomplish (e.g. the methods of Quantz, C. P. E. Bach, L. Mozart). The entire aesthetic of this period represents a thirsting, never satisfied, to create a code—ideally all-embracing, if not by the generality of its rules then at least by their number—that will fix the status of a taste felt to be definitive. On the other hand, the extreme refinement of that taste also makes of it a system which is in very unstable equilibrium and which must therefore be protected at all costs against overreaching, which would spell its ruin.

C. P. E. Bach's *Versuch*, together with his contribution to the evolution of musical notation, raises him beyond question to the high point of the orbit traced by this construct—both theoretical and applied—of musical expression. The microcosm of his artistic activity clearly reveals the paradox of the century, in his almost unique attempt to formulate with quite perfect unambiguity the ambiguous essence of musical meaning, to catch the natural by way of the artificial, to protect expression from the free-running expression of an art rather too much democratized. The artist becomes artificer.

---

[2] B. G. E. Lacépède, 'Poétique de la musique', *Bibliothèque universelle des dames*, XIe classe (Paris, 1787), VI–VIII.

## Notation, Revealer of Aesthetic Awareness

A musician's subjective awareness of his own originality can most often be measured by examining his notation.[3] It would seem that the invention of new signs shows a specific creative need which is no longer content with the available array of performance symbols and traditions. Clearly, it matters first of all to be able to make oneself understood in practice. But that very effort uncovers in turn, on a second level as we might say, an aspect of the artist's conscience: the distance between the essence of his intuition and its chances, as he sees them, of being effectively perceived by the world for which he intends it. These notational schemes do indeed reveal the shakiness of the system, the instability of an artistic construction which must try to survive in an atmosphere that the composer considers unsuitable. Taking the matter one step further, one may say that these devices, considered in their number and their complexity, allow us to evaluate the composer's awareness of the degree to which the nature and the intelligibility of his ideas depend on the detail of their realization in sound. 'Imperfectly performed, a certain piece loses all its meaning': that can certainly not be said of a Haydn sonata or a Goldberg variation, but one does wonder if it might not be applicable to many of the sonatas and fantasias of C. P. E. Bach. That is somewhat the conclusion reached by an overall study of his personal, 'didactic' participation in the aesthetic of his century.

Let us first note a few telling symptoms of this growing union between the notated and its issuance into the world of sound. In the *Versuch* C. P. E. Bach states that a mediocre composition can be improved by a fine performance.[4] One could write a dissertation on that statement alone, but a preliminary observation would be that the statement is true only if one takes it that the performer completes the composition, or to put it differently, that the score is to all intents a neutral, intermediary stage leading to performance. It is only a springboard in the process which therefore requires the sensibility of a performer in order to be realized. But the score has already occasioned a value-judgement (it is called 'mediocre'). By what criteria? Can one answer the question by reversing it and asking—still with reference to the Berlin aesthetic—whether a good composition can be made unattractive by a bad performance? The simple fact that Bach wrote his *Versuch* lets one answer affirmatively in all certainty. Within the performance style he is describing, the interpreter clearly plays a fundamental role with regard to the value and the final effectiveness of the musical process, and consequently the written form

---

[3] See Etienne Darbellay, 'Tradition and Notation in Baroque Music', *The Oral and the Literate in Music*: Third ICTM Colloquium 1985 (Tokyo, 1986), 57–68.

[4] *Essay*, p. 153.

must, if it is to be deemed valid, contain more than only potentially those idiosyncracies that are to characterize its release into the musical gesture. Many musicians and theoreticians before him had emphasized the performer's participation and role; none, however, had done so, as he and the Berlin School in general did, with such a wealth of precision and such awareness of how the aesthetic meaning of the message is related to its realization. It therefore almost naturally follows that if one studies what makes up the specific qualities of a fine performance, one can thereby have a set of criteria likewise applicable to an evaluation of the composition itself (the score). Within the Berlin aesthetic context the very tenor of the musical idea is, as it were, completely set by the accent and the tone of its shape in sound. It is as if the fitness of that tone could be verified against an extra-musical criterion, one that is therefore common to both composition and performance.

The question comes down to what conditions are required for a performance to be judged as effective, or in other words what aspects of those conditions C. P. E. Bach took to be capable of notation on a score and of codification in a theory. The answer can come from examining the *Versuch* and his own use of notation. I shall try to do this by showing the systematic and highly co-ordinated aspect of the numerous precepts and recommendations with which he studded the *Versuch*.

## Die 'wahre' Art das Clavier zu spielen

It is significant that in the very title of his treatise on musical practice C. P. E. Bach included a value-judgement: the 'true' way. This possibly polemical stance is confirmed throughout the book; one finds in it a number of precepts rather than recommendations, stated with the same commanding conviction of their universal applicability, whether it is a matter of an axiom that reveals a whole aesthetic philosophy, such as 'A musician cannot move others unless he too is moved,'[5] or the statement of a point about the applicability of a particular sound shape ('Example 3, set with this ornament, is the true home of the turn, for a substituted trill, whether it is placed over or after the first note, is unconditionally false' [allezeit falsch]).[6] The categorical tone, found throughout a volume which is nevertheless quite unlike a beginners' primer (where commands are more effective than recommendations), betrays both the sense of an anarchic historical situation on which a style needs to be imposed and a clear-sighted forthrightness with regard to the existence of a universal artistic truth that can be systematically cast in rules.

C. P. E. Bach finds himself totally isolated, in his age, so he reacts against that isolation. His favourite instrument (the clavichord) sets him on the periphery of the large concert and of the fashionable; there opera, vocal music, and large

<hr />

[5] Ibid., p. 152.          [6] Ibid., p. 120.

vocal and instrumental ensembles predominate. Clavier music itself is a very special case, one rather overlooked in the musical life of 1750. The sonata[7] is considered an uninteresting subdivision of the more effective instrumental forms, which it is supposed to represent 'in miniature'.[8] The expressive ideal is clearly the imitation of nature, 'nature' being the human voice and its expressive capabilities as shaped by language. Moreover, C. P. E. Bach is truly the only person, as performer, to attain the expressive magic that the most perspicacious of his contemporaries acknowledge in him (one thinks of the reports from Marpurg, Reichardt, and Burney, among others).

This sociological isolation of the musician, both by the forms and the genres he uses and by the nature of his favourite instrument, favours on the other hand the emergence of an unshakeable aesthetic conviction regarding the modernity and the ultimate value of the style he advocates. A style which depends so much in its very essence on performer's refinements, needs, in order to survive in a rather inadequate environment, solid foundations in theory and a firm base in its codification in writing.

## A Hierarchical System using Algorithms

It will be quickly apparent that the process of codification can be grasped in two phases. The *Versuch* gives, on the one hand, general rules in the form of a priori propositions or algorithms and, on the other, rules for their application that regulate sub-categories of possible cases. In other words, one can speak of a true theory of stylistic practice by virtue of the fact that the construction thus built is hierarchical (a particular category of practical cases is always explained in connection with an a priori proposition, and a number of those propositions are valid recursively at various levels of the composition) and generalizable (a limited group of rules tends to cover virtually all possible cases that one is likely to meet in practice). That kind of idealized model, applied to a field as shifting and incalculable as the 'phenomenal' manipulation of musical time, is somewhat surprising. It presumes an incredible consistency in the notation itself, given the fact that a good many of its moorings have to be properly coded in the notated message in order to be recognized as such.

Performers . . . must try to capture the true content of a composition and express its appropriate affects. Composers, therefore, act wisely who in notating their works include terms, in addition to tempo indications, which help to clarify the meaning of a piece. However, as worthy as their intentions might be, they would not succeed in preventing a garbled performance if they did not also add to the notes the usual signs and marks relative to their execution.[9]

---

[7] It is not necessary to recall here Fontenelle's celebrated reprimand or the contents of the article 'Sonate' in Rousseau's *Dictionnaire de musique* (Paris, 1768), among other examples.

[8] See Lacépède, 'Poétique', ii. 232 ff.    [9] *Essay*, pp. 153–4.

That is what one does observe in C. P. E. Bach's notation. Before his time, as far as one can tell, such preciseness had never been attained on so well-ordered a basis.

# Articulation

Let us take a look at one or two examples of this system. In the chapter on performance there is an exhaustive examination of every kind of musical articulation, détaché and legato, with specific indications of the rules, the notation symbols that supplement or confirm them, and the particular cases, identified by precise criteria, that allow *ad hoc* treatments.[10] Then all unspecific cases are covered by a general rule plus a particular exception:

Tones which are neither detached, connected, nor fully held [the cases previously listed] are sounded for half their value, unless [exception] the abbreviation *Ten.* (hold) is written over them, in which case they must be held fully. Quarters and eighths in moderate and slow tempos are usually performed in this semidetached manner. They must not be played weakly, but with fire and a slight accentuation.[11]

It could hardly be put more precisely, and one will have real trouble finding cases in the music that have not been covered by that algorithm. The broadening of the rule at the end of the paragraph is worth noting. What appears to be a limitation (moderate tempos) is a stipulation for practice: the faster the tempo, the less applicable the rule. So it is a matter of making sure that the rule will be taken not as evidence concerning the détaché articulation of a faster tempo (a concern, obviously, to play rapid passages clearly), but rather as a full-blown expressive idiom. And indeed, if we look at a piece, for instance Rondo 1 ('Andante un poco') of the fifth collection 'für Kenner und Liebhaber' (H. 268/W. 59, 2; see Examples 2*e* and 2*f* below), we will not find a single note whose relative length (as articulated) is not perfectly deducible from these rules and from the notation. The quarter-note that ends the opening motif is indeed marked, throughout the piece, 'ten.', without which it would be détaché, like the eighth notes. In measures 28 ff., the rule for appoggiaturas applies and the 'ten.' is not needed; in the other cases they are semi-détaché.

The same rondo supplies us with an example of what appears a priori to be a redundancy in the information. The series of sixteenth-note appoggiaturas in measure 3, synchronized with the eighth-notes (détaché) in the bass, are slurred in pairs. In fact, the *Versuch* stipulates that 'Passages in which passing notes or appoggiaturas are struck against a bass are played legato in all tempos even in the absence of a slur'.[12] As a matter of fact, the rule here does not necessarily prescribe articulating pairs, but only playing legato. Consequently

---

[10] Ibid., pp 154 ff.          [11] Ibid., p. 157.          [12] Ibid., p. 155.

that articulation is what the slurs mean, not the legato (which is automatic). The desired effect, clearly, is that of the clash of a harmonic dissonance.

As for the practice of the semi-détaché, even if it is a matter of a common practice later in the period, the Boolean logic of the remark is evident. Insofar as a symbol or a rule specifically marks every context for playing legato, it is taken for granted (logically but, at least for a modern performer, not intuitively) that passages lacking them are to be played neutrally, half-way between legato and staccato. The remark is like the 'or else' branch of a two-pronged decision-process, 'if . . . then . . . or else'. Beyond its intuitive necessity, it gives rise to a new logical branching relative to the modifier 'ten.'. From a psychological point of view, its position as 'or else' underscores a posteriori the particular action of the rules previously stated. The slur identifies not only a group (specific melodic coherence relating certain notes to one another) but also a set physical action, relative to the dynamic of the first note and to the shortened duration of the last, implying tenuto for the notes between (with some variation according to whether they belong to a developing harmonic grouping).

## Dynamics

In connection with the discussion about dynamic markings, Bach takes up, although critically and selectively, a theory of Quantz's that is quite representative of our argument. It concerns an attempt to connect dynamic shadings and harmonic contexts by a rule for performance.[13]

In general it can be said that dissonances are played loudly and consonances softly, since the former rouse our emotions and the latter quiet them. . . . An exceptional turn of a melody which is designed to create a violent affect must be played loudly. So-called deceptive progressions are also brought out markedly to complement their function. A noteworthy rule which is not without foundation is that all tones of a melody which lie outside the key may well be emphasized regardless of whether they form consonances or dissonances and those which lie within the key may be effectively performed piano, again regardless of their consonance or dissonance.[14]

That rule generalizes several particular remarks about dynamics or the accenting of clearly defined harmonic-melodic contexts, such as the appoggiatura or the figures like it. 'Patterns of two and four slurred notes are played with a slight, scarcely noticeable increase of pressure on the first and third tones.'[15] 'A profusion of appoggiaturas with their release is particularly good in affettuoso passages since the releases usually expire pianissimo.'[16] 'With regard to execution we learn . . . that appoggiaturas are louder than the following tone. . . .'[17] 'With respect to loudness and softness, the performance

---

[13] See ibid., p. 163 n. 32, in connection with Quantz's point of view on this subject.
[14] Ibid., p. 163.     [15] Ibid., p. 154.     [16] Ibid., p. 95.     [17] Ibid., p. 88.

of our embellishment [the double-dotted appoggiatura] is the same as that of the simple appoggiatura; the retarded principal tone is played softly and the retarding tone loudly.'[18] Those observations all lean toward expressing a dynamic principle that could be summed up in the *Gestalt* view of figure-ground. In the process developing, what drives the change is the form, and the axis of reference against which the change is perceived is the background. Whatever is properly form is capable of being brought out by a strong dynamic. Dissonance perturbs the harmonic system and therefore produces a move towards its stabilization; notes outside the current key (dissonant or not) reorient the key and open the way to a move towards stabilizing the orbit of the perturbed key.

Once again, C. P. E. Bach succeeds in setting up a decision algorithm, this time concerning dynamics. But one difference from the preceding algorithm must be noted: its principles are rooted in a more fundamental structural element of the composition, the intervallic relationships. Here the rule establishes that the dynamics might somehow be entirely deducible from the music itself, which was not the case for the rules about the relative durations of a conventional kind. It stems from a natural aesthetic conception in which it is dissonance in the broad sense (whatever breaks the harmony, whatever disturbs the equilibrium of the system) that drives the music's unfolding. Without it there would be sheer silence. Indeed, the perturbations are what are brought to the centre of attention (the intensity of the volume, the noise); the resolutions of them fade away into silence. In this regard it must also be noted that C. P. E. Bach clearly distinguishes this built-in dynamics, directly connected to the affects, from the conventional Baroque 'terraced' dynamics, which is arbitrarily applied and which concerns only the stacking of the levels of sound independently of their context.

It is not possible to describe the contexts appropriate to the forte or piano because for every case covered by even the best rule there will be an exception. The particular effect of these shadings depends on the passage, its context, and the composer, who may introduce either a forte or a piano at a given place for equally convincing reasons. In fact, complete passages, including their consonances and dissonances, may be marked first forte and, later, piano. This is a customary procedure with both repetitions and sequences.[19]

This terraced dynamics really belongs more to the realm of playing with the music, manipulating sound levels so as to organize the musical process not according to the intensity required by a particular expressive sense but by an attempt to make a distancing in time perceptible, just as the film-maker does by dissecting space. The analogy with space is clearly at the source of this particular experience where the perceived audible intensity of the event is a function of the distance between it and its perceiver (as in the principle of the

[18] Ibid., p. 351.          [19] Ibid., p. 163.

echo). It is a way of using a potential and imaginary layering of past and present to establish and highlight two musical segments that are distinguished in this way by their belonging to distinct moments. It is, indeed, the most elementary kind of 'repeat with variation'. So it is not surprising that these procedures, scarcely suitable for producing emotional affects by themselves (unless perhaps by analogies—the distant echo of an emotional scene, for example), should not be among the main concerns of C. P. E. Bach, who is, on the contrary, constantly seeking to maintain the emotive intensity of a musical present moment constantly renewed.

## The Variation of the Reprises

The obvious priority given to the handling of the musical moment for purposes of raw, immediate expression as opposed to using generative cells of long-span formal structure (which will be in particular the basis of the Classical Viennese composers' conception, either intuitive or explicit), or in other words the working-out of a musical idiom aiming essentially at the immediate effectiveness of expression may be most clearly demonstrated in the area of reprise-with-variations, much cultivated and written about by C. P. E. Bach. A realm so unregulated and important with regard to the eventual actualization of the musical idea was bound to attract the attention of a composer so much aware of his dependence on the interpreter. It was therefore hardly possible that in his *Versuch*, as well as in his particular approach to notation, he would leave it simply to the whim of the performer. His whole argument, whether theoretical or by example, affirms first and foremost the composer's prerogatives. What a modern mind finds obvious was less so in his time, and for two reasons: the one, practical, was the status of the interpreter, not yet rigidly defined by tradition; the other had to do with the special nature of the musical meaning, nearly totally dependent on expression, that he wished to promote.

It is indispensible nowadays to alter repeats. One expects it of every performer. . . . Almost every thought is expected to be altered in the repeat, irrespective of whether the arrangement of the piece or the capacity of the performer permit it. But then it is just this altering which makes most hearers cry BRAVO, especially when it is accompanied by a long and at times exaggeratedly ornate cadenza.[20]

Aiming to impress the audience was, then, acknowledged as a normal practice; composer and interpreter were accomplices in the alchemy of embellishment, the former supplying the raw material, a thread of ideas that

---

[20] C. P. E. Bach's preface to his *Sechs Sonaten mit veränderten Reprisen* (H. 126, 136–40/W. 50, 1–6). of 1760, translated in *Essay*, p. 166 n. 40, and in the edition by Etienne Darbellay (Winterthur, 1976).

the latter was responsible for transmuting, except that he most often made it unrecognizable. The interpreter had a function much closer to the composer's than is the case today (except in certain contemporary works), which is hardly surprising inasmuch as the composer was most often himself the performer in solo music. In trying to clearly distinguish each one's function, C. P. E. Bach thereby established the status of the composer as producer of a relatively 'completed' message of which the performer became the 'prophet'. There, indirectly, lies the most novel aspect of his contribution, giving rise—for the instructor that he was—to new algorithms, based this time on an aesthetic hierarchy of meanings.

If, on the other hand, the practice of the reprise-with-variation is admitted without question, that kind of repeat must be reconciled with the new sense of what composition is, weighted entirely on the side of expression: an ongoing communication between interpreter and hearer without avowed reference to a formal structure situated outside this transient relationship. In other words, the responsibility that now falls to the performer is twofold. As is shown by the algorithms for decoding (discussed above) that C. P. E. Bach presents him with, he must be, so to speak, slavishly faithful to the notation code, the only guarantee—if it is correctly interpreted—of communicating the meaning. But at the same time he must, insofar as that meaning likewise resides in the necessity for a repeat to be reinterpreted, renew it by the art of transforming it without playing it falsely. C. P. E. Bach the instructor must then yield; no positive rule can now be found to programme the performer, and the composer is entirely in his hands. The only escape is by way of aesthetic directives and examples—in which regard C. P. E. Bach is eloquent.

'Play from the soul, not like a trained bird!':[21] that is perhaps the most general, most significant instruction in the *Versuch*. The complex skein of rules with which that instruction is set about might seem to be so many threads hampering the bird's flight. It would be better to see them as the markers that define its flight path, the *Empfindungen* trail laid out for it by the composition. If in the course of the flight it comes time to vary a repeat, to trace a spiral whereas the code, with its one dimension, can only define a circle, the problem becomes really acute. It must be admitted firstly that covering the same ground is not a redundancy, whereas the whole phenomenological pathway of Berlin composition appears precisely to avoid the circle in favour of the line or, put differently, appears to shun the constructivist, geometry-heeding structures in the form (other than those dictated by the already established structural redundancies of the tonal idiom of the age) and to favour the pure expressive line along which the affective can come into being; and secondly that no matter how carefully one chisels the sounds that encase a particular affect as if it were the symbol of itself and itself alone, one grants it at the same time a status of being dependent on a deeper level of which it is apparently only one of

[21] *Essay*, p. 150.

the appearances, one that is realized insofar as (*a*) the performer is likely to be able to express it again in another form in the repeat and (*b*) the performer consequently has the means of identifying it outside himself as being both the fixing of a moment totally characterized emotionally and, at the same time, the potential representation of another expressive moment to whose meaning it might be reducible. The paradox is plain: the composition exists, so to speak, entirely in its written code, which must be as exhaustive as possible in order to programme the performer all but unequivocally in its course; but this same performer must be free to recognize in that course another possible course that will maintain the identity of something (the composition) which, for its part, is not notated. That other, further thing, which is the music, the idea, and is not the notes that are its setting—what exactly is it like? In what way can one musical object be extended into another which is reducible to the first? What is the admissible transformational distance between two musical objects such that these distinct objects can still be associated with one another or, perhaps, associated with a common term, indeterminate as regards the audible contour but inducible by the musical intelligence?

C. P. E. Bach's aesthetic response to that question, more alive and insistent than ever, is clear: 'A musician cannot move others unless he too is moved'. That is the description of a general affect to which the particular affects of the course are hierarchically subordinated. Consequently, the performer's first task is to discover that affect:

What comprises good performance? The ability through singing or playing to make the ear conscious of the true content [*nota bene*: there is a true—verifiable—determinate content] and affect of the composition. Any passage can be so radically changed by modifying its performance that it will be scarcely recognizable [that is to say, separated from its source, which is the affect, which seems to imply an asymptotic direction towards the truth that is to be discovered] . . . Good performance, then, occurs when one hears all notes and their embellishments played in correct time with fitting volume produced by a touch which is related to the true content of a piece.[22]

Here lies the aesthetic 'key' to the era (in Langer's sense).[23] It is a matter of 'portraying rage, anger, and other passions', for example, or 'the briskness of allegros . . . the tenderness of adagios'.[24] Those are the affects that the performer must understand and identify. They are as coded and conventionally catalogued as can be, and mostly they are set by the indications of tempo and expression at the beginning of the piece. 'In order to arrive at an understanding of the true content and affect of a piece, and, in the absence of indications, to decide on the correct manner of performance . . . it is advisable that every opportunity be seized to listen to soloists and ensembles; the more so because these details of beauty often depend on extraneous factors.'[25] One

[22] Ibid., p. 148.
[23] See Susan K. Langer, *Philosophy in a New Key* (Cambridge, Massachusetts, 1950), chap. 1.
[24] *Essay*, p. 149.    [25] Ibid., p. 150.

could cite many more passages. The musical work is a deciphering grid, a catalogue of feelings which guarantee its holistic value. Artistic truth does not exist in the structure of the work itself as a combination of sounds but rather takes its measure, considered as composition, from how close it comes to the nature of the feeling it means to represent and, considering performance, by its pertinence to the means applied to locating and reconstituting the feelings identified according to their coding in sound. The musical gesture, the pure expressivity of the means used are consequently as important for the result to be obtained as is the intrinsic 'quality' of the composition, insofar as they are both brought together at the close of the path by the expression produced and by its impact (the impression) on the hearer. With that as one's view, it is legitimate to state that a mediocre composition can be improved by a fine performance, but also that a passage may be 'scarcely recognizable' when it is disfigured by an inadequate performance (and thus constitute a failure of communication, a foreign body with regard to the affect that measures it). Here C. P. E. Bach's formulation must be stressed: to 'recognize a passage' implies perhaps the ability to identify a passage previously heard (a point relative to the structural side of musical form), but surely even more the ability to perceive the emotional meaning of which it is intended to be the central thread. One of the *Versuch*'s quite rare mentions of the formal unity of a work is the one that ends the first volume (a remark to which C. P. E. Bach likewise alludes in his preface to the collection of *Sechs Sonaten mit veränderten Reprisen*, referred to above):

All variations must relate to the piece's affect, and they must always be at least as good as, if not better than, the original. For example [sentence added in 1787], many variants of melodies introduced by executants in the belief that they honor a piece, actually occurred to the composer, who, however, selected and wrote down the original because he considered it the best of its kind. . . . Constant attention must be given to preceding and succeeding parts; there must be a vision of the whole piece so that the variation will retain the original contrasts of the brilliant and the simple, the fiery and the languid, the sad and the joyful, the vocal and the instrumental. . . . Despite the present popularity of elaborate variations, it is of first importance always to make certain that the lineaments of a piece, by which it is recognized, remain unobscured.[26]

In short, both composition and performance are to be taken as the two sides of a common process which is measured according to affect, with the exception that a further relationship of subservience exists for the performance with regard to the composition that it extends, whether it is in the unambiguous actualization of the code or in its reworking, varied and marked out by the affect to which the code relates. As for the composer, he too chooses from among the formulas that come to his mind those which seem to him best suited to embodying his affect ('because he considered it the best of its kind'). It is not

---

[26] Ibid., pp. 165–6.

so much that he constructs a form as that he assembles one. Rather than let himself be surprised by the ineffable evidence of an idea that he will develop organically according to its dynamic potentialities, he will look to assuring the continuity and the coherency of a statement in sound founded on (and verified by) a pin-pointed emotion that will control the unfolding of musical time along the well-laid tracks of a sensible rhetoric properly identified.

If one now wishes to see more clearly what those 'lineaments' consist of— those reductions which are of great semantic interest for the work and which are obviously the basis of the technique of repeat-with-variations, the fundamental form that guarantees their identity and also points out to them the right direction for the sound to take along its course—one's only recourse is either musical analysis or, preferably, an examination of the repeats-with-variation offered by C. P. E. Bach himself. Among these latter, the 1760 collection, *Sechs Sonaten mit veränderten Reprisen* (see Example 1), is certainly the most instructive.

By comparing the original sections and their repeats, one can easily see that these variations for which C. P. E. Bach sets the model do not consist of adding a few ornaments or diminutions, but rather represent real thematic reworkings of an essentially harmonic content. The new working-out may either enhance or amplify the harmonic-melodic direction indicated by the original contour (Example 1a), or also sometimes shift the centres of gravity of these contours by rather fundamentally reorienting the syntax (the 'linking of ideas') of two complementary segments so as to cover them both with a single expressive gesture (Example 1b). In Example 1a, the initial state is already a melodic gesture that comments upon a lineament that is harmonic in nature, a gesture that can be read as a movement of the dominant to the subdominant in an extended appoggiatura; in the repeat the twists and turns of chromatic appoggiaturas suggest a more strongly marked harmonic constellation in G minor, thus accenting a complex harmonic departure that had already been present (at least potentially) beforehand. In Example 1b the first state presents two clearly delimited affirmations in D minor, harmonically complementary (measures 3–4 are a heightening of measures 1–2) but syntactically separate; the second state creates a syntactic link between them, both by effecting a movement of measures 21–2 towards the next two measures (23–4) through an open melodic connection and by shifting the centre of harmonic gravity toward these measures. Measure 22 is 'put in parentheses' by the piano marking, and the new right-hand melodic progression in the antecedent produces the unfolding of the forte gesture in the consequent.

It is not my intention to multiply examples here, nor to analyse them in detail. Suffice it to underscore the kind of alchemy at work, in which one discovers the fundamental importance of the underlying harmonic motion (the lineament), which sets very nearly all the other parameters: rhythm, melody (complex combinations of appoggiaturas and figuration), and dyna-

*Etienne Darbellay*

Example 1. Sonata in D minor H. 139/W. 50, 4. 'Reprisen-Sonaten' (Berlin, 1760)

*a* i, mm. 8–10, 34–6
*b* iii, mm. 1–4, 21–4

mics. The thinking is therefore not thematic or motivic, properly speaking, but harmonic. The underpinning of the affect seems to be a kind of tone colour in a given tempo (of prime importance); various secondary harmonic attractions come into play which take on a syntactic form quite firmly set in the melodic and rhythmic elaborations that they give rise to. One is tempted at this point to remember what C. P. E. Bach said about improvisation—or the way to compose what he considers the pinnacle of art in the subject, the 'freie Fantasien'.[27] On top of a carefully considered harmonic scheme, one works out the various particular affects in the way one constructs an utterance, one punctuates the harmonic lineament syntactically with the help of the other ingredients of the language.

[27] Ibid., pp. 430–45.

## The Gesture in Sound

The projection of these basic lineaments on to the screen of musical time moves past an essential aspect of performance not yet mentioned, that of another 'anthropomorphism' of musical form along with affect, one that resembles the musical analogue of its apprehensible manifestation in space: gesture, the motion by which a feeling takes on a visible shape for the outside viewer. For C. P. E. Bach, this aspect is properly a part of the quality of the performance, and is even necessarily superimposed upon it, as if the audible event pure and simple were not enough to communicate the affect. 'Those who maintain that all of this can be accomplished without gesture will retract their words when, owing to their own insensibility, they find themselves obliged to sit like a statue before their instrument.'[28]

The idea of gesture takes on a complex polymorphism in the context of the Berlin aesthetic. It is, first and foremost, the visible human sign of emotion, or more simply expression, as manifestation in space of a psychological content. The emotional unfolding of affect is thus rendered by the movement-in-time of the audible events which mimic it in the musical phrase: that is to say, tempo. Applied by a performer, tempo in turn takes on the character of a physical manifestation that one could call a 'manual dance-mime' on the part of the performer at the keyboard. It is a second state of the musical gesture, which returns to its original in space through the transformation of the process of musical communication. Further, and of the same order, it is the physical expression that affect dictates to the one who performs it and who thus rediscovers and makes manifest the emotion originally worked out by the composer.

The remarkable part of this whole process is clearly not the relatively simplistic and unsophisticated logic of its philosophical assumption ('A musician cannot move others unless he too is moved'),[29] but rather the consistency with which C. P. E. Bach tries to reveal and code it. By bringing together ideas that C. P. E. Bach emphasizes at various places in the *Versuch* and elsewhere, one can reconstruct an algorithmic system of relatively simple strategies for composition.

Based essentially on harmonic relationships, the affects depend primarily on the tempo (or density of events hierarchically qualified by time-unit). They are accentuated by the musical dynamics and articulation. A sonata movement is above all a 'movement', that is to say a piece of music bearing a dominant affect, a 'humour', stipulated by the analogical tempo marking ('adagio', 'affettuoso', etc.). To this dominant affect the particular affects are hierarchi-

---

[28] Ibid., p. 152. See also Marpurg's comment, ibid. n. 9.
[29] On this problem, see in particular Peter Kivy, *The Corded Shell—Reflections on Musical Expression* (Princeton, 1980).

cally subordinate. The unity, the coherence of the movement depends essentially on the relationship of meaning that ties these particular affects to the dominant affect ('All variations must relate to the piece's affect') which generates them, and consequently on the steadiness of the tempo.

But the success (and indeed the quality or value) of the composition and its performance is measured by how well they establish communication with the hearer. To the degree that the communication density is proportional to the potency and the characterization of the *Empfindungen*, the success increases with the variety and the appropriateness of the affects.[30] That is why the Berlin aesthetic places prime importance on that very variety. Hence it is logical for a sonata to be inferior to a fantasia since the latter, often free in tempo and without metre, is not a slave, in its expression, to the many-sided working-out of a dominant affect:

It is principally in improvisations or fantasias that the keyboardist can best master the feelings of his audience. . . . Unbarred free fantasias seem especially adept at the expression of affects, for each meter carries a kind of compulsion within itself. At least it can be seen in accompanied recitatives that tempo and meter must be frequently changed in order to arouse and still the rapidly alternating affects. Hence, the metric signature is in many such cases more a convention of notation than a binding factor in performance. It is a distinct merit of the fantasia that, unhampered by such trappings, it can accomplish the aims of the recitative at the keyboard with complete, unmeasured freedom.[31]

But that is also the trouble with the fantasia; namely, it lacks the 'syntactic' safeguard of meaning (linking of ideas) that was represented by faithfulness to a set tempo, thanks to which the composer could control the performer with regard to his way of playing, a key aspect of the utterance. The fantasia can now be no better than schematically notated, and so it represents the breaking-point of an aesthetic which, in order to promote a perfect understanding of the emotional message, applies itself to drawing up a typology of that message sufficiently rationalized to be entirely enclosed in the coding of the score.

*Empfindsamkeit* sets up, in fact, two levels of communication between musician and hearer, analogous in nature but distinct in value. The first, which is almost of the instructional order, is the sonata. In it, affect can be almost totally coded, and thereby taught. Steady metre and tempo guarantee its effectiveness, insofar as the composer can, through the coding, effectively control the delivery of the utterance and—if one admits the close correlation between delivery and meaning (by way of the gesture in sound)—can in some way programme the performer so as to optimize communication. Once the overall tempo is established, that of each particular affect is, in large measure, set (it can be 'recognized', as we have seen). The very existence of the second

---

[30] The idea is outlined in the preface to the collection of 1760. See *Sechs Sonaten*, ed. Darbellay, xii, and n. 20 above.

[31] *Essay*, pp. 152–3.

level, that of notated improvisation, is enough to confirm the aesthetic priorities of *Empfindsamkeit*. It is called superior because, being freed from the pre-established metre and tempo, it allows that ideal spontaneity that the pure communication of affect requires, whatever its nature from moment to moment. Indeed, it reduces the normative action of musical time, deprived of its 'metric magnetism', to the bare phenomenological manipulations of the present and the immediate past; it moves yet further from what was left by way of structural organization of the form that stemmed from metric constraints, generating symmetries and parallelisms in the scope of the sonata. This is the musical domain that comes closest to the semantic communication of spoken language (C. P. E. Bach cites recitative). From this perspective one can see free fantasia as what emerges at the far end of the sonata training-ground. Its consistency is now guaranteed only by the intelligibility of the harmonic relationships[32] and by the pertinence at a given point of the gesture in sound that is taking shape.

I shall not cite the numerous remarks in the *Versuch* about tempo and its relationship to affect.[33] As for the preciseness of the coding *per se*, the reader may take cognizance of the sources or also, in the case of the 1760 sonatas, the commentaries in the edition previously cited.[34] I shall limit myself here to a few brief examples illustrating what could be called the choreographing of the gesture in sound by the coding, with the further remark that the examples are not special cases but illustrate, rather, C. P. E. Bach's customary practice.

One of the most prominent aspects of C. P. E. Bach's musical utterance is its immediate clarity. One sees a temporal segmenting of the events that never leaves any doubt as to their logical syntactic sequence. Each fragment is a 'word' perfectly intelligible in its 'sentence'. Furthermore, one is struck by the absence of the implied (other than harmonically). The unambiguousness of the meaning is disturbed by hardly any secondary polyphonic layer not synchronized with the momentary gesture in sound. On the contrary, everything converges towards making sense of a movement, of a gesture. Each 'commentary' inserted, each phrase, whatever its source, helps accentuate the initial contour of the idea and set its unswerving sense of direction. This total symbiosis of the ingredients results in a convergence, never departed from, of the gesture in sound, with the result that one must in the last analysis give up any notion of accompanied melody. Rare indeed are the instances where one can say of the left hand that it is accompanying or merely sustaining the right and creating a neutral layer of sound that might, without doing any harm, find an equivalent substitute. Normally the two hands work together to produce the overall gesture. Their functions are distributed not only in response to an obvious mechanical necessity (a given note cannot be played by either hand

---

[32] Ibid., pp. 430–4.     [33] See *Sechs Sonaten*, ed. Darbellay, iii–ix.
[34] See *Sechs Sonaten*, ed. Darbellay, xiv, concerning the notation of the editor Winter, and the discussion of the manuscript emendations in the critical notes.

indifferently) but also in order to give it its very meaning. The rhythmic drive of which each note, by its harmonic-melodic situation, is the outcome, cannot be 'visibly' translated and thus expressed choreographically as a gesture unless it is a particular hand that plays, even though from the viewpoint of mechanical ease of execution the other hand would have been more appropriate. One would have no difficulty drawing up a typology of the characteristic gestures coded in this way by C. P. E. Bach. They are everywhere to be found, with a frequency that increases with his stylistic development.

In Example 2*a*, the left hand bears, or leads, the right hand's resolution of the appoggiatura towards silence, in a gesture to be met again, for instance, in the Allegro of the second sonata of the same collection (Example 2*b*). The movement of broken ascending thirds in Example 2*c* would have been as intelligible musically if notated as in Example 2*d*; to the eye, and affecting the synergy of the audible and physical means in the working-out of the gesture,

Example 2. 'Kenner und Liebhaber', vol. 5 (Leipzig, 1785)
*a* Sonata in E minor, H. 281/W. 59, 1, iii, m. 1
*b* Sonata in B flat major, H. 282/W. 59, 3, i, m. 5
*c* Rondo in G major, H. 268/W. 59, 2, m. 9
*d* Notation of *c* transformed
*e* Rondo in G major, H. 268/W. 59, 2, mm. 1–2
*f* Rondo in G major, H. 268/W. 59, 2, mm. 32–3

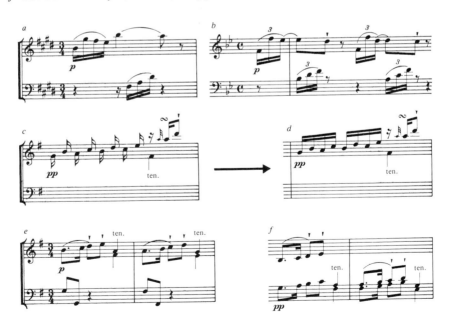

its division between the two hands changes its meaning radically, since the two hands pursue one another before splitting apart in the sudden opening up of the gesture.[35] Examples *2e* and *2f* show the same affect in its initial formulation and a later repeat, respectively. In both cases, the splitting of the final chord between the two hands (as coded by the wedges) contains incipiently its eventual breaking apart by rhythmic fragmentation (Example *2c*). It is not, properly speaking, a chord, but rather—thanks to the coding—a point of harmonic convergence for the gesture, one which is potentially divided, from the viewpoint of sound, and divided in fact, spatially, by the gesture.[36]

## Epilogue

Taken together with the algorithms of the *Versuch*, C. P. E. Bach's musical notation far exceeds in precision and thoroughness everything before it and much in the notations of later composers. It is conceived to embrace all the practical aspects of performance considered pertinent to reaching a fixed aesthetic goal, from *Bebung* to the broadest effects of articulation, from the overall dynamics to that of each particular note, and even factors until that time considered purely mechanical (fingering, assignment to one hand or the other). One can observe, however, that after him notation will progress a step further. Composers will notate intentions that cannot be realized in practice (something that C. P. E. Bach never does). For instance, in piano music there will be seen a crescendo on a single note, or there will be verbal remarks intended to make the performer think of helpful associations of images. On the other hand, a number of aspects thought by C. P. E. Bach to be essential to the meaning of the message will later be treated with indifference, made to depend upon the performer's subjective sense or confined to his instinctive under-standing of tradition; these will include the ornaments (as is already the case among the Classical composers), and the articulatory devices (legato, staccato), which will acquire harder or automatic quality. In other words, after C. P. E. Bach the general development of notation seems to be towards a subjective, analogical representation of audible poetic form, either because that form is deemed to be truly notatable only as a sketch left to the performer's inspired interpretation or because it holds within itself multiple potentialities for realization in sound, which are all taken as equally apt for translating the intention of the composer. (One cannot but be struck by the difference in approach that separates the dictatorial practice of the *Versuch* from the relativism which, some fifty years later, will imbue the dedicated virtuosos' approach to the same problem. The existence of such a 'method of methods' as

[35] A similar example is in H. 139/W. 50, 4, i, measure 13.
[36] Several similar cases are in H. 126/W. 50, 5, iii, e.g. measures 32 ff.

that of Fétis–Moscheles (1840) is a case in point.) At every hierarchical level of his system of notation, C. P. E. Bach tries to eliminate the ambiguities, close the circle, confirm on one level what was already present on another. A forte marking confirms the emphasis of a dissonance, a slur shows where to place an initial stress and a closing articulation. Every symbol meant to affect how the music is to be taken can actually be played, and is tied directly to the musical diction. (Future Romantic notation will, on the contrary, often fall back on these symbols in order to open up other horizons. The notation will suggest more than encode.)

This aspect of positivist pragmatism in C. P. E. Bach's notation matches in fact that of his aesthetics. To the degree that one is persuaded of a language's unambiguousness, it must be possible to codify it exactly. And indeed, C. P. E. Bach handles 'words', and the words have, above all, a meaning. If disfigured, they are no longer recognizable. 'Now music is nothing but an artificial language through which we seek to acquaint the listener with our *musical ideas*,' wrote Quantz.[37] J. A. P. Schulz, writing specifically of C. P. E. Bach, went further: 'Most of them [his sonatas] speak so clearly that one thinks he is hearing not so much notes as an understandable language that rouses and maintains our imaginations and feelings.'[38] There is, then, a 'true way' to utter them and to assemble them. If it were not that a computer is ill-fitted to feel them and to make them visible through gestures, they could almost be catalogued in an electronic memory and programmed for acceptable repro-duction. Here is a telling restriction: it is precisely their breaking out into the gesture in sound that is perhaps what is most vital in one's understanding of the utterances of *Empfindsamkeit*: the non-programmable part of that utter-ance (remarkably coded by C. P. E. Bach though it is). While that part of the utterance is the most original contribution of the school, it is also what, from a viewpoint immanent within the composition, reduces the school's originality. Each segment (or word) can find a satisfactory substitute which does not contradict the intention but does modify its gesture (as one can see in the repeats-with-variations). And it is by means of this release that a mediocre work can be improved upon by its performance, or that an excellent work can be made unrecognizable and thereby impoverished. It is also what, in the last analysis, supplies both composition and performance with the common ground of appreciation, by evoking standards of value that are applicable to both alike.

One could finally turn the paradox around and declare that the music of the school, although it is the one that benefits from the most precise coding and is therefore theoretically the most suited to computer transcription, is the one that submits to it least well. One can certainly programme more successfully

---

[37] Johann Joachim Quantz, *On Playing the Flute*, trans. Edward R. Reilly (New York, 1966), 120.

[38] 'Sonata, i', in J. G. Sulzer's *Allgemeine Theorie der schönen Künste* (Leipzig, 1771–4), 1095.

(or with less loss) a fugue of J. S. Bach than a fantasia or a sonata of C. P. E. Bach. The profusion of the phenomenal coding of the Berlin School therefore clearly shows the fragility of the message, its dependence on the gesture in sound that is to transmit it, an immoderate, Utopian attempt to put into one musical profile a thorough catalogue, an identification of all the themes of the fluid and evanescent world of emotion apprehended ever afresh. This drive to use all the devices of logical formalism, in order to make one utterance enclose a universal entity (emotion) that is in its essence not discursive, typically stems from an Enlightenment way of thinking and locates the Berlin School at the far extreme from Romanticism. The success of a composition-performance is measured by the pleasure it gives—BRAVO—and consequently its ability to communicate to the audience, on the basis of a psychological common ground, an emotion suitably disguised in formulas of sound. (The Italians, so much decried by J. A. P. Schulz, preferred surprise and the artifices of dazzlement and embellishment.) Pleasure is a function of the variety and the relevance of the 'emotions' put to use, and of the coherent tone of the sensible utterance. It is a matter of channelling the 'flood of tears' in order not to drown the sublime. . ..

# C. P. E. Bach and the Early History of the Recapitulatory Tutti in North Germany

Shelley G. Davis

CARL PHILIPP EMANUEL BACH began writing his keyboard concertos in the early 1730s and had completed the majority of them by the late 1750s. In 1793 Heinrich Christoph Koch, the celebrated theorist, still cited Bach's concertos as exemplars for the genre.[1] While it is true that Koch was most probably acquainted with Bach's Hamburg concertos of the late 1760s and early 1770s,[2] the ideal concerto plan that he describes is found in many of the earlier concertos; Koch may indeed have had in mind some of Philipp Emanuel's concertos of nearly forty years earlier.[3] The theorist was obviously not alone in his admiration for Philipp Emanuel and, with regard to many aspects of the concerto, may have reflected an attitude still prevalent among knowledgeable musicians in the generations of Haydn and Mozart.[4]

In the twentieth century, most of the interest in C. P. E. Bach's concertos has been scholarly. Studies by Hugo Daffner (1906) and Hans Uldall (1927, 1928) have formed the matrix for more modern investigations by Charles R. Haag,

---

[1] *Versuch einer Anleitung zur Composition*, 3 vols. (Leipzig, 1782–93, repr. Hildesheim, 1969), iii, 332, 337.

[2] On p. 335, Koch refers to the possible appearance of a slow introduction at the beginning of the concerto, a practice Philipp Emanuel had adopted in the first movements of two of his Hamburg concertos, H. 469/W. 41 (1769) and H. 475/W. 43, 5 (1771/2).

[3] At least with regard to symphonies and string quartets, there is no reason to believe that Koch was behind the times: in his symphony discussion, he referred to works by Haydn and Dittersdorf (iii. 310), and in his description of the quartet, he cited practices by Haydn, Pleyel, Hoffmeister, and Mozart (iii. 326). Koch's admiration for Bach's concertos may indeed have reflected a widely held contemporary view. David Schulenberg, in *The Instrumental Music of Carl Philipp Emanuel Bach* (Ann Arbor, 1984), 28, 133, maintains that Koch refers to C. P. E. Bach's concertos specifically with regard their to similarities to classical tragedies, viz., the dramatic effect of solo-and-chorus opposition.

[4] High regard for C. P. E. Bach appears to have obtained through some even later generations as well. Beethoven's continuing admiration for him is documented in letters, dated 26 July 1809, 15 Oct. 1810, and 28 Jan. 1812, to the firm of Breitkopf & Härtel. For an English translation, see Emily Anderson, ed., *The Letters of Beethoven*, 3 vols. (London, 1961), i. 235 (Letter 220), 298–9 (Letter 281), and 355 (Letter 345). See also Arnold Schering, *Geschichte des Instrumentalkonzerts bis auf die Gegenwart*, 2nd edn. (Leipzig, 1927), 142, esp. n. 1.

Leon Crickmore, and most recently, Jane R. Stevens and Rachel W. Wade.[5] As attention to the eighteenth-century concerto has increased, scholarship has broadened to include eighteenth-century theory regarding the concerto.[6] One area that remains of particular interest concerns the tonic restatement in the post-Baroque concerto,[7] the area that subsequently became known as the recapitulation. Study of the tonic restatement in Philipp Emanuel's concertos is significant generally because it provides a basis for measuring the strength of symmetry in a tonal plan[8] and specifically because it gives us insight into the originality of a most creative musical mind.

Philipp Emanuel's treatment of the restatement is enhanced in two ways: the boldness of the harmonic excursions in the tonally contrasting middle section (characteristic among some other and later North Germans as well), and the relatively clear and balanced proportions of the main tonal areas (perhaps more characteristic of Bach than of several other composers in his immediate circle). It was possibly these factors that subsequently encouraged Koch to compare the tonic restatement in first-movement concerto form to the third main period of a symphony.[9] Significantly, Koch's recognition of C. P. E. Bach's concertos as paradigms existed despite Bach's early use of a formal plan that may be analysed as having five, rather than Koch's four, main ritornello statements.[10] Actually, Bach favoured several formal plans; however, the one that Koch described was used with relative consistency by Bach and was also the one most frequently employed in the general repertory bridging the generation between C. P. E. Bach and Mozart.

The present study will be concerned mainly with Philipp Emanuel's first twenty concertos, those written between the 1730s and the mid-1740s. This

---

[5] The main studies are Hugo Daffner, *Die Entwicklung des Klavierkonzerts bis Mozart* (Leipzig, 1906), esp. 24–36; Hans Uldall, *Das Klavierkonzert der Berliner Schule* (Leipzig, 1928), esp. 24–68, and 'Beiträge zur Frühgeschichte des Klavierkonzerts', *ZfMw*, 10 (1927–8), 139–52; the comparatively recent studies include Charles R. Haag, The Keyboard Concertos of Carl Philipp Emanuel Bach, Ph.D. diss., University of California at Los Angeles, 1956; Leon Crickmore, 'C. P. E. Bach's Harpsichord Concertos', *ML*, 39 (1958), 227–41; Jane R. Stevens, The Keyboard Concertos of C. P. E. Bach, Ph.D. diss., Yale University, 1965; and Rachel W. Wade, *The Keyboard Concertos of Carl Philipp Emanuel Bach* (Ann Arbor, 1981). See also Stevens, 'Formal Design in C. P. E. Bach's Harpsichord Concertos', *Studi musicali*, 15 (1986), 257–97.

[6] See especially Jane R. Stevens, 'An 18th-century Description of Concerto First-movement Form', *JAMS*, 24 (1971), 85–95; for a related discussion, but extending into 19-century theory, see Stevens, 'Theme, Harmony, and Texture in Classic–Romantic Descriptions of Concerto First-movement Form', *JAMS*, 27 (1974), 25–60.

[7] For recent discussions of the restatement in post-Baroque concertos, see Pippa Drummond, *The German Concerto: Five Eighteenth-century Studies* (Oxford, 1980), 300, and Shelley Davis, 'H. C. Koch, the Classic Concerto, and the Sonata-form Retransition', *JM*, 2 (1983), 45–61.

[8] Symmetry (artistically balanced proportions) in the tonal design, of course, is the basis of the sonata-form ideal. 'Restatement' here means the return of the tonic and of primary thematic material.

[9] For Koch's comparison of the third solo (restatement) in a concerto to the third main period (recapitulation) in a symphony, see his *Versuch*, iii. 339.

[10] Uldall referred to the five-ritornello plan in *Klavierkonzert*, p. 18, and in 'Beiträge', 145; later, Crickmore cited this design in 'C. P. E. Bach's Harpsichord Concertos', 230–3.

period may have been witness to the first hints by Bach and others of what was later to become the recapitulatory tutti in the first-movement design of concertos written in Mozart's generation. The investigation will focus primarily on questions of overall form and will include only peripheral reference to activity in the smaller dimensions of phrase and theme.

The restatements, especially the ones seen most clearly in the outer movements of Bach's early concertos, may be arranged in two groups: those in which the return is initiated by the orchestra ('tutti restatement') and those in which the return begins with a solo statement ('solo restatement').

## Tutti Restatement: Five-ritornello Plan

Tutti restatements typically may be found in some of the opening movements of Bach's earlier concertos, and these usually occur in the five-ritornello–four-solo design mentioned above.[11] Figure 1 illustrates the harmonic outline of this design, with R representing a ritornello statement and S representing a solo section. The actual process of modulation usually occurs in the solos. $R_1$ generally remains in the tonic, although other keys may be suggested in passing; $S_1$ modulates to the second key, typically the dominant (or relative major), and $R_2$ maintains the second key. Modulation occurs in the central portion of the movement, which follows.[12] Here the soloist has many sequences, sometimes in dialogues with the tutti. Since $S_3$ sometimes tends to be relatively short and generally modulates back to the tonic from a distant key, it frequently has a function similar to what was later to become a sonata-form retransition.[13] The restatement then begins with a comparatively brief tutti, $R_4$. Often, the entire last section is not as extended as either the opening tonic–dominant statements or the central area of modulation; however, since only one key is emphasized, tonal balance may still be perceived. This final

Figure 1

$$R_1 \quad S_1 \quad R_2 \quad S_2 \quad R_3 \quad S_3 \quad R_4 \quad S_4 \quad R_5$$

| statements of I & V | central area | return of I |
|---|---|---|
| (or i & III) | of modulation | |

[11] Clear examples of this five-ritornello–four-solo design in Bach's early concertos may be found in the first movements of H. 407/W. 5, H. 410/W. 7, H. 414/W. 11, H. 418/W. 15, H. 420/W. 17, and H. 421/W. 18.

[12] If modulation appears in $R_2$, the central area of modulation begins there rather than with $S_2$; such an occurrence is not characteristic in Bach's concertos, although other keys may occasionally be suggested in $R_2$.

[13] On the resemblance of $S_3$ to a retransition, see Schulenberg, *Instrumental Music*, pp. 29, 131–2, 135; on the ternary nature of Bach's designs, p. 131.

ritornello–solo group, which reaffirms the tonic, has been likened to the recapitulation of a sonata form.[14] In general, the five-ritornello–four-solo plan is an expansion of designs found in some presumably late concertos by Vivaldi.[15]

Many North German composers, especially those of Bach's generation, favoured this plan. For example, it was characteristic of concertos by Christoph Schaffrath (1709–63), the harpsichordist in the service of Princess Anna Amalia. Schaffrath had been a member of Frederick the Great's Kapelle until about 1744 or 1745, and may have been succeeded in that post by Christoph Nichelmann.[16] In the six Schaffrath concertos inventoried for this study, all have this five-ritornello–four-solo plan in their opening movements, and four employ it in their finales as well.[17] The broad scope of this ritornello plan made it particularly effective for movements in quicker tempo; thus it appears in the first movement of an F major keyboard concerto by Johann Gottlieb Janitsch as well as in the first movement of a D major keyboard concerto by Johann Gabriel Seyffarth, both in the collection of the Staatsbibliothek Preussischer Kulturbe-sitz at Berlin.[18]

A somewhat different application of this design appears in several concertos for violin or flute by Franz (František) Benda and at least four keyboard concertos by his younger brother, Georg Anton (Jiří Antonín). Both lessen the weight of $R_3$ by making it shorter and by withholding primary thematic material. It maintains its identity as a structural ritornello (as opposed to an orchestral participant in a solo–tutti dialogue) because it is set off at both borders by clear cadences, because it is non-sequential, and because it is lengthier than the tuttis in the dialogues that surround it. But when it is compared with analogous ritornellos in concertos by Schaffrath, the one by

[14] For example, Drummond, in *The German Concerto*, pp. 300, 301, 316, refers to the area of tonic return in C. P. E. Bach's concertos in terms of 'recapitulation'.

[15] See Vivaldi's violin concertos Ryom 173 (C major), i, Ryom 176 (C major), i, Ryom 244 (D minor), i and iii, Ryom 342 (A major), iii, Ryom 361 (B flat major), i, and Ryom 381 (B flat major), i. A somewhat similar design appears in the finale of J. S. Bach's A major concerto BWV 1055, arranged for keyboard.

[16] See the preface to Schaffrath's *Concerto in B flat for Cembalo and Strings*, ed. Karyl Louwenaar (Madison 1977), vii.

[17] See D-brd B, Mus. ms. 19750/2 (A major), i and iii, 19750/4 (E minor), i, 19750/6 (E flat major), i and iii, 19750/8 (A minor), i and iii, 19750/10 (B flat major), i, and D-ddr Bds, Ms Am. B. 492 (B flat major), i and iii. For an early discussion of Schaffrath, see Uldall, *Klavierkonzert*, pp. 69–72. The A major concerto D-brd B, Mus. ms. 19750/2, probably by Schaffrath, has been attributed to J. C. Bach in an edition by Adolf Hoffmann, Corona Werkreihe für Kammerorchester, 73 (Wolfenbüttel and Zurich, 1963); the same attribution appears in D-brd B, Mus. ms. Bach St 487. For this concerto's incipits, see Charles Sanford Terry, *John Christian Bach*, 2nd edn. (London, New York, and Toronto, 1967), 300/1–3 (references in this form indicate page number and number of incipit on the page).

[18] Shelf-marks Mus. ms. 11109 (Janitsch); Mus. ms. 20776, 20665 (Seyffarth). 20776 provides parts for keyboard, horns, oboes, and strings. 20665 gives only the violin I part, with an appended note, dated 4 Feb. 1965, by J[ean] K[essler] Wolf: 'The Cembalo part for this Concerto is catalogued under/Bach?/Mus. ms. Bach St 624'.

Janitsch, and some early Bach examples, it occupies a position considerably less prominent in the overall design. This tendency to assimilate $R_3$ into $S_2$–$S_3$ gives the central area of modulation an even stronger solo emphasis and further heightens the contrast to $R_4$, the beginning of the tonic return. The result of this tendency is an approximation of a four-ritornello–three-solo design in which the entire central modulatory area becomes a unified $S_2$.[19] Such a quasi-three-solo format and the concomitant tutti restatement somewhat resemble the concerto plan found in a great majority of Mozart's piano concertos and thus may be interpreted as a relatively progressive handling of the form. To judge from style features, it is possible that at least some of the Georg Benda concertos were written several years after those discussed previously.

## Solo Restatement: Four-ritornello Plan

Solo restatements are often found in the finales of Bach's early concertos,[20] and they appear in a four-ritornello–three-solo design that has become the subject of much scholarly attention, since it was the one extensively described in the third volume of Koch's *Versuch*.[21] It may be illustrated as in Figure 2. $R_3$ may be shorter and less defined thematically than the main orchestral statements that precede it. According to Koch's description,[22] it is functionally similar to what later theorists would refer to as a sonata-form retransition: its purpose is to lead the musical flow, by means of melodic sequence, back to the

---

[19] Incipits for the Franz Benda concertos may be found in Douglas A. Lee, *Franz Benda (1709–1786): A Thematic Catalogue of his Works* (New York, 1984). See the finale of Concerto II-4 ('before 1762'; see Lee, *Franz Benda*, p. 13, D minor; p. 15, E minor) and the first movement and finale of II-11 ('before 1763'; see Lee, *Franz Benda*, p. 16, G major; p. 11, C major); ed. Jan Racek and Vratislav Bělský, Musica Antiqua Bohemica, 80 (Prague, 1979), 1, 60. Regarding Georg Benda, see the first movement and finale of a B minor concerto (Breitkopf catalogue, pt. IV (1763), 18, no. 1) and the finale of an F minor concerto (Breitkopf, pt. IV (1763), 18, no. 4); both of these concertos may be found in Racek and Bělský, eds., Musica Antiqua Bohemica, 45 (Prague, 1960). Two other examples include the first movement of a G major concerto (Breitkopf, pt. IV (1763), 18, no. 3), ed. Racek and Bělský, Musica Antiqua Bohemica, 77 (Prague, 1976), and the first movement and finale of a G minor concerto (Breitkopf, suppl. V (1770), 29), ed. Racek and Václav Kaprál, Musica Antiqua Bohemica, 10 (Prague, 1950). A similar design by C. P. E. Bach occurs in the finale of H. 410/W. 7. See Barry S. Brook's reprint edition of the Breitkopf catalogue, *The Breitkopf Thematic Catalogue: The Six Parts and Sixteen Supplements, 1762–1787* (New York, 1966).

[20] Examples in the early concertos may be found in H. 404/W. 2, i; H. 405/W. 3, i and iii; H. 406/W. 4, iii; H. 407/W. 5, iii; H. 412/W. 9, i and iii; H. 415/W. 12, iii; H. 416/W. 13, i and iii; and H. 421/W. 18, iii.

[21] Koch, *Versuch*, iii, 333–9.

[22] Ibid. 338–9: 'Mit dem Schlusstone tritt wieder ein kurzes Ritornell ein, welches den, schon bey der Sinfonie beschriebenen Nebenperioden macht, welcher vermittelst eines melodischen Theils, der durch die Progression, oder durch die Fortsetzung einer in demselben enthaltenen metrischen Formel erweitert wird, die Modulation wieder in den Haupton zurückführt, in welcher dieses Ritornell mit dem Quintabsatze schliesst, damit das dritte Solo der Hauptstimme wieder im Hauptone anfangen kann.'

## Figure 2

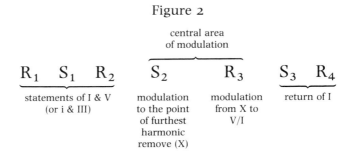

central area
of modulation

R₁  S₁  R₂        S₂              R₃              S₃  R₄

statements of I & V    modulation       modulation       return of I
(or i & III)          to the point      from X to
                      of furthest        V/I
                      harmonic
                      remove (X)

tonic from the point of furthest harmonic remove, generally the minor submediant or mediant when the movement is in a major key.[23] Of all the orchestral statements, this ritornello, especially owing to its relative brevity, comes closest to being integrated into the three-part superstructure of the solo, and, harmonically, it still functions as part of the central modulatory area. This overall format was often used during the second half of the eighteenth century, and it was favoured especially among Mannheim composers. In North Germany, it was frequently employed by the Grauns in their keyboard concertos. At least six of the keyboard concertos attributed to 'Graun' in the Staatsbibliothek Preussicher Kulturbesitz at Berlin have it in their first movements or finales, and sometimes in both.[24] It also occurs in both outer movements of Nichelmann's A major concerto of 1740 as well as in the first movement of his E major concerto of 1758.[25] Occasionally it appears in a slow movement, such as the D minor Andantino quasi allegretto of an F major keyboard concerto by Georg Benda,[26] and the E minor Adagio of an E major

[23] For a discussion of the point of furthest harmonic remove, see Leonard G. Ratner, *Classic Music: Expression, Form, and Style* (New York and London, 1980), 225–7. In C. P. E. Bach's concertos, the solo part sometimes supports the tutti modulation with figuration, maintaining activity (beyond continuo function) up to its own restatement, as in the finale of so early a concerto as H. 404/W. 2. This solo preparation for the solo return results in a design that approximates the three-ritornello–two-solo plan later to be used by J. C. Bach and to become a favourite of Johann Samuel Schroeter in London during the 1760s and 1770s. Christoph Nichelmann used this design in the finale of his 1758 E major keyboard concerto (see n. 25 below). Perhaps the most noteworthy instances occur in two famous violin concertos by Mozart, K. 218 in D and 219 in A (the 'Turkish'), both from 1775. This type was the one described by most late 18th-century theorists, and eventually Koch himself adopted it in his *Musikalisches Lexikon* (Frankfurt am Main, 1802), cols. 349–55. For a comparatively recent discussion of these theorists, see Stevens, 'Theme, Harmony, and Texture', pp. 25–43.

[24] D-brd B, Mus. ms. 8271/2 (D major), i and iii; 8271/3 (G major), iii; 8271/4 (G major), i; 8272/1 (=8271/5; C major), iii (see Breitkopf, pt. IV (1763), 19, collection III no. 3, attributed to C. H. Graun); 8272/2 (C major), i and iii; and 8282/1 (G major), iii.

[25] See Douglas A. Lee, *Christoph Nichelmann: A Thematic Index* (Detroit, 1971), concertos I and III. In the first movement of Concerto I, the soloist does not begin the restatement with its (typically) independent main theme.

[26] Incipit in Breitkopf, suppl. XII (1778), 40; modern edition, Musica Antiqua Bohemica, 77.

violin concerto by Franz Benda in the manuscript collection at the Library of Congress.[27]

Johann Christian Bach employed this design more frequently than any other in the keyboard concertos that he wrote prior to his Op. 1 set (published in London in 1763). Typically, in the last part of $R_3$, the young Bach brought back thematic material that had appeared in the later part of $R_1$, making especially smooth the transition to the restatement in $S_3$. Five of his harpsichord concertos, dating from between 1750 and 1754, when Christian was under the artistic wing of Philipp Emanuel, survive at the Staatsbibliothek Preussischer Kulturbesitz in Berlin as a group of holographs under one cover with the shelf-mark Mus. ms. Autogr. Bach P 390. Of these, two emphasize a modulatory third ritornello, and two others contain it in one each of their movements.[28]

Christian may also have returned to this plan later. There is a print of an E flat major keyboard concerto by 'Jean Chretien' Bach issued at Paris, 'Gravé par Madame Annereau / Mis au Jour par M$^r$ Bailleux'. This print, with the heading 'I$^{er}$ Concerto' and the subsequent reference 'Oeuvre XIV', bears no specific indication of date. The incipit for the first movement did appear, however, in the 1781 supplement to the Breitkopf catalogue, and the concerto was also advertised in Bailleux's catalogue, possibly as early as *c.*1777.[29] The designs of the first movement and finale conform to Koch's *Versuch* description.

## Tutti Restatement: Four-ritornello Plan

Of the remaining formats C. P. E. Bach tended to favour, one stands out, mainly because it anticipates the overall ritornello-solo plan associated with a convention of Mozart's generation. The movement is often, but by no means

[27] Shelf-mark M 1012 .B45P Case; dated 'before 1764' in Lee, *Franz Benda*, II–6.

[28] Ed. Richard Maunder in *Keyboard Concertos I: Six Early Concertos* (New York and London, 1985), vol. 32 of The Collected Works of Johann Christian Bach, 1735–1782, ed. Ernest Warburton. A modulatory third tutti occurs in the first movements and finales of nos. 1 and 3, in the finale of no. 2, and in the second movement of no. 5.

[29] See Terry, *John Christian Bach*, 301/1–3, and Breitkopf, suppl. XIV (1781), 53. For reference(s) in Bailleux's catalogue, see Cari Johansson, *French Music Publishers' Catalogues of the Second Half of the Eighteenth Century* (Uppsala, 1955), Fac. 10 (1782) and possibly Fac. 6 (1777?). If this concerto was newly written for publication in Paris, it is then possible that Bach changed his style from the London sets to accommodate a different public's expectations. In London, Bach favoured two new formats: a three-ritornello–two-solo plan reflecting strong sonata influence and chamber style; and a four-ritornello–three-solo plan with tutti recapitulation, subsequently adopted by Mozart. In this Bailleux print, as well as in his two bassoon concertos (perhaps written during the 1770s for the Mannheim bassoonist Georg Wenzel Ritter), Bach changed (back?) to a style that may have been more appropriate to the tastes of different locales. See Terry, *John Christian Bach*, p. 288/1–6 (bassoon concertos), and also the comments by R. Maunder in The Collected Works of Johann Christian Bach, vol. 36 (1986), ix. The opening tutti in the finale of the E flat bassoon concerto ends in the dominant, providing an unusually clear example of a true double-exposition form.

Figure 3

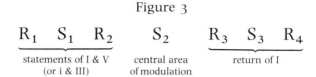

$$R_1 \quad S_1 \quad R_2 \qquad S_2 \qquad R_3 \quad S_3 \quad R_4$$

statements of I & V          central area          return of I
(or i & III)                 of modulation

always, in a slow tempo; it may be that this type was able to sprout most easily in surroundings where symphonic breadth and extensive ritornello structure give way to expressive melody and relative simplicity of texture. There is a sizeable group of Philipp Emanuel's very early keyboard concertos—seven out of the first twenty—containing movements in which the third ritornello, in a four-ritornello plan, begins in the tonic with the main theme (see Figure 3).[30] Bach's angular harmonic style tends to make his handling of $R_3$ a bold stroke. What the end of $S_2$ may occasionally lack in preparation for the tonic entrance of $R_3$ is counterbalanced by the dramatic contrast of the harmonic shift from mediant, submediant, or (sub)dominant to tonic. In general, the impression of

Example 1. Keyboard concerto in E flat major, H. 404/W. 2, ii, mm. 72–8. D-brd B, Mus. ms. autogr. Bach P 354

---

[30] H. 404/W. 2, ii; H. 406/W. 4, i; H. 410/W. 7, ii; H. 411/W. 8, i, ii, iii; H. 412/W. 9, ii; H. 413/W. 10, i; and H. 419/W. 16, i.

arrival at the beginning of $R_3$ is convincing, as in the C minor slow movement of the E flat major harpsichord concerto H. 404/W. 2 (see Example 1).[31] Rachel Wade has postulated that the Huberty print of this concerto, which dates from *c.* 1762, may actually represent the original (1734) version.[32] It is noteworthy that the Huberty print has the same formal design for this movement as does the 1743 revision.[33]

The elegant proportions of the F sharp minor Adagio from the A major concerto H. 410/W. 7 of 1740 provide a perfect four-ritornello concerto plan in miniature, with $R_3$ about half the length of $R_1$. By contrast, in the B minor Adagio from the G major concerto H. 412/W. 9 of 1741/2, $R_3$ is unusually brief, but Bach compensates by supplying it with an effective preparation harmonically.[34]

Third-tutti restatements also occur in some fast movements of Bach's concertos. An early instance may be found in the first movement of the A major concerto H. 411/W. 8 of 1741 (see Example 2). In the finale of the same concerto, there is a direct shift from the minor submediant at the end of $S_2$ to the tonic at the entrance of $R_3$, producing what has been referred to by Jan LaRue as a 'bifocal' harmonic relation.[35] This change of key centre, without any preparation, had been characteristic of significant structural changes within or between movements in late Baroque works. Its appearance in this context therefore signals what had traditionally been an important formal event (see Example 3). These early concertos demonstrate that in the fast movements, as in the adagios, Bach used a wide variety of procedures immediately preceding the entrance of $R_3$, from an absence of preparation, as in Example 3, to a very brief modulatory scalar descent, as in the first movement of H. 413/W. 10 of 1742, to a relatively extended zone of activity that resembles a full-blown retransition, as in the first movement of H. 419/W. 16 of 1745 (see Example 4).

It may be with a variant form in the finale of H. 413/W. 10 that Bach employs one of his most intriguing designs. $S_2$ concludes in the minor submediant (G minor); $R_3$ then begins on the path back to B flat major, the tonic, in the manner described by Koch in his *Versuch*. However, once the tonic is reached, rather than having the soloist enter with the restatement, Bach reserves this crucial moment for the orchestra, which indeed does present the primary theme in the tonic. This combination of Koch *Versuch* and tutti-

---

[31] Other examples include H. 406/W. 4, i; H. 411/W. 8, ii and iii; and H. 427/W. 23, ii.

[32] See Wade, *Keyboard Concertos*, pp. 25, 57–8, 90.

[33] I am indebted to Rachel Wade, who graciously afforded me access to copies of this print and many of the other C. P. E. Bach sources cited in this paper.

[34] Later examples include the slow movements of H. 425/W. 22, H. 465/W. 39, and H. 477/W. 44.

[35] See Jan LaRue, 'Bifocal Tonality, An Explanation for Ambiguous Baroque Cadences'. *Essays on Music in Honor of Archibald Thompson Davison by his Associates* (Cambridge, Mass., 1957), 173–84.

Example 2. Keyboard concerto in A major, H. 411/W. 8, i, mm. 191–201. D-ddr Bds, Mus. ms. autogr. Bach P 352

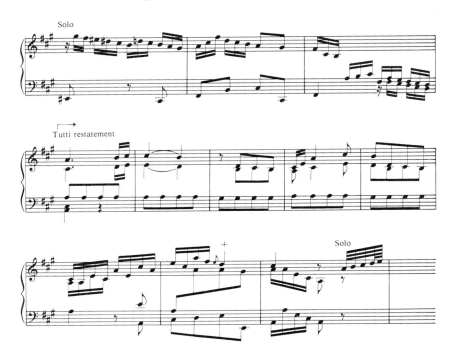

Example 3. Keyboard concerto in A major, H. 411/W. 8, iii, mm. 162–8. D-ddr Bds, Mus. ms. autogr. Bach P 352

Example 4. Keyboard concerto in G major, H. 419/W. 16, i, mm. 143–57. D-brd B, Mus. ms. Bach St. 499

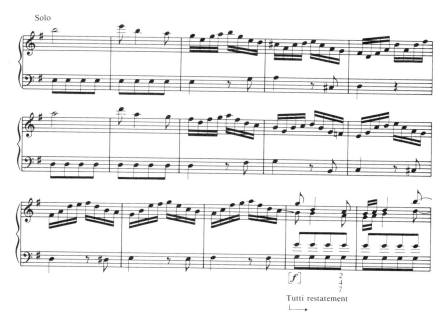

Tutti restatement

restatement types provides an unusual design that was to find favour, but at a much later date, with Dittersdorf and Leopold Anton Koželuh.[36]

In general, the clarity of the tonic return, after a harmonic odyssey, reinforces an impression of harmonic symmetry for the last ritornello–solo section in these early concertos and further heightens the effect of a tripartite structure. Thus, Bach's harmonic treatment is probably the most telling single factor in conveying to us the resemblance of these four-ritornello–three-solo structures to the concerto designs of Mozart's generation over forty years later.

While most of J. C. Bach's Berlin concertos, written during the early 1750s, make use of the plan described by Koch in his *Versuch* (as mentioned above),

---

[36] This combination was also employed by Giornovichi, Lolli, and Franz Anton Hoffmeister. Wagenseil, who was unusually imaginative in this zone of activity, used it on occasion, as in the first movement and finale of the C major keyboard concerto, listed by Helga Scholz-Michelitsch in *Das Orchester- und Kammermusikwerk von Georg Christoph Wagenseil: thematischer Katalog* (Vienna, 1972) as no. 341. Bach's use of it appears to be too early to have been influenced by Wagenseil. The combination also crops up every so often in concertos by J. C. Bach, as in the finale of the G major keyboard concerto from the Berlin autographs, D-brd B, Mus. ms. autogr. Bach P 390, no. 5; see Terry, *John Christian Bach*, 299/4.

Example 5. J. C. Bach, keyboard concerto in G major, i, mm. 131–8. D-brd B, Mus. ms. autogr. Bach P 390 (No. 5)

two concertos, nos. 4 in E major and 5 in G major, contain movements that are noteworthy owing to their use of a third-tutti restatement.[37] The E major concerto has the third-tutti restatements in both its first movement and finale, but it is in the opening movement of the G major concerto that Bach provides the most impressive retransition. From the point of furthest harmonic remove, the minor mediant (B minor), the music moves through a series of keys to the major subdominant, from which key the flow rebounds easily to V/I. The use of

[37] Terry, *John Christian Bach*, pp. 298/10, 299/1, 2. The four-ritornello–three-solo type with R₃ reprise and its sonata-form implications are discussed in Uldall, *Klavierkonzert*, pp. 107–8, with reference to J. C. Bach.

the subdominant to brake the momentum in this manner definitely looks forward to procedures found in Christian's Op. 13 London concertos. In Example 5, the last part of the retransition, including the arrival at the subdominant, is presented.

An F minor concerto, variously attributed to Wilhelm Friedemann and Carl Philipp Emanuel as well as to Johann Christian Bach, is listed by Terry in his monograph on J. C. Bach[38] and appears as no. 486 in Helm's C. P. E. Bach catalogue. Helm dates this concerto *c*.1753 and indicates that it is probably by Christian and was merely revised by Philipp Emanuel.[39] While the first movement conforms to Koch's *Versuch* description, in the finale, the second solo concludes the central area of modulation with a cadence on the dominant, approached by an implied diminished-seventh chord under a fermata proceeding to a trill on v/v (G minor) and finally to the resolution on an open C in octaves and a rest. The unwritten cadenza is followed directly by $R_3$, the tutti restatement, on the tonic (F minor). This zone of punctuation is more elaborate than the typical bifocal juxtaposition and may be a stylistic link to the later type with full retransition at the conclusion of $S_2$.

Apparently experiments at the time they were conceived, these movements appear as remarkable projections into a later musical syntax and, in fact, could well have furnished much of the intellectual matrix from which Christian drew inspiration for the fully developed recapitulatory designs in the London concertos, particularly the Op. 7 and Op. 13 sets. The first movements of two F major oboe concertos by Christian, both believed to have been written during the early 1760s, as well as the first-movement torso of a flute concerto in D major, dated 1768, all have $R_3$ recapitulations preceded by fully evolved retransitions.[40]

Other North German composers who made significant use of this four-ritornello–three-solo plan in their keyboard concertos include Nichelmann, the Grauns, Georg Benda, and especially Christian Friedrich Schale. Douglas A. Lee has shown that Nichelmann (1717–61/2), among the early North German composers of keyboard concertos, was forward-looking in various

---

[38] Terry, *John Christian Bach*, p. 301/4–6.

[39] In D-brd B, Mus. ms. P 680, this concerto is attributed to Wilhelm Friedemann Bach; in D-brd B, St 482, the cover has the inscription, in Nichelmann's hand, '. . . dal Sgr. *J. C. Bach* . . . riveduto dal Sgr. C. F. E. Bach'; on D-brd B, St 483, the title-page has the attribution '. . . von Joh. Cretien bearb. in Berlin unter E. Aufsicht'; in D-ddr LEb, Gorke-Slg. 40, 'Concerto/ da/ J. C. Bach'. In Breitkopf, pt. IV (1763), 18, collection III no. 2, the work is attributed to C. P. E. Bach. In an edition by W. Szarvady (Leipzig) [n.d., c. 1890(?)] it is attributed to Philipp Emanuel; W. Smigelski's edition (Hamburg, 1959) attributes it to Wilhelm Friedemann; and in the edition by R. Maunder in The Collected Works of Johann Christian Bach, vol. 32 (1985), it is assigned to Johann Christian. For further discussion of this concerto, see Uldall, *Klavierkonzert*, pp. 66, 89–91, and Wade, *Keyboard Concertos*, pp 15–17, 124–5, 274–6.

[40] See Terry, *John Christian Bach*, pp. 287/4–6 (this work is listed as doubtful in *New Grove*, i. 875) and 290/6 (oboe concertos), and 286/7 (flute concerto). For a discussion of their background and dates, see Maunder's edition of the woodwind concertos in The Collected Works of Johann Christian Bach, vol. 36 (1986), vii ff.

aspects of style, including his handling of phrasing, harmonic rhythm, thematic independence of the soloist with regard to primary material, and, in a broader dimension, the attention given the restatement in the total design.[41] In an A major concerto dated 1740, Nichelmann employed a third-tutti restatement in the somewhat foreshortened slow (middle) movement.[42] In another A major concerto (undated),[43] Nichelmann used recapitulatory tuttis in both the first movement and the finale. In the first movement, which has a relatively long reprise by Nichelmann's standards, $R_3$, the tutti restatement, enters without prior retransitional preparation. In the finale, however, which has a characteristically short restatement,[44] the recapitulatory tutti is prepared and helps establish this concerto as a truly progressive work.

The Grauns apparently employed a variety of formal designs, but they favoured a four-ritornello–three-solo plan for their fast movements, and as already noted, showed a slight preference for the Koch *Versuch* type, in which the restatement begins with $S_3$. However, at least five of the keyboard concertos from the Graun collection at the Staatsbibliothek Preussischer Kulturbesitz in Berlin employ the design in which $R_3$ begins the restatement.[45] An F major concerto, attributed to Carl Heinrich in the Breitkopf catalogue of 1763 and to Johann Gottlieb in a 1762 Walsh print,[46] provides additional examples in its slow movement and finale. Well-proportioned four-ritornello–three-solo designs occur in the B flat major Largo and the concluding Allegretto. In both movements, a brief additional internal ritornello in the central area of modulation appears shortly before the tutti restatement, and this design may be related to the transitional five-ritornello–four-solo type discussed above in connection with Franz and Georg Benda.

In the E major violin concerto attributed to Franz Benda in an eighteenth-century manuscript at the Library of Congress, mentioned above, the first movement has a recapitulatory third tutti without prior harmonic preparation, creating a bifocal relation from a cadence in G sharp minor as v/vi to the primary theme in E. In the keyboard concertos by Georg Benda, there

---

[41] For further discussion, see Douglas A. Lee, 'Christoph Nichelmann and the Early Clavier Concerto in Berlin', *MQ*, 57 (1971), 647, 649–50, 652–3.

[42] Lee, *Thematic Index*, Concerto I. A scored version appears in Douglas A. Lee, 'The Instrumental Works of Christoph Nichelmann', Ph.D. diss., University of Michigan, 1968, Appendix IV, 4–45.

[43] Lee, *Thematic Index*, Concerto IV, Douglas A. Lee in *Christoph Nichelmann: Clavier Concertos in E Major and A Major* (Madison, 1977).

[44] See also Concerto XIII (A major) in Lee, *Thematic Index*; ed. Carl Bittner as *Christoph Nichelmann: Konzert für Cembalo*, Nagels Musik-Archiv, 145 (Hanover, 1938).

[45] D-brd B, Mus. ms. 8272/1 ( = 8271/5; C major), i (see Breitkopf, pt. IV (1763), 19, collection III no. 3); 8272/3 ( = 8271/1 = 8282/5; B flat major), i and iii (see Breitkopf, pt. IV, 19, collection I no. 3); 8272/4 (B flat major), i and iii (see Breitkopf, pt. IV, 19, collection III no. 1); 8282/2 (D major), i and iii; and 8282/4 (A major), iii. All Breitkopf attributions are to C. H. Graun.

[46] See Breitkopf, pt. IV, 19, collection II no. 1. In Hugo Ruf's edition (Heidelberg, 1959; based partly on Mus. ms. 8283 (D-brd B?), it is attributed to C. H. Graun.

sometimes appears a relatively clear example of a four-ritornello–three-solo design with recapitulatory third tutti, especially in the works that may have been composed at somewhat later dates. It occurs not only in some of the slow movements, notably that of the familiar F minor concerto,[47] but also in several fast movements. In an F major concerto, listed in the 1778 supplement to the Breitkopf catalogue,[48] Benda in the first movement employed the traditional, harmonically unprepared entrance of $R_3$, with its bifocal relation. In the finale of a G major concerto, however, he used a more progressive retransitional preparation for the tutti entrance of the restatement, despite this concerto's earlier listing in the Breitkopf catalogue (1763).[49] The comparatively forward-looking treatment of this movement may be the result of it being a finale and thus relatively free from some of the conventional formal strictures associated with opening movements.

In the two keyboard concertos issued by E. B. Schwickert at Leipzig in 1779, Benda adopted a newer and less weighty style in which sonata-form elements become more explicit, especially in the finales, where internal repeats are used.[50] In all six movements, tuttis are radically shortened. The first movements of both concertos, as well as the slow movement of the second, have recapitulatory third tuttis with retransitional harmonic preparation. Significantly enough, there remain vestiges of the brief inner tutti within the central area of modulation, a tutti referred to above in the discussion of the Bendas' characteristic approach to the five-ritornello–four-solo format.

Of all the North German composers after C. P. E. Bach, it was perhaps Christian Schale (1713–1800), cellist at the Berlin royal chapel from 1741 and first cathedral organist from 1763, who most favoured the third-ritornello restatement in the fast movements of his concertos.[51] Although several of Schale's concertos in D-brd B employ the type with a harmonically unprepared entrance of $R_3$ in one or more of their movements,[52] others display an impressive handling of the third tutti preceded by full retransitional preparation.[53] Perhaps the most advanced of these is the B flat major concerto with the shelf-mark Mus. ms. 19758/5. In the first movement, Allegro non

[47] The Larghetto is in A flat major; modern edition, Musica Antiqua Bohemica, 45. Another $R_3$ restatement occurs in the C major Andante con moto of the G major concerto (also in Musica Antiqua Bohemica, 45). The incipit for the F minor concerto appears in Breitkopf, pt. IV (1763), 18, no. 2; that for the G major concerto is in Breitkopf, suppl. XII (1778), 41, no. 2.

[48] Suppl. XII, p. 40; modern edition, Musica Antiqua Bohemica, 77.

[49] Pt. IV, 18, no. 3; modern edition, Musica Antiqua Bohemica, 77.

[50] US Wc M 1010.B445 Case. See Breitkopf, suppl. XII (1778), 41, and n. 47 above. These designs are reminiscent of some concerto movements by Tartini, such as the first movement and finale of the F major violin concerto, Dounias 67, and the finale of the A minor violin concerto, Dounias 115.

[51] In the slow movements, Schale favoured the abridged three-ritornello–two-solo type in which $S_2$ begins with the primary theme in the tonic.

[52] D-brd B, Mus. ms. 19758/1 (G major), i and iii; 19758/3 (G major), i; 19758/4 (F major), iii.

[53] D-brd B, Mus. ms. 19758/4 (F major), i; 19758/5 (B flat major), i and iii; 19758/7 (C minor), i and iii.

Example 6. C. F. Schale, keyboard concerto in B flat major, iii, mm. 120–31. D-
brd B, Mus. ms. 19758/5

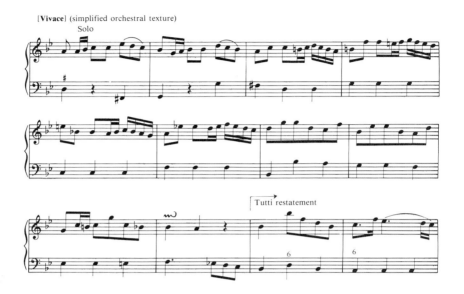

troppo, and the finale, Vivace, Schale provided clear retransitional material in
the solo part directly before the recapitulatory tutti. In the Allegro, the soloist
effects a smooth transition from vi to V/I in a four-measure linking passage; in
the Vivace, Schale extends the harmonic transition to ten measures (see
Example 6). The manuscript copy of this concerto does not specify a date;
however, it is quite possible that this concerto's gently curved melodies,
comparatively balanced phrasing, and well-proportioned overall design, and
especially its well-co-ordinated treatment of the retransitional zone, suggest
that it is a relatively late work by this unusually long-lived composer.[54]

Although an exploration of the repertory outside North Germany and the
surroundings of the court of Frederick the Great lies beyond the scope of this
study, it may be appropriate for purposes of overall perspective briefly to
consider one remarkable handling of concerto form occurring in Naples.
Before the 1740s, appearances of a tutti restatement in a four-ritornello form
were generally isolated and sometimes tentative, creating problems in
definition. The movements were short and, unlike those of Bach, cramped

---

[54] The slow movements of the concertos by Janitsch and Seyffarth cited in n. 18 above also
employ $R_3$ restatements.

harmonically and somewhat out of proportion when compared with the dimensions characteristic of later designs. However, occasionally a movement emerged that gave exceptional promise of things to come.

As Douglass Green has pointed out, some of the most attractive of the early possibilities crop up in several violoncello concertos by Leonardo Leo, dating from 1737 and 1738.[55] Progressive designs sometimes occur in the slow first movements of these four- and five-movement works, which use a graceful and refined melodic style. Possibly owing to their brevity, these movements seldom stray far from home harmonically. In the D major concerto,[56] the second tutti modulates back to the tonic from the dominant, so that the second solo begins again in the tonic. Moreover, the second solo is so brief that it creates the impression of being a retransition. The first movement of the 1737 A major concerto,[57] a truly impressive work owing to its emphasis on rhythmic variety and melodic grace, has a design more suggestive of later concerto form, even though the first tutti and solo occupy an unusually large portion of the entire movement. However, Leo again adheres to a limited harmonic palette, and the feeling of arrival at the beginning of the third tutti is thereby weakened, despite the forward-looking preparatory dominant pedal. In general, these movements project an impression of what Green refers to as 'sonatina' form.[58] Thus, the formal similarities that these attactive concerto movements exhibit with later designs do not appear quite as convincing as do some of the early C. P. E. Bach examples, at least with regard to the forcefulness of the restatement. Nevertheless, they stand nearest Philipp Emanuel's concertos as some of the earliest and most elegant examples of a format that was not to become established as the norm for at least half a century.

In sum, with searching intellect and fertile imagination, C. P. E. Bach displayed a rich variety of procedures with his handling of form in the early keyboard concertos. Certainly, some of his procedures anticipate stylistic features characteristic of later generations.[59] However, it would be misleading to gauge the ultimate worth of Bach merely in terms of how 'progressive' he

[55] See Douglass Green, 'Progressive and Conservative Tendencies in the Violoncello Concertos of Leonardo Leo', *Geiringer Festschrift*, pp. 261–71.

[56] Composed in 1737; modern editions include those of Francesco Cilèa (Milano, 1934) and Felix Schroeder (London, Zurich, and Stuttgart, [n.d.; Preface, 1958]).

[57] Modern editions include those of Eugen Rapp (Mainz, 1938) and Renato Fasano (Milano, 1967).

[58] Green, 'Progressive and Conservative Tendencies', p. 271 n. 12.

[59] Bach's (and other mid-century composers') concerto ritornellos are increasingly affected by the tripartite nature of the nascent sonata principle. The changing functions of these ritornellos provide fascinating insights into the transitional genres between the ideal Baroque concerto and its Classic counterpart. Mid-century appearances of the tutti in a retransitional guise (later described by Koch) or in a recapitulatory mode (later exemplified in Mozart's piano concertos), both in the sonata-form sense, may be viewed as steps along the path to the integration of opening-tutti thematic material in the solo recapitulation. This trend led eventually to the opening tutti's thematic pervasiveness in Beethoven's concerto developments and the dominance of the orchestra in Beethoven's recapitulations.

*Shelley G. Davis*

was. Perhaps we may gain the best perspective of his accomplishment by judging his music on its own merits and enjoying his probes into the future as ancillary benefits and as testaments to the timelessness of his art. It is then that we may most clearly view his contributions, not as those of a 'precursor' or as an 'early' Classicist, but rather as those of a consummate musician who represents an early, if not actually the first, high point in the history of the eighteenth-century keyboard concerto.

# C. P. E. Bach and the Trio Old and New*
## Michelle Fillion

DURING the two central quarters of the eighteenth century the trio was transformed in theory and practice. North German theoretical discussions of the term 'trio' from Scheibe to Koch agree that it denotes primarily a compositional principle—the elusive art of writing in three parts—and mention exact instrumentation or number of performers only secondarily if at all. But beyond this basic agreement, the standard of perfection in trio writing shifted noticeably. For Scheibe in 1740, the most characteristic trio form (what he called 'das eigentliche Trio') was one in which three equal but independent parts engage in a serious fugal expansion.[1] A decade later, Quantz upheld the equality of the two upper parts, while playing down the role of extended imitation in favour of exchange.[2] Schulz, writing in the early 1770s, differentiated between works for three obbligato instruments (*sonate a tré*) and those in three parts (trios), but concentrated on the latter. For him, the 'highest level of perfection' was represented by the freely imitative chamber trio, a rare combination of three equal but complementary parts that engage or oppose one another in an affective dialogue of the passions, 'ein vollkommen leidenschaftliches Gespräch'. But Schulz was unable to overlook the emerging treble-dominated trio with subservient accompaniment, a difficult genre to handle if, as he claimed, it is to avoid the emptiness of the inexpressive trios cultivated by 'our young composers today'.[3] H. C. Koch's definition of 1793 duplicates the essence of Schulz's masterful analysis, but not without regret for the demise of the grand old trio in the wake of the homophonic style.[4] This homophonic trio, most often scored for two violins and unfigured bass, forces a

* The research for this study was partially funded by a faculty research grant from McGill University, Montreal. I also wish to express my gratitude to the libraries that assisted me, especially the music archive of the Gesellschaft der Musikfreunde in Wien (Dr Otto Biba), and the Staatsbibliothek Preußischer Kulturbesitz, Berlin (Dr Rudolf Elvers) and their co-operative staffs. Dr Elvers kindly granted me permission to reproduce segments of autograph P 357.

[1] Johann Adolph Scheibe, *Der Critische Musikus*, 2nd edn. (Leipzig, 1745; repr. Hildesheim, 1970), section 74 (20 January 1740), 676.

[2] Johann Joachim Quantz, *On Playing the Flute*, trans. Edward R. Reilly (New York, 1966), 317.

[3] Johann Abraham Peter Schulz, 'Trio', in Johann Georg Sulzer, *Allgemeine Theorie der schönen Künste*, 2nd edn. (Leipzig, 1792–94), as cited in Hubert Unverricht, *Geschichte des Streichtrios* (Tutzing, 1969), 94–6.

[4] Heinrich Christoph Koch, *Versuch einer Anleitung zur Composition* (Leipzig, 1782–93; repr. Hildesheim, 1969), iii. 322–5. For more detailed background on the mid-century trio, the reader is referred to Unverricht, *Geschichte des Streichtrios*, to which I am likewise indebted.

shift of meaning on the word 'trio': no longer for three independent lines, it becomes a basically two-part work for three players, as noted by Schulz.

The theorists lagged behind contemporary practice, for the homophonic trio was vigorously cultivated after mid-century, especially in Italy and Vienna, until it fell prey to the string quartet in the 1770s. Further obscuring an already confusing picture is the emergence during this period of chamber music with obbligato keyboard, especially the trio for violin or flute and realized harpsichord, initially a translation of the Baroque trio sonata to two instruments, and the *terzetto* or sonata for keyboard 'with the accompaniment of violin and cello', the close ancestor of the mature Classical piano trio. The middle third of the century, when these new obbligato keyboard forms interacted with one another and with the long standing tradition of string trios with or without continuo, is, as David Fuller has shown, a formidable and apparently inpenetrable tangle that separates J. S. Bach's trios from those of Haydn and Mozart.[5]

In this tangled mass, C. P. E. Bach's chamber music offers an ideal opportunity to study the trio in transition. Here is a substantial number of works composed over the period 1731–77, the critical mid-century years, by a composer of major historical significance. Unlike the music of most early Classical composers, Bach's is well documented, with many fastidiously prepared autographs, excellent authentic copies, and authorized first editions, the whole lot resting more or less securely on a now lost authentic catalogue, the contents of which survive in the published estate catalogue (*NV*) of 1790.[6] In a gesture of uncommon mercy, this catalogue includes accurate information on date and place of composition, scoring, and arrangements. But except in E. F. Schmid's classic study of over fifty years ago, *Carl Philipp Emanuel Bach und seine Kammermusik*, this large and important repertoire has not received the attention that it deserves. The sheer difficulty of getting one's hands on the music and, until recently, the lack of bibliographical control of the sources, can explain this situation. As yet, the only critical edition is that of H. 525–30/W. 89 by E. F. Schmid.[7] And the existence of multiple scorings and a rash of works or versions questionably attributed to C. P. E. Bach necessitate, in the absence of critical editions, examination of the original manuscript sources. E. Eugene Helm's new thematic catalogue has made the task of locating and evaluating these sources possible.[8]

---

[5] David Fuller, 'Accompanied Keyboard Music', *MQ*, 60 (1974), 222–45.

[6] Rachel Wade, *The Keyboard Concertos of Carl Philipp Emanuel Bach* (Ann Arbor, 1981), 5–8.

[7] *Sechs Trios für Klavier, Violine und Violoncello*, 2 vols. (Kassel, 1952). Hugo Ruf has prepared a series of reliable performing editions of most of the Berlin sonatas, published by the Deutscher Ricordi Verlag [Lörrach/Baden], but these are unfortunately not widely available. The bulk of the other editions, often proclaimed to be 'für den praktischen Gebrauch bearbeitet', can so obscure the original text as to be virtually useless.

[8] *Thematic Catalogue of the Works of Carl Philipp Emanuel Bach* (New Haven, in preparation), a typescript of which the author kindly shared with me.

The *Nachlass-Verzeichniß* tells us that, like the theorists, Bach conceived of the term trio in its broadest sense. Under the heading 'TRII' are listed forty-three works in chronological order, including trio sonatas, obbligato duo sonatas, and 'Claviersonaten' with accompaniment for a violin and cello—that is, works for either three lines or three players.[9] Table 1 shows the spread of Bach's trios, divided into six periods of intensive activity. Wotquenne's numberings conveniently differentiate the scorings, for obbligato duo sonatas and keyboard trios have two-digit numbers (W. 71–8, 83–91 = H. 502–15, 522–34), while the trio sonatas have three digits (W. 143–63 = H. 567–90); the numbers in parentheses in the table refer to authentic alternate scorings. Of the forty-three 'Trii', twenty-seven are works with obbligato keyboard (marked with an asterisk). The first fourteen of the works with obbligato keyboard are from the Berlin years, although H. 502 and 503 are revisions of Leipzig works. Until H. 590 of 1756, Bach's last trio sonata, the obbligato duos are generally alternate versions of trio sonatas; thereafter, Bach wrote only obbligato duos, ending with H. 515 of 1766. After a ten-year hiatus, the 'Hamburg Bach' published his three sets of modern accompanied sonatas in keyboard trio scoring (H. 522–34/W. 89–91).

Bach's trios with obbligato keyboard, scored for obbligato duo or keyboard trio, are the focus of this study. Not only do they cover the entire span of Bach's trio production, but, as a new genre with intimate ties to both the old trio sonata and the new Classical keyboard trio, they offer a unique opportunity to view the trio in transition. Four key issues suggest themselves: identification of the corpus of authentic works and alternate scorings as trio sonatas; the chronological and textual relationships between these alternate versions; the stylistic evolution of the Berlin obbligato duos, especially regarding form and texture, and their relation in these respects to the Hamburg trios; and the extent to which this process reflects changing theoretical concepts of the trio.

Source information in conjunction with the *NV* citations define the corpus of Berlin obbligato duos as the fourteen works listed in Table 2a. Only six of these (bracketed) have authentic alternate versions as trio sonatas,[10] which are

---

[9] Three additional entries in *NV* (nos. 24, 31, and 46), bringing the total number of 'Trio' entries to forty-six, have been omitted as extraneous to this study. I shall use 'trio' as a generic term for the principle of composing for three lines, regardless of number of performers. More specifically, 'trio sonata' carries its usual meaning as a work for two high melody instruments and continuo; 'obbligato duo sonata' denotes a work that either transfers a trio sonata to more or less fully obbligato harpsichord and one melody instrument, or mimics that texture in an originally composed work for two instruments but three real lines, at least ideally; 'keyboard trio' means a work for obbligato keyboard, violin, and cello which is said to be in 'accompanied keyboard' style when its string parts are subordinate to the keyboard.

[10] Additionally, H. 503 exists in a trio sonata version as H. 596 for flute, violin, and continuo in a single corrupt and heavily articulated manuscript in US Wc, but the necessary range adjustments in transferring the right hand of the keyboard to the flute result in a few stylistic infelicities that affirm Helm's designation of the version as 'doubtful or spurious'. Helm also reports doubtful obbligato duo versions of trio sonatas H. 570/W. 146 and H. 587/W. 159 (H. 542 and 543); doubtful duo versions of H. 584/W. 158 (D-brd B St 253) and H. 578/W. 161, 2 (St 260, 572) also exist.

Table I

## C. P. E. Bach's trios

| | | | | Date from (NV) |
|---|---|---|---|---|
| I. | 1731–5 | 8 works composed in Leipzig or Frankfurt-furt; renewed ('erneuert') in Berlin, 1746–7 | | |
| | | H. 502* | W. 71* | 1731/1746 |
| | | H. 503* | W. 72* | 1731/1747 |
| | | H. 567–71 | W. 143–7 | 1731/1747 |
| | | H. 572 | W. 148 | 1735/1747 |
| II. | 1745–9 | 8 works composed in Potsdam | | |
| | | H. 573 (=H. 504*) | W. 149 (=W. 73*) | 1745 |
| | | revision of works in group I | | 1746–7 |
| | | H. 574, 576, 577 | W. 150, 154, 155 | 1747 |
| | | H. 575 (=H. 505*) | W. 151 (=W. 83*) | |
| | | H. 578 | W. 161, 2 | 1748 |
| | | H. 579 | W. 161, 1 | 1749 |
| | | H. 580 (=H. 506*) | W. 162 (=W. 84*) | |
| III. | 1754–6 | 8 works composed in Berlin | | |
| | | H. 583=581 (=H. 508*) | W. 157=152 (=W. 85*) | 1754 |
| | | H. 582, 584 | W. 156, 158 | |
| | | H. 585 (=H. 507*) | — (=W. 74*) | |
| | | H. 586 (=H. 509*) | W. 153 (=W. 86*) | 1755 |
| | | H. 587, 588 | W. 159, 163 | |
| | | H. 590 | W. 160 | 1756 |
| IV. | 1759 | H. 510* | W. 88* | 1759 |
| V. | 1763–6 | 5 obbligato duos composed in Potsdam and Berlin | | |
| | | H. 511–14* | W. 75–8* | 1763 |
| | | H. 515* | W. 87* | 1766 |
| VI. | 1775–7 | 13 published accompanied sonatas composed in Hamburg | | |
| | | H. 522–4* | W. 90, 1–3* | 1775; pub. 1776 |
| | | H. 525–30* | W. 89, 1–6* | 1775–6 (Helm); pub. 1776 |
| | | H. 531–4* | W. 91, 1–4* | 1777; pub. 1777 |

aligned with their duo counterparts in Table 2*b*. In the latter, *NV* usually cites both scorings (though H. 505 and 585, authenticated by virtue of their sources, are inexplicably absent), with the first-cited scoring indicated in my table by underlining of the *NV* rubric.[11] The authenticity of the Hamburg trios is supported by full autographs and *NV* citations (H. 522–34).

[11] As in H. 580/W. 162 and H. 506/W. 84, entered in *NV*, 38, as: '2 Flöten und Baß; ist auch für die Flöte und Clavier gesezt'.

Table 2

### a

#### Berlin obbligato duo sonatas

| H. | W. | Scoring | Key | Basis of authenticity |
|---|---|---|---|---|
| 502 | 71 | cemb/vn. | D | NV36: A Wgm copy partly autograph* |
| 503 | 72 | cemb/vn. | Dm | NV36: A Wgm copy partly autograph |
| 504 | 73 | cemb/vn. | C | NV37†: B Bc copy with autograph title-page (Schmid) |
| 505 | 83 | cemb/fl. | D | B Bc is partly autograph; not in NV |
| 506 | 84 | cemb/fl. | E | NV38: autograph (D-brd B) |
| 507 | 74 | cemb/vn. | D | NV39: A Wgm copy partly autograph |
| 508 | 85 | cemb/fl. | G | NV38: A Wgm copy partly autograph |
| 509 | 86 | cemb/fl. | G | NV39: 2 Michel copies |
| 510 | 88 | cemb/gamba | Gm | NV40: autograph (D-brd B); partly autograph copy A Wgm |
| 511 | 75 | cemb/vn. | F | NV40: autograph (D-brd B) |
| 512 | 76 | cemb/vn. | Bm | NV40: autograph (D-brd B) |
| 513 | 77 | cemb/vn. | Bb | NV40: autograph (D-brd B) |
| 514 | 78 | cemb/vn. | Cm | NV40: autograph and sketches (D-brd B) |
| 515 | 87 | cemb/fl. | C | NV41: sketches (D-brd B) |

### b

#### Authentic alternative trio sonata versions

| H. | W. | Scoring | Basis of authenticity |
|---|---|---|---|
| 573 | 149 | fl./vn./b.c. | NV37†: autograph (D-brd B) |
| 575 | 151 | fl./vn./b.c. | NV38: autograph (D-brd B) |
| 580 | 162 | 2 fl./b.c. | NV38 |
| 585 | — | 2 vn./b.c. | not in NV; autograph once belonged to M. Pincherle, location now unknown (Helm); A Wgm copy of duo version orig. marked '2 Violini' by Bach |
| 581 | 152 | fl./vn./b.c. | NV38: autograph reference to this scoring on autograph of H. 583 (W. 157) |
| 583 | 157 | 2 vn./b.c. | |
| 586 | 153 | fl./vn./b.c. | NV39 |

* Source information from Helm.

† Simultaneous citation of both scorings in NV: 'Flöte oder Clavier, Violine und Bass.'

The question of priority of scoring in the six revised sonatas is a crucial one. With the exception of H. 506, all the full autographs transmit the trio sonata version (see Table 2); duo versions have, at best, only autograph title-pages. In general, the primary *NV* citation tends to refer to the trio sonata scoring as well. Although Rachel Wade has shown in relation to the concertos that it is dangerous to assume that the citation form in *NV* automatically implies actual order of composition,[12] the coincidence of primary *NV* entry and autograph is a powerful argument for the precedence of the trio sonata versions H. 573, 575, and 583. Wade has also observed that Bach seldom recopied the autograph himself when revising.[13] Remarks on the autograph title-pages of copies of H. 504 and 507 also support the priority of the trio sonata version.[14]

The autograph of the trio sonata H. 575,[15] in which the bass is figured only where the violin part drops out and flute and bass remain (i.e., corresponding to the flute solos with continuo accompaniment in H. 505), seems to suggest that it was copied from the duo version. This figuring pattern, common in the obbligato duo autographs, is repeated in none of Bach's other trio sonata autographs in collection P 357: the latter are either completely figured or, as in H. 573, completely unfigured. The autograph hand in which these figures are added, however, is shaky and markedly different from that of the rest of the autograph, suggesting that the trio sonata autograph was initially unfigured (like H. 573), and that Bach later added the figures in preparing the revision as a duo.

With H. 506/W. 84, which is supported by an autograph, we have the only clear candidate for the duo version as the primary one. All other evidence points against this assumption, however. As we see in Facsimile 1, its autograph is entitled 'Trio [*deleted*: für 2 flöten, oder] fürs Clavier und eine flöte'. The copy in A Wgm (XI 36267) has an autograph wrapper calling it a 'Sonata a 2 Flauti Traversi e Basso', although another title-page inside, in the copyist's hand, corrects this to 'Clavier und eine flöte'. The bizarre and exceptional placement of the instruments in the autograph, with the flute sandwiched between the staves of the keyboard part (see Facsimile 1), is surely related to the fact that the right-hand keyboard part of H. 506 is equivalent to the first flute part of H. 580.

The autograph of H. 506 is composed of three separate bifolios, with a distinct change in paper and handwriting occurring at the beginning of the

[12] See Wade, *Keyboard Concertos*, p. 106, in relation to concertos H. 468/W. 165 for oboe and H. 467/W. 40 for harpsichord.

[13] Ibid. p. 86.

[14] Schmid, *Kammermusik*, p. 110 n. 6, reports a copy of H. 504/W. 73 in B Bc (27.907) including Bach's comment on the autograph title-page: 'fürs Klavier ausgeschrieben'; the autograph title-page of H. 507/W. 74 in A Wgm (XI 36265) was corrected by Bach to read '1 Violino' instead of the deleted '2 Violini'.

[15] The autographs of this and 15 other Berlin obbligato duos and trio sonatas are assembled in a large collection once owned by Georg Pölchau, now in D-brd B, Mus. Ms. Bach Autogr. P 357.

Facsimile 1. Trio in E major H. 506/W. 84, i. Autograph, D-brd B, Mus. ms. Bach P 357, fo. 43, title and first system

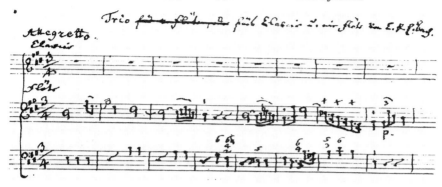

third bifolio; here Bach's shaky, crumpled hand gives way to his assured hand. In the first two movements, the autograph agrees almost completely with the partly autograph copy of the duo (A Wgm, XI 36267), but differs markedly from the text of the trio sonata version (B Bc, 6363; D-brd B, St 241). The duo regularly has added notes in the keyboard left hand, sometimes also in the right, to amplify the texture and to complete chords, especially in keyboard solos. As we see in Facsimile 2 (where notes are added to the left hand and measures 82–3 of the right), these added notes are neatly entered in fair copy; in the opening of the second movement, however, a few appear to have been added later. At the beginning of the third bifolio (second movement, measure 16), the added notes are quite messily forced into the completion of the movement. The finale has few such added notes in the autograph, though the A Wgm copy is full of them, added in Bach's characteristically wispy, unsteady hand, which contrasts markedly with the assured elegance of the copyist. It

Facsimile 2. Trio in E major H. 506/W. 84, i, mm. 81–8. Autograph, D-brd B, Mus. ms. Bach P 357

appears, therefore, that Bach composed the trio sonata version in 1749. Some time later, he took the autograph of the trio sonata and revised it so extensively that it needed recopying to a point half-way through the second movement. The rest of the second movement was revised directly in the trio sonata autograph, but the finale was left largely untouched for the moment. Bach entered the revisions to the third movement into the A Wgm copy, and these were dutifully included when the same copyist made a second copy (D-brd B, St 478).[16] Thus, all six of these obbligato duos are later revisions of original trio sonatas.

The implications of this conclusion widen when we consider that in revising four of these sonatas—H. 504, 505, 508, and 509—Bach simply transferred one of the two melody lines and the bass part to the keyboard.[17] As a result of these transfers, the flute consistently receives the higher of the two treble lines in a duo with flute, the violin the lower in one with violin, with the keyboard right hand assuming the remaining part.[18] There are no further alterations beyond the elimination of the now superfluous indications 'tasto solo' and 'unisono' and the continuo figures for all but solos of the melody instrument. By contrast, H. 506 and 507 introduce some important revisions. We have already seen the additions that Bach made to the former: they show his concern for the slightly different demands of the obbligato duo, and suggest that he may have intended such filling-out to be applied to his other duos in this context.[19] In H. 507 the former first violin part is occasionally retouched to suit the harpsichord better. And the second movement (Andante), with its elaborate ornamentation of the trio sonata's basic melodic framework, provides yet another example of Bach's practice of ornamental revision or *Auszierung* so common in other forms of his music (Example 1).[20]

These six sonatas provide clear testimony to the intimate connection between the trio sonatas and obbligato duos of the Berlin years. But the older form left its mark on all of the Berlin obbligato duos, even the original works. This connection is congruent with his father's practice, and with that of the Graun brothers.[21] But it would be a vast over-simplification to see the Berlin

[16] According to Paul Kast, *Die Bach-Handschriften der Berliner Staatsbibliothek*, ed. W. Gerstenberg (Tübinger Bach-Studien, vols 2/3; Trossingen, 1958), this copyist may have been Johann Stephan Borsch (c.1744–1804); Wade, *Keyboard Concertos*, p. 318, states that Borsch's hand is also found in Berlin copies of the concertos H. 421, 442, and 444/W. 18, 32, and 34.

[17] The same procedure was prescribed by Bach in the authentic edition of the trio sonatas H. 578–9/W. 161, 1 and 2 by Balthasar Schmid's widow (Nuremberg, 1751) in which 'die eine von den Oberstimmen auch auf dem Flügel gespielet werden kan.'

[18] The only exception is H. 506/W. 84, derived from a trio sonata for two flutes; here the first flute part has gone to the keyboard right hand.

[19] Schmid, *Kammermusik*, p. 112, also reaches this conclusion, though from a different angle.

[20] Wade, *Keyboard Concertos*, pp 85–102; Darrell Berg, 'C. P. E. Bach's "Variations" and "Embellishments" for his Keyboard Sonatas', *JM*, 2 (1983), 151–73.

[21] David Sheldon, 'The Transition from Trio to Cembalo-Obbligato Sonata in the Works of J. G. and C. H. Graun', *JAMS*, 24 (1971), 395–413; Hans Eppstein, 'J. S. Bachs Triosonate G-dur (BWV 1039) und ihre Beziehungen zur Sonate für Gambe und Cembalo G-dur (BWV 1027)', *Mf*, 18

Example 1. H. 507/W. 74 (obbligato duo) and H. 585 (trio sonata) ii, mm. 39–45. H. 507, *A Wgm*, XI 36265 (partly autograph); H. 585, ed. F. Nagel (Möseler, 1972)

sonatas as mere remnants of a past tradition, contrasting with the modern accompanied keyboard sonatas H. 522–34/W. 89–91 of the 1770s. The Berlin duos bear out that shift in focus suggested by the theorists; beginning as pure trios, they gradually shift to duo texture, all the while shedding Baroque formal and textural features in favour of those of early Classical chamber music.

(1965), 126–37. In Eppstein's monograph, *Studien über J. S. Bachs Sonaten für ein Melodieinstrument und obligates Cembalo* (Uppsala, 1966), 29–33 and *passim*, he argues that Bach's obbligato duos, though rooted in the trio, contain a number of exceptional movements that belie the assumption that these works are merely trios translated for two players. Eppstein's claim is corroborated by Fuller, 'Accompanied', p. 230.

The Leipzig duos revised in Berlin, H. 502 and 503/W. 71 and 72, are apparently the only duo sonatas that Bach originally conceived as chamber music with keyboard until the late 1750s.[22] Perhaps this explains why they are so markedly different from their successors, so eclectic in style. With very few, fleeting exceptions, their keyboard parts are obbligato throughout, and are at times quite idiomatic. The relationship between keyboard and violin is varied to the point of being almost an inventory of textural possibilities, ranging from motoric homophonic figuration to the purest of trio textures. The fugal movement touted by Scheibe is not in evidence; it is replaced by quick binary movements rooted in the dance suite, including a bourrée and two menuettos (H. 502, second and fourth movements) and a mildly imitative gigue (H. 503, second movement).[23] The dances, with their energetic rhythms, homophonic texture, and short, vivacious themes organized in compact forms, contrast with the serious, imitative slow movements. These, too, are varied, including a lament with an echo-like imitative dialogue supported by an ostinato bass (H. 502, first movement) and a violin cantilena poised above an idiomatic keyboard obbligato of strong rhythmic profile (H. 502, third movement; see Example 2); the latter suggests that the son had learned his lesson from the remarkable slow movements of his father's obbligato duos with violin (especially BWV 1014 and 1016, first movements).[24] The opening Adagio of H. 503 would undoubtedly have received the approval even of such tough critics as Scheibe and Schulz: it has a compact form organized around three central ritornellos, which are separated by long passages of pure contrapuntal dialogue between the upper parts, a serious *Gespräch* supported by the measured tones of the bass (see Example 3).

The next six duos, the arrangements of trio sonatas, tell us as much about Bach's changing concept of the trio sonata as they do about his obbligato duo style, but they also establish certain stylistic norms that Bach transferred to his original obbligato duos of the 1760s. These six works fall into two

---

[22]  Ed. Hugo Ruf (Lörrach/Baden, 1954).

[23]  This gigue, called simply 'Allegro', is consistently placed in the sources as the second of three movements, which is rather puzzling in view of its character and length. The best source, A Wgm, XI 36308, with an autograph title-page, adds the remark 'No. 3' under its tempo indication in both parts, almost certainly in Bach's hand. Can this mean that Bach changed his mind about the order of the movements, and wished to place the gigue last?

[24]  On these two latter movements, see Eppstein, *Studien*, pp. 41–2. As recorded in *NV*, 67 and 68, C. P. E. owned copies of J. S. Bach's sonatas for obbligato harpsichord and violin (BWV 1014–19) and of one for flute (BWV 1031). Throughout his life he retained a deep respect for these works, especially the slow movements, which he expressed in a letter to J. N. Forkel on 7 Oct. 1774: 'The 6 keyboard trios are among the best works of the dear late father. They sound very good even now and give me much pleasure, regardless of the fact that they are over 50 years old. There are some adagii among them which one cannot compose more melodiously at the present time,' cited by Christoph Wolff, in 'Johann Sebastian Bach: The Six Violin Sonatas, BWV 1014–1019', trans. F. A. Bishop (Telefunken, Das alte Werk, 6.35310–00–501; Hamburg, 1976); original text cited in C. H. Bitter, *Carl Philipp Emanuel und Wilhelm Friedemann Bach und deren Brüder*, 2 vols., (Berlin, 1868), i. 338.

Example 2. Sonata in D major H. 502/W. 71, iii, mm. 1–4. *A Wgm*, XI 36264 (autograph wrapper); ed. Ruf (1954)

Example 3. Trio in D minor H. 503/W. 72, i, mm. 5–10. *A Wgm*, XI 36308 (autograph title-page); ed. Ruf and Hoffmann (1954)

chronological groups: the three sonatas from the mid- to late 1740s (H. 504–6/W. 73, 83, and 84), and the three from the mid-1750s (H. 507–9/W. 74, 85, and 86).

The first three are conservative works in which a severe, undifferentiated equality of the upper parts prevails. Only H. 504 has any thematic entries in the bass; elsewhere, the two upper parts engage in constant exchange that, in spite of paired entries and sequential imitation, can often be reduced to a basic two-part soprano–bass model.[25] The strengths and weaknesses of this style are captured in the first movement of H. 504, a model of Bach's trio style of the 1740s.[26] In spite of its restriction to only three ritornellos, this through-composed movement attains considerable length by virtue of the extent of its main theme and its heavy reliance on sequential expansion. As we see in Example 4, the long theme, spawned by heavy-duty motivic work, is immediately answered at the fifth in measure 8; here the accompanying violin resorts to little imitative fillers and parallel motion, which mimic the impulses of a contrapuntal countersubject. Although passages of unabashed chordal

Example 4. Sonata in C major H. 504/W. 73, i, mm. 1–30. Ed. Ruf (1957); autograph of H. 573/W. 149, D-brd B, Mus. ms. Bach P 357

---

[25] David Schulenberg, *The Instrumental Music of Carl Philipp Emanuel Bach* (Ann Arbor, 1984), 32.

[26] Ed. H. Ruf (1957); Schmid, *Kammermusik*, pp. 129–30, treats this movement as a 'Musterbeispiel melodischer Evolution'.

homophony are few (such as the closing theme, measures 28–30), two-part writing prevails; even the exchanges are often the product of alternation rather than dialogue (as in measures 15–21). Repetition results whenever the upper parts reverse roles (as in measures 18–21 or 28–30). Close imitative sequence, or what Marpurg called 'canonische Nachahmung',[27] provides the movement's most contrapuntally active moments (as in measures 21–7), though extensive independent three-part writing is rare. Because of the reliance on sequence, the rhythm is continuous and repetitive.

The stylistic elements of this movement—continuous ritornello form arranged around tonic–dominant paired entries of a long theme, separated by long, expansive passages of imitative sequencing or repetition born of role exchange, and homogeneous, continuous rhythm—recur in all first and second movements in this group. Only the finales depart from this model in their use of clear, rhythmically vital monothematic sonata forms and more consistently treble-dominated homophony. One is struck by the essential differences between these works and H. 502 and 503, with their wide variety of textures and styles and, in slow movements, their thorough three-part writing. Perhaps in these later works there is a new strength born of consistency, but this is offset by the structural problems posed by the sprawling ritornello forms, stagnant rhythms, and excessive reliance on sequential repetition. The themes (especially the periodic theme of H. 506, first movement) seem to call out for contrasting episodes to break the rhythmic

[27] *Abhandlung von der Fuge* (1753), i. 13, as cited by Schulenberg, *Instrumental Music*, p. 14.

continuity. Essentially, the demands of thematic material and form seem at odds with one another.[28]

In the three duos of the mid-1750s Bach appears to have been looking for solutions to this basic tension between theme and structure, and he incorporated some of his discoveries in later sonatas. The sinfonia H. 507 is Bach's only 'accompanied keyboard sonata' among all these obbligato duos, and if the trio sonata version is also authentic, his only trio sonata in the ultra-modern treble-dominated homophonic style deplored by Koch. It is an amiable *Liebhaber* sonata with the earmarks of the style, including short phrases, simple diatonic harmony, easy lyricism, a rondo finale—and no sequential alternation. The keyboard part is obbligato throughout, lacking patches of continuo writing, and quite idiomatic in places; the violin constantly accompanies the keyboard, usually in lower thirds or sixths. Bach returned to this texture only in the Hamburg keyboard trios.

In H. 508 and 509 the role of ritornello form and overlapping imitative sequences is greatly reduced in favour of sonata form and homophonic texture, the manner previously restricted to finales. Symptomatic of this freer texture is Bach's shift to the title 'Sonata' in the authentic sources of these two and almost all subsequent obbligato duos, contrasting with the 'Trio' that he more often used in the earlier works.[29] This terminological shift reflects Marpurg's prescription that the former title be used 'when the texture is not limited to a specific number of voices, . . . the latter when the texture is held to a specific number of voices.'[30] As in the earlier duos, flute and keyboard share the dominating role equally, but the homophonic element is further enhanced. The accompanying instrument often moves in parallel motion with the melody line or bass (Example 5), emphasizing the two-part texture. When sequences are used, they tend to be non-overlapping. H. 508 also uses a lot of literal repetition with instrumental alternation (Example 6), most notably in the paired tonic entry of the main theme that replaces the Baroque tonic–dominant subject–answer form. Only its second movement is in ritornello form, but its ongoing motivic growth promotes coherence. Several of the sonata-form movements also emphasize motivic work, replacing the earlier focus on sequence. The sprawling ritornello forms of the 1740s here give way to moments of exemplary clarity, as in H. 508, i, promoted especially by Bach's careful control of phrase and period structure and the greater economy of his forms.

---

[28] Schulenberg, *Instrumental Music*, pp. 74–5, discusses this weakness specifically in relation to first-theme construction.

[29] However, the best copies of the earlier H. 502/W. 71 and H. 505/W. 83, with autograph title-pages, use the title 'Sonata', and the autograph of the gamba sonata H. 510/W. 88 of 1759, a conservative three-part work, is designated 'Trio'.

[30] *Clavierstücke mit einem practischen Unterricht*, ed. Marpurg, vol. I (Berlin, 1762), 6, as quoted by Fuller, 'Accompanied', p. 230.

Example 5. Sonata in G major H. 508/W. 85, i, mm. 23–30. *A Wgm*, XI 36262
(autograph title-page); ed. Scheck and Ruf (1955)

The remarkable sonata in G minor for harpsichord and viola da gamba of 1759[31] is the first original obbligato duo since H. 502 and 503/W. 71 and 72, but its style follows rather from the trio sonata derived works of the 1750s, with much figured bass in keyboard left hand and virtually no differentiation of instrumental style. Though conservative in these respects, it continues in other ways the experimentation of the preceding works. The outer movements are powerful mono-motivic sonatas based on themes that, though preserving the old tonic–dominant entry pattern, are vital and distinctive. They are also notable for their variety of texture, from strict three-part imitation to long passages of parallel homophony. The second movement is an especially good example of Bach's use of motivic development to replace sequential repetition as the major expansive device. It is based on a sinuous chromatic theme; one is tempted to question whether Brahms, who owned a copy of this work (A Wgm, XI 36270), could have had it at the back of his mind when composing the slow movement of the Horn Trio Op. 40. Throughout this movement, the motivic, rhythmic, and metrical elements of the theme are transformed incrementally in a subtle process of developing variation, culminating in the masterful expansion in the recapitulation (measures 47 ff).

The five sonatas of the 1760s tend as a whole to be even more homophonic, often resorting to a true two-part texture with or without accompanying

---

[31]  Ed. Ruf (Mainz, 1969).

Example 6. Sonata in G major H. 508/W. 85, i, mm. 116–29. *A Wgm*, XI 36262 (autograph title-page); ed. Scheck and Ruf (1955)

middle part. One sees a new emphasis on aspects of performance in the number and variety of ornamentation and articulation indications, and in the more idiomatic treatment of the harpsichord—including flattering characteristic figuration and chords in the right or left hand of every one of these works (see Example 7). Moreover, the amount of figured bass in the keyboard is dramatically reduced, and in the third movement of H. 513, the second of H. 514, and H. 515 completely eliminated, returning to the totally obbligato writing of H. 502 and 503. Several of the slow movements are in ritornello form, and the yoke of the Baroque trio sonata weighs ponderously on the sprawling outer movements of the C minor sonata H. 514. But in general, terse sonata form is the rule.

Most exceptional, however, is Bach's increasing differentiation of keyboard

Example 7. Sonata in F major H. 511/W. 75, iii, mm. 75–80; i, mm. 66–9. D-brd B, Mus. ms. Bach P 357 (autograph)

and violin style, seen in Example 8 from H. 513 where the motoric string figuration answers *empfindsam* keyboard solos. This role separation in style and material is even more evident in the slow movement of H. 514 and the opening movement of the sonata in B minor H. 512.[32] In the latter, the harpsichord has driving figuration in unvarying thirty-second-note groupings, alternating in a constant concertante dialogue with the violin, which is

---

[32] H. 512/W. 76 ed. Ruf (Mainz, 1965); H. 514/W. 78 ed. Ruf (Mainz, 1982).

Example 8. Sonata in B flat major H. 513/W. 77, i, mm. 36–44. D-brd B, Mus. ms. Bach P 357; ed. Ruf (1956)

extremely varied in rhythm and heavy with ornamentation and articulation markings. The lyrical, fantasy-like violin line is just as insistent in avoiding repetition as is the dry keyboard part in maintaining it. This movement shows Bach thinking in terms of treating the instruments according to their inherent capabilities, rather than as abstract lines in a three-part texture.

At the end of this group comes H. 515 for flute and fully obbligato keyboard, a thoroughly *galant* work in which keyboard and flute are featured more or less equally but share the treble line alternately.[33] It is a finely proportioned work, Classical in its short, balanced phrases enlivened by appoggiaturas, slurs, and short ornaments, and its lucid, compact sonata forms. Brilliant, grateful to both flute and keyboard, at times graceful, melancholy, or lively, it brings Bach's Berlin sonatas to the very threshhold of the accompanied sonatas of the next decade.

Nine years later, Bach approached a new form of chamber music with keyboard, the sonata for keyboard with the optional accompaniment of violin and cello. He wrote to J. N. Forkel in September of that year that in writing these works he 'finally had to bow to fashion and write sonatas for keyboard that are easy, and that one can simply play alone without missing anything,' thus inviting some biting criticism from J. F. Reichardt.[34] The three sets of

[33] Ed. G. Scheck and H. Ruf (Lörrach/Baden, 1955).
[34] Bach's letter quoted by Schmid, *Sechs Klaviertrios*, 'Commentary', p. 34.

sonatas W. 89–91 (1775–7) are modern keyboard trios in accompanied sonata style. With the exception of several works in W. 89, their string parts are, as Bach suggested, entirely dispensable and quite rudimentary, and relate to the keyboard in the ways outlined by William S. Newman in his classic introduction to the accompanied clavier sonata.[35] But on closer examination, some of these sonatas, especially H. 525, 526, and 528, are not as new as Bach suggested to Forkel, for they continue the process of transformation of the trio already initiated in the works of the mid–1750s and 1760s.

Example 9 illustrates this. Here the texture differs from the earlier sonatas primarily in the *consistent* predominance of the keyboard (previously seen only in H. 507) and the high incidence of unison writing between violin and keyboard right hand (the cello possesses no real independence from the keyboard left hand in any of these works). This is, for sure, an essential difference. But many features also recall the sonatas of the 1760s: the fully obbligato keyboard part; the predominantly two-part keyboard texture, with occasional turns to a fuller sonority in the right or left hand; the continuo-inspired bass line; and the idiomatic keyboard figuration. The passages of three-part homophony (such as measures 7–8, 19–20) are no different from the kind of parallel writing that is found in all the obbligato duo sonatas (increasingly in those of the 1750s and 1760s). And the derivation of the sequential alternation in measures 13–16, rare but not unique in these sonatas, is obvious. The undeniable differences are primarily of degree rather than substance.

We have seen that C. P. E. Bach's Berlin sonatas offer an opportunity to study the gradual transformation of the trio that is unparalleled in the works of other

Example 9. Sonata in C major H. 526/W. 89, 2, iii, mm. 1–20. Ed. Schmid (1952)

---

[35] William S. Newman, 'Concerning the Accompanied Clavier Sonata', *MQ*, 33 (1947), 327–49.

important Classical composers. Beginning in a style that owes much to his father's obbligato duos, Bach's earlier trios still betray many Baroque elements: ritornello form organized around long themes in tonic–dominant paired entries, expansion by imitative sequence, treatment of the melody instruments as interchangeable bearers of pure lines, and patches of basso continuo in the keyboard. His earliest trios are never as contrapuntal as his father's—or as Scheibe's ideal—and the homophonic element already evident in the works of the 1740s intensifies in those of the next decade, to the extreme of one experiment in the accompanied sonata. His obbligato duos of the 1750s and 1760s demonstrate increasingly confident handling of sonata form and motivic development, as well as the gradual emergence of such Classical features as fully obbligato keyboard and idiomatic, differentiated instrumental writing. The *galant* style of H. 515 anticipates the Hamburg trios in all their aspects except absolute dominance of the keyboard.

David Fuller has challenged us to locate musical evidence to refute the 'myth' that accompanied keyboard music 'belongs to a different genus from trios in which two of the parts are played on a keyboard and the third on a melody instrument.'[36] A recent statement of this alleged myth comes in Hans Hering's 1970 article, in which J. S. Bach's obbligato duos are held to be historically irreconcilable with the accompanied sonata.[37] C. P. E. Bach's trios with obbligato keyboard answer this challenge with evidence that the accompanied sonata, at least in Bach's case, grows out of the obbligato duo. In these works we witness, in essence, the gradual emergence of the new trio from the old in a fascinating, if not always successful, fusion of Baroque and Classical means.

[36] Fuller, 'Accompanied', p. 227.
[37] 'Das Klavier in der Kammermusik des 18. Jahrhunderts: Versuch einer Orientierung', *Mf*, 23 (1970), 27.

# The Stylistic Anomalies of C. P. E. Bach's Nonconstancy

## Pamela Fox

THE novel unpredictability and imaginative unorthodoxy of Carl Philipp Emanuel Bach's music exert a magnetic attraction upon scholars, performers, and listeners. For the last two centuries critics of Bach's music have produced countless evaluations and opinions, ranging from positive assessments of his idiosyncrasies to accusations of incoherent and illogical compositional practice. There are several reasons for the conflicting nature of critical comment concerning the large output that Bach produced over more than half a century: differences result from one's historical viewpoint, one's point of analytic departure, and, most importantly, the specific work under examination—indeed, the individual movement, or portion, thereof in question.

As a result of a flexible compositional philosophy, Bach exhibited 'multilingual' musical abilities. His choice of stylistic expression fluctuated, dictated by professional requirements, changing musical tastes, and the need for personal artistic outlet. Even a limited sampling of Bach's output exposes this compositional variety, which ranges from strictly contrapuntal works to *galant* movements of a popular, unassuming character and unusual works whose heterogeneous and asymmetrically arranged phrases contain contrasting melodic materials, textures, harmonies, and dynamics. Since this variety permeates Bach's entire career, his style evades segmentation into clear periods or stages of morphological progression. As Helm states, 'his gradual (though never total) abandonment of contrapuntal and continuous-expansion techniques was not matched by a corresponding adoption of the regular phraseology and slow harmonic rhythm of the Classical style.'[1]

There is evidence of certain concentrations of activity, such as the process of 'renewing' earlier works which Bach undertook in the 1740s[2] or the large

---

[1] *Helm/Grove*, p. 851. General acknowledgement of Bach's stylistic diversity is made by Rachel Wade, *The Keyboard Concertos of Carl Philipp Emanuel Bach* (Ann Arbor, 1981), 59–60, and Darrell Berg, 'The Keyboard Sonatas of C. P. E. Bach: An Expression of the Mannerist Principle', Ph.D. diss., State University of New York at Buffalo, 1975, 205. Because of this diversity, establishment of chronology on purely stylistic criteria is risky (especially with regard to varied and alternate versions); Berg discusses this problem in reference to Etienne Darbellay's edition of the *Sechs Sonaten mit veränderten Reprisen für Clavier*, H. 136–9, 126, 140/W. 50 (Winterthur, 1976) in 'C. P. E. Bach's "Variations" and "Embellishments" for his Keyboard Sonatas', *JM*, 2 (1983), 165–72.

[2] Works designated as *erneuert* in *NV*; versions intended to replace earlier efforts.

number of pedagogical and character pieces written for keyboard during the
1750s and 1760s.[3] Also evident is an extremely broad developmental context,
featuring the experimental and increasingly bold style which emerges
throughout the 1740s,[4] the long 'plateau' of 'refinement' during the 1750s
and 1760s,[5] and the increased emphasis during the later Hamburg years on
aphoristic motifs, connected movements, and more radical harmonic adven-
ture, bringing many instrumental works closer to his improvised fantasia
ideal.[6] Yet even the trend toward examining C. P. E. Bach's music 'on its own
terms' betrays the self-contradictory analytic peculiarities with which such an
inherently diverse *oeuvre* is fraught.[7]

Bach's stylistic vacillations explain the sharp contrasts of style which occur
between numerous works in close compositional proximity. Two keyboard
sonatas written in 1765, H. 186/W. 55, 4 and H. 187/W. 55, 6, both later
published in the first 'Kenner und Liebhaber' collection (1779), differ so
decidedly that their nearness in time seems almost incredible. The first
movement of H. 186 (opening quoted in Example 1) is a 247-measure sonata
movement in a quick tempo featuring a pervasive motivic unity and economy
unusual, if not unique, in Bach's instrumental output. Many writers have
singled out the tightness yet appealing symphonic breadth of this movement[8]
as stylistic proof that when so motivated, Bach could produce a regularly
phrased, developmental sonata form in which his methods of surprise, textural
variety, dynamic shadings, and harmonic pacing are complementary elements within an integrated form–content structure rather than disparate
factors which unpredictably coexist within the expected binary encasement.[9]

In most sonata movements, as illustrated in H. 187, i (opening quoted in

---

[3]  See the article by Darrell Berg in this volume.

[4]  See the article by David Schulenberg in this volume.

[5]  Berg, 'Keyboard Sonatas', p. 101. Also quoted in David Schulenberg, *The Instrumental Music of
Carl Philipp Emanuel Bach* (Ann Arbor, 1984), 6.

[6]  The last ten years of Bach's life offer the highest concentration of his personal style,
particularly the last rondos and fantasias. Berg, 'Keyboard Sonatas', p. 106, discusses the resultant
effect on late sonatas.

[7]  The approach to Bach's music 'on its own terms' has been adopted by several writers,
including Ekkehard Randebrock, *Studien zur Klaviersonaten Carl Philipp Emanuel Bachs* Ph.D. diss.,
Westfalische Wilhelms-Universität, 1953, who is cited and supported on this issue by William S.
Newman, *The Sonata in the Classic Era*, 3rd edn. (New York, 1983), 430. Charles Rosen also
proposes this principle in *The Classical Style: Haydn, Mozart, Beethoven*, rev. edn. (New York, 1971),
115. Schulenberg, *Instrumental Music*, p. 3, acknowledges his debt to Rosen and adopts the
approach as a basis for his entire study.

[8]  Charles Rosen, *Sonata Forms* (New York, 1980), 171–2; Michael Broyles, 'The Two
Instrumental Styles of Classicism', *JAMS*, 36 (1983), 233–4; Schulenberg, *Instrumental Music*, pp.
103–5, 131, 140; A. Peter Brown, 'Approaching Musical Classicism: Understanding Style and
Style Change in Eighteenth-century Instrumental Music', *CMS*, 20/1 (spring 1980), 18–30.

[9]  Extended discussions of the problematic relationship between form and content in Bach's
works include Berg, 'Keyboard Sonatas', pp. 88–158; Schulenberg, *Instrumental Music*, pp. 99–
146 and *passim*; Pamela Fox, 'Melodic Nonconstancy in the Keyboard Sonatas of C. P. E. Bach',
Ph.D. diss., University of Cincinnati, 1983, 212–57.

Example 1. Sonata in A major H. 186/W. 55, 4, i, mm. 1–17. 'Kenner und Liebhaber', vol. 1 (Leipzig, 1779)

Example 2), Bach apparently did not regard form as a source of dramatic and expressive potential, but rather as a necessary formal stereotype into which he crowded intense moment-to-moment activity.[10] Though the opening movement is shorter than H. 186, (136 measures with repeats), the complexity of melodic and rhythmic particulars creates the impression of a much longer movement. Uncertainty prevails in the first section, through the exploitation of non-thematic melodic materials, irregular phrases, capricious dynamics, and unusual sequential passages which obscure clear tonic–dominant polarity. Though Bach avoids predictability in the exposition, he presents almost exactly the same material in the mid-section, here more appropriately what Ratner has termed a 'modified exposition' than a development,[11] and in the recapitulation—producing an extremely tautological utilization of unusual ideas. Conversely, the opening movement of H. 186 continually pushes forward and offers the greatest concentration of tension in the mid-section, rather than focusing on a succession of small contrasting ideas that are subject to two structural repetitions.

The unusual character of H. 187's opening Allegro moderato is maintained throughout the remaining two movements. The Andante opens with a long, unaccompanied communicative melody, and also features expressive appoggiaturas and quirky dynamic extremes (measure 12); the final Allegro di molto illustrates Bach's unconventional manipulations of two-part texture through its rhythmic changes of pace, continually varied figured patterns, and registral shocks. The last two movements of H. 186, however, do not continue the expectation of regularity established by the opening Allegro. Instead of providing an appropriately clear tonic closure to the first movement, Bach ends with a declamatory passage that cadences on F sharp minor, the key of the second movement. This section, though incongruous with the character of the first movement, provides a transition of mood to the quiet and florid expressivity of the Poco adagio and the playful, slightly unpredictable concluding Allegro.

Bach's stylistic fluctuations, therefore, appear on many levels: between entire works from various periods of Bach's life and those in close compositional succession, between individual movements of single works, and even

---

[10] Bach does not discuss binary forms in the *Versuch*, except for an indirect reference to the mandatory repeats which necessitate the process of varying reprises (*Essay*, pp. 165–6). Bach's lack of attention to binary form and his statements that repeats are 'expected' indicate an important mid-18th century deference towards the formal conventionality accepted in sonata composition. This outlook was consciously recognized and even joked about by Johann Friedrich Reichardt, as quoted in Newman, *Classic*, p. 599: 'How often we [J. A. P. Schulz and I] later laughed over our orthodoxy at that time with regard to the forms sanctified by the Berlin school. As I played my sonata for Schulz up to the second section of the last movement, he would say to me: Now only a good modulation into a related key is lacking, plus a felicitous return in the main key to a restatement of the preferred places in the first section, and the sonata is *comme il faut.*'

[11] Leonard Ratner, *Classic Music: Expression, Form, and Style* (New York, 1981), 234.

Example 2. Sonata in G major H. 187/W. 55, 6, i, mm. 1–15. 'Kenner und Liebhaber', vol. 1 (Leipzig, 1779)

within single movements. As Berg states, 'Emanuel Bach often combined styles informally in his sonatas, juxtaposing orchestral and vocal styles, alternating melodious, homophonic passages with rhapsodic passages in *brisé* style.'[12] Though stylistic mixture within single movements occurs throughout Bach's career, it reaches an apex in the experimental works of the late 1740s, such as the sonata in B flat major H. 51/W. 65, 20, written in 1747. In the opening movement (see Example 3), Bach not only mixes homophonic texture, Baroque sequential-contrapuntal treatment, and his personalized traits of octave displacement, rhythmic dissimilarity, and irregular phraseology, but he deliberately divorces them from their expected contexts: the opening melody-and-accompaniment texture counters stereotypical harmonic simplicity and clarity through the immediate introduction of chromaticism and harmonic uncertainty, and the sequential-contrapuntal passage in measures 13–16, usually associated with a faster harmonic rhythm, statically sustains a single chord.

Such conscious and intellectualized manipulations of expectation clearly attest to Bach's cognizance of and compositional control over several stylistic languages, rather than exposing a 'chaotic background of Baroque workmanship and tradition and half-understood classic and *galant* aspirations.'[13] Despite the plethora of descriptive labels employed, Hans Engel captures the nature and consequences of the compositional choices that faced Bach as a mid-eightenth-century composer:

His [Bach's] style ranges from that of his father to Graun and to the classicism of Haydn and Mozart; there is a gradual fermentation of the old mighty language of the high Baroque period with the North German gallant style . . . to which was added the pathos of storm-and-stress and the cantabile of the sentimental style—this multitude of stylistic elements did not occur in succession but grew up in Bach's output side by side and in combination.[14]

An understanding of the stylistic anomalies which result from Bach's 'side by side and in combination' approach facilitates interpretation of the frequently contradictory nature of critical commentary about his works. Helm, for example, characterizes many of C. P. E. Bach's non-repetitive melodies as 'non-tunes', stating that Bach 'will do anything to ensure that nobody is going to go around humming his melodies.'[15] Helm thereby highlights Bach's innovative 'post-Baroque but anti-Classical' concept of

[12] Darrell Berg, ed., *The Collected Works for Solo Keyboard by Carl Philipp Emanuel Bach*, 6 vols. (New York, 1985), vol. 1, xiii.

[13] Rosen, *The Classical Style*, p. 48.

[14] Hans Engel, *The Solo Concerto*, Anthology of Music, ed. Karl Gustav Fellerer, vol. 25 (Cologne, 1974), 22. Also quoted in Wade, *Keyboard Concertos*, p. 59.

[15] E. Eugene Helm, 'To Haydn from C. P. E. Bach: Non-tunes', *Haydn Studies: Proceedings of the International Haydn Conference, Washington, DC, 1975*, ed. Jens Peter Larsen, Howard Serwer, and James Webster (New York, 1981), 384.

Example 3. Sonata in B flat major H. 51/W. 65, 20, i, mm. 1–23. D-brd B, Mus. ms. Bach P 775 (Michel, rev. C. P. E. Bach)

(Cont over).

melody[16] while minimizing the importance of his clear forms whose 'participation in the ubiquitous development of eighteenth-century sonata form are only incidental to their effect.'[17] Charles Rosen expresses the opposing belief:

> C. P. E. Bach's treatment of the striking and memorable motif, however, was crucial for the history of the sonata forms. . . . In other words, the themes of C. P. E. Bach are capable of transformation, of 'development,' and remain sufficiently memorable for their identity to be clear through the transformations. Both the strikingly individual motif and development by transformation exist in Baroque style, but it was C. P. E. Bach above all who made them available for sonata style and showed how they could be used in the creation of forms.[18]

Though Rosen's remarks certainly appertain to works such as H. 186, which he cites as his stylistic model, Helm's comments apply to a much larger portion of Bach's output. Both bring to the fore the hazards in offering valuable broad stylistic statements that also adequately reflect Bach's diversity, a problem which compels writers to qualify or even contradict their own remarks.

In his brief autobiography, Bach directly acknowledged 'the variety that has been observed in my works', and delineated two fundamental stylistic determinants: public tastes (encompassing his patrons, pupils, and the music-purchasing public), and his personal musical and aesthetic preferences. He also quantitatively substantiated that most of his pieces (at least those written before 1773) catered to the public category.[19] Bach articulated his differing compositional approach towards pieces destined for publication in his 'advice from the heart' to Johann Christoph Kühnau in 1784: 'In things that are to be

---

[16] Preface to C. C. Gallagher and E. Eugene Helm, eds., *Carl Philipp Emanuel Bach: Six Symphonies*, The Symphony, 1720–1840, ed. Barry S. Brook and Barbara B. Heyman, Series C, Vol. 8 (New York, 1982), xiv.

[17] Ibid, xii.

[18] Rosen, *Sonata Forms*, pp. 137–8.

[19] William S. Newman, 'Emanuel Bach's Autobiography', *MQ*, 51 (1965), 371.

published—and thus are for everyone—be less artistic and give more sugar.... In things that are not to be published, allow your diligence full rein.'[20]

It is, none the less, a complicated and often subjective process to partition his works into distinct 'public' and 'private' stylistic categories solely on the basis of whether or not they were published. The extremes are easily established: many titles, particularly for keyboard solo, definitively convey their public and/or pedagogical intent, and the improvisatory freedom and communicative expressivity of a work such as the unpublished 1787 *Fantasie* for keyboard and violin, H. 536/W. 80, personally, labelled 'C. P. E. Bach's Empfindungen',[21] dominate or tinge many other unpublished instrumental compositions. Yet, some of the most concentrated examples of his unique expression were published in the six collections of sonatas, rondos, and fantasias 'für Kenner und Liebhaber', which Helm speculates were 'written to please himself in spite of criticism over their difficulty and declining numbers of subscribers.'[22] In 1782 Bach even wrote to Breitkopf declaring that he had written the fantasias H. 277/W. 58, 6 and H. 278/W. 58, 7 'so that after my death one could see what a *Fantast* I was.'[23] Moreover, it is misleading to assume that Bach's personal style was entirely excluded from works intended for publication;[24]

[20] Letter dated 31 Aug. 1784, written after Kühnau had sent Bach a cantata for perusal: 'Erlauben Sie mir, dass ich Ihnen, aus wahrem guten Herzen, eine Lehre fur Künftig geben darf. Bey Sachen, die zum Druck, also für Jedermann, bestimmt sind, seyn Sie weniger künstlich und geben mehr Zucker.... In Sachen, die nicht sollen gedruckt werden, lassen Sie Ihrem Fieisse den vollkommenen Lauf.' Printed in La Mara [Ida Marie Lipsius], *Musikerbriefe aus fünf Jahrhunderten* (Leipzig, 1886), i. 208–9; also quoted in and translated in Wade, *Keyboard Concertos*, p. 56.

[21] This designation appears in the autograph of the *Clavier-Fantasie mit Begleitung einer Violine* H. 536/W. 80, D-brd B, Mus. ms. Bach P 361, but not on the autograph of the version for solo keyboard, H. 300/W. 67, D-brd B, Mus. ms. Bach P 359.

[22] *Helm/Grove*, 850.

[23] 15 Oct. 1782: 'Meine Feunde woliten durchaus zwey Fantasien mit dabey haben, damit man nach meinem Tode sehen könne, weicher Fantast ich war.' Quoted in Hermann von Hase, 'C. P. E. Bach und Joh. Gotti. Im. Breitkopf', *BJ*, 8 (1911), 97; Translated in Schulenberg, *Instrumental Music*, p 6.

[24] Though it is tempting to take many of Bach's remarks literally, interpretive caution must be exercised: his sharp business acumen included the ability to say the right things to the right people at opportune moments. Consider Bach's letter to Breitkopf, 23 Sept. 1785, concerning the C major sonata H. 209/W. 60, which Breitkopf subsequently published. Bach described it as 'ganz neu, leicht, kurz u. beynahe ohne Adagio, weil dies Ding nicht mehr Mode ist' ('entirely new, easy, short and almost without an Adagio, since such a thing is no longer fashionable'; see *Suchalla/Briefe*, p. 191). Bach's use of the adjective 'neu' in this instance refers to his belief that this sonata was currently saleable, not to its recent composition, since it was written in 1766. Similar interpretive difficulties arise with regard to Bach's remarks of 19 Dec. 1779 to Breitkopf, concerning the publication of the sonatas H. 246/W. 56, 2, H. 269/W. 56, 4, and H. 270/W. 56, 6: 'Der Inhalt dieser Sonaten wird ganz und gar von allen meinen Sachen verschieden seyn; Ich hoffe für Jedermann.' Peter Schleuning, *Die freie Fantasie. Ein Beitrag zur Erforschung der Klaviermusik des 18. Jahrhunderts* (Göppingen, 1973), 273–6, believes that these sonatas (and all his other published works) could not represent his personally satisfying style since they were 'für Jedermann'; yet perhaps, especially considering the unique nature of these works, Bach was hoping they would sell and thereby represent a narrowing of the gap between *Kenner* and *Liebhaber*.

even his *Leichte Sonaten* (H. 162–3, H. 180–3/W. 53, 1–6) were given special reviews for their serious quality of content in comparison with those of his contemporaries,[25] and Forkel felt that Bach could not completely suppress his personal style, since 'the irresistible force of his inner nature overcomes any obstacle which stands in the way of his outpouring of communication.'[26]

The public–private issue also relates to two important and interwoven strands of Bach's personality: the practical versus the perfectionist. Though his practicality actually facilitated his stylistic flexibility by allowing him to see the potential in imposed restrictions, when his practical gifts as a performer and pedagogue collided with his compositional penchant for perfectionist detail, he was placed in a unique and sometimes uncomfortable position between improvisatory freedom and notated prescription which, judging from the multitude of revised and alternate versions, he could never reconcile. Many layers of the complicated network of revised and alternate versions can be unravelled with the aid of Bach's own record-keeping and through careful comparison of autographs and study of filiation, yet the practical–perfectionist conflict persisted even into his habit of proof-reading copyists' manuscripts. Bach not only corrected his copyists' mistakes (even in Michel's generally excellent copies)[27] but 'jealously guarded his prerogative as a composer to settle even the smallest details of his works'[28] by making compositional alterations—crossing out entire measures, changing isolated notes, clarifying the polyphonic foundation through changes in stemming, and adding dynamics, slurs, accidentals, and ornaments.[29]

Thus the key to understanding Bach's multi-faceted personality and output lies in the acceptance of non-uniformity. In his own words: 'I have never liked excessive uniformity in composition and taste.'[30] Carl Philipp Emanuel Bach's compositional approach was 'nonconstant'[31]—a term which succinctly

[25]  As in Johann Adam Hiller's review of Bach's *Leichte Sonaten* in *Wöchentiiche Nachrichten und Anmerkungen die Musik betreffend*, 4 vols. (Leipzig; 1766–70), i. 132: 'Die Sätze sind alle ernsthaft; keine Menuetten und Polonoisen, wodurch man immer nur eines einseitigen Beyfall erhält, der einem Componisten wie Bach nicht sehr am Herzen liegen kann, da leicht ein jeder der nur ein paar Noten neber-oder über einander zu setzen weist in diesem Feld Aufsehen zu machen denkt.'

[26]  Forkel, *Musikalisch-kritische Bibliothek*, 3 vols. (Gotha, 1778–9), ii. 275: '. . . und seine innere unaufhaltsame Wirksamkeit überwältigt jede Hinderniss, die in seinem Ausbruch oder seiner Mittheilung im Wege steht.' Quoted and translated in Berg, 'Keyboard Sonatas', p. 63.

[27]  As in, for example, Bach's numerous corrections in Michel's copy of the sonata in C major H. 46/W. 65, 16, D-brd B, Mus. ms. Bach P 775.

[28]  Wade, *Keyboard Concertos*, p. 100.

[29]  Plentiful evidence of such alterations is contained in the large keyboard manuscripts D-brd B, Mus. ms. P 772 and P 789. Dating of such autographic insertions is naturally exceedingly difficult. The presence of Bach's characteristic tremour, frequently cited as calligraphic proof for dating works of his latter years, cannot be used solely. From its appearance in the early to mid-1740s, it is most evident within cramped spaces where Bach was making corrections (especially the free-hand drawing of staff lines in an erased passage) and on long beams.

[30]  Newman, 'Autobiography', p. 371.

[31]  'Nonconstancy' is proposed here in preference to the negative connotations associated with inconstancy (fickle, unfaithful, etc.). The term also relates well to the steady stream of 'non-', 'un-',

describes his aesthetic vantage-point, the stylistic anomalies which resulted from his practical and flexible abilities, and the ever-changing, capricious, and kaleidoscopic musical surface manifest in his personally satisfying works. 'Nonconstancy' also captures the essence of a key motivating principle behind Bach's works—variation, which operates at nearly all levels of his compositional process, from its harmonically founded base to his continual small changes in surface detail.

The source of Bach's nonconstancy lies in the combination of three traits commonly associated with the effusion of genius: thorough technical mastery, acute powers of musical observation, and capacity for musical expression. Though Bach's technical mastery is pervasively evident in his compositions and in the *Versuch*, he is not simply a craftsman. As Lowinsky summarizes: 'the idea that the genius, unlike the mere craftsman, can transcend rules without committing errors, and that in doing so he can make new revelations, is a leitmotif in the history of the concept of musical genius.'[32] 'Transcendence of rules' to produce 'new revelations' is especially applicable to C. P. E. Bach. The philosophy of composition that he inherited from his father centred on the presence of a firm harmonic foundation and the coherent surface elaboration of the principal notes of the bass line, yet it is the nonconstant foreground—particularly the melody combining pitch contour and rhythmic excitation, unfolding in textural variety, and carefully shaded with dynamics—that discloses his genius.[33] The play of unpredictable surface against coherent and predictable substructure ensures both adherence to and transcendence of compositional rule, and empowers Bach's ingenuity to create highly unusual and original works from the same basic vocabulary that resulted in much stereotyped music by so many composers during his lifetime.

As a highly gifted musical observer and analyst, Bach was by his own admission 'able to derive some good . . . even if it is only a matter of minute details'[34] from all music, and urged the judicious study of scores. 'True

and 'anti-' words frequently applied to Bach, such as 'non-repetitive', 'non-evolutionary', 'non-tune', 'unpredictable', 'unstandardized', 'uncommon', 'anti-Classical', 'anti-Baroque', etc. See also Fox, 'Melodic Nonconstancy', pp. 7–8 and *passim*.

[32] Edward Lowinsky, 'Musical Genius—Evolutions and Origins of a Concept', *MQ*, 50 (1964), 322.

[33] Schulenberg, *Instrumental Music*, p. 46, expresses the opposite opinion when discussing Bach's two recompositions of the entire three-movement sonata H. 150/W. 51, 1 to produce H. 156/W. 63, 35 and H. 157/W. 63, 36: 'Both of the varied versions, however, maintain almost exactly the same phrasing and foreground voice-leading as the original; it is as though they were intended to show that the melodic surface is irrelevant to the rhythmic and harmonic structure of the piece.' Yet through these recompositions, the diverse nature of Bach's animative melodic process is revealed; each is progressively more nonconstant. Even if the melodic material is considered to be basically an embellishment of the structural bass notes, Bach's position with regard to expressive content is clear: 'No one disputes the need for embellishments . . . They connect and enliven tones and impart stress and accent; they make music pleasing and awaken our close attention. Expression is heightened by them. . . . Without them the best melody is empty and ineffective.' (*Essay*, p. 79). [34] Newman, 'Autobiography', p. 371.

masterpieces should be taken from all styles of composition, and the amateur should be shown . . . how far a work departs from ordinary ways, how venturesome it can be, etc.'[35] He exhibited the ability to seek out and personalize novelty, as Johann Georg Sulzer explained: 'The man of genius sees more than other people do in those things that interest him, and he discovers more easily the securest means of achieving his aim.'[36] These keen observational abilities were brought to life by his intense inner capacity for expression. The famous vivid descriptions by Burney and Reichardt of his clavichord improvisations point to his depth of involvement in conveying his inspiration,[37] which Jean-Jacques Rousseau equated with imagination:

> The true *pathétique* lies in the impassioned accent which is not determined by rules, but which the genius finds and the heart feels without art's being able to formulate its law in any manner whatsoever.[38]

A similar thought is reflected in Bach's famous remark that 'a musician cannot move others unless he too is moved.'[39]

It was, therefore, Bach's high level of aesthetic consciousness that engendered his philosophy of obtaining and maintaining the listener's close attention through the variety and novelty associated with nonconstancy. As Alexander Gottlieb Baumgarten stated in 1750:

> When however a thought is new, it is then different from the thoughts I have ever had, consequently the thought becomes clear by virtue of this very difference. For since everyone possesses the desire to increase his knowledge, novelty arouses the desire to gain this new idea, and we exert our attention energetically. Thus the idea becomes clear and vivid. Thus novelty is absolutely essential if one wants to obtain aesthetic liveliness.[40]

Bach himself directly equated the concept of nonconstancy with conveyance of *Akkeft*:

> It is understood, for example, that the portrayal of simplicity or sadness suffers fewer

---

[35] C. P. E. Bach, letter to Forkel, 15 Oct. 1777; *Suchalla/Briefe*, p. 250. Also cited in *Essay*, p. 441 n. 8.

[36] J. G. Sulzer, 'Genie', *Allgemeine Theorie der schönen Künste*, 4 vols., 2nd edn. (Leipzig, 1792; fac. edn., Hildesheim; 1967), ii. 363.

[37] Charles Burney, *Carl Burney's . . . Tagebuch seiner musikalischen Reisen*. vol. 3: *Durch Böhmen, Sachsen, Brandenburg, Hamburg und Holland*, trans J. J. C. Bode (Hamburg, 1773), fac. repr., ed. Richard Schaal, Documenta Musicologica, Series 1, vol. 19 (Kassel, 1959); and *Dr. Burney's Musical Tours in Europe*, ed. Percy A Scholes, 2 vols. (London, 1959), ii. 219; J. F. Reichardt, 'Noch ein Bruchstück aus J. F. Reichardt's Autobiographie; sein erster Aufenthalt in Hamburg', *AMZ*, 16 (1814), col. 28.

[38] J. -J. Rousseau, 'Pathétique', *Dictionnaire de musique* (Paris, 1768); trans. in Lowinsky, 'Musical Genius', p. 328.

[39] *Essay*, p. 163.

[40] Alexander Gottlieb Baumgarten, *Aesthetica*, 2 vols. (Frankfurt an der Oder, 1750, 1758), i. 330–1; trans. in Bellamy Hosler, *Changing Aesthetic Views of Instrumental Music in the 18th-century Germany* (Ann Arbor, 1981), p. 95.

ornaments than other emotions. He who observes such principles will be judged perfect, for he will know how to pass skillfully from the singing style to the startling and fiery (in which instruments surpass the voice) and with his constant changing rouse and hold the listener's attention.[41]

It is possible to isolate the specific stylistic manifestations of nonconstancy by studying Bach's attention-arousing means of accomplishing immediate listener involvement at a work's inception and his methods of demanding continued attention throughout. In some instances the music proceeds so variably and unpredictably that Bach avoids creating expectations; in other works he deliberately establishes an expectation only to defeat it soon thereafter, achieving nonconstancy when the expectation of regularity is skilfully denied fulfilment.

In order to effectively utilize 'new and energetic ideas and phrases' within a church symphony, Johann Adolph Schelbe recommended that 'the very beginning of such a symphony must display something novel and unfamiliar.'[42] Bach employs several principal means of engrossing the listener in the opening phrase. Frequently he establishes the expectation of stability and regularity with a forceful motif that is rhythmically and harmonically straightforward, but then immediately defeats this expectation since he seldom repeats the motif within the opening phrase (and sometimes not in several subsequent phrases), continually turning instead to new ideas. Since the opening motif does not return to affirm its presence or establish its memorability, the listener's expectation of its recall is thwarted. Helm's 'non-tune' designation refers to this lack of motivic recall, and he cites the opening of the sixth Prussian sonata, H. 29/W. 48, 6 (see Example 4).[43] The short two-measure opening motif is followed by rests and an upbeat scalar passage marked 'forte', consistent with his advice that 'an exceptional turn of a melody which is designed to create a violent affect must be played loudly.'[44] Rather than leading to a restatement of the opening motif, this is followed by a passage of static triplets. Bach uses the regularity of these six measures in an irregular manner which further confuses the listener about the movement's motivic behaviour.

Sometimes Bach creates a 'non-tune' by following a strong opening motif with melodic dissolution through the integration of bass and treble. Although all of Bach's melodies are closely bound to their bass lines, this technique yields treble lines which are so reflective of the harmony that they are fused to the bass in an almost conversational manner.[45] The treble line is disjointed

---

[41] *Essay*, pp. 80–1.

[42] Johann Adolph Scheibe, *Der critische Musikus*, 2nd edn. (Leipzig, 1745), 600; trans. in Hosler, *Changing Views*, p. 58.

[43] Helm, 'To Haydn from C. P. E. Bach', p. 384.

[44] *Essay*, p. 163.

[45] Berg, 'Keyboard Sonatas', pp. 102–3, describes treble/bass integrations as an 'atomization of the Gallant style'.

Example 4. Sonata in A major H. 29/W. 48, 6, i, mm. 1–15. 'Prussian Sonatas'
(Nuremberg, 1742/3)

through frequent rests, which are filled in by left-hand interjections creating a
stop-and-start capriciousness. The third movement of H. 59/W. 62, 10 of
1749 (opening quoted in Example 5), opens with a strong triadic motif
suggesting a concerto-like propulsion, yet this rhythmic and tonal strength is
negated by treble–bass integration in the second measure. Bach recalls the
opening motif in pseudo-inversion in the fourth measure, only to dissolve the
texture a second time. Such integrations of bass and treble also appear as
textural interruptions which halt motivic continuity, as in the first movements
of the 1773 symphonies H. 657/W. 182, 1 and H. 658/W. 182, 2, and the last
movement of the 1748 duet for flute and violin H. 598/W. 140.

Several works, such as the sonatas H. 243/W. 55, 5 (1772) and H. 245/W.
55, 3 (1774),[46] open in the wrong key. The first eight measures of H. 243 (see
Example 6) present a series of expectational defeats; Bach begins in the minor

---

[46] Also discussed in Rosen, *The Classical Style*, pp. 112–15.

Example 5. Sonata in C major, H. 59/W. 62, 10, iii, mm. 1–6. *Musikalisches Mancherley* (Berlin, 1762)

dominant, and the placement of both hands in the upper staff creates a shallow effect which adds to the immediate instability. This short opening motif is repeated in D minor in the second measure, and followed by two measures of cadential material (measures 3–4). When the tonic finally arrives in the fifth measure, its sequential nature still fails to provide any melodic satisfaction.

Whether Bach opens a movement nonconstantly, through attention-awakening novelty, or constantly, through regularity of motivic recall, he frequently maintains, heightens, or rekindles alertness through defeats of expectation in second and later phrases. Having prepared the listener for the beginning of a new thought through closure with rests, fermatas, or both, Bach offers surprising contrast by the use of an unexpected harmony (elision of function, sudden change of mode, abrupt modulation, etc.), which is compounded by melodic, rhythmic, or textural shock. Bach recommends such harmonic artistry and rare progression: 'those who are capable will do well when they depart from a too natural use of harmony to introduce an occasional deception,'[47] adding that 'so-called deceptive progressions are also brought out markedly to complement their function.'[48] *Verwunderung*, the wonderment or surprise created by the unexpected,[49] not only arouses attention but also clarifies the emotional content of a piece through what Baumgarten termed 'elucidation by the contrary':[50]

All differences, dissimilarities, and inequalities are relations. Accordingly, if one thinks at the same time of two things opposite to each other, he thinks not merely of each one

[47] *Essay*, p. 439.  [48] Ibid., p. 163.
[49] Hosler discusses *Verwunderung* as the subject of heated 18th-century aesthetic controversy; see *Changing Views*, pp. 20–2, 29, 58–60, 94–6.  [50] *Ibid.*, p. 95.

Example 6. Sonata in F major, H. 243/W. 55, 5, i, mm. 1–8. 'Kenner und
Liebhaber', vol. 1 (Leipzig, 1779)

in itself, but also at the same time of the relations of a thing. Consequently the thought
becomes thereby very clear and can accordingly become more vivid.[51]

The last movement of H. 281/W. 59, 1 (1784) illustrates this type of
contrast well (see extract in Example 7). After a clear cadence in measure 16
with prominent arpeggiation of tonic harmony, the stability of which is
prolonged by a fermata, Bach turns suddenly to F major—the Neapolitan of
the tonic—with both hands in a contrasting upper register at the dynamic
level pianissimo. This two-measure motif (measures 17–18) is treated
sequentially in a series of expectational defeats until the tonic returns in
measure 26, when Bach has consequently reawakened attention and clarified
the tonic by 'contrary' diversion.

Bach extends this concept in order to sustain attention through the final
measure of a piece. In the second movement of the *Probestücke* sonata
H. 74/W. 63, 5 of 1753 (see extract in Example 8), massive homophonic
chords alternate with unaccompanied upbeat motif common to Bach's
instrumental recitative style (measure 19), and exacting dynamic gradations
exaggerate the textural contrasts. The listener awaits the resolution of this

[51] Baumgarten, *Aesthetica*, i. 1, 295; trans. in Hosler, *Changing Views*, p. 95.

Example 7. Sonata in E minor H. 281/W. 59, 1, iii, mm. 15–26. 'Kenner und Liebhaber', vol. 5 (Leipzig, 1785)

Example 8. Sonata in E flat major H. 74/W. 63, 5, ii, mm. 19–20. 'Probestücken' (Berlin, 1753)

accumulated tension, yet the expectation of dramatic culmination is totally thwarted, as the movement expires in a low register on an empty third at the dynamic level *ppp*.[52]

As is evident in many phrase-to-phrase defeats of expectation, Bach utilizes rhythm as an attention-maintaining device by prolonging action through elaborated or unelaborated fermatas, by suspending action through silencing rests, or by changing the rhythmic pace with formal tempo designations or the notation of varying levels of rhythmic activity. Though the extent of application varies, these rhythmic obfuscations are integral to Bach's entire output in all genres.

In accordance with his own advice that fermatas 'are often employed with good effect, for they awaken unusual attentiveness,'[53] Bach applies them liberally and is careful to remind performers that 'at times a note without the sign may be held for expressive reasons.'[54] He divides the discussion of notated fermatas into two main types: those which require improvisatory elaboration and those which remain undecorated simply by being held as long as is appropriate to the nature of the individual *Affekt*.[55] Regardless of whether a fermata is elaborated or unelaborated, or whether it occurs at the conclusion of a movement or at an internal point of rest, a suspension of action results. The suspension is accomplished quite simply in undecorated fermatas by the temporary prolongation of melodic, rhythmic, and harmonic action. In the case of decorated fermatas, the beat is held in abeyance during the free unfolding of an improvisatory melodic elaboration.[56] Quantz cautions against the excessive use of cadenzas which would 'weary the listener', emphasizing the importance of the elaborated closing fermata's ability 'to surprise the listener unexpectedly once more at the end of the piece, and to leave behind a special impression in his heart.'[57] Bach's most disruptive use of fermatas occurs when two or more appear in close succession, as in the first movement of the sixth Württemberg sonata H. 36/W. 49, 6 (1747), measures 14–17, which Bach cites specifically as an example of 'a retard'.[58]

Clearly related to and often appearing in conjunction with fermatas are the dramatic silences created by the frequent and varied employment of rests. Rests appear in many values, ranging from short silences of an eighth- or sixteenth-note to more substantial quarter- and half-note rests. Bach occasionally demands a longer period of silence by writing an entire measure of rest, and in a few instances he inserts an expectant pause of two full measures.[59] Though he recommends that rests be given their exact time

---

[52] Bach creates similar effects through unusual octave displacements at final cadences in the sonatas H. 282/W. 59, 3, ii (1784) and H. 286/W. 61, 2, i (1785–6).

[53] *Essay*, p. 143.          [54] Ibid.          [55] Ibid., p. 161.          [56] Ibid., p. 165.

[57] Johann Joachim Quantz, *On Playing the Flute*, trans. and ed. Edward R. Reilly (New York, 1966), 180.                                                        [58] *Essay*, p. 160.

[59] See, for example, H. 38/W. 62, 4, iii (1744), measures 48–57, where Bach isolates a small phrase by providing two measures of rest on either side of a three-measure unit.

value,[60] Bach seems determined to conceal the beat by following many rests (particularly those of shorter value) with syncopations or 'disoriented upbeats'.[61] Thus not only is the basic pulse interrupted or halted, but its resumption is unclear as well. Periods of silence in Bach's music, whether they consist 'only of the momentary omission of a previously established pulse'[62] or a long period of rest, heighten attentiveness and effectively provide rhythmic nonconstancy.

While fermatas and rests tend to disrupt metric flow through the prolongation and cessation of action, Bach obscures the pulse over a longer period of time by changing the rhythmic pace. Since he defines 'the pace of a composition' as being 'based on its general content as well as on the fastest notes and passages contained in it',[63] he alters this pace in two main ways: either through an actual change in tempo designation, or through a sudden shift from faster to slower subdivisions of the beat or vice versa to produce contrasting rates of notated rhythmic activity.

Changes in tempo designation often involve a temporary switch from a faster to a slower tempo, such as an inserted adagio measure in an allegro or moderato movement. Occurring most frequently at the ends of movements or phrases, adagio insertions ensure the gradual expiration of action. The reverse, however, is also found, as in the second movement of the concerto H. 441/W. 31, where violent fortissimo 'presto' measures interrupt the communicative recitative adagio. An unusual utilization of changing tempo designations appears in the first movement of Bach's sonata H. 46/W. 65, 16 of 1746 (see Example 9). Though this sonata lacks a formal second movement, Bach builds one into the final section of the first movement by changing tempo every one to three measures, alternating between 'adagio', 'andante' and 'allegro'. Each tempo has its own melodic idea and recurs in a variety of keys.

Berg refers to Bach's proclivity toward changes of notated pace as 'convulsive accelerations' and 'abrupt decelerations'.[64] Constantly shifting subdivisions of a basic pulse are accomplished by the apposition of minute asymmetrical values with periods of simple quarter-note regularity or perpetual sixteenth-note motoric propulsion. Another type of notated change of pace corresponds to Bach's description of tempo rubato in the *Versuch*: 'Its indication is simply the presence of more or fewer notes than are contained in the normal division of the bar.'[65] His criteria for tempo rubato concern harmony, rhythm, and melody: he states that one hand adheres strictly to the beat while the other plays against the beat (conspicuously evident in syncopation across the bar-line), that dissonance is more appropriate than consonance, that slow values are recommended, and that sad or caressing melodies are the best.[66] Bach's realization of these guidelines, as in H. 173/W.

---

[60] *Essay*, p. 150.   [61] Berg, 'Keyboard Sonatas', p. 125.   [62] Ibid., p. 123.
[63] *Essay*, p. 151.   [64] 'Keyboard Sonatas', p. 123.   [65] *Essay*, p. 161.
[66] Ibid.

Example 9. Sonata in C major H. 46/W. 65, 16, i, mm. 108–18. D-ddr Bds, Mus. ms. Bach P 1131 (autograph)

57, 6, measures 18–23 (see Example 10), provides another example of the transformation of a performance practice into a compositional device.[67]

Two of Bach's most celebrated compositional mannerisms also contribute to nonconstancy: the hyperactive complexity of melodic detail which characterizes many treble lines in a basic two-part texture, and the communicative instrumental speech-like passages which employ various melodic, rhythmic, and textural mannerisms of vocal recitative. Written-out embellishments conveying the feeling of spontaneous variation avoid establishing expectations: changes of register and direction abound, appoggiaturas and suspensions shift pitch and rhythmic emphasis, leaps in the melodic line are filled in through conjunct motion, and small subdivisions of the beat result in a lack of

[67] Curt Sachs, *Rhythm and Tempo* (New York, 1953), 307–9, discusses Bach's views as a 'redefinition' of the 'authentic concept' of tempo rubato.

Example 10. Sonata in F minor H. 173/W. 57, 6, i, mm. 18–23. 'Kenner und Liebhaber' vol. 3 (Leipzig, 1781)

rhythmic transition and recall. Naturally, Bach's process of transforming a melody (sometimes already quite complex) into a more detailed filigree is most evident in the compositions furnished with varied reprises or which exist in revised or alternate versions, but complexity of melodic detail appears even in Bach's early works[68] as a key part of his nonconstant style; it is used pervasively in some movements[69] and as nonconstant contrast in otherwise constant works.

Though much attention has been devoted to the aesthetic intent of Bach's instrumental recitatives,[70] the degree to which recitative influences and infiltrates his melodic style has not been fully explored. His own vocal recitatives and most obvious instrumental simulations, such as the second movements of the first Prussian sonata H. 24/W. 48, 1 (1740), and the concerto in C minor H. 441/W. 31 (1753), furnish ample models.[71] Generally all parts but one are suspended rhythmically for emphasis on the melodic line,

---

[68] e.g. the revised 1744 version of the sonata in G major, H. 8/W. 64, 2, in the Michel copy, with further autograph changes by C. P. E. Bach, (D-brd B, Mus. ms. Bach P 775).

[69] As in the 1773 symphony H. 661/W. 182, 5, i; and the quartet in D major H. 538/W. 94 (1788).

[70] Bach's instrumental recitative style has been cited as an illustration of 'das redende Prinzip in der Musik' by Arnold Schering, 'C. Ph. E. Bach und das redende Prinzip in der Musik', *Jahrbuch der Musikbibliothek Peters*, 45 (1938), 13–29. Helm approaches the subject insightfully in 'The "Hamlet" Fantasy and the Literary Element in C. P. E. Bach's Music', *MQ*, 58 (1972), 277–96.

[71] The second movement of H. 441/W. 31 is particularly important, since Bach provided a realized version of the second movement recitative (D-brd B. Mus. ms. Bach P 711, autograph). In a letter of 28 Apr. 1784 to Grave, Bach explained: 'The Concerto in C minor was formerly one of my showpieces. The recitative is given approximately as I played it.' Printed in Carl Hermann Bitter, *Carl Philipp Emanuel und Wilhelm Friedemann Bach und deren Brüder* (Leipzig, 1868; repr., Leipzig and Kassel, 1973), ii. 303; translated in Wade, *Keyboard Concertos*, p. 97.

which is constructed in some adaptation of the upbeat pattern ♪ ♪ ♫
Common melodic intervals include the minor seventh, diminished fifth, perfect
fourth (particularly the manneristic concluding descending fourth), and half-
step appoggiaturas. Punctuating chord strokes in the accompaniment appear
in conjunction with melodic characteristics and sometimes alone as well.
Recitative influence is present in small self-contained passages, as in the third
movement of the sonata H. 59/W. 62, 10 (1749), and some movements are
based entirely on embellished upbeat figures (the second movements of H.
247/W. 57, 2, H. 189/W. 65, 42, and H. 658/W. 182, 2).

A characteristic recitative intrusion occurs in the first movement of the
sonata H. 21/W. 65, 11 (1739), as a recall of the main motif in measure 55 is
disturbed through small upbeat figures (see Example 11). After the arrival on
an augmented sixth chord in measure 58, suspension of activity is ensured by
an entire measure of rest, and resumption of metric regularity is held in
abeyance when the piece resumes in measure 60 by a cadenza-like flourish
over a dominant pedal. Through careful study of such recitative influences, it is
possible to recognize that small interrogative upbeat motif become a pervasive
and natural part of Bach's melodic style, affecting nearly all works to some
degree.

Just as recitative influences are incorporated as disruptions within a normal
melody-and-accompaniment texture, Bach also creates textural diversions

Example 11. Sonata in G minor H. 21/W. 65, 11, i, measures 55–62.
D-brd B, Mus. ms. Bach P 775 (Michel, rev. C. P. E. Bach)

within a two-part disposition, without endangering the underlying coherence of the voice-leading, by manipulating and changing the role of each voice. The nonconstant effect of these techniques is determined by their function, duration, and relationship to surrounding materials. *All'unisono* passages, monophonic interruptions of unaccompanied melody, octave displacements, homophonic interruptions, and highly varied figural patterns are employed to avoid textural and melodic predictability. The fantasia H. 289/W. 61, 3, (written in 1786 and published in 1787 in the sixth 'Kenner und Liebhaber' collection) illustrates the combined effect of such techniques (opening quoted in Example 12). The work opens with a constant sixteenth-note motion in a two-part texture dominated by right-hand figuration, which dissolves in measure 5 through integrations of bass and treble and is rhythmically obfuscated by small rests. Two forceful forte arpeggiated homophonic interruptions in measure 6 contrast with the piano expiration in the previous measure and offer a metre change and quickening of pace[72] through a rapid descending scalar run. This is answered immediately by an ascending gesture; such immediate juxtapositions of ascending and descending scales or arpeggios convey a whimsical mood in many instrumental works.

Having thus established the piece's novel conduct, Bach seems to follow his own advice by inserting all'unisono passages:

Imagine a situation: A composer works industriously over a piece, lavishing on it every last resource of melody and harmony. At a certain point he feels that his audience must be roused with something different. He searches enthusiastically for a passage whose splendor and majesty shall be pronounced and striking. He decides to discard the beauty of harmony for awhile; the passage shall be played in unison; it alone is to occupy the thoughts and actions of the performers.[73]

*All'unisono* writing is indeed applied frequently and effectively in many different contexts in Bach's works, from strong opening symphonic unisons to brilliant closing tuttis and lyrical ritornello-like passages, and, as in this most disruptive and nonconstant example, in small interruptive parcels. Bach turns to a free recitative-like passage in measure 21, and ultimately to an entire measure of rest in measure 30 to maintain the high level of listener involvement.

Bach's nonconstant techniques have been isolated here like pieces in a jigsaw puzzle, but ultimately their combinations and interactions must be studied in each individual work. None the less, extracting his idiosyncrasies reveals his originality and suggests that we not only seek (often through

---

[72] In the autograph (US Wc, ML 96.B18) it is evident that Bach originally intended to enhance the notated change of pace by also providing a tempo change. Erasure of an 'allegro' marking is evident throughout the piece at the metre changes to 3/4.

[73] *Essay*, pp. 313–14.

Example 12. Fantasia in B flat major H. 289/W. 61, 3, mm. 1–32. US Wc, ML 96.B18 (autograph)

subjective criteria) the works that wholly represent his personal style,[74] but also utilize this collection of techniques to seek the stamp of individuality in all his works. As Schulenberg states, 'a systematic analysis of Emanuel Bach's instrumental music will contain a good deal that is relevant to the music of his contemporaries as well,'[75] but thoroughgoing study also uncovers what is uniquely his.

A large number of keyboard composers have been associated with the C. P. E. Bach style, including North and central German contemporaries and others who were geographically further removed.[76] Such association is based on the existence of certain stylistic traits, including written-out varied reprises, similarity in type and application of ornaments, dotted rhythms, *all'unisono* writing, diverse figuration techniques, avoidance of Alberti bass, greater harmonic depth and variety, and an enriched texture.[77] Careful, comprehensive comparison shows that these elements, when present, are almost always used in conjunction with constancy-producing characteristics such as more attention to balanced and symmetrical formal structures, greater normality of key relationships and preparations, greater similarity of rhythmic values, less melodic complexity, fewer manipulations of two-part texture, and less defeat of expectation. Bach's creation of nonconstancy was therefore a highly original achievement that was both enduring and inimitable. His continuous search for compositional ingredients which could adequately mirror the soul's ever-shifting sensibility is echoed in Sulzer's equation of change with perfection:

This predilection for change contributes very much to the gradual perfection of man. For it sustains and augments his activity and causes a daily increase in his ideas, wherein man's true inner wealth consists. . . . The more one has enjoyed the pleasure of changing and diverse ideas, the stronger will be his need and consequently his striving to increase them. Therefore it happens that man gradually learns to use each inner and

---

[74] A. Peter Brown, *Joseph Haydn's Keyboard Music: Sources and Styles* (Bloomington, 1986), 219, applies Bach's public and personal distinctions strictly when considering the question of influence: 'If any of his works had an ascertainable stylistic impact on another composer, they would have to belong to the second [personal] type.'

[75] Schulenberg, *Instrumental Music*, p. 31.

[76] These stylistic associations have been based on self-admission, 18th-century observation, or 20th-century comparative analysis, and most commonly include the following composers (in chronological order): Johann Nikolaus Tischer (1707–74); Johann Adolph Scheibe (1708–76); Wilhelm Friedemann Bach (1710–84); Adolph Carl Kunzen (1720–81); Friedrich Gottlob Fleischer (1722–1806); Christlieb Siegmund Binder (1723–89); Christian Franz Severin Hägemann (c.1724–1812); Johann Gottfried Müthel (1728–88); Johann Christoph Friedrich Bach (1732–95); Nathanael Gottfried Gruner (1732–92); Ernst Wilhelm Wolf (1735–92); Friedrich Wilhelm Rust (1739–96); Hardenack Otto Conrad Zinck (1746–1832); Johann Wilhelm Hässler (1747–1822); Christian Gottlob Neefe (1748–98); Franz Seydelmann (1748–1806); Johann Nikolaus Forkel (1749–1818); Daniel Gottlob Türk (1750–1813); Johann Friedrich Reichardt (1752–1814).

[77] Berg, 'Keyboard Sonatas', pp. 66–87, discusses these characteristics, and similar style traits are utilized in Newman, *Classic*, to point out Bach's influence (pp. 371–2, 377, 380, 383, 391, 408–9, 413–14, 429–30, 576–90, and *passim*).

outer capacity, each ability, so that in order to become everything he is capable of he gradually approaches the condition of perfection.[78]

Even in the few autobiographical glimpses into Bach's character that we have been afforded, it seems clear that Sulzer's concept of change explains Bach's stylistic vacillations and result anomalies, his toleration for imposed restrictions and obeisance to public taste, the restless, perfectionist changes in detail, and the surface peculiarities which set him apart in his own day and which continue to attract our interest and devotion.

[78] Sulzer, 'Mannigfaltigkeit', *Allgemeine Theorie*, iii. 361; trans. in Hosler, *Changing Views*, p. 149.

# A Supplement to C. P. E. Bach's Versuch: E. W. Wolf's Anleitung of 1785

## Christopher Hogwood

C. P. E. BACH's *Versuch* has rightly enjoyed more than two centuries of unchallenged pre-eminence amongst keyboard methods. Described as 'the school of all schools',[1] carrying impressive (if possibly apocryphal) recommendations from Mozart, Haydn, Beethoven, Weber, Clementi *et al.*, and justifiably praised for its breadth and clarity, it nevertheless offers surprisingly little specific information on the mechanics of actually playing the clavichord.

Until a few years ago, its position as 'the best of clavichord tutors' for the anglophone student was maintained by its being the *only* standard text available in a full and idiomatic translation (by William J. Mitchell); with the appearance of Raymond H. Haggh's exemplary translation of Türk's *Klavier-schule* in 1982[2] a *'terminus ad quem'* has been established from which to survey the widely varying instruction that was offered to the *Clavier*-player.

Uncertainty over the implications of the term *Clavier* in the latter half of the eighteenth century has obscured the actual intent of much of the information that was peculiar to the clavichord, and confused the modern student seeking pertinent instruction for this increasingly popular instrument. The *Versuch* uses both *Clavier* and *Clavichorde*, but refers to the fortepiano as *Flügel*. Increasingly from 1753, however, and during the latter half of the century, *Clavier* was used specifically in tutors and on title-pages to mean clavichord.[3]

A partial listing of the clavichord literature that followed the *Versuch* might include:

| | |
|---|---|
| Forkel, J. N. | *Von der wahren Güte der Clavichorde* (MS D-brd B) |
| Hensel, J. D. | *Ausübende Clavierschule* (1796?) |
| Kleeburger, J. A. | *Nöthigste Fragen das Clavier betreffend* (1788) |
| Kittel, J. C. | *Notenbuch* (MS US Wc, MT 224. K62 Case) |

---

[1] Remark attributed to Haydn, although A. Peter Brown doubts whether Haydn had access to the treatise in the 1750s, as Dies implies in his biography; see *Joseph Haydn's Keyboard Music: Sources and Styles* (Bloomington, 1986), 219.

[2] *School of Clavier Playing by Daniel Gottlob Türk*, trans. Raymond H. Haggh (Lincoln and London, 1982).

[3] See Cornelia Auerbach, *Die Deutsche Clavichordkunst des 18. Jahrhunderts*, 3rd edn. (Kassel, 1959), 44–62, for a summary of the evidence, and Eva Badura-Skoda, *Prolegomena to a History of the Viennese Fortepiano*, Israel Studies in Musicology, vol. 2 (Jerusalem, 1980), for the implications of the terms *Clavier* and *Flügel* at the end of the century.

| Laag, H. | *Anfangsgrunde zum Clavierspielen und Generalbass* (1774) |
| Löhlein, G. S. | *Clavier-Schule* (1765) |
| Marpurg, F. W. | *Die Kunst das Clavier zu spielen* (1750) |
| | *Anleitung zum Clavierspielen* (1755) |
| Merbach, G. S. | *Clavierschule für Kinder* (1782) |
| Milchmeyer, I. P. | *Die wahre Art das Pianoforte zu spielen* (1797) |
| Petri, J. S. | *Anleitung zur praktischen Musik* (1767) |
| Rellstab. J. C. F. | *Anleitung für Clavierspieler* (1790) |
| Rigler, F. | *Anleitung zum Klavier* (1779) |
| Sander, F. S. | *Kurze und gründliche Anweisung zur Fingersetzung für Clavierspieler* (1791) |
| Wiedeburg, M. J. F. | *Der sich selbst informirtende Clavierspieler* (1765–75) |
| Wolf, G. Fr. | *Kurzer aber deutlicher Unterricht im Klavierspielen* (1783) |

Following the model of the *Versuch,* many of these methods concentrate on essential skills of notation, fingering, *Manieren,* and figured bass (often treated as an approach to harmonic understanding and composition rather than as an accompaniment device, as in C. P. E. Bach's work). Only small sections deal (often indirectly) with the technical and mechanical details of performing music in the *empfindsamer Stil* on the clavichord; almost all skirt the actual problem of describing the varieties of touch and articulation, the practical effect of the quick retraction of the finger from the key,[4] the actual sequence of notes used in playing a series of chords in arpeggio style, the technique used to produce both the *Bebung* and the *Tragen der Töne,* and the way changes of tempo and dynamic affect the execution of the set *Manieren.*

These gaps can be filled by reference to one source, which has been largely overlooked because it forms an introduction to 'Eine Sonatine, Vier affectvolle Sonaten und Eine dreyzehnmal variirtes Thema, das sich mit einer kurzen und freien Fantasie anfängt und endiget. Fürs Klavier componirt von Ernst Wilhelm Wolf', published by the Leipzig firm of Johann Gottlob Immanuel Breitkopf in 1785 (RISM W 1818, exemplar in US Wc).[5]

Wolf's qualifications to provide a 'Vorbericht (als eine Anleitung zum guten Vortrag beym Clavierspielen)' are stated with reassuring modesty in his opening paragraph (natural talent and hard work), though a passing mention of his association with C. P. E. Bach (p. 151) explains his relevance to the present volume. In fact he was closely connected to the Berlin *Clavier* School, married Franz Benda's daughter Maria Caroline in 1770 (and thus, for a while, had Johann Reichardt as brother-in-law), and eventually turned down an offer

---

[4] Confusingly called *Schnellen* by Bach (*Essay,* p. 43), and associated only with the terminations of trills (see *Essay,* pp 101, 112).

[5] M23. W 853; other copies in A Wn; D-ddr LEm; DK Kmm, Kv.

from Frederick the Great to succeed C. P. E. Bach, preferring the position of Kapellmeister at the 'Musenhof' of the Duchess Anna Amalia in Weimar. In an intellectual environment created by the presence of Goethe, Herder, Wieland, and Kotzebue, he developed his philosophical ideals of an aesthetic that combined *Empfindsamkeit* with an unusual respect for the older masters and a partiality for the popular idiom of the *Singspiel*.

He published many sets of sonatas between 1765 and 1787, and a posthumous collection appeared in Berlin in 1793 (described even then as 'pour le clavichorde ou le fortepiano').[6] The usual designation was 'fürs Clavier', although the most attractively engraved set, *Sei Sonate per il Clavicembalo* (1774), dedicated to his patroness, had the added elegance of a dedication and title-page in Italian; nevertheless, the graded dynamic markings in these works identify them also as clavichord music.

Türk's *Klavierschule* (p. 361) commends one sonata from the 1779 set for its progammatic contrast of moods, depicting 'an estranged married couple of the common folk' (it was possibly modelled on C. P. E. Bach's 'Gespräch zwischen einem Sanguineo und Melancholico' H. 579/W. 161, 1), but the most direct compliment to the Bachian manner is the deliberate grouping of *Fantasie* and *Affekt* in the title of the 1785 collection. To this he attached the summary of advice on clavichord-playing that was (and still is) needed, since 'nothing has been said for some time' (p. 137).

Wolf's aim was to provide young players and those who had no access to teaching with the ground rules for connecting emotion, *Affekt*, accent, dynamic, and ornamentation to the abstract principles of 'pure feeling' and *Empfindsamkeit*. His explanations are deliberately simple, and his technical instruction is specific and graphic. As in so many writings on style at this period, there is an undercurrent of disillusionment with the contemporary taste. This disillusionment intrudes only rarely, with his lavish recommendation of the music of the old masters, including J. S. Bach's preludes and fugues, which had little popularity in 1785 (p. 155), and his argument that the art of *Manieren* be preserved in print as a type of endangered species (p. 143).

Philosophically also he is an odd compound; he follows Sulzer (and his musical advisers Kirnberger, Schulz, and Koch) in the relationship of art to nature—a view decried as old-fashioned and moralistic by Goethe and the remainder of the Weimar intellectuals—but is one of the first musical writers to admit the existence of 'the sublime' in music five years later (but see n. 12 below).

In his practical advice he takes for granted a basic knowledge of harmony, and avoids the well-worn topic of fingering, which had already been more than adequately covered by the *Versuch* and Marpurg's two methods and exempli-

---

[6] Subscribers to the various sets include C. P. E. Bach, the Benda family, Eckard, Fasch, the Strasburg clavichord-maker Silbermann and Westphal's music company in Hamburg.

fied in Kirnberger's four-volume anthology, fingered 'mit der Bachischen applicatur' (Berlin, 1762–6).[7]

With only a passing reference to rhetoric ('long and short syllables as in speech'), Wolf deals with the use of 'accents' to articulate the various formal components of melody. (Definitions of the troublesome terms *Einschnitt, Abschnitt* and *Periode* are given by Kirnberger in *Die Kunst des reinen Satzes*, vol. 2 (1776–9), and repeated in his contribution to Sulzer's *Allgemeine Theorie der schönen Künste*.) The distinction between 'internal' and 'external' accents and dynamics, although pedantically expressed (pp. 139–40), gives a rule-of-thumb approach for applying Mattheson's parsing of musical discourse, and, as Wolf implies, makes up for the fact that few composers indicated more than the 'unexpected' accents; his readers, and the modern performer, need to know the degree and placement of the 'expected' nuances.

Ornaments are treated in conjunction with accent, harmony, and tempo. Wolf adds the *Rolle* to the expected list, with examples to indicate that it always begins on the written note. The 'invariable' short appoggiatura is capable of differing effects, but Wolf is firm in his view that its real length should be indicated in the notation (pp. 149–50).

To explain the actual effect of the finger 'sliding off' the front of the key, he devises a simple and explicit form of vocalization to represent the clear percussive finish that the clavichord mechanism allows. Players will recognize the difference between the dead effect of the tangent simply blocking the sound (a lazy 't't'), and the small grunt produced by an energized release ('t'nt').

Three nuances detailed by Wolf are peculiar to the clavichord: they each involve additional manipulation of the key without removing the finger. Of these, the unnamed 'double nuance on one note' (p. 153) is related to the appoggiato (p. 150), which in turn, repeated, becomes the *Bebung*, the most familiar nuance which Wolf graphically describes in his hints for performing his own *Fantasie* (p. 154). While no other writer mentions the 'double nuance on one note', the appoggiato is frequently described elsewhere—either as an ornament, or as a manner of execution often called *das Tragen der Töne* (rendered in modern translations, not entirely accurately, as 'portato').

C. P. E. Bach, comparing 'die neuern Forte piano' and 'das Clavichord' writes: 'I hold that a good clavichord, except for its weaker tone, shares equally in the attractiveness of the pianoforte and in addition features the *Bebung* and *Tragen der Tone* which I produce by means of added pressure after each stroke'.[8] He later (p. 157) reiterates that both these effects 'apply only to the clavichord'.

Franz Rigler (*Anleitung zum Klavier*, 1779) suggests that one 'puts some weight on the key and sustains it a little'; Marpurg adds exotic competition by

---

[7] Wolf did, however, include fingering in his *Sechs leichte Klavier-Sonaten* (1786).
[8] *Essay*, p. 36.

remarking that it works 'only on the clavichord, or even better on a Bogenflügel by Hohlfeld'.[9] Only in Türk is the ambiguity of the notation explained: 'the dot indicates the pressure which every key must receive and by the curved line the player is reminded to hold the tone out until the duration of the given note has been completed.' In a note he adds further warning that the dot does not signify detached or staccato: 'when one tone progresses to another there will be no interruption of the sound' (p. 343, p. 421 n). This interpretation, so rarely heard today, is relevant not only to the full *empfindsamer Stil*, and the *Clavier* works of C. P. E. Bach, but also to the keyboard music of Mozart and Haydn, much of which still remains to be discovered as clavichord repertoire incognito.[10]

The problems of translating Wolf's technical and abstract terms are typical of most German writing of this period; for the more notorious (*Einschnitt, Abschnitt, Manieren, Intresse, Affekt, abstossen, abglitschen*) terminological details are given in editorial footnotes. A fully documented and discriminating overview of the whole topic is provided by Raymond Haggh in his commentary to Türk's *Klavierschule*.

Where applicable, page references have been made to English translations of standard texts: C. P. E. Bach, *Essay on the True Art of Playing Keyboard Instruments*, translated by William J. Mitchell (New York, 1949) and D. G. Türk, *School of Clavier Playing*, translated by Raymond H. Haggh (Lincoln and London, 1982).

For help and advice with this translation I would like to thank James Day, John Halliday, Heather Jarman (Cambridge), and Michael O'Brien (Washington, DC).

# A Guide to Good Performance on the Clavichord

It is always good when one can share with others not only those talents bestowed upon one by Nature but also what one has learned through practice and experience. I do not, therefore, look for thanks in using this appropriate opportunity to offer a few clarifying remarks to those who are truly serious about playing the clavichord but lack either verbal or written instruction on good clavichord performance and especially in the techniques required for playing clavichord music—on which nothing has been said for some time. I only ask that my readers be able to play with a good sense of rhythm (the

---

[9] Marpurg, *Anleitung zum Klavierspielen*, 30. The Berlin mechanic Johann Hohlfeld had devised a form of bowed piano (the *sostenente piano*) in 1754. Türk commended his improvements to this 'piano-violin' (p. 10), and C. P. E. Bach composed the sonata in G major (H. 280/W. 65, 48) for this hybrid.

[10] But see the discussion of keyboard idiom in Brown, *Keyboard Music*, p. 159 (although his final example from Hob. XVII: 6 would not qualify under Türk's description).

primary requirement of proper performance) and that they understand the essentials of figured bass.

Good performance in all music, not only in clavichord playing, depends on the use of good taste to achieve the right level of interest ['Intresse'][11] inherent in each type of piece. The appropriate level of interest which a piece can have for us has been reached when anyone listening with a good ear and a modicum of musical knowledge can easily appreciate and enjoy its true outer and inner ['ausserlich und innerlich'] character. An inaccurate and unstylish performance, on the other hand, can completely conceal the true nature of a piece.

Because differing musical characters ['characteristics'] aim not simply to provide a beautiful melodic or vocal line but primarily serve to portray human emotions and passions, it is necessary for every clavichord player and every musician to:

(a) analyse the way the emotions develop in all their various shades and acquire a thorough understanding of beautiful melody;

(b) learn to enter into those emotions and passions portrayed in the pieces;

(c) become sufficiently familiar with all that is necessary for a proper performance and for the expression of these characters and beautiful melody.

Together with rhythm, accents are the main characteristics of good performance. Every musical character has its own inherent manner of execution and requires its own special accents. Sublime ['Erhaben'][12] joy is expressed through fiery tones and strong accents; tenderness, on the other hand, requires soft, quiet tones, delicate accents, and so on.

Since the emotions are apt to change frequently, so accents are no less subject to the same frequent change; even within a single piece some musical periods, phrases, or smaller units ['Perioden, Einschnitte, (oder Sectionalzeilen)'],[13] must be played more strongly, while others are played more softly according to the rise and fall of the mood ['Affekt'].

Lack of space forbids a lengthy elaboration here upon the execution of each individual musical character. I will only briefly point out what nature and art have told us about strong and weak accents, as well as anything else pertaining to the technical skills neccesary to play the clavichord well.

[11] Wolf's use of 'Intresse' suggests both 'degree of involvement' and 'degree of communication', but cannot entirely be covered by 'intensity'.

[12] 'Erhaben' is rendered as 'sublime' throughout, despite the tone of exaggeration to modern ears, in order to maintain contact with the Theory of the Sublime. Wolf appears to have been the first to maintain that the sublime could exist in music (he was followed by Christian Friedrich Michaelis, in the *Berlinische musikalische Zeitung*, 1805), a concept denied five years later by Kant in his *Kritik der Urteilskraft*. See *Music and Aesthetics in the Eighteenth and Early Nineteenth Centuries*, ed. Peter le Huray and James Day (Cambridge, 1981), 214 ff. and 286 ff.

[13] See Türk, pp. 504–11 for a discussion of these terms, their connection with rhetoric, and relevant quotations from Kirnberger, Sulzer, Marpurg, etc.

Music has strong notes and weak notes, just as speech has long and short syllables. They are distinguished from each other by strong and weak accents; this is something we can only learn by intuition.

Now according to our natural sensitivity ['Empfindung'], and the natural attack required by different notes, the strong notes require a stronger accent than the weak notes following them; yet in a strong manner of performance, even the weak notes stay within the bounds of what is strong, and in a weak manner of performance the strong notes do not exceed the limits of what is weak. These types of accents are called internal accents.

There are cases, however, where weak notes require a stronger accent. These are mainly those which differ from the others because of the prevailing harmony. e.g.:

Here, the harmony C–E–G of the last quarter in the first measure, marked *a*), differs from the G–B–D harmony of the previous quarters, and calls for a stronger accent on the weak note.

Likewise, the initial notes of a new phrase ['Abschnitte'] receive a stronger accent. e.g.:

Here, as the first notes of new phrases or motifs ['Ab- oder Einschnitte'], the notes at (*b*) and (*c*) receive a stronger accent. These accents are called external accents. The word *tenuta* is usually written over such notes, whether they are in the melody or the bass, or even the inner parts, indicating that they should be sustained with consistent strength for their full length.

A strong note can sometimes be very short without losing its strong accent. Likewise, a weak note can be longer and still receive a weak accent.

In such cases we say that the strong notes are internally long and externally short, and that the weak notes are internally short and externally long.[14] (In vocal composition much depends upon this distinction, and therefore many people who are not themselves composers can easily misjudge the degree of accent.)

Further, all notes preceded by an accidental are accented, since they are dissonant with the notes before and after them and create a sense of uneasiness which makes us long for a consonance to arrive. The accent heightens this so that the consonance falls all the more restfully upon our ears, satisfying the expectation and resolving the uneasiness gracefully and pleasurably. e.g.:

Also, all syncopated notes:

And all tied notes:

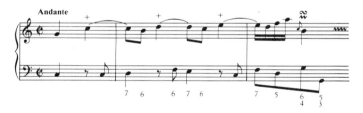

(In the first example the + indicates the syncopated notes, and in the second, the tied notes.)

Yet, as stated earlier, the accents must be such that the limits of what is strong or weak are never exceeded, or the result could easily sound affected[15]—something abhorrent to the Man of Reason ['der vernünftige Mann']. Accents, like all ornaments, apply to the bass as much as they do the treble, so diligent practice is required of both hands.

The technique for getting the best tone out of the instrument in playing syncopations and tied notes is to strike them with suitable force, and sustain the key with a stiff finger for their full value without relaxing, withdrawing the finger from the key just before striking the next note. There are, however, varying degrees of strength and weakness, some of which are indicated, and

[14] Türk (p. 91) uses the same terminology, implying emphasis rather than duration.
[15] Wolf's use of 'Affectation' is unusual in a period that held the theory of Affekt.

some of which can only be transmitted to the player's fingers through natural sensitivity. They must be practised accordingly.

The strongest dynamic level is indicated with 'fortissimo' or *ff*, and the softest with 'pianissimo' or *pp*,[16] written either above or below the notes.

The normal dynamic level is indicated with 'forte', or *f*, and half-strength with 'mezzoforte' or *mf*.

The normal level of softness, the opposite of 'forte', with 'piano' or *p*.

In addition to *ff* one should add 'sforzando' (which is currently very popular), and to *pp* one should add 'smorzando'.

In the former case, the notes thus indicated must always be played louder than the preceding or following notes; the latter, however, requires such a delicate touch that the vibrating string creates only the slightest whisper in the air which, like a spirit ['vehiculo'] from afar, breathes on the ear with a clear, living tone.

All of these shades and nuances can be realized most successfully ['mit dem glücklichsten Erfolg'] on good clavichords.

Neither the crescendo (when the forte swells like a rising flood), nor the diminuendo (in which the volume must give way gradually to extreme quiet like a downward sloping plan) should be overlooked here.[17]

The French use the symbol ⊏⊐ for crescendo, and ⊏⊐ for diminuendo, but these signs are only suitable for a rapid increase or decrease in volume. It is better to indicate a slow, gradual increase or decrease, therefore, by writing the words above or below the notes.

There are also cases where forte and piano are not to be played simultaneously in the bass and treble, but offset (always, though, at the right place in the measure and the right tempo). e.g.:

In order to afford greater variety of nuance in pieces, nature has provided the opportunity for the invention of ornaments,[18] which are indicated by the following signs above or below the notes [see Facsimile I]:

---

[16] Although C. P. E. Bach agrees that 'two or more of the letters standing together denote greater softness' (*Essay*, p. I62), he also used *pp* as an abbreviation for 'più piano'.

[17] Cf. Schubart's descriptions of the effects of such dynamic changes in *Ideen zu einer Ästhetik der Tonkunst* (Vienna, I806).

[18] 'Manier' is translated as 'ornament' throughout, rather than 'embellishment', and is used by Wolf to include the slur, the arpeggio, and tempo rubato.

Christopher Hogwood

Facsimile 1. Table of ornaments from E. W. Wolf, *Vorbericht* (als eine *Anleitung zum guten Vortrag beym Clavierspielen*) (Leipzig, 1785)

Trill ['Triller']                                                                    *tr* or /wↄ
Trill from above ['Triller von oben']                                  Cwↄ
Trill from below ['Triller von unten']                                 ʘʌ
Short trill ['Pralltriller']                                                        /ʌʌ or ʌ
Inverted trill, or mordent ['verkehrte Triller, oder Mordent']     /ʌʌ or /ʌ
Turn ['Doppelschlag']                                                          ∿
Inverted turn ['verkehrte Doppelschlag']                             ↻
Trilled turn ['prallende Doppelschlag']                                ≋

Turn ['Rolle']¹⁹

Inverted turn ['verkehrte Rolle']
Appoggiaturas ['Vorschläge'] and all other ornaments are notated in small notes.

A further elaboration of these signs would be useful to young clavichord players. Even though Bach and Marpurg have already explained them, I see that in most pieces, with the exception of occasional grace-notes, the only ornaments indicated by most composers are turns and trills. I have recorded all these ornaments because I consider them to be the most natural and the best and am therefore passing them on for the benefit of young clavichord players who do not know them. Also, since the use of ornaments in performance is a constituent of good taste, I feel justified in publishing them in order to prevent their being completely forgotten.

Their realizations in full notation are as follows:

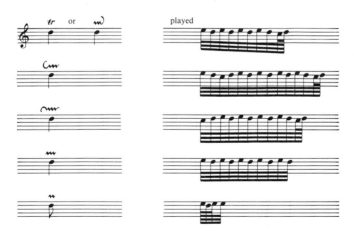

¹⁹ In Türk (p. 276) this is described as a 'quick turn' or 'groppo' and distinguished by the fact that (as Wolf indicates) it begins on the written note.

Appoggiaturas

Two-note prefixes [Doppelvorschläge]

Three-note prefixes [Dreyfache-]

Four-note prefixes [Vierfache Vorschläge]

Slide [Schleifer]

Double-slide [Doppelschleifer]

Each of these ornaments, besides adding interest to the performance, has its own special function.

The trill emphasizes the approach to a perfect cadence most agreeably, thus:

At half-closes and for certain other breaks in the phrase ['Einschnitten'],[20] the trilled turn, short trill, mordent, and turn ['Doppelschlag'] serve the same function:

Appoggiaturas, being strong notes and therefore taking strong accents, beautify the melody by making difficult intervals easier and softening the harsher intervals. All ornaments executed correctly and at the right time can both intensify dissonances as well as soften them. Their length depends upon the length of the note to which they belong.

Still more shadings can be obtained from the

détaché ['Abstossen'][21] and from
slurring (the drawing-together of the notes)
appog[g]iato
*Bebung*
tempo rubato
arpeggio etc.

Détaché playing [shortening the value of the notes] is indicated by dots •••••• or short vertical dashes ıııı over or under the notes;

the slur with curved lines; ⌒ ⌣

the appoggiato by curved lines and dots, either above or below: or by the word itself; ⌒•• ⌣••

the *Bebung* by small dots close together; •••••••

tempo rubato has no abbreviation, and arpeggio is indicated by the word itself.

In today's style of brilliant playing, the détaché is very common; in allegro the runs are all played detached, if not expressly forbidden by the slur, as often

[20] 'Einschnitt' = section, segment, caesura, etc (see Türk, pp. 506 ff. for a full documentation of such terms in musical analysis).

[21] 'Détaché' and 'detached' are used for 'Abstossen' for grammatical ease; like many of his contemporaries Wolf avoids the term 'staccato'.

happens.[22] With dotted rhythms, the détaché can be used both in adagio and allegro—the difference being that in adagio only the short note after the dotted note is played detached, while the dotted note is held for its full value. e.g.:

(For clarity, dots have been added above the notes to be played detached.) Sometimes, depending on the circumstances and according to one's feelings and taste, the dotted notes may be lengthened somewhat and the short notes shortened an equal amount. The finger is retracted from the key at the end of the long note, just before the short note is struck. e.g.:

Generally this figure is written so:

In allegro, however, the dotted notes as well as the following notes are played detached.[23]

The best way of playing this type of melodic figure at the clavichord, one which sufficiently differentiates the détaché from the normal style of articulation, and one which produces the best tone, is this: one strikes the key with a stiff finger (as when playing a syncopation), and then immediately draws the finger back towards the player so that it slides off[24] the front, and the key quickly springs back up. The tone, when thus struck on good clavichords sounds rather as if the consonants 't'nt!' were sounding along with it; this 't'nt!' has a better effect than the 't't' one gets when the finger releases the key without the slide-off.

The détaché and the slide-off are also used on:

1. the final two notes of a trill or short trill;
2. the final note of a mordent in allegro;
3. all four notes of a turn;
4. the final four notes of the trilled turn, when followed by a rest:

---

[22] Cf. p. 153, where Wolf describes the 'normal' touch as neither détaché nor slurred.

[23] Neither the *silences d'articulation* indicated here, nor the change of articulation imposed by tempo are mentioned by C. P. E. Bach: 'Short notes which follow dotted ones are always shorter in execution than their notated length. Hence it is superfluous to place dashes or dots over them'. (*Essay*, 157).

[24] 'Abglitschen' = slide-off, a technique described by many writers (e.g. C. P. E. Bach, *Essay*, p. 43).

In a fiery allegro, I would play the turns in the following, and similar passages thus:

Here the turn expresses a kind of ardour and defiance. If the passage were performed in a slower tempo and piano, the turn would add tenderness to the note, and so on.

The effect of the turn and of many other ornaments depends upon the nature of the melody as much as it does upon the loudness or softness of the performance, the tempo, or the execution of the ornament itself.

With dotted notes, the turn comes on the dot after the note, and is played as follows: the dotted note is slurred on to the first note of the turn, the finger is retracted from the key in the manner of the slide-off, and the remaining three notes are played completely détaché:

The trilled turn is often too strident for an adagio, and for better effect it should be played in this way:

In the following passage where the turn comes on the second half of a note, it is more effective slurred:

Yet the following note must be played with a stiff finger ['mit straffen Finger'] if its proper accent is to sound.

Another kind of détaché occurs in an accompanying bass line, either in andante when the bass moves in simple eighth-notes, or in allegro when it moves in quarter-notes. e.g.:

These notes are sounded for only half their written length, with the finger being retracted from the key as in the détaché, without sounding contrived (unless the bass itself is a singable melody, in which case there would be no détaché or slide-off). Played detached in this way, the metre is more distinct and the melody in the upper voice is clearer.

Let us move on now to the slur or drawing-together of the notes. This ornament is the opposite of the détaché, and is used particularly in pieces of a gentle character, both allegro and adagio. It adds an individual quality and serves to beautify cantabile passages. Even in allegro it has a good effect, especially in imitating swift, natural motion, such as the rush of the wind, the roar of the sea, and so on.

All appoggiaturas are slurred to their following note. Two, three, four, and more notes can also be slurred together. The first of the slurred notes, whether strong or weak, always receives the stronger accent:

(This is the interpretation in serious music. The opposite would be like accenting the final letter of a syllable in vocal music and trying to break up the syllable, for two or more notes slurred together always mean no more than one syllable in speech. e.g.:

This is a technique for caricature, and not under discussion here.)

In performing the more serious type of slurring, one holds the finger down on the note where the slur begins until after the next note has been struck, and only then releases it gently. With several notes slurred together each finger does likewise. Where the slur ends, however, and a new one begins, the finger leaves the key on the last note of the slur before striking the next.

A dot or a small dash above the second, third, etc. note of a slur indicates that these notes are to be detached, while those beginning the slur still receive the stronger accent. (The + here indicates the stronger accent, the letters *a,b,c,* and *d* the weaker.)

Just as there has to be an exception to every rule, this cannot be without exception either. In some cases, with notes of a longer duration, or in a serious adagio, the note beginning a slur can have a milder accent without disturbing the seriousness of the performance:

This has the effect of someone taking a deep breath and releasing it with a loud sigh.

One sees from this how the performance of allegro and adagio, and of notes of longer and shorter length, can be different and relative, without upsetting the true character of the piece.

   Many melodic figures require their own particular type of execution. In the following allegro figure, for example, the finger stays on the key during the appoggiatura until the note after the appoggiatura is actually struck; it must then slide off the key with a push in order for the key to spring back into position quickly, as in the détaché. The last two notes of this figure are then detached, giving them the necessary liveliness and a more 'speaking' manner of expression:

Notice that this appoggiatura, called an invariable appoggiatura ['unveränderlicher Vorschlag'], is very short.[25] Here it is no longer than a thirty-second-note; before quarter-notes it is only a sixteenth-note. Yet, as with all appoggiaturas, its real value must be indicated if the music student is to learn

---

[25] A similar distinction is observed by C. P. E. Bach, Marpurg, J. A. Hiller (*Anweisung zum musikalischen-richtigen Singkunst*, 1774), and Türk; the latter takes Quantz to task for failing to distinguish between the 'long variable' and the 'short invariable' appoggiatura. See Türk, pp. 467–8.

to differentiate it from other appoggiaturas. There is something pleading and supplicating about its effect in an adagio; something severe in an allegro:

Yet in an allegro the appoggiatura can have a coaxing effect:

There are also cases where the bass is slurred and the treble is detached, or vice versa, where the treble is slurred and the bass is detached. In the first allegro of the fourth sonata included here (in measure 13 of the second half), there is such a passage where the bass carries the theme in slurred notes, while the treble provides a brilliant counterpoint in detached notes above; in measure 20, the treble takes over the theme, and the bass takes up the counterpoint.

We come now to an ornament which combines slurring and an extra pressure, the appoggiato, indicated thus:

It is to be played in the following manner: after striking the first note marked 'appoggiato', one applies an additional pressure to the key with a stiff finger, and then holds the note for its full length at a constant strength; all subsequent notes are struck in a similar fashion and, as far as possible, without changing finger ['mit einem Finger'], so that the tone sounds as if the consonants 't'h!' were sounding along with it. (This ornament, like the slur and the détaché, can be readily realized on the fortepianos ['Flügel'] by Silbermann of Strasburg, although without the nuance of tone.)[26]

### *The* Bebung

The execution of the *Bebung* is distinguished by a rather slow quivering of the finger on the key. However, it cannot be brought out successfully on all clavichords; its fullest effect, which gives a feeling of uneasiness, apprehension and—according to the character of the piece—earnest zeal, can be achieved only on those instruments where the tangents can raise the strings in the air without damage, when pressure is applied to the key. Old Bach ['Vater Bach'] in Hamburg really does wonders with this ornament on his favourite clavichord (to which I was actually a witness two years ago).[27] It can be used in the sonata mentioned above at measure 18 of the first half movement, at measure 35 of the second half of this movement, and elsewhere.

### *Tempo rubato*

This type of ornament is used in adagio as well as allegro. Often composers will write it out in full notation, since it consists of anticipating as well as retarding and thus is a consistent form of melodic figuration, much the same as syncopation in present-day music. As an ornament of performance or as an effect in playing, it makes its best impact in adagio. The bass keeps strictly to the rhythm; while the melody in the right hand is retarded. The values of some notes are lengthened, the values of others are shortened. Also, at the suitable places, one or more notes may be added producing an irregular number of notes to the beat. The rhythm of the melody may wander back and forth, though it must always meet up with the bass at bar-lines, at downbeats.[28]

Certain melodic figures can rightly be included here: such as quintuplets— meaning that in the length of a quarter-note, five sixteenth-notes are played in

---

[26] It is difficult to reconcile Wolf's description of the *Tragen der Töne* with his suggestion that it can be realized on the fortepiano, since without the extra pressure it can be no more than a tenuto.

[27] Cf. the well-known description by Charles Burney of his visit to Bach in Hamburg: 'M. Bach was so obliging as to sit down to his *Silbermann clavichord*, and favourite instrument, upon which he played three or four of his choicest compositions, with the delicacy, precision, and spirit, for which he is so justly celebrated among his countrymen. In the pathetic and slow movements, whenever he had a long note to express, he absolutely contrived to produce, from his instrument, a cry of sorrow and complaint, such as can only be effected upon the clavichord, and perhaps by himself.' (*The Present State of Music in Germany, the Netherlands, and United Provinces*, London, 1775, pp. 269–70.)

[28] Wolf gives no illustration of the tempo rubato; this example is taken from the first movement of the 2nd sonata in the 1785 publication.

such a way that no single note is faster than another; and septuplets—meaning that in the length of a quarter-note, seven sixteenth-notes are played this way.[29] They are either written out or else added impromptu in performance, though only by virtuosi. They take the following form:

I must also say something about the arpeggio because it requires its own particular manner of performance. The word is generally understood to mean that the notes of the chords, so indicated, are struck not simultaneously but one after the other.

More precisely, one should note that in the execution of this ornament, the lowest bass note is struck first, followed by the other notes upwards, more or less in the tempo of a moderate allegro. As soon as the highest treble note is touched, the other notes then follow downwards in the same way, and so on, each finger, both upwards and downwards, remaining on the key it has just struck until it is time to strike it again. As soon as the full value of the chord has elapsed, only those notes in the right hand are to be played downwards in succession; the left hand begins immediately again with the lowest bass note of the next chord in the same way, and so on.[30]

This type of performance does not lend itself easily to being written-out. Still, if one can imagine the fingers being held down and free groupings of sixteenth-notes being distributed throughout the measure, it might appear on paper something like this:

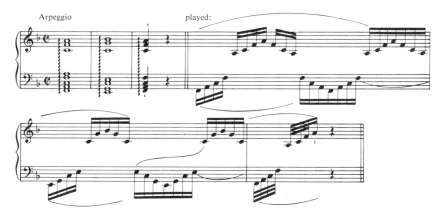

[29] C. P. E. Bach's definition of tempo rubato as 'simply the presence of more or fewer notes than are contained in the normal division of the measure' (*Essay*, p. 161) might cover both the

Passages in this style can be found in the *Fantasie* that opens and closes the variations after the sonatas in this collection.

One final aspect of good performance should be mentioned here, and that is the way that, in adagio and cantabile movements, two nuances can be made on a single note; one strikes the key more strongly at first, then relaxes the finger pressure immediately so that the tone goes on resonating more softly.

Just as the performance as a whole presupposes a pure sense of feeling, so also does the realization of the finest nuances, which defy notation. These nuances represent the limit of what composition can prescribe, since it deals in rules for what is fixed and definite, but cannot specify for what is optional or extempore ['willkürliche'].

Different metres require a different kind of performance style, just as the different musical genres do, and this performance style is something which always derives from a pure sense of feeling and rhythm. (See the section on performance in Sulzer's *Allgemeine Theorie der schönen Künste*.)[31]

I would add here a few more instances where what I have already said can be applied to the accompanying sonatas, etc.

The first movement of the sonatina, which expresses simple pleasure and innocence should be performed cantabile, that is, slurred and rather softly. In the second movement, as this pleasure becomes slightly more animated, so should the performance.

The first movement of the first sonata has a sublime character about it, and therefore all the notes should be played with full volume, except where the piano indications forbid it. The second movement has a masculine, cheerful character, somewhat tempered with a note of gentleness. This masculine cheerfulness requires a performance that is lively, yet controlled, and therefore the forte passages are best executed with a natural touch, neither détaché nor slurred, but rather clear and articulate. The arpeggio passages should be slurred.

The first movement of the second sonata is full of seriousness and intense emotion ['Affekt'], interwoven with milder threads of gentleness and consolation. To achieve the right energetic effect, the passage-work is to be articulated and détaché, while the other sections[32] should be slurred.

---

'syncopated' and the 'irregular' type, though his instructions later speak of 5, 7, and 11 notes without musical example.

[30] Cf. C. P. E. Bach, *Essay*, p 159, which simply states that the arpeggio 'calls for a chord broken upward and downward several times'.

[31] See Peter le Huray and James Day, ed., *Music and Aesthetics*, pp. 120–39.

[32] 'Sätze' = either parts of the same movement, or of the other movements.

The two adagios found among the sonatas provide good opportunity for the use of tempo rubato.

The short *Fantasie* before the theme and variations should be performed this way: the passage up to the first fermata ⌒ goes at great speed and all the notes are to be played very loud and clearly articulated. At the fermata, the long trill should be played leaving one with some uncertainty about its resolution. The line then plunges down, as it were, to the second fermata, on which there is a *Bebung*, which should sound like someone quickly catching his breath. After a pause of about four heartbeats ['Pulsschlagen'][33] long, the arpeggio begins, slowly and with pathos, with strict contrasts between forte and piano until the raging allegro breaks out and climbs upwards, only to turn gradually down to the third fermata (everything is détaché, the fingers executing a slide-off). Again, a long and deliberate trill is made which leads as if it were exhausted into the opening of the theme and variations.

The second *Fantasie* calls for a similar interpretation. However, when the allegro has reached the high D flat, after the *Bebung*, it begins more or less in the tempo of an andante. Then, gaining speed gradually, it falls to the low E, makes another pause (the length of which can only be determined by intuition), moves reflectively into the adagio, and ends resolutely in the final arpeggio.

It would be going too far to examine every detail in each movement and every sonata, or to discuss every nicety of character and performance (which, as I have already said, cannot all be notated anyway). I would only hope that I have presented, as best I can, the most suitable styles of playing and the various shadings that a good performance requires.

Whoever wishes to pursue further melodic and rhetorical figures must understand pure composition ['der reine Satz'],[34] and be a composer himself. One can only add clarity to what has been said already. When performed in this way, these pieces will contain their full level of interest for our feelings.

At rests, the finger should always be taken off the key, so that the strings do not go on sounding and produce false harmonies and so that the [next] accent does not give an impression of laziness.

I hope that in all of this something has been said which has not been said before, and that this meagre amount can direct the thinking of aspiring clavichordists and provide enough opportunity for useful practice.

# Appendix

A knowledge of chords and harmonic progressions is something to be

---

[33] Either beats or (since the *Fantasie* is without a definite metre) heartbeats.
[34] Possibly a reference to Kirnberger's *Die Kunst des reinen Satzes in der Musik* (1771–9).

recommended to young clavichord players, and for all student musicians, for without this knowledge it is really not possible to play any piece properly or gracefully. Although many do not realize the truth of this, I am as completely convinced of it as I am of the creation of the sun; and in this regard the scores of the great masters are the most reliable teachers.

It should not be assumed that I have failed to appreciate the subtle modulations of the Italians—and the Germans who derive from them—or the simplicity and practical aesthetic of a Gluck (who nevertheless is not a classic model, as one can prove by examples), or the gentle spirit of a Hiller, the serious mood of a Haydn—the great virtuosity and wit of the French on their instruments, and so on; I value the talent of every musician very highly. Quite apart from these, I cannot finish without mentioning those pieces which appear to be true inspirations, those which stand like nature recreated, or a second Creation for our wonder and edification; the longer we look at these works, and the more often we hear them, the more we become aware of the beauty, the strength and the glory of works such as Handel has presented us in his *Messiah*, or Bach in the 'Heilig' chorus.[35] Whoever studies these sublime masterpieces diligently and practises the preludes and fugues[36] of J. S. Bach for technical mastery at the clavichord, can expect them to be truly useful, in terms of the art of harmony and sublime expression. On the other hand, anyone who merely wishes to gather a collection of beautiful, gently flowing melodies will find a wealth of such material in the operas of Hasse.

The melodies of these admirable masters are, of course, no longer the sweetest to the fashionable ear; yet one must bear in mind that the newest of melodies, like the most up-to-date fashions, age in time; everything on this earth, including composers (except for Nature herself), is subject to ever-changing fashion.

True good taste, however, whether it be a matter of individual temperament or national inclination, is grounded not in the newest of melodies, but in the fundamental truth inherent in the expression of human sensibilities and passions, and in an awareness of the beauties of song—a beauty whose power is such that it even touches the nerves of insensible animals, is always beautiful, and yet is an attribute of music that can be found in no other form of art.

Anyone who has acquired a true sense of taste will find the latest melodies, which betray little evidence of good taste in their inventors, to be nothing more than writing in the sand. Had Rousseau (whom our learned Herr Forkel was able to counter with nothing more apt than the words of Luther)—had he

---

[35] Probably C. P. E. Bach's *Heilig* H. 778/W. 217, which the composer himself described as his 'swan song in this genre', see Hans-Günter Ottenberg, *C. P. E. Bach*, trans. P. J. Whitmore (Oxford, 1987), p. 177.

[36] 'Fugen und Praeludia'. J. S. Bach during his time at Weimar (1708–17) had produced a quantity of organ preludes and fugues (as well as the *Orgel-Büchlein*). Whether Wolf knew of this repertoire or whether he refers to *Das wohltemperierte Clavier* is unclear.

managed to progress further in harmony and composition than he actually did, would surely have regarded harmony as the most significant part of composition, instead of an 'invention gothique et barbare'. (See *Magazin der Musik* [edited by Carl Friedrich Cramer], vii (July) and viii (August) 1783. Hamburg in der Musikalischen Niederlage, page 855: [article] *Von der Theorie der Musik, etc. Eine Einladungsschrift zu musikalischen Vorlesungen.* Also the article in French on harmony in Rousseau's *Diction[n]aire de Musique*, volume 1).[37] (I must point out that although harmony, as understood by the composer, can be discovered or found, though not invented, by man, it can be created by God alone.)

I cannot resist telling a brief anecdote here which is very apt in the context of this appendix. Not long ago, a composer in *** told me that he had performed Handel's *Messiah* and *Alexander's Feast*. He complained at length about the old-fashioned and antiquated arias, assuring me, with a meaningful expression, that in his opinion—and this is significant—for the sake of his very refined public he should have dressed the repeats up in the style of the newest, current taste. Since I couldn't bring myself to compliment him, I remained silent. I felt like the painter must surely have felt who, on his travels, came across the portrait of Dr Luther by Lucas Cranach in the newly renovated University Church of Wittenberg and noticed to his amazement that bright new, garish colours had been applied to Luther's face. I was forced to conclude that this composer, the public in *** and the churchwardens of the University Church in Wittenberg share the same taste. (See: *Beschreibung einer Reise durch Deutschland, und die Schweiz. Im Jahre 1781 Von Friedrich Nicolai*, volume 1, page 27. Berlin and Stettin 1783.) (Also on the subject of Handel's *Messiah*,

---

[37] Rousseau presented the extended argument that 'When we reflect, that of all the people of the earth who all have a music and an air, the Europeans are the only ones who have harmony and concords, and who find this mixture agreeable; when we reflect, that the world has continued so many years, without, amongst the cultivation of the beaux arts throughout mankind in general, any one's having known this harmony; that no animal, no bird, no being in nature, produces any other concord than the unison, no other music than melody; that the eastern languages, so sonorous, so musical; that the Greek air, so delicate, so sensible, exercised with so much art, have never guided these voluptuous people, fond of our harmony, that without it, their music had such prodigious effects, that with it, ours is so weak; that lastly, it was reserved for the northern nations, whose rough and brutal organs are more touched with the eclat and noise of the voice, than with the sweetness of the accent, and the melody of the inflections, to make this vast discovery, and to give it as a foundation of all the rules in art; When, I say, we pay attention to the whole of this, it is very difficult not to suspect that all our harmony is but a gothic and barbarous invention, which we should never have followed if we had been more sensible of the true beauties of art, and of music truly natural.' (Rousseau, *Dictionnaire*, trans. William Waring, London, 1779, 191).

Forkel, remembered now primarily for his biography of J. S. Bach, produced as the first of his musical writings a prospectus *Über die Theorie der Musik* in 1777, which was later reprinted by Cramer in his short-lived *Magazin* in 1783. Forkel rejects the proposition of Rousseau by matching 'a good man with a better man', and argues, by quotation from the *Encomnio musices* of Luther, that the heart of man delights in a multiplicity of sounds, and sees therein the glory of God. Whoever cannot agree on this point, Luther concludes, is 'ein grosser Klotz' (*Magazin*, pp. 905–6 n.)

one should read what [Johann Gottfried] Herder, General Superintendent [at Weimar], has said in his *Briefen, das Studium der Theologie betreffend*, volume 3, page 301).[38]

Since these sonatas go no higher than $D^3$ and no lower than bass C, they can be played on any clavichord made this century.[39]

Weimar, October 1784

Wolf's retelling of Nicolai's anecdote manages to lose the sting in the tail of the original, which makes a point that will not be lost on those engaged today in historical re-creation and its pitfalls:

A well-known painter was eager to see the picture of Luther by Lucas Cranach, which had remained intact when the church burnt down. He was taken there, but was astonished to discover a face that was full of bright new, garish colours. On asking the reason for this, the sacristan replied: 'Since the whole church was being renovated and re-gilded, the churchwardens had this famous picture repainted by Mr *** from ***.' The painter was silent; but on looking round a little more, he noticed the picture of Melanchthon still completely in its old colours. He asked, with a smile, why then this picture had not also been repainted. 'Oh,' replied the sacristan, 'Experts assure us that it is only a copy, so we don't feel inclined to spend money on it.'

[38] At Herder's instigation, Wolf had conducted a performance of *Messiah* in Weimar on 13 May 1780; Goethe attended, and afterwards noted in his diary that it had given him 'new ideas for declamation'. Herder's *Briefen* include an enthusiastic account of the sublimity and universality of Handel's theme, and a poetic description of the main numbers from *Messiah*. His excellent German translation was used for a later performance of the work, on 7 Jan. 1781.

[39] C. P. E. Bach (*Essay*, p. 36) recommends that a clavichord should have 'at the very least' a range from 'the great octave C to the three-lined *e*', although there were instruments of a larger range in Germany. See Raymond Russell, *The Harpsichord and Clavichord*, 2nd edn. (London, 1973), Donald H. Boalch, *Makers of the Harpsichord and Clavichord 1440–1840*, 2nd edn. (Oxford, 1974), and Hubert Henkel, *Clavichorde* (Leipzig, 1981), for specifications and illustrations.

# C. P. E. Bach in the Library of the Singakademie zu Berlin

## Elias N. Kulukundis

PRIOR to World War II, the city of Berlin contained a number of important collections of printed and manuscript music. The most significant of these was, of course, the music division of the Preussische Staatsbibliothek. Another very interesting and little-studied collection was the library of the Singakademie zu Berlin. Its extensive holdings were oriented around its principal activities—the fostering of choral singing and the teaching of orchestral performance. They included manuscript and printed music from all periods, with instrumental and vocal music by composers active in Berlin during the reign of King Frederick the Great prominently featured. Unlike the other great collections in Berlin, which largely survived the war (although they were split between several locations), the library of the Singakademie has substantially disappeared. This is a great loss for the student of North German music in the eighteenth century.

The fate of the library is actually not clear. An air raid in November 1943 caused considerable damage to the buildings housing the Singakademie and may have destroyed or damaged portions of the library. In 1945, the buildings were seized by military authorities and later rebuilt as the Maxim-Gorki Theater.[1] Items from the library were sent to Silesia for safe keeping.[2] Which manuscripts were involved is uncertain; nothing has since been accounted for. A few items, including one work by C. P. E. Bach, remained behind and were rediscovered long after the war was over.[3] In 1974 these manuscripts were transferred to the Staatsbibliothek Preussischer Kulturbesitz on permanent loan.[4]

The holdings of the Singakademie library were never systematically studied nor was a catalogue ever published. S. W. Dehn prepared a handwritten listing of the J. S. Bach materials in the library in the early 1850s.[5] A comprehensive

---

[1] Werner Bollert, ed., *Sing-Akademie zu Berlin: Festschrift zum 175 jährigen Bestehen* (Berlin, 1966), 134.

[2] Bollert, *Sing-Akademie*, p. 20.

[3] Erwin R. Jacobi, 'Das Autograph von C. P. E. Bachs Doppelkonzert in Es dur', *Mf*, 12 (1959), 488–9.

[4] Rudolf Elvers, letter to the author, Berlin, 22 Oct. 1986. I would like to thank Dr Elvers for his kindness in responding to my questions so comprehensively.

[5] 'Johann Sebastian Bachs Vocal- und Instrumental-Musik in der Bibliothek der Singakademie zu Berlin', D-ddr Bds, Mus. ms. theor. Kat. 429.

catalogue of the vocal music in the collection was contemplated in the 1930s. Work on this catalogue was actually completed; publication was prevented, however, by the financial crisis of those years, and the completed card catalogue disappeared along with the manuscripts themselves.[6] A few scholars in the years before World War II sought out the riches of the collection in the course of preparing their dissertations,[7] referring to specific manuscripts in the course of their discussions. Many other scholars appear to have ignored the Singakademie altogether, contenting themselves with sources in more accessible libraries.[8] Until recently, the references in these few studies were the only detailed public record of any of the collection's holdings.[9]

In 1966, the Singakademie celebrated the 175th anniversary of its founding. For the occasion, Werner Bollert put together a commemorative book which includes essays on various facets of the activities of the Singakademie throughout its history.[10] Among these is an essay by Friedrich Welter discussing the library and surveying its former holdings.[11] Welter actually worked in the library under Professor Georg Schumann between 1928 and 1932; he was directly responsible for preparing the materials for the aborted publication of the vocal music catalogue and was, by his own admission, one of the few people then alive who had a first-hand recollection of the scope and extent of the collection.[12] He was therefore particularly well qualified for his task. Furthermore, he possessed at the time a copy of the so-called 'Zelter Catalogue',[13] which he had received as a gift from Dr Schumann.[14] The 'Zelter Catalogue' was a handwritten document prepared in the course of the settlement of a lawsuit brought by the heirs of C. F. Zelter against the Singakademie. It contained brief descriptions of many of the holdings of the library at the time of Zelter's death.

The scope of the Singakademie collection was broad. It contained collections

---

[6] Friedrich Welter, 'Die Musikbibliothek der Sing-Akademie zu Berlin', in Bollert, *Sing-Akademie*, p. 33.

[7] Max Falck, *Wilhelm Friedemann Bach* (Leipzig, 1914); Hans Uldall, *Das Klavierkonzert der Berliner Schule* (Leipzig, 1928); Heinrich Miesner, *Philipp Emanuel Bach in Hamburg* (Leipzig, 1929); Ernst Fritz Schmid, *Carl Philipp Emanuel Bach und seine Kammermusik* (Kassel, 1931).

[8] Hugo Daffner, *Die Entwicklung des Klavierkonzerts bis Mozart* (Leipzig, 1906); Carl Mennicke, *Hasse und die Gebrüder Graun als Symphoniker* (Leipzig, 1906); Lucien Kamienski, *Die Oratorien von Johann Adolf Hasse* (Leipzig, 1912); Rudolf Gerber, *Der Operntypus Johann Adolf Hasses und seine textlichen Grundlagen* (Leipzig, 1925).

[9] In his *Biographisch-bibliographische Quellen-Lexikon der Musiker und Musikgelehrten der christlichen Zeitrechnung bis zur Mitte des 19. Jahrhunderts*, (Leipzig, 1898–1904), Robert Eitner occasionally includes a reference to a source from the Singakademie library; but the paucity of such references and the omission of most of the materials known to have been in the library at one time suggest that Eitner was not really familiar with the Singakademie collection.

[10] Bollert, *Sing-Akademie*. I would like to thank Dr Rachel Wade for bringing this publication to my attention.

[11] Welter, 'Musikbibliothek' (see n. 6 above).          [12] Welter, 'Musikbibliothek', p. 33.

[13] 'Katalog musikalisch-literarischer und praktischer Werke aus dem Nachlasse des Kgl. Prof. Dr. Zelter'.

[14] Welter, 'Musikbibliothek', pp. 33, 45 n. 4.

of arias and keyboard music, chamber music, symphonies, and concertos for various combinations as well as accompanied and unaccompanied vocal music, theoretical treatises, librettos, and newspapers. Most of this material consisted of printed editions and early manuscripts, though some autographs were also included. Some of the secondary sources were undoubtedly unique copies; others may have contained unknown variants of otherwise well-known works. The emphasis was on music of composers who flourished before 1800.[15] With the exception of some Beethoven chamber music and miscellaneous compositions by Zelter, Mendelssohn, and Nicolai—all actively connected with the Singakademie—no nineteenth-century composers appear on Welter's list. This may in part reflect the conservative taste of Zelter, during whose term as director of the Singakademie the bulk of the collection was assembled. More probably, it reflects the nature of the document Welter was using. The 'Zelter Catalogue' dates from the 1830s; nineteenth-century materials in the library were probably acquired after its compilation, and all record of them has disappeared.

The collection included manuscripts and publications of religious music by Palestrina, Lassus, and Benevoli, Handel and Caldara, Leo, Durante, and Lotti, Mozart and Haydn, Mendelssohn and Nicolai as well as oratorios, Passions, and cantatas by C. H. Graun, Hasse, Telemann, Agricola, and Kirnberger. Concertos and symphonies of Mozart and Haydn, Stamitz and Vanhal, Corelli and Handel, Tartini and John Stanley appeared together with works by the Bach family, Quantz, Schaffrath, Müthel, and Reichardt. Operas were present both in full and vocal scores—King Frederick William III presented important sets of publications of operas by Handel and Lully—as well as collections of arias and songs, chamber music, and works for solo keyboard. The library's extraordinary holdings of J. S. Bach materials were sold to the Preussische Staatsbibliothek in 1854;[16] the 'Alt-Bachisches Archiv' remained, however, as well as a number of miscellaneous manuscripts of Bach's choral music, primarily nineteenth-century performance materials used by the Singakademie itself.[17] Only the music of Heinrich Schütz was conspicuous by its absence.

One of the most important parts of the Singakademie collection was its holdings of music by C. P. E. Bach. These covered the whole range of Bach's output: symphonies, sonatas, chamber music, songs, concertos, and choral music. These included numerous autographs, contemporary manuscript copies, and printed editions as well as Bach's 1772 autograph catalogue of his keyboard sonatas. The extent of these holdings is not surprising in view of the

---

[15] All references in this and the following paragraph to the contents of the Singakademie library are taken from Welter, 'Musikbibliothek', pp. 36, 39–43, unless otherwise noted.

[16] Georg Schünemann, *Die Singakademie zu Berlin 1791–1941* (Regensburg, 1941), 126.

[17] Alfred Dürr, *Kritischer Bericht*, NBA, Series I, vol. 27 (Kassel, 1968), 54; Alfred Dürr and Leo Treitler, *Kritischer Bericht*, NBA, Series I, vol. 18 (Kassel, 1967), 27, 77, 192.

important role played by C. F. Fasch, C. F. Zelter, Georg Pölchau, and Sara Levy
in the establishment and expansion of the Singakademie library. Carl Friedrich
Fasch was the founder and first director of the Singakademie and, from 1756,
an associate of Bach at the court of King Frederick the Great.[18] C. F. Zelter was
Fasch's successor at the Singakademie and an enthusiastic admirer of Bach's
music all his life.[19] Georg Pölchau, another admirer and one of the first great
collectors of Bach's music, was librarian at the Singakademie from 1833 until
his death in 1836.[20] Sara Levy, née Itzig, a participant in the activities of the
Singakademie as well as one of Zelter's principal financial angels, was a
personal friend of Bach and his family, and, in her youth, had been the
favourite student of Bach's brother Wilhelm Friedemann.[21]

The Singakademie's holdings of music by C. P. E. Bach included more than
one hundred keyboard sonatas in manuscript copies and early editions, trio
sonatas, fourteen symphonies to some of which Zelter added wind parts, eleven
'concertos' for solo flute and bass, and assorted other works. The most
important part of the collection was the holdings of Bach's choral music, the
manuscripts of keyboard concertos, and the autograph scores of two of the
1788 quartets, H. 538/W. 94 and H. 539/W. 95. All these materials were
studied in depth by Heinrich Miesner, Hans Uldall, and Ernst Fritz Schmid.[22]
Thanks to their research and to Welter's comments, it is possible to reconstruct
specifics of the C. P. E. Bach holdings of the Singakademie library in some
detail.

The remainder of this article will focus on these holdings, recapitulating and
evaluating what is known about them from references in Welter's article and
in the studies of Miesner, Uldall, Schmid, and Falck. A reconstructed listing of
the C. P. E. Bach sources formerly in the Singakademie library will follow, with
shelf-marks where available. The discussion and ensuing source list will be
organized by category, following the order of the works as they appear in the
catalogue in *Helm/Grove*.

## Keyboard Music

Welter's article is the only source to make reference to manuscripts of Bach's
keyboard music in the Singakademie library. His descriptions are sketchy and
extremely general. He mentions that the collection contained sources for more
than one hunded works—sonatas, sonatinas, and isolated pieces—mostly in
manuscript but also including some unspecified printed editions. Specifically
noted are a collection of thirteen 'books' and another of fourteen 'books', the

---

[18]  Adrian Adrio, 'Fasch', *MGG*, vol. 3, cols. 1847–61.
[19]  See the article by Hans-Günter Ottenberg in this volume.
[20]  Schünemann, *Singakademie*, pp. 72–3; Miesner, *Bach in Hamburg*, p. 50.
[21]  The Singakademie library also contained important holdings of the music of W. F. Bach,
much of it in autograph or unique copies.
[22]  See n. 7 above.

latter including accompanied as well as solo material; a collection of keyboard works in the hand of C. F. Fasch; a set of six keyboard fugues, again in Fasch's hand; and the autograph of Bach's 1772 catalogue of his keyboard sonatas.

## Concertos

The Singakademie library may have contained as many as fifty manuscripts of keyboard concertos by Bach. Uldall's dissertation is the principal source for information about these works. He lists thirty-seven separate works—there are two copies of the G major concerto H. 419/W. 16—and notes two other works wrongly attributed to Bach.[23] Most of these manuscripts were copies, though Uldall includes of autographs among the unspecified scores and parts.[24] His list does not specify, however, which of the sources may have been wholly or partially autograph, nor whether any of the sets of parts may have originated in Bach's personal library. The only autograph manuscript of a concerto definitely known to have been in the Singakademie collection was the score of the concerto in E flat major for harpsichord, fortepiano and orchestra H. 479/W. 47, which was among those few manuscripts that by chance survived the war.[25] Contemporary copies included a manuscript of a G minor concerto in the hand of J. F. Agricola and a G major concerto in the hand of Fasch.[26]

Uldall says little about the sources he consulted. His principal concern is the evolution of Bach's concerted style and its relationship to and influence on the music of his contemporaries. In the course of his discussions, however, he notes the presence of nineteenth-century cadenzas in two of the Singakademie sources—manuscripts of the concertos in E flat major H. 404/W. 2 and D major H. 414/W. 11—and of horn parts in the manuscript of the C minor concerto H. 448/W. 37.[27] He also fails to mention the wind parts of the D major concerto H. 433/W. 27, and this suggests that the sources he consulted did not include them.[28] His count of thirty-eight authentic and two spurious works does not tally with Welter's notation of 'about 50' nor with a subsequent unexplainable notation in the 'Zelter Catalogue'—is it a duplication?—relating to '50 Conc. Sonaten und Sinf.' in manuscript parts.[29] These last may possibly be trio sonatas.

A considerable number of the concerto manuscripts undoubtedly came from

[23] The two spurious works are concertos in F minor and E flat major, possibly by J. C. Bach. See Uldall, *Klavierkonzert*, pp. 66, 89.

[24] Uldall, *Klavierkonzert*, p. 25.

[25] Uldall, *Klavierkonzert*, p. 52; Jacobi, 'Autograph', pp. 488–9; Rudolf Elvers, letter to the author, 22 Oct. 1986. The present shelf-mark of the manuscript in D-brd B, where it is on permanent loan, is N. Mus. S A 4.

[26] Welter, 'Musikbibliothek', p. 38.

[27] Uldall, *Klavierkonzert*, pp. 27, 31, 44–5.

[28] Uldall, *Klavierkonzert*, p. 37.

[29] Welter, 'Musikbibliothek', p. 38.

the collection of Sara Levy.[30] These include the autograph of the E flat major concerto H. 479/W. 47.[31] Inasmuch as reasonably good sources for nearly all of Bach's keyboard concertos survive—autograph scores and parts in the Staatsbibliothek Preussischer Kulturbesitz and the Deutsche Staatsbibliothek; and contemporary parts, mostly in the hand of Michel, one of Bach's more reliable copyists, in the Westphal collection in Brussels—the disappearance of the Singakademie manuscripts does not represent an irreparable loss.

The Singakademie apparently possessed no manuscript copies of Bach's concertos for flute, oboe, or violoncello. Uldall cites no source references from the Singakademie in his discussions of these works, and Welter makes no mention of them at all. Welter does make reference to '11 Conc. flauto traverso solo e Basso'. Helm and Schmid both cite these works in their catalogues of Bach's compositions as flute concertos.[32] Rachel Wade, citing Welter's listing of the catalogue entry, believes they are actually copies of the flute sonatas H. 550–6, 560–61, 564, and 548/W. 123–31 and 133–4.[33]

Neither Uldall nor Welter notes the presence in the Singakademie library of any sources, either printed or manuscript, for the sonatinas for keyboard(s) and orchestra. E. F. Schmid, however, records copies of the Winter editions of the sonatinas H. 458, 461, and 462/W. 106–8.[34]

## Chamber Music

The sources of Bach's chamber music in the Singakademie consisted both of printed editions and manuscripts, frequently in multiple copies. The latter were primarily eighteenth-century copies, interesting for their association with particular copyists and for any textual variants they may have contained, but otherwise seemingly unimportant. Schmid's listing of sources for the works he studied—the principal surviving reference—is extremely detailed; it specifies more than fifty manuscript copies of twenty-nine different works in the Singakademie library.[35] Welter writes only generally about the chamber music in a postscript to his brief recapitulation of sources for the keyboard concertos, and offhandedly in his summary of sources for the keyboard music.

---

[30] Most of the manuscripts from the Sara Levy collection were clearly marked on the outer cover as well as in the 'Zelter Catalogue'. See Welter, 'Musikbibliothek', p. 36, and Schmid, *Kammermusik*, p. 44.

[31] The manuscript was presented to the Singakademie in 1813 (Rudolf Elvers, letter to the author, 22 Oct. 1986).

[32] *Helm/Grove*, p. 858; E. F. Schmid, 'Bach, Carl Philipp Emanuel', *MGG*, i. col. 933. Helm assigns the works the catalogue number H. 482.

[33] Rachel Wade, letter to the author, 4 June 1986.

[34] Schmid, *Kammermusik*, p. 166.          [35] Schmid, *Kammermusik*, pp. 161–71.

He mentions autograph manuscripts of the Hamburg quartets as well as manuscript collections of unspecified trios, of thirteen sonatas for keyboard, melody instrument and bass, of eleven 'concertos' for flute and bass, of accompanied keyboard sonatas, and of the mysterious '50 Conc. Sonaten und Sinf. in St. Ms.' mentioned above.

Two groups of sources are, however, of exceptional interest: three trio sonatas from the collection of Sara Levy, which are not included in either *NV* or Wotquenne's catalogue and which Schmid considers, from the source of the manuscripts, may be authentic works of the Berlin period;[36] and the autographs and early copies of the three quartets of 1788, H. 537–9/W. 93–5, again from the Sara Levy collection.[37] All trace of these quartets, Bach's last important chamber works, had disappeared until Schmid rediscovered the Singakademie sources and, subsequently, a series of reliable copies made for J. J. H. Westphal and now in the Library of the Conservatoire Royal de Musique de Bruxelles, Brussels, Belgium.

Welter records the presence in the Singakademie of autographs for all three quartets.[38] Schmid is quite explicit in noting that the score of the first quartet, H. 537/W. 93, is not an autograph.[39] In describing the manuscripts in his edition of the quartets, Schmid notes the existence of several pagination sequences, which suggest that the autograph score of the first quartet was originally attached to the other two.[40] It is possible that the compilers of the 'Zelter Catalogue' mistook the contemporary copy of the first quartet for an autograph. It is also possible that, at the time the catalogue was compiled, the autograph of the first quartet was still joined to its sister works and became separated from them at a later time.

Schmid interestingly records no copies of any of the sonatas for flute, oboe or viola da gamba, and bass, H. 548–56, 560–61, and 564/W. 123–31 and 133–7, in the Singakademie library. This raises again the question of the '11 Conc. flauto traverso solo e Basso'. Rachel Wade's suggestion (based on the catalogue entry recorded by Welter) that these were actually sonatas rather than concertos is all the more plausible in the context of the apparent absence of these works from the Singakademie collection. If this is indeed the case, then it is likely that Schmid never examined these manuscripts, perhaps because he was put off by the title.

[36] Schmid, *Kammermusik*, pp. 120–1. Only one of these works appears to have survived in another copy: a sonata in F major, in the Thulmeier collection in Berlin, with the composer's name originally given as 'Bach jun' and then altered to W. F. Bach. Falck, *W. F. Bach*, p. 116, doubts any association of this work with W. F. Bach.

[37] Schmid, *Kammermusik*, pp. 44, 139. Schmid prepared an edition of the three works, based primarily on the Singakademie sources, which was completed in 1936 and published by Bärenreiter, Kassel, in 1952.

[38] Welter, 'Musikbibliothek', p. 38.

[39] Schmid, *Kammermusik*, pp 44, 164.

[40] See n. 37.

## Symphonies

Welter mentions two lots of symphonies, some in score and some in parts but all in manuscript.[41] One group consisted of six symphonies, in G major, E flat major, D major, B minor, B flat major, and A major, to which C. F. Zelter added wind parts. These are probably the six symphonies H. 657–62/W. 182, notwithstanding the erroneous key designation of the second- and third-listed works.[42]

The second group contained eight works, of which no details are given. Elsewhere on the same page, Welter notes a collection of thirteen symphonies including works by W. F. Bach, C. P. E. Bach, and Kirnberger. The five by W. F. Bach, assigned the shelf-mark 1385 in the Singakademie library, were discussed in some detail by Max Falck.[43] The possibility exists that the above-mentioned eight symphonies of C. P. E. Bach were kept with these works by his brother, in which case they would have been assigned the same shelf-mark. This meshes nicely with the total of thirteen symphonies given by Welter, but takes no account of Kirnberger. Falck[44] mentions an overture by Kirnberger also kept with the W. F. Bach symphonies. The compilers of the 'Zelter Catalogue', Welter's probable source, may well have been careless in counting the number of works kept under the shelf-mark, or they may have omitted Kirnberger's overture from their count since it was not expressly titled 'symphony'. The possible association with works of his brother and Kirnberger suggests that the C. P. E. Bach symphonies in question were probably his earlier works in the genre, H. 648–52 and 654–6/W. 173–7 and 179–81, rather than the late Hamburg symphonies, H. 663–6/W. 183.

## Choral Music

The most important of the C. P. E. Bach materials in the Singakademie library were certainly the manuscripts of choral music. These included most of the Passions and inauguration cantatas as well as *de tempore* church music and occasional works. The manuscripts fell into two groups: autographs and contemporary copies. The autograph material consisted of full scores for entire works as well as compositional materials for isolated portions of other works. The non-autograph material—by far the larger part—consisted primarily of

---

[41] Welter, 'Musikbibliothek', p. 38.

[42] The correct keys are probably E major and C major respectively. The works are not listed in the order they appear in *NV*. It is possible that the references to D major and E flat major symphonies may also mean the symphonies H. 651/W. 176 and H. 654/W. 179, both of which circulated in versions without wind instruments.

[43] Falck, *W. F. Bach*, pp. 121 ff.　　　　　　　　　　　　　[44] Falck, *W. F. Bach*, p. 125.

complete sets of performing parts. These parts were the actual parts Bach used in the Hamburg churches, and were kept in his library during his lifetime. Much of this material was specifically dated—the year when a manuscript was used was often noted on the outer cover—and works for particular occasions were datable from other sources. The material was all acquired from Bach's estate by Georg Pölchau and sold by him to Abraham Mendelssohn; it reached the Singakademie through Sara Levy, who was Abraham Mendelssohn's aunt by marriage.[45] All materials for a given work appear to have been stored together in the Singakademie library,[46] much as they probably were in Bach's home.

During his lifetime, Bach apparently kept a close hold on this material, frequently reusing portions of it on different occasions or in different contexts. A few copies were prepared after his death for J. J. H. Westphal;[47] and a few manuscripts acquired by Pölchau, chiefly autograph scores, remained in his possession and passed with his collection to the Preussischer Staatsbibliothek. But no other copies of the rest of this material appear to have ever existed, meaning that the Singakademie sources were to a considerable extent *unica*. Since Bach's primary duties in Hamburg involved the provision of music for the city's churches, the disappearance of this material seriously affects our understanding of Bach's activities during the last twenty years of his life.

Fortunately, Heinrich Miesner examined these sources in some detail and summarized his observations in his dissertation. He gives a general description and chronology of the works and their then-surviving sources, selected incipits, and a limited discussion of questions of form and style, often with particular reference to parodied or borrowed material. He identifies those sources that are wholly or partly autographs, notes those years or circumstances when performance materials may have been reused,[48] and even lists singers mentioned specifically in the parts. We are therefore not completely uninformed about the works and their sources.[49]

What we know about the sources, however, is that which Miesner felt was important, interesting, or relevant to the points he was making. He appears to have been very meticulous in researching and recording this data, and there

[45] Mendelssohn's wife was the daughter of Sara Levy's sister Babette. See Schünemann, *Singakademie*, p. 71; Rachel Wade, *The Keyboard Concertos of Carl Philipp Emanuel Bach* (Ann Arbor, 1981), 44; Stephen Clark, 'The Occasional Choral Works of C. P. E. Bach', Princeton University, Ph.D. diss., 1984, 18. I am grateful to Dr Clark for making his dissertation available to me.

[46] This is implied by the listings in Miesner, *Bach in Hamburg*, pp. 64–7 and 87–9.

[47] Now in B Bc. See Alfred Wotquenne, *Catalogue de la Bibliothèque du Conservatoire Royal de Musique* (Brussels, 1898–1912), i. 136–9.

[48] The dates when materials were used were noted on the outer cover of manuscripts. See Miesner, *Bach in Hamburg*, p. 77.

[49] In 'Occasional Choral Works', Stephen Clark has been able to reconstruct a surprisingly broad and comprehensive picture of these works from Miesner's comments, the few surviving sources, and an extensive body of surviving texts, notwithstanding the disappearance of most of the music.

are no grounds to question his findings. But we do not know what he may have overlooked either by chance or intention. There remain a great many questions about the music and the manuscripts to which we would have liked answers.[50]

The disappearance of the C. P. E. Bach materials formerly in library of the Singakademie zu Berlin is a great misfortune for the scholar, the archivist, and the bibliographer. The manuscripts of the concertos may have contained authentic variants and included parts from Bach's own library. These last would be of paramount importance to an editor since they frequently contain Bach's final thoughts about a work. The 1772 autograph catalogue of keyboard sonatas is critical to the authentication and dating of Bach's sonatas, even though much of the information it contains may well have been included in *NV*. The manuscripts of Bach's vocal music—containing actual performing materials as well as autographs—were necessarily the principal source for the assessment of Bach's church music and the performance of his daily duties in Hamburg. Their loss necessitates that generalizations must be arrived at from examination of the few sources that have survived. Many interesting questions regarding Bach's attitude toward his duties and the composition of occasional church music can only be partially answered. With the possible exception of his brother Wilhelm Friedemann, the evaluation of the work of no other composer appears to have been so seriously affected by the disappearance of the Singakademie collection.

---

[50]  Welter's list of sources for Bach's choral music corresponds closely with the aggregate of the references in Miesner, *Bach in Hamburg*. Welter includes references to published as well as unpublished materials, and to manuscripts of works for which Miesner cited only sources in other libraries or to which Miesner made no reference whatsoever. Welter's descriptions are summary and are not always accurate.

# Sources of C. P. E. Bach's Music formerly in the Library of the Singakademie zu Berlin

## Keyboard Music

H. 75.5, 99–102/W. 119, 2–7     1755     6 keyboard fugues: MS, copied by C. F. Fasch
More than 100 unidentified pieces (see text)

## Concertos

| | | | |
|---|---|---|---|
| H. 403/W. 1 | 1733/44 | Concerto in A minor | MS: D II 1465 |
| H. 404/W. 2 | 1734/43 | Concerto in E flat major | MS: D II 1472 a; includes a cadenza from 1819 |
| H. 405/W. 3 | 1737/45 | Concerto in G major | MS: D II 1472 |
| H. 406/W. 4 | 1738 | Concerto in G major | MS: D II 1467 |
| H. 408/W. 46 | 1740 | Concerto in F major, 2 keyboards, orchestra | MS: D II 1472 i; includes horn parts |
| H. 409/W. 6 | 1740 | Concerto in G minor | MS: D II 1465 |
| H. 411/W. 8 | 1741 | Concerto in A major | MS: D II 1468 |
| H. 412/W. 9 | 1742 | Concerto in G major | MS: D II 1465 |
| H. 413/W. 10 | 1742 | Concerto in B flat major | MS: D II 1472 |
| H. 414/W. 11 | 1743 | Concerto in D major | MS: D II 1472 t; includes a cadenza from 1819 |
| H. 415/W. 12 | 1744 | Concerto in F major | MS: D II 1466 |
| H. 417/W. 14 | 1744 | Concerto in E major | MS: D II 1472 |
| H. 418/W. 15 | 1745 | Concerto in E minor | MS: D II 1472 |
| H. 419/W. 16 | 1745 | Concerto in G major | 2 MS copies: D II 1472 and D II 1465 |
| H. 420/W. 17 | 1745 | Concerto in D minor | MS: D II 1472 |
| H. 421/W. 18 | 1745 | Concerto in D major | MS: D II 1472 |
| H. 422/W. 19 | 1746 | Concerto in A major | MS: D II 1465 |
| H. 423/W. 20 | 1746 | Concerto in C major | MS: D II 1467 |
| H. 427/W. 23 | 1748 | Concerto in D minor | MS: D II 1466 |
| H. 429/W. 25 | 1749 | Concerto in B flat major | MS: D II 1472 |
| H. 433/W. 27 | 1750 | Concerto in D major | MS: D II 1472; lacks wind, brass and drum parts (?) |
| H. 434/W. 28 | 1751 | Concerto in B flat major | MS: D II 1467 |
| H. 437/W. 29 | 1753 | Concerto in A major | MS: D II 1472 |
| H. 440/W. 30 | 1753 | Concerto in B minor | MS: D II 1472 |
| H. 441/W. 31 | 1753 | Concerto in C minor | MS: D II 1470 |
| H. 442/W. 32 | 1754 | Concerto in G minor | MS: D II 1471 |
| H. 443/W. 33 | 1755 | Concerto in F major | MS: D II 1472 |

| | | | |
|---|---|---|---|
| H. 444/W. 34 | 1755 | Concerto in G major | MS: D II 1469 |
| H. 446/W. 35 | 1759 | Concerto in E flat major | MS: D II 1465 |
| H. 448/W. 37 | 1762 | Concerto in C minor | MS: D II 1467; includes horn parts |
| H. 454/W. 38 | 1763 | Concerto in F major | MS: D II 1472 |
| H. 458/W. 106 | 1763 | Sonatina in C major | Winter edition |
| H. 461/W. 107 | 1764 | Sonatina in D minor | Winter edition: 2 copies |
| H. 462/W. 108 | 1764 | Sonatina in E flat major | Winter edition |
| H. 469/W. 41 | 1769 | Concerto in E flat major | MS: D II 1472 |
| H. 470/W. 42 | 1770 | Concerto in F major | MS: D II 1472; includes horn parts (?) |
| H. 472/W. 43, 2 | 1771 | Concerto in D major | MS: D II 1466 |
| H. 473/W. 43, 3 | 1771 | Concerto in E flat major | MS: D II 1466 |
| H. 476/W. 43, 6 | 1771 | Concerto in C major | MS: D II 1466 |
| H. 479/W. 47 | 1788 | Concerto in E flat major, harpsichord, fortepiano, orchestra | Autograph score: D II 1473 a |
| H. 482 | (?) | Collection of 11 'concertos' flute, bass | See under Chamber Music |
| Spurious | | Concerto in F minor | MS: D II 1472 z; by J. C. Bach (?) |
| Spurious | | Concerto in E flat major | 2 MS copies: D II 1472 v; by J. C. Bach (?) |

## Chamber Music

| | | | |
|---|---|---|---|
| H. 502/W. 71 | 1731/46 | Sonata in D major, keyboard, violin | MS: 1 copy |
| H. 503/W. 72 | 1731/47 | Sonata in D minor, keyboard, violin | MS: 2 copies |
| H. 504/W. 73 | 1745 | Sonata in C major, keyboard, violin | MS: 4 copies |
| H. 505/W. 83 | 1747 | Sonata in D major, keyboard, flute | MS: 1 copy |
| H. 507/W. 74 | 1754 | Sinfonie in D major, keyboard, violin | MS: 2 copies |
| H. 509/W. 86 | 1755 | Sonata in G major, keyboard, flute | MS: 2 copies |
| H. 510/W. 88 | 1759 | Sonata in G minor, keyboard, viola da gamba | MS: 3 copies |
| H. 511/W. 75 | 1763 | Sonata in F major, keyboard, violin | MS: 2 copies |
| H. 512/W. 76 | 1763 | Sonata in B minor, keyboard, violin | MS: 2 copies |
| H. 513/W. 77 | 1763 | Sonata in B flat major, keyboard, violin | MS: 2 copies |

| | | | |
|---|---|---|---|
| H. 522–4/W. 90 | 1775 | 3 sonatas, keyboard, violin, violoncello | Composer's edition: 2 copies |
| H. 525–30/W. 89 | 1778 | 6 sonatas, keyboard, violin, violoncello | Hummel edition: 2 copies |
| H. 531–4/W. 91 | 1777 | 4 sonatas, keyboard, violin, violoncello | Composer's edition: 2 copies |
| H. 537/W. 93 | 1788 | Quartet in A minor, keyboard, flute, viola, bass | MS: Z D 1649 a, score and parts |
| H. 538/W. 94 | 1788 | Quartet in D major, keyboard, flute, viola, bass | Autograph score: Z D 1649 a<br>MS parts: Z D 1649 a |
| H. 539/W. 95 | 1788 | Quartet in G major, keyboard, flute, viola, bass | Autograph score: Z D 1649 a<br>MS parts: Z D 1649 a |
| H. 548, 550–6, 560–1, 564/W. 123–31, 133–4 (?)=H. 482 | 1735/86 | 11 sonatas, flute and bass, titled 'Concertos | MS |
| H. 567/W. 143 | 1731/47 | Trio sonata in B minor, flute, violin, bass | MS: 1 copy |
| H. 568/W. 144 | 1731/47 | Trio sonata in G major, flute, violin, bass | MS: 1 copy |
| H. 569/W. 145 | 1731/47 | Trio sonata in D minor, flute, violin, bass | MS: 2 copies |
| H. 570/W. 146 | 1731/47 | Trio sonata in A major, flute, violin, bass | MS: 2 copies |
| H. 571/W. 147 | 1731/47 | Trio sonata in C major, flute, violin, bass | MS: 1 copy |
| H. 572/W. 148 | 1735/47 | Trio sonata in A minor, flute, violin, bass | MS: 2 copies |
| H. 576/W. 154 | 1747 | Trio sonata in F major, two violins, bass | MS: 4 copies |
| H. 577/W. 155 | 1747 | Trio sonata in E minor, two violins, bass | MS: 1 copy |
| H. 578/W. 161, 2 | 1748 | Trio sonata in B flat major, flute, violin, bass | MS: 5 copies |
| H. 579/W. 161, 1 | 1749 | Trio sonata in C minor, two violins, bass | MS: 2 copies |
| H. 584/W. 158 | 1754 | Trio sonata in B flat major, two violins, bass | MS: 2 copies |
| H. 588/W. 163 | 1755 | Trio sonata, bass flute, viola, bass | Winter edition: 1 copy<br>MS: 4 copies |

Elias N. Kulukundis

| | | | |
|---|---|---|---|
| H. 590/W. 160 | 1756 | Trio sonata in D minor, two violins, bass | *Musikalisches Mancherley* edition: 2 copies |
| Uncertain | | Trio sonata in E flat major, flute, violin, bass | MS: 2 copies, E 1954/55 o; |
| | | | $\dfrac{\text{E } 1954/55 \text{ m}}{\text{I}}$ |
| Uncertain | | Trio sonata in E major, flute (violin), violin, bass | MS: E 1954/55 h |
| Uncertain | | Trio sonata in F major, flute, violin, bass or flute, keyboard | MS: D 1702 e |
| Arrangements (spurious): | | | |
| H. 507/W. 74 | | Sonata in D major, arranged for two violins, viola, bass | MS: E 1954/55 k |
| H. 507/W. 74 | | Sonata in D major, arranged for two violins, bass | MS: D 1699 v |
| H. 510/W. 88 | | Sonata in G minor, arranged for keyboard, violin | MS: 2 copies, E 1954/55 r; D 1700, 1 |

## Symphonies

Collection of eight symphonies, probably:

| | | | |
|---|---|---|---|
| H. 648/W. 173 | 1741 | Symphony in G major | MS: 1385 (?) |
| H. 649/W. 174 | 1755 | Symphony in C major | MS: 1385 (?) |
| H. 650/W. 175 | 1755 | Symphony in F major | MS: 1385 (?) |
| H. 651/W. 176 | 1755 | Symphony in D major | MS: 1385 (?) |
| H. 652/W. 177 | 1756 | Symphony in E minor | MS: 1385 (?) |
| H. 654/W. 179 | 1757 | Symphony in E flat major | MS: 1385 (?) |
| H. 655/W. 180 | 1758 | Symphony in G major | MS: 1385 (?) |
| H. 656/W. 181 | 1762 | Symphony in F major | MS: 1385 (?) |

Collection of six symphonies, with wind parts added by C. F. Zelter, probably:

| | | | |
|---|---|---|---|
| H. 657/W. 182, 1 | 1773 | Symphony in G major | MS |
| H. 658/W. 182, 2 | 1773 | Symphony in B flat major | MS |
| H. 659/W. 182, 3 | 1773 | Symphony in C major | MS |
| H. 660/W. 182, 4 | 1773 | Symphony in A major | MS |
| H. 661/W. 182, 5 | 1773 | Symphony in B minor | MS |
| H. 662/W. 182, 6 | 1773 | Symphony in E major | MS |

### Songs and Secular Cantatas

| | | | |
|---|---|---|---|
| H. 670–84, 687, 689–92/W. 199 | 1762 | *Oden mit Melodien* | Draft for a revised  . republication of the 1762 printed edition, with autograph (?) notations |
| H. 697/W. 232 | 1765 | *Phyllis und Thyrsis* | Winter edition |
| H. 735/W. 200, 22 | | *Die Grazien* | Autograph score |

### Choral Music

*Major Choral Works*

| | | | |
|---|---|---|---|
| H. 772/W. 215 | 1749 | *Magnificat* | MS |
| H. 775/W. 238 | 1769 | *Die Israeliten in der Wüste* | Composer's edition |
| H. 778/W. 217 | 1778 | *Heilig* (for two choruses) | Composer's edition (?) |
| H. 779/W. 239 | 1783 | *Klopstock's Morgengesang am Schöpfungsfeste* | Composer's edition (?) |
| H. 780, 871/W. 204 | 1786 | *Zwei Litaneyen* | Schiørring edition |

Arrangement:

| | | | |
|---|---|---|---|
| H. 778/W. 217 | | *Heilig* (for two choruses), arranged for one chorus by C. F. Zelter | MS score (Zelter?) |

*The Passions*

| | | | |
|---|---|---|---|
| H. 782 | 1768–9 | St Matthew Passion | Autograph score (fragmentary?); complete set of parts |
| H. 783 | 1769–70 | St Mark Passion | Complete set of parts |
| H. 784 | 1770–1 | St Luke Passion | Complete set of parts |
| H. 785 | 1771–2 | St John Passion | Complete set of parts |
| H. 786 | 1772–3 | St Matthew Passion | Complete set of parts |
| H. 787 | 1773–4 | St Mark Passion | Complete set of parts |
| H. 789 | 1775–6 | St John Passion | Complete set of parts; 12 pages of autograph material including a chorus and 4 chorales. |
| H. 790 | 1776–7 | St Matthew Passion | Complete set of parts; 11 pages of autograph material including 1 chorus, 1 arioso, 1 aria, and fragments of recitatives |
| H. 791 | 1777–8 | St Mark Passion | Complete set of parts |
| H. 792 | 1778–9 | St Luke Passion | Complete set of parts |

| | | | |
|---|---|---|---|
| H. 793 | 1779–80 | St John Passion | Complete set of parts (?); 1 chorus, MS score. |
| H. 794 | 1780–1 | St Matthew Passion | Autograph score of final chorus |
| H. 795 | 1781–2 | St Mark Passion | Complete set of parts |
| H. 796 | 1782–3 | St Luke Passion | Complete set of parts; autograph score for 1 chorus, 1 accompagnato, and 1 aria |
| H. 797 | 1783–4 | St John Passion | Complete set of parts |
| H. 798 | 1784–5 | St Matthew Passion | Autograph score for 4 choruses, 3 arias, 1 arioso, and 1 accompagnato |
| H. 799 | 1785–6 | St Mark Passion | Complete set of parts; autograph score for 4 arias, 1 accompagnato, and 1 chorus |
| H. 800/W. 234 | 1786–7 | St Luke Passion | Complete set of parts |
| H. 801 | 1787–8 | St John Passion | Complete set of parts; autograph score for 5 arias, 1 accompagnato, 1 chorale, and 1 chorus |
| H. 802/W. 235 | 1788 | St Matthew Passion | Complete set of parts |

*Easter Cantatas*

| | | | |
|---|---|---|---|
| H. 803/W. 244 | 1756 | *Gott hat den Herrn auferwecket* | MS |
| H. 804/W. 242 | 1778 | *Jauchzet frohlocket* | Complete set of parts |
| H. 805/W. 241 | 1780 | *Nun danket alle Gott* | MS (incomplete?) |
| H 807/W. 243 | 1784 | *Anbetung der Erbarmer* | MS (parts?) |
| H. 808 | 1768 | *Sing Volk der Christen* | Complete set of parts |
| H. 808 | 1771 | *Ist Christus nicht auferstanden* | Complete set of parts |

*St Michael's Day Cantatas*

| | | | |
|---|---|---|---|
| H. 809/W. 248 | 1769 | *Den Engeln gleich* | Complete set of parts |
| H. 810/W. 245 | 1772 | *Ich will den Namen des Herrn preisen* | Complete set of parts |
| H. 812/W. 247 | 1775 | *Siehe ich begehre* | Complete set of parts; autograph score for choral fugue |
| H. 814/W. 246 | 1785 | *Der Frevler mag die Wahrheit* | Complete set of parts (?) |

*Christmas Cantatas*

| H. 815/W. 249 | 1775 | *Auf schicke dich* | (?) |
| H. 816 | 1772 | *Ehre sei Gott in der Höhe* (also for St Michael's Day) | Complete set of parts |

*Cantatas for Other Feasts*

Pentecost:

| H. 817 | 1769 | *Herr lehr uns thun* | MS |
| | 1787 | unknown title | MS |

Visitation:

| H. 819 | 1768 | *Meine Seele erhebet* | MS: parts (?) |

Ascension:

| | (?) | unknown title | MS |

7th Sunday after Trinity:

| | (?) | *Der Himmel allenthalben ist des Herrn* | Complete set of parts |

*Inauguration Cantatas*

| H. 821 a | 1769 | for Palm | Autograph score of Part I; MS score of Part II |
| H. 821 b | 1771 | for Klefecker | Autograph score; complete set of parts |
| H. 821 d | 1772 | for Häseler | Complete set of parts |
| H. 821 e | 1772 | for Hornbostel | Complete set of parts (?); MS score of opening chorus and one aria |
| H. 821 f/W. 252 | 1773 | for Winkler | Complete set of parts; autograph score of Part II |
| H. 821 h | 1777 | for Gerling | Complete set of parts; autograph score, lacking opening chorus |
| H. 821 i | 1778 | for Sturm | Autograph score |
| H. 821 k | 1782 | for Jänisch | Autograph score; complete set of parts for Part II |
| H. 821 l/W. 250 | 1785 | for Gasie | Complete set of parts |
| H. 821 m/W. 253 | 1785 | for Schäfer | Complete set of parts |
| H. 821 n | 1787 | for Berkhan | Autograph score of Part I; complete set of parts for Part II |
| H. 821 o | 1787 | for Willerding | Autograph score; complete set of parts |

*Occasional Cantatas*

| | | | |
|---|---|---|---|
| H. 823 | 1786 | Dedication cantata for the tower of St Michael's Church | Complete set of parts (?) |
| H. 824 e | 1785 | Hymn to Friendship, *Danket dem Herrn* | Autograph score of Part I |

*Other Choral Music*

| | | | |
|---|---|---|---|
| H. 825/W. 207 | | *Veni Sancte Spiritus* | Soprano part only |
| H. 827/W. 218 | | *Heilig* (for one chorus) | MS |
| H. 828/W. 219 | | *Sanctus* | MS |
| H. 829/W. 216 | 1770 | *Spiega Hammonia fortunata* | MS score with autograph notations |
| H. 830/W. 221 | 1771 | Chorus: *Mein Heiland, meine Zuversicht* (for the 10th Sunday after Trinity) | Text only (?) |
| H. 832/W. 223 | 1777 | Chorus: *Zeige du mir deine Wege* (for the 8th Sunday after Trinity) | MS |
| H. 835/W. 227 | 1783 | Chorus: *Leite mich nach deinem Willen* | MS |
| H. 837/W. 229 | 178? | Chorus: *Meinem Leib wird man begraben* (for a funeral) | MS |
| H. 855/W. 220 | | *Veni Sancte Spiritus* (spurious—Telemann?) | Complete set of parts |
| H. 856 | | *Selig sind die Toten* (for a funeral; spurious—Telemann?) | Complete set of parts |
| W. 224 | 1775 | Chorus: *Lass mich nicht deinem Zorn empfinden* | MS |
| W. 230 | 1782 | Chorus: *Wann der Erde Gründe beben* | MS |
| | 1785 | Chorus: *Umsonst empörte der Hölle sich* | MS |
| | (?) | Chorus: Psalm VIII, *Herr unser Herrscher* | MS |

# C. P. E. Bach and the Free Fantasia for Keyboard: Deutsche Staatsbibliothek Mus. Ms. Nichelmann 1N

### Douglas A. Lee

THE free fantasia for solo keyboard which began to appear in the mid-eighteenth century, with J. S. Bach's Chromatic Fantasia (BWV 903) as progenitor, embodied many of the changes in musical style characterizing that era. A move toward sensitivity had focused increasing attention on the solo keyboard as a medium which could easily and effectively address that trend; the free fantasia offered a stylistic format which encouraged, even required, a maximum of individuality, often in a highly personal vein. The idiomatic keyboard patterns prevailing in most fantasias reflected an instrumental medium well developed in its facility and capability for a wide range of musical gestures. In all of this, the free fantasia eschewed the stereotyped designs and patterns which had come to be the hallmark of much music of the late Baroque. Fantasias were now only infrequently paired with strict contrapuntal pieces, as had been usual in the earlier fantasia and fugue tradition; they relied on keyboard resources rather than adapting to the manuals the structure and thematic materials of the concerto grosso; and they appealed to the prevailing aesthetic of sensibility in their marked contrasts of mood and key and dramatic changes of dynamic levels.

Beyond these considerations, the free fantasia—meaning one without barlines in most if not in all its sections—signified a change in musical leadership from the court and church to the stylized music-making of the middle class. The individual could 'fantasize' in private, before a small group of professional musicians, for a group of amateurs, or for a concert of middle-class urban society. The genre came to be a type of composition which could stand alone, or could be identified as an independent process appropriate for inclusion within a larger work.

Carl Philipp Emanuel Bach was the most important composer of such works. In many ways he was a musical spokesman for the era, particularly in his music for solo keyboard. His sonatas should by no means be regarded as stereotypes, yet they did follow a broad design common to much instrumental music of the time. The free fantasia may be regarded as particularly significant within his keyboard works in that it frequently offers more insight into his musical thought than is readily perceived in his sonatas. Note that he devoted a complete chapter to the fantasia in his famous *Versuch* and included a complete fantasia at the conclusion of that work for illustration.

Bach's impact on what we have come to call Classical style receives increasing attention, but recognition of his free fantasias for solo keyboard, a numerically small portion of his catalogue, has not kept pace with his growing historical stature. He was in close touch with contemporary literary figures in North Germany, as well as with Diderot and the *encyclopédistes* in France.[1] Perhaps it was in that vein that he had responded to the famous writing war in Paris in the 1750s with his own *Versuch*, published in two parts in 1753 and 1762.

The Fantasia in E flat addressed here remains as a manuscript copy in D-ddr Bds (Mus. Ms. Nichelmann 1 N), as the last item in a collection of keyboard works by Christoph Nichelmann (1717–62), the cembalist who shared continuo duties with Bach at the court of Frederick the Great between 1745 and 1755. The manuscript shows no attribution, but the collective catalogue number led to its inclusion in the published thematic catalogue of Nichelmann's works,[2] an error which this study is designed to correct. My continued interest in this particular work led to suspicions concerning the earlier attribution to Nichelmann, and those concerns were shared with Eugene Helm, at that time compiling a new and complete catalogue of C. P. E. Bach's works; as a result the Fantasia was included in Helm's list of works of uncertain authenticity. The intent here is to establish that the work is not by Nichelmann but by C. P. E. Bach, and that the one known manuscript represents the composer's autograph, copied before 1749.

The musical text of the Fantasia includes four sheets of heavy paper, the last containing only one keyboard system. No watermark is discernible, but the colour, thickness, and texture of the paper are typical of others used for music copying in North Germany in the mid-eighteenth century. Individual sheets measure 330 mm. vertically and 223 mm. in width, and each is ruled from left to right by a single-staff rastrum into seven double-staff keyboard systems. The manuscript represents a fair copy, with the few erasures attributable to simple copying errors.[3]

The single title 'Fantasia' appears at the head of the musical text (see Facsimile 1); no performing medium is specified, but the work is clearly intended for a keyboard instrument. At least one traveller reported hearing Bach 'play his compositions [sonatas?] on the clavier and his fantasias on the

---

[1] See Ernst Fritz Schmid, *Carl Philipp Emanuel Bach und seine Kammermusik* (Kassel, 1931), 44–5.

[2] Douglas A. Lee, *The Works of Christoph Nichelmann: A Thematic Index* (Detroit, 1971), 68.

[3] I am indebted to Professor Pamela Fox for generous assistance in providing details of this manuscript.

fortepiano'.[4] Bach's own comments designate the clavichord and pianoforte as preferred instruments for performing works such as the one under discussion. 'The best instruments for our purpose [improvisation and the free fantasia] are the clavichord and pianoforte. Both must be well tuned. The undamped register of the pianoforte is the most pleasing and, once the performer learns to observe the necessary precautions in the face of its reverberations, the most delightful for improvisation.'[5]

In refuting Nichelmann's authorship of the work one must first acknowledge that there is no strong reason to support the attribution. That the Fantasia is gathered with other verified works by Nichelmann means little, considering the usual condition of eighteenth-century manuscript collections. If this Fantasia were by Nichelmann, it would be unique among his compositions, with no other works approaching it in style or musical sophistication. The calligraphies of Bach and Nichelmann do show many similarities in broad characteristics, but these are not surprising considering that the two were nearly the same age, that they had been students at the Thomasschule in Leipzig at the same time, studying under the same music master (J. S. Bach), and that they shared a position at the royal court in Berlin, where they were engaged in many of the same musical activities. Yet detailed examination shows some distinct differences between Nichelmann's script and that represented in this Fantasia.

A typical autograph by Nichelmann, the score of a concerto for keyboard and strings in E (D-ddr Bds, Amalienbibliothek 588), shows a distinct style of handwriting (see Facsimile 2). Nichelmann's G clefs are quite open, while the G clef in the Fantasia (see Facsimile 1) is closed. His F clefs are closer in design, but that in the Fantasia shows a distinctive tail extending to the right in a style which, as we will see, is typical of Bach's earlier script.

Naturals by Nichelmann are consistently square, showing sharp angles at the corners. Those in the Fantasia lack a sharp corner on the right and might be called 'round-shouldered'. 'Forte' markings offer further contrast. Those by Nichelmann consistently comprise a single letter *f* followed by two dots (as in a colon) to designate the abbreviation from 'forte', and consist of three strokes of the pen, including the stem, cross-beam, and a separate reinforcing stroke at the top. Comparable dynamic markings in the Fantasia are made with two strokes, one for the stem and one for the cross-beam, with no following dots.

On the other hand, similar comparisons of calligraphy offer some positive correlations with Bach's manuscript. The formation of the natural signs on the first page of the Fantasia score matches that found in Bach's script from throughout most of his life.[6] Of even greater importance, the F clef in the

---

[4] From Elsie von der Recke's *Reisen durch Deutschland*, p. 201, quoted in Cornelia Auerbach, *Die deutsche Clavichordkunst des 18. Jahrhunderts*, 3rd edn. (Kassel, 1959), 49.

[5] *Essay*, p. 431.

[6] See the facsimile of the Allegro assai in E minor, H. 188/W. 58, 4, in *The Collected Works for Solo Keyboard by Carl Philipp Emanuel Bach*, ed. Darrell Berg (New York, 1985), i. 145.

Facsimile 1. Fantasia in E flat major. D-ddr Bds, Mus. ms. Nichelmann
                                    1 N

Fantasia, with its pronounced, heavily inked tail (noted above), matches the F
clefs in works copied by Bach during the 1740s and earlier, but this style of clef
was replaced by a different one in Bach's manuscript style after 1749. For
comparisons with autograph facsimiles generally accessible at present, note
the F clef in the sonata in E flat from 1737, revised in 1743 (H. 17/W. 65, 8)
and the sonata in F from 1749 (H. 60/W. 65, 24).[7] Both the F clef and the
brace in the Fantasia and in these works cited correspond as closely as one
could expect when comparing multiple figures from the same hand.

The C minor Fantasia which appeared as the last of the eighteen sample
pieces for Part I of the *Versuch* has been regarded as Emanuel Bach's first work
in this genre. He could have written that Fantasia long before the publication
date of 1753, but the calligraphic evidence descirbed above leaves little
question that the E flat Fantasia considered here was copied before 1749. Until
evidence surfaces of any previous fantasia by C. P. E. Bach, it is reasonable to

---

[7] Ibid., iii. 205–11; iv. 33–5.

Facsimile 2. Christoph Nichelmann, Concerto for keyboard and strings in E major. D-ddr Bds, Amalienbibliothek 588

assume that this Fantasia represents our composer's earliest preserved effort in this genre.

To turn to the admittedly precarious terrain of musical style: Example 1 outlines the structure of the Fantasia in the same manner as did Bach when sketching the Fantasia in D which he appended as an illustration for his closing chapter on the free fantasia in his *Versuch*, Part II. Here, three quasi-ritornello sections, derived from arpeggiation, outline the work, as is the case in other Bach fantasias. The first and last of these sections open with a similar keyboard pattern, establishing a balance which is reinforced by a correspondence in their bass lines: both ascend a third, the first from E flat to G, and the third from C to E flat. The middle ritornello section exploits a different keyboard pattern, but is still based on arpeggiation, and the bass line still ascends to the upper third, this time from E natural to G.

Example 1. Structural bass line of the Fantasia in E flat major

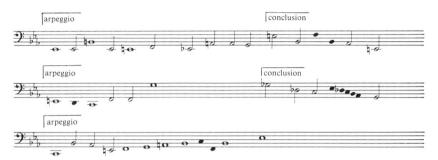

These three sections of arpeggiation are separated by two areas of disruptive chords, dotted rhythms, and intermittent recitative, their resemblance enhanced by the similar structural lines concluding their bass parts: both bass lines descend through a fourth, a semitone, and a further fourth (the first is an augmented fourth). Much of the musical activity in these areas derives from continuing modulation; the recitative sections exploit a series of sevenths offering little in the way of stable tonal reference, and this ambiguity is often increased by enharmonic spellings of diminished-seventh harmonies.

Bach's own comments in his *Versuch* concerning the fantasia in general could have been written as a description of this particular work. 'As a means of reaching the most distant keys more quickly and with agreeable suddenness no chord is more convenient and fruitful than the seventh chord with a diminished seventh and fifth, for by inverting it and changing it enharmonically, a great many chordal tranformations can be attained.'[8] Many other comments by Bach are equally pertinent, but the following are particularly notable. 'A free fantasia consists of varied harmonic progressions which can be expressed in all manner of figuration and motives.'[9] 'At the start the principal key must prevail for some time so that the listener will be unmistakably oriented. And again before the close it must be well prolonged as a means of preparing the listener for the end of the fantasia and impressing the tonalities upon his memory.'[10]

Some further observations warrant consideration. Bach was known to be more careful than other composers in cataloguing his works, particularly those which he felt had commercial value. It has been shown with reasonable certainty that most of Bach's estate catalogue (*NV*) was prepared in part from

---

[8] *Essay*, p. 438.          [9] Ibid., p. 430.          [10] Ibid., p. 431.

his index of his own works,[11] but this fantasia is not included. Bach's index was prepared in his later years, while this Fantasia originated in an earlier part of his life; its omission from any catalogue could have been a simple matter of faulty memory.

C. P. E. Bach's correspondence with friends, printers, and other individuals involved in the sale or distribution of his compositions shows that he was a thoroughly practical business man. That quality, as well as others of his views on the free fantasia, was expressed in a letter to Johann Nikolaus Forkel (1749–1818), dated 10 February 1775.

One will have from me now six or seven fantasias, [counting] the eighteenth test piece in C minor. I don't deny that I would have liked to do something [more] in this sphere, perhaps were I not so totally inept in the matter. But I have a hoard of them which belong . . . to the treatment of the fantasia in the second part of my *Essay*; moreover, how many [players] are there who like, understand, and play [these works] well? . . . I have little interest in this, even less than for the keyboard sonata with an accompanying instrument in the current humdrum manner. Yet these latter mediocrities can be more lucrative than the darkest fantasia.[12]

Our best information concerning the dating of Bach's works shows that by 1775 he had written well over six or seven fantasias.[13] Here again the memory of a busy and prolific composer could account for the omission of the E flat Fantasia from his work-list; but equally plausible explanations are his scepticism about the interest and capabilities of players in coping with such a work, plus his doubts over the commercial values of this as musical property. Obviously the composer's reservations were strong enough in 1775 to engender the conscious suppression of some of his fantasias, which derived from his assessment of public reception more than from his interest in them or his regard for the musical substance of such works.

There is a possible explanation for the present cataloguing in the Deutsche Staatsbibliothek. It was at one time in the possession of Friedrich August Grasnick (1798–1877), a collector who also owned many manuscripts of J. S. Bach which had been copied by Nichelmann, along with many of Nichelmann's own autographs. Grasnick's collection of autographs was purchased by the Berlin Royal Library in 1879; very likely it was during this time that the E flat Fantasia, without signature, was erroneously included among Nichelmann's compositions.[14]

---

[11] Darrell M. Berg, 'Towards a Catalogue of the Keyboard Sonatas of C. P. E. Bach', *JAMS*, 32 (1979), 276–303.

[12] Carl Hermann Bitter, *Carl Philipp Emanuel und Wilhelm Friedemann Bach und deren Brüder* (Berlin, 1868), i. 341; *Suchalla/Briefe*, p. 243.

[13] *Helm/Grove*, p. 857, and Renate Selinger-Barber, *Die Klavierfantasien Carl Philipp Emanuel Bachs*, MA thesis, Universität Hamburg, 1984, 59.

[14] Hans-Joachim Schulze, 'Der Schreiber "Anonymous 400"—ein Schüler Johann Sebastian Bachs', *BJ*, 58 (1972), 104–17; and Douglas Johnson, Alan Tyson, and Robert Winter, *The Beethoven Sketchbooks: History, Reconstruction, Inventory* (Berkeley and Los Angeles, 1985), *passim*.

The addition of one more work to the catalogue of a major figure in the history of music may not alter our view of that composer or of the period in which he worked; certainly it is not unusual for manuscripts of the eighteenth century to be mislaid, misattributed, or forgotten. But it is through the assembling of previously unknown musical materials that we arrive at, or at least approach, a better understanding of the prevailing musical processes of a particular period, and this is particularly important in the case of a time of changing musical styles such as the mid-eighteenth century. There remains little reason to doubt that the E flat Fantasia is a work by C. P. E. Bach, copied in his own hand before 1749. Considering Bach's position in the history of this genre and the degree to which this style of writing reflected changing musical thought of the time, a work standing at the very threshold of the transition warrants our most careful attention.

# C. P. E. Bach and Carl Friedrich Zelter

## Hans-Günter Ottenberg

THE music of the 'Hamburg Bach' attracted the attention of Carl Friedrich Zelter at an early stage, and continued for decades to hold a certain fascination for this Berlin musician and master mason, with profound consequences in the short term for the taste of the wider public. Zelter was drawn towards C. P. E. Bach as a composer, as a practical musician, as a theorist, and as a collector of music, and this attraction can in turn be closely linked with the reception of J. S. Bach's music in Berlin in the late eighteenth century and the first third of the nineteenth. It is scarcely surprising, then, that Bach scholars should for some time now have given considerable attention to this wider area of research,[1] though without, admittedly, singling out the topic 'Zelter and C. P. E. Bach' for special treatment.

If an attempt is made in what follows to outline Zelter's appreciation of the personality and the output of J. S. Bach's second son, this is done in the understanding that many new and unexplored avenues of research on this subject will continue to open up in the future. It is no more possible, on the basis of the few surviving examples, to conduct an exhaustive survey of Zelter's instrumental output, and in particular to assess whether it shows any signs of Bach's influence, than it is to reconstruct from what little remains of the 'Anwesenheitsbücher' of the Berlin Singakademie[2] an accurate picture of the performance of Bach's music. Nor is a great deal known about the range, composition, or present whereabouts of Zelter's musical library, which contains a great many of Bach's works, and was among the finest and most valuable in Berlin. Research in this area is particularly complicated since, owing to the loss of the greater part of the library of the Singakademie, crucial evidence is missing concerning the route by which many of Bach's original manuscripts were handed down. The ideas put forward in this paper are

---

[1] See in this connection Georg Schünemann, 'Die Bachpflege der Berliner Singakademie', *BJ*, 25 (1928), 138–71, and *Die Singakademie zu Berlin 1791–1941* (Regensburg, 1941); Erwin R. Jacobi, 'C. F. Zelters kritische Beleuchtung von J. N. Forkels Buch über J. S. Bach, aufgrund neu aufgefundener Dokumente', *International Musicological Society Congress Report*, 11 (Copenhagen, 1972), 462–6; Hans-Joachim Schulze, *Studien zur Bach-Überlieferung im 18. Jahrhundert* (Leipzig and Dresden, 1984), especially chap. 4, 'Überlieferung in Berlin', pp. 128–45.

[2] According to information kindly supplied by Dr Rudolf Elvers, director of the *Musikabteilung* at D-brd B, the surviving 'diaries' (*Tagebücher*) of the Berlin Singakademie go back no further than 1828. The volume containing records from 1828 to 1847 has the shelf-mark Mus. SA 290. Nothing is known about the whereabouts of the 'diaries' from 1791 to 1827.

derived principally from two hitherto largely neglected essays by Zelter on the sons of Bach, currently housed in the Goethe- und Schiller-Archiv in Weimar.[3]

In a later version of his *Kurzer Lebenslauf*, dated 1 November 1793 and published twenty years afterwards almost word for word in Gerber's *Neues historisch-biographisches Lexikon der Tonkünstler*,[4] Zelter writes: 'I was fortunate enough to obtain a few scores by C. P. E. Bach and Hasse at the very beginning. By studying these masters I made early acquaintance with two essential features of a good work of art—order and unity. Thereby I acquired some skill in lending lightness to my ideas and a certain fluency to my inner parts . . . My models, Bach and Hasse, were my idols; I prayed to them, worked and suffered for them, and I consoled myself by them.'[5]

By this stage (c.1774–5), Zelter had already taken lessons in harpsichord and organ playing from Johann Ernst Rosskämmer the younger, organist of the church in Dorotheenstadt, and he was anxious now to acquire the technical skill for composition.[6] At times he even toyed with the idea of going to Hamburg, in order 'to enjoy tuition from Bach'.[7] There are two handwritten remarks to this effect in Zelter's *Selbstbiographie*.[8] His earliest attempts at composition took the form of a few sonatas, symphonies, and a sacred work; this is implied in a passage contained in Zelter's biography of Fasch.[9]

It cannot be established which of Bach's works the young Zelter knew, or to what extent they influenced his early style, since not one of his works from this period has survived. The concerto in E flat for viola and orchestra,[10] written c. 1779 and thus the earliest known instrumental work by Zelter, belongs

---

[3]  Zelter's writings on C. P. E. Bach have the shelf-mark GSA 95/I, 4. Their contents are quoted and analysed in detail below.

[4]  Ernst Ludwig Gerber, *Neues historisch-biographisches Lexikon der Tonkünstler*, 4 vols. (Leipzig, 1812–14), vol. 4, col. 633.

[5]  *Carl Friedrich Zelters Darstellungen seines Lebens zum ersten Male vollständig nach den Handschriften*, ed. Johann-Wolfgang Schottländer (Weimar, 1931), 4: 'Ich war so glücklich, gleich im Anfange einige Partituren von Carl Philipp Emanuel Bach und Hasse zu bekommen. Durch das Studium dieser Meister lernte ich zuerst zwei wesentliche Eigenschaften guter Kunstwerke— Ordnung und Einheit—kennen. Dadurch gewann ich eine Art von Fertigkeit, meinen Gedanken Leichtigkeit und meinen Mittelstimmen einigen Fluß zu geben. . . . Meine Modelle, Bach und Hasse, waren meine Gottheit; zu diesen betete ich, für diese arbeitete ich,—litt ich; mit diesen tröstete ich mich.'

[6]  For biographical data see in particular Zelter, *Darstellungen*.

[7]  Ibid., p. 317: 'Bachs Unterricht zu genießen'.

[8]  Schottländer comments upon the passage, 'I now made up my mind to receive proper instruction in harmony from Fasch, who was so busy, however, that he could not take on any pupils' (p. 128) as follows: 'at this point in the autograph [of the original *Selbstbiographie*] there appears for the second time a marginal comment of great biographical interest written in pencil in Zelter's hand: "examination and journey to Hamburg, my intention being to enjoy tuition from Bach" '. Zelter, *Darstellungen*, p. 317.

[9]  Carl Friedrich Zelter, *Carl Friedrich Christian Fasch* (Berlin, 1801), 24. The passage in question is also quoted below (n. 24).

[10]  The manuscript of this work is in B Bc. Manuscript copies were circulated by J. C. F. Rellstab of Berlin. Printed editions have been issued by R. Jauch, E. Lüdeke, and D. Hallmann.

clearly within the tradition of the North German concerto, although the use of an instrumental recitative in the finale is a thoroughly Bachian feature. The expressive thematic material of the Adagio, with its powerful dynamic contrasts, echoes the concerto slow movements of the 'Hamburg Bach'. It must be remembered that C. P. E. Bach's music, especially the keyboard and orchestral works, was widely circulated in the last decades of the eighteenth century in both manuscript and printed copies,[11] and also that Bach was regarded as an authority in musical circles in the city where he had worked for so many years. So it is easy to understand how Zelter came to take an interest in this composer.

Recognizing the inadequacy of his efforts to teach himself, Zelter took lessons in composition from Carl Friedrich Christian Fasch between 1784 and 1786, though not without initial opposition to the idea from the latter.[12] It seems probable that Zelter came into further contact with Bach's music during this period, for C. P. E. Bach was one of Fasch's own artistic idols.[13] The two were friends, in fact, and had been employed in the same capacity in Frederick the Great's musical establishment.[14] The founder of the Berlin Singakademie contributed to Bach's *Musikalisches Vielerley* (1770)[15] and possessed manuscript copies of some of his works, though he was later to destroy almost all of these together with works of his own.[16]

It is safe to conclude, on the evidence of the many references to Bach contained in Zelter's biography of Fasch, that Zelter also obtained much biographical information and other details concerning Bach from Fasch. In the same way Zelter was to rely heavily on what he had learned from his revered teacher in the memorial speech for Frederick the Great that he delivered in Königsberg on 17 January 1809.[17]

[11] In connection with the history of music in Berlin in the 18th century see the literature listed in Hans-Günter Ottenberg, ed., *Der Critische Musicus an der Spree. Berliner Musikschrifttum von 1748 bis 1799* (Leipzig, 1984), 380–3, and especially E. Eugene Helm, *Music at the Court of Frederick the Great* (Norman, Oklahoma, 1960). Detailed information concerning C. P. E. Bach sources in Berlin and their provenance is given in Ernst Suchalla, *Die Orchestersinfonien Carl Philipp Emanuel Bachs nebst einem thematischen Verzeichnis seiner Orchesterwerke* (Augsburg, 1968); Rachel W. Wade, *The Keyboard Concertos of Carl Philipp Emanuel Bach* (Ann Arbor, 1981); and the prefaces of Darrell M. Berg, ed., *The Collected Works for Solo Keyboard by Carl Philipp Emanuel Bach*, 6 vols. (New York, 1985).

[12] A brief account of the composer and harpsichordist C. F. C. Fasch is given in Helm, *Music at the Court*, pp. 208–15.

[13] Several allusions to this are made in Zelter's biography of Fasch. See Zelter, *Fasch*, pp. 16, 23–4, 47. According to a report by Kirnberger, Fasch was also a first-rate performer of C. P. E. Bach's keyboard music: 'I have never heard Sebastian's music better played than by him, and the music of the Hamburg Bach he played even better.' (Quoted in Zelter, *Darstellungen*, p. 128.) Fasch also took out a subscription for some of Bach's published works, e.g. the six *Flügel-Concerte*, H. 471–6/W. 43 (1772) and *Herrn Doctor Cramers übersetzte Psalmen mit Melodien zum Singen bey dem Claviere* H. 733/W. 196 (1774).

[14] Fasch was appointed to the post of second harpsichordist early in 1756.

[15] He contributed two keyboard sonatas, in F and C.     [16] See Zelter, *Fasch*, p. 39.

[17] See Carl Hermann Bitter, *Carl Philipp Emanuel und Wilhelm Friedemann Bach und deren Brüder*, 2 vols. (Berlin, 1868), i. 181–2.

In the composition of character pieces, which formed a part of his training,[18] Zelter had further cause to study the example of Bach. These miniatures, each supplied with an arresting French title, enjoyed quite extraordinary popularity in Berlin,[19] and Zelter must at least have known *La Coorl*, the third movement of the keyboard sonata in A minor, H. 143/W. 65, 33.[20] His own *La Malade*, published in Rellstab's *Clavier-Magazin für Kenner und Liebhaber*[21] in 1787 (i.e. immediately after the period of study with Fasch) is characterized by strongly individualized thematic ideas, although it suffers from overuse of sequence and a stereotyped modulatory scheme (at one point a passage of 26 measures is devoted to a single idea), so that the initial promise of the material is not fully realized. The extent to which Zelter's technically and musically demanding *Sonata per il Clavicembalo solo* in C minor (1790)[22] is indebted to C. P. E. Bach's keyboard style merits closer study.

Such stylistic influence should not be overestimated, however; the superiority of a composer enshrouded with the aura of an *Originalgenie* was more likely to inhibit than to stimulate the creative inspiration of a young musician, and it is clear that this was the case from a remark by Fasch which Zelter quotes. Although the name of the young composer mentioned in the following extract is not given, there can be no doubt, in view of the similarity of content with that of the passage quoted earlier from the *Kurzer Lebenslauf*,[23] that it is Zelter who is meant.

To a young man who had asked Fasch for instruction he put the question: what have you already composed? The reply was: that he had written symphonies, sonatas, and a sacred work, in which he would have broken every rule, had he not acquired a certain light from the scores of Bach and Hasse, on whose style he was keen to model his own. There you have chosen dangerous models, Fasch replied, which you are unlikely to surpass. You will be much safer if you can get started on a path of your own, for there is

---

[18] In his *Selbstbiographie* Zelter writes: 'Finally we turned our attention to three-part writing, which I had to practise not in the normal manner with an instrumental trio, but with voices alone to a text, which was one of the most difficult tasks imaginable. After this I moved on to the so-called character pieces and French dances. . . .' (Zelter, *Darstellungen*, pp. 155–6).

[19] See Hans-Günter Ottenberg, *Carl Philipp Emanuel Bach*, trans. Philip Whitmore (Oxford, 1987), 102, and the article by Darrell Berg in this volume.

[20] See Zelter, *Fasch*, p. 8, and also below.

[21] *Clavier-Magazin für Kenner und Liebhaber*, first quarter (Berlin, 1787), 5–8 (see RISM for details). In giving the date of composition as 1792, both Martin Geck, 'Zelter, Carl Friedrich', *MGG*, vol. 14, col. 1210, and Raymond A. Barr, 'Zelter, Carl Friedrich', *New Grove*, xx. 665, are incorrect. That this anthology belongs entirely to the tradition of *Musikalisches Mancherley* (1762–3) and of Bach's *Musikalisches Vielerley* (1770) is evident from a remark by a contemporary of Zelter, who calls it 'a keyboard periodical containing many character pieces like those of Bach'. Quoted in *Bemerkungen eines Reisenden über zu Berlin vom September 1787 bis Ende Januar 1788 gegebenen öffentlichen Musiken* (Halle, 1788), 29.

[22] According to the *Selbstbiographie* this was published in 1790 by Rellstab in Berlin, perhaps as Op. 3. See Zelter, *Darstellungen*, pp. 3, 305.

[23] Zelter, *Darstellungen*, p. 4, see n. 5.

nothing more for us to search out along their path; at best we can follow after them, but they are forever blocking the way.[24]

C. P. E. Bach's music continued to be performed in Berlin even after his departure for Hamburg in 1768. His works were cultivated in various aristocratic and middle-class musical circles, for example by Princess Anna Amalia of Prussia[25] and by the Jewish banker Itzig, whose daughter Sara Levy (née Itzig) was to be one of the most enthusiastic collectors of Bach's music.[26] The fact that much of his keyboard music was readily available in comtemporary printed editions and manuscripts, or that there were as many as five editions of his *Gellert-Lieder* within Bach's own lifetime,[27] suggests that his music was widely cultivated in domestic circles too. His larger works were also performed occasionally in the Prussian capital. Reichardt attended a performance of the *Passions-Cantate* in St Peter's Church in 1774,[28] and in 1779 the people of Berlin had an opportunity to hear Bach's *Heilig*, as we know from one of Kirnberger's letters.[29]

So it is easy to understand how Zelter would also have come to know and to treasure the music of C. P. E. Bach as a performer. In the 1770s he played the violin in the amateur orchestra directed by Carl Friedrich Sebaldt, a registrar in the Royal Treasury.[30] According to a remark in Zelter's *Selbstbiographie*, this

---

[24] Zelter, *Fasch*, p. 24: 'Einen jungen Mann, der um Faschens Unterricht bat, fragte er: was er schon componirt hätte? Die Antwort war: daß er Sinfonieen, Sonaten und eine Kirchenmusik gemacht hätte, wobei es ihm an jeder Regel gefehlt haben würde, wenn er nicht durch die Partituren des Bach und Hasse, nach welchen er sich gern bilden wollte, einiges Licht bekommen hätte. Da haben Sie sich ein paar gefährliche Männer zu Mustern gewählt, sagte er, die Sie schwer übertreffen werden; Sie werden aber weit sicherer Ihren eignen Weg gehen, wenn Sie einen Eingang finden können, denn auf jenem Wege ist für uns nichts mehr zu suchen, man kann höchstens nachfolgen und sie stehen einem überall im Wege.'

[25] The music library of Princess Anna Amalia of Prussia included many works by C. P. E. Bach. See the following items from the Amalien-Bibliothek: 53–4, 85–9, 92–101, 107–10, 115, 170, 215?, 479, 505, 554–5, as listed in Eva R. Blechschmidt, *Die Amalien-Bibliothek, Musikbibliothek der Prinzessin Anna Amalia von Preussen (1723–1787). Historische Einordnung und Katalog mit Hinweisen auf die Schreiber der Handschriften* (Berlin, 1965).

[26] Sara Levy, neé Itzig, was a subscriber to some of C. P. E. Bach's works. She took out a subscription to the six collections 'für Kenner und Liebhaber', to the six *Flügel-Concerte*, H. 471–6/W. 43, and to *Klopstocks Morgengesang am Schöpfungsfeste*, H. 779/W. 239, among other works.

[27] They appeared in 1758, 1759, 1764, 1771 and 1784.

[28] See Johann Friedrich Reichardt, *Briefe eines aufmerksamen Reisenden die Musik betreffend*, vol. 1 (Frankfurt am Main and Leipzig, 1774), 111–12.

[29] He wrote to Forkel in 1779 as follows: 'Bach's *Heilig* was performed here, and the fugue lasted exactly 11 minutes. I disapproved, because it completely ruined it. Herr Bach in Hamburg, to whom I declared that 5 minutes was the maximum duration appropriate for it, sent me the following letter [of 16 Dec. 1779, quoted in Bitter, *Carl Philipp Emanuel*, ii. 300] and put the time at 3 minutes, and it seems to me that 4 minutes would be ideal, but 11 minutes is enough to drive anyone mad.' (Quoted in Bitter, *Carl Philipp Emanuel*, ii. 323). See also Heinrich Miesner, *Philipp Emanuel Bach in Hamburg* (Leipzig, 1929), 97. C. P. E. Bach's *Passions-Cantate* was also performed several times in Berlin, for there are three librettos of this work in existence that were printed there. See Stephen L. Clark, 'The Occasional Choral Works of C. P. E. Bach', Ph.D. diss., Princeton University, 1984, 53.

[30] Zelter, *Darstellungen*, pp. 109–11.

orchestra 'performed the most difficult symphonies, concertos, and overtures by Bach, Graun, Goldberg, Müthel, Benda, Handel, Wolf, Geminiani, Vivaldi, Tartini, Hasse, Kirnberger, and Quantz . . . in a correct and natural manner'.[31]

It is possible that the high opinion of Bach's music which Zelter was often to express in later years originated during this period. From 1787 to 1788 Zelter was the leader of Johann Carl Friedrich Rellstab's *Concert für Kenner und Liebhaber*,[32] performing works by Gluck, Hasse, Naumann, J. A. P. Schulz, C. P. E. Bach, etc. In April 1787 the latter's *Magnificat* was performed, a work which had been composed nearly forty years earlier.[33] The anonymous author[34] of *Bemerkungen eines Reisenden über zu Berlin vom September 1787 bis Ende Januar 1788 gegebenen öffentlichen Musiken* deplores the poor quality of the choral singing, but is otherwise full of praise for the performance,[35] in particular Zelter's playing: 'It is Zelter who actually directs the performance; he is an attentive and discreet violinist who at the same time plays with great power.'[36] The writer adds that symphonies by Bach and Haydn were performed as well.[37] Guttmann suspects that there may have been a performance of C. P. E. Bach's *Heilig* and of his oratorio *Die Israeliten in der Wüste* in the course of this series of subscription concerts.[38] To summarize, then, Zelter would have become acquainted with a great many of Bach's works even before joining the Singakademie in 1791.

In 1800 Zelter succeeded Fasch as director of the Berlin Singakademie. In the ensuing years this choral society and the Ripienschule, the orchestra associated with it, performed many of Bach's compositions. There seems to have been a particular concentration on works by Bach from 1813 onwards,[39] made possible mainly by the constant enlargement of the library of the

---

[31] Ibid., p. 110: 'schwersten Sinfonien, Konzerte und Overtüren der Bach, Graun, Goldberg, Müthel, Benda, Händel, Wolf, Geminiani, Vivaldi, Tartini, Hasse, Kirnberger und Quantz . . . sicher und näturlich aufgeführt.'

[32] See Schünemann, *Singakademie*, p. 6.

[33] See O. Guttmann, *Johann Karl Friedrich Rellstab. Ein Beitrag zur Musikgeschichte Berlins* (Berlin, 1910), 30. A score of the *Magnificat* in Rellstab's hand was included in Zelter's estate (i.e. the Singakademie library). See Guttmann, *Rellstab*, p. 30. It appears that there had also been earlier performances of this work in Berlin, or so the existence of parts dating from between 1750 and 1770 would suggest. See the preface to C. P. E. Bach, *Magnificat*, H. 772/W. 215, ed. G. Graulich (Neuhausen-Stuttgart, 1971).

[34] Probably the Weimar court Kapellmeister Ernst Wilhelm Wolf.

[35] *Bemerkungen eines Reisenden*, p. 36.

[36] Ibid., pp. 33–4: '[Dieser] ist der eigentliche Anführer; er ist ein aufmerksamer und discreter Violinist, der dabei große Kraft hat.'

[37] Ibid., p. 40: 'The first and most difficult of Bach's four published orchestral symphonies [H. 663/W. 183, 1] I heard performed here, and indeed it was such that a better performance, while it might be imagined, would scarcely be possible. One can hear that this orchestra is aflame with spirit and love for art.'

[38] Guttmann, *Rellstab*, p. 31.          [39] See Schünemann, *Singakademie*, pp. 44–5.

Singakademie. At this point Zelter's merits as a collector of Bachiana enter the picture.[40]

Even if this passion for collecting was chiefly directed towards meeting the practical needs of the Singakademie, providing for the constant enlargement of its repertoire, and for the setting up of a musical archive at some future stage,[41] Zelter still managed at the same time to derive from a thorough study of this unique treasure a profound knowledge of musical history, for which he left ample evidence in his correspondence with Goethe and elsewhere. Zelter's musical library was both extensive and valuable; since, however, he was not always careful to distinguish between his private possessions and those of the Singakademie, there were to be complicated negotiations between his heirs and the leadership of the choral society after Zelter's death in 1832.[42] On 30 May 1810 Zelter wrote to Georg Poelchau in Hamburg as follows:

My collection of valuable antiquities, the posthumous disposal of which I have already begun to plan, has grown remarkably in recent times, and I have just purchased for myself the best items from the Kittel publishing firm in Erfurth,[43] and when you come to Berlin you will have the pleasure of finding a catalogue with the names of more than a thousand fine composers, and the greatest and most excellent works that the best of them have produced: the works of the Bachs, Handel, Hasse, Graun, Leo, Lotti, Rosenmüller, Geminiani, Marcello, Durante, etc., all practically complete, except that I haven't any manuscripts at all, nor anything by Seb. Bach or C. P. E. Bach.[44]

In the same letter Zelter had thanked Poelchau for sending two choruses by the Bachs, father and son. In looking through these manuscripts, one a copy of the chorale movement 'Vom Himmel hoch da komm' ich her' from the *Magnificat*, BWV 243, and the other a copy of a late version of the 'Et misericordia eius' from C. P. E. Bach's *Magnificat*, Zelter had discovered some errors, and so he

[40] In the course of his work on a catalogue of the Amalien-Bibliothek (D-ddr Bds. Mus. ms. autogr. theor. C. F. Zelter, 5) from 1800 to 1802, Zelter came to know a great many of C. P. E. Bach's works. See n. 25 above.

[41] Zelter and Poelchau were strong supporters of the idea of setting up such an 'Archiv der musikalischen Kunst'. See Karl-Heinz Köhler, 'Die Musikabteilung', *Deutsche Staatsbibliothek 1661–1961*, pt. 1, 'Geschichte und Gegenwart' (Leipzig, 1961), 243, and also K. Engler, *Georg Poelchau und seine Musiksammlung. Ein Beitrag zur Überlieferung Bachscher Musik in der ersten Hälfte des 19. Jahrhunderts*, Ph.D. diss., Tübingen, 1984, 2 ff.

[42] See Schünemann, *Singakademie*, pp. 71–2.

[43] J. C. Kittel had died the previous year. In connection with this music collector from Erfurt see Schulze, *Studien zur Bach-Überlieferung, passim*.

[44] D-ddr Bds, Mus. ep. C. F. Zelter, 58. Also quoted in Schünemann, *Singakademie*, pp. 68–9: 'Meine Sammlung trefflicher alter Sachen über die ich schon eine Verfügung nach meinem Tode entworfen habe, hat in den letzten Zeiten einen merklichen Zuwachs erhalten, auch habe ich kürzlich aus dem Kittelschen Verlag zu Erfurth das Beste an mich gekauft und Sie sollen sich freuen wenn Sie nach Berlin kommen, ein Namenregister von mehr als Tausend braven Componisten vorzufinden und von den Besten das Meiste und Vorzüglichste was sie geleistet haben. Die Werke der Bach, Händel, Hasse, Graun, Leo, Lotti, Rosenmüller, Geminiani, Marcello, Durante u.a. ganz oder beynahe complett nur an Handschriften von Seb. Bach u. C. P. E. Bach habe ich gar nichts.'

asked Poelchau straight away if he might on future occasions borrow the original manuscripts. In this request may be seen one of Zelter's guiding principles: the importance of source study as a basis for judgements of a stylistic, aesthetic, or technical nature. Without such sound and painstaking study of the works and their sources, Zelter could not have maintained his reputation as a first-rate Bach scholar, and an expert also on the music of C. P. E. Bach. Later in the same letter Zelter wrote, 'Your intention to bequeath your musical treasures to the Singakademie is divinely inspired, and I cannot commend it highly enough.'[45]

Georg Schünemann has described in detail the dissemination of Poelchau's library which then began.[46] Parts of it he sold in 1811 to Abraham Mendelssohn, who in turn passed them on to the Singakademie. Zelter wrote to thank him on 29 June 1811:

My excellent friend, you have earned yourself great and prolonged thanks for the magnificent treasures which the Singakademie will preserve in your honour. I cannot answer your question fully, since no catalogue was included with the material. I have looked through it all already, but the cataloguing must await my return, and then you too will receive a complete list. Meanwhile I enclose the printed catalogue[47] of Bach's estate. You can see from this what I have received: namely the items underlined in red.'[48]

Altogether forty-two items by J. S. Bach, together with compositions by W. F. and J. C. Bach, Zelenka, Hasse, C. H. and J. G. Graun, C. F. C. Fasch, etc., as well as twenty-four works by C. P. E. Bach are indicated in red crayon by Zelter in this copy of the *Nachlass-Verzeichniß*. The works by Bach which the Singakademie could have performed are mainly vocal compositions, among them the *Magnificat*, H. 772/W. 215, the *Passions-Cantate*, H. 776/W. 233, the settings of the Passion according to St Matthew (1768–9) and St Luke (1786–7), H. 782 and H. 800/W. 234, and the Easter cantata *Gott hat den Herrn auferweckt*, H. 803/W. 244. In subsequent years further works by Bach found their way from Poelchau's growing collection into the possession of Zelter and the Singakademie. In the course of the disputes over Zelter's estate, moreover,

[45] Ibid., and in Schünemann, *Singakademie*, p. 69: 'Ihren Vorsatz der Singakademie Ihre musikalischen Schätze zu vermachen ist ein Göttergedanke, den ich nicht genug loben kann.'
[46] Ibid., pp. 68–71. A brief account of the C. P. E. Bach material, particularly the concertos, formerly owned by the Berlin Singakademie is given in Wade, *Keyboard Concertos*, pp. 43–4. See also the article by Elias Kulukundis in this volume.
[47] The copy of *NV* mentioned in Zelter's letter is currently in D-ddr Bds, Db. 312.
[48] D-ddr Bds, Mus. ep. C. F. Zelter, p. 42, and in Schünemann, *Singakademie*, pp. 69–70: 'Sie haben mein trefflicher Freund, sich einen großen und langen Dank verdient für die herrlichen Schätze, welche die Singakademie zu Ihren Ehren aufbewahren wird. Ihre Frage kann ich nicht ganz befriedigen, da kein Verzeichniß bey den Sachen war. Durchgesehen habe ich schon alles doch die Katalogirung muß anstehn bis nach meiner Zurückkunft, dann soll auch Ihnen ein Verzeichniß eingehändigt werden. Das gedr. Verzeichniß lege ich einstweilen bey, von Bachs Verlaßenschaft. Hieraus können Sie sehn, was ich empfangen habe: es sind die roth angestrichenen Sachen.'

it was established that Poelchau had sold a large group of works by C. P. E. Bach to Abraham Mendelssohn between 1805 and 1808.[49] He in turn gave them to Sara Levy, who subsequently left the vocal items to the Singakademie and the instrumental works to the Ripienschule.[50] Some remnants of Fasch's estate had also survived, including an anthology containing keyboard works by the 'Hamburg Bach', and also six keyboard fugues,[51] both in Fasch's hand.[52]

In 1835, then, after the dispute with Zelter's heirs had been settled, the Singakademie had at its disposal an extraordinarily well-stocked library of C. P. E. Bach's music, quite on a par with the collection of Bach manuscripts in Poelchau's library. Welter's fine catalogue[53] of those works by C. P. E. Bach still owned by the library of the Singakademie in 1930 contains examples of works in every genre in autographs, manuscript copies, and printed editions.[54]

Some items from Zelter's collection of Bachiana found their way into Goethe's possession. On 11 April 1815 Zelter wrote to his friend in Weimar:

This may serve as a good opportunity to send you a few autographs of remarkable men. And even if you should already possess something in the hands of these men, the items themselves are of historical and artistic significance, especially the one by Sebastian Bach[55] and the one by Kirnberger.[56] You can find an explanation of the piece entitled 'La Coorl' in *Faschens Leben*.[57]

The last-named work is identical with the third movement of C. P. E. Bach's keyboard sonata in A minor, H. 143/W. 65, 33, one of the relatively few solo works to survive in Bach's own hand. This sonata was included in Goethe's collection of autographs, and is now located in the Goethe- und Schiller-Archiv in Weimar.[58] The manuscript consists of two folios (i.e. four sides of music),

---

[49] Schünemann, *Singakademie*, p. 71.   [50] Ibid.

[51] Possibly a copy of the *Six fugues pour le piano-forte* published by N. Simrock, (H. 99–102, and the second movement of H. 75.5/W. 119).

[52] See Friedrich Welter, 'Die Musikbibliothek der Sing-Akademie zu Berlin. Versuch eines Nachweises ihrer früheren Bestände', *Sing-Akademie zu Berlin*, ed. W. Bollert (Berlin, 1966), 38.

[53] Ibid.

[54] See the article by Elias Kulukundis in this volume.

[55] It is not known which piece by J. S. Bach is meant here.

[56] According to H.-J. Schreckenbach, ed., *Goethes Autographensammlung. Katalog* (Weimar, 1961), 120, no. 869, this refers to a manuscript of contrapuntal exercises and a three-part invention in E minor.

[57] See Zelter, *Fasch*, p. 8. Quoted in *Der Briefwechsel zwischen Goethe und Zelter*, ed. M. Hecker, 3 vols. (Leipzig, 1913–18), i. 415–16; 'Die gute Gelegenheit mag dazu dienen, Dir einige Autographa merkwürdiger Hände zu überschicken. Und sollte auch von diesen Händen schon etwas in Deiner Sammlung sein, so sind die Stücke selbst in geschichtlich-artistischer Hinsicht bedeutend, besonders das Stück von Sebastian Bach und das von Kirnberger. Über das Stück mit der Überschrift "La Coorl" findest Du in "Faschens Leben" Aufschluß.'

[58] No. 33 in Goethe's collection of autographs; shelf-mark GSA 33/33. See also Schreckenbach, *Goethes Autographensammlung*, 10, no. 60. The history of this manuscript and of the hands through which it has passed must await further investigation.

measuring 21 cm by 34.5 cm. The sequence of movements is as follows: Allegretto—Adagio ma non troppo: *La Guillelmine*—Tempo di Minuetto: *La Coorl*. The inscription 'No. 106', which appears in Bach's hand at the top left-hand corner of the first page (see Facsimile 1), evidently refers to an earlier catalogue of Bach's works—possibly to the *Katalog von seinen Klavierwerken bis 1772*,[59] for this work is listed as no. 113 in *NV* under the heading 'Clavier Soli'. At the end of the last page Zelter has noted: 'This sheet is written entirely in the composer's hand.' The titles *La Guillelmine* and *La Coorl* are mentioned neither in *NV* nor in Wotquenne's thematic catalogue, though they do occur in some contemporary manuscript copies.[60] Zelter apparently knew this sonata before 1801, for he refers to it in his biography of Fasch.[61]

The extensive holdings of the Singakademie library made it possible to perform a wide-ranging repertoire of choral music, and so many a work from the past was revived for the present. While at first a cappella music predominated, it was not long before choral works with instrumental accompaniment were added to the repertoire, particularly after the establishment of the Ripienschule in 1807. The masters of Italian vocal polyphony of the sixteenth and seventeenth centuries, J. S. Bach (the long association of the Berlin Singakademie with the music of the elder Bach had begun with study of the motets, and was to reach a peak with the memorable performance of the *St Matthew Passion* in 1829), Handel, Caldara, Fux—these composers were all represented in the repertoire of the Singakademie, and they indicate the historical breadth of its outlook. At the same time contemporary works and those of the recent

[59] According to Welter, 'Musikbibliothek', p. 38, this catalogue was among the autographs owned by the Singakademie. The position of the catalogue number 106 corresponds to that used in some of Bach's other keyboard works, e.g. the D major sonata H. 56/W. 65, 22 (D-brd B, Mus. ms. Bach P 776). Darrell Berg links the figure 54 found in this source with *NV*; see 'Towards a Catalogue of the Keyboard Sonatas of C. P. E. Bach', *JAMS*, 32 (1979), 282. A similar attempt to link the sonata in A minor H. 143/W. 65, 33 with *NV* does not work, hence the author's reference to a further possible catalogue.

[60] Second movement: D-ddr Bds, Mus. ms. 30385 and D-brd Kll, Mb 50–10: *La Guillelmine*; third movement: D-ddr Bds, Mus. ms. 30385: *La Coorl*. See also E. Eugene Helm, 'The "Hamlet" Fantasy and the Literary Element in C. P. E. Bach's Music', *MQ*, 58 (1972), 293 n. 24.

[61] Zelter, *Fasch*, p. 8. Further evidence that autographs by C. P. E. Bach were sent to Goethe is provided by Zelter's letter to the poet of 17 Mar. 1822: 'Included with the Bach sonatas there is also an autograph—a collector's item which alone is worth more than the entire manuscript written by the former Kapellmeister of Gotha, Stölzel.' (*Der Briefwechsel zwischen Goethe und Zelter*, vol. 2, 161.) By 'Bach sonatas' Zelter means C. P. E. Bach's organ sonatas H. 84–7 and 133–4/W. 70, which were intended for practical use by the Berka inspector of baths, J. H. F. Schütz (1779–1829), who was a competent organist and harpsichordist. Schütz had also received music from Zelter before. On 6 July 1816 Zelter observed in his diary: 'To the latter [Organist Schütz] the 6 fugues by C. P. E. Bach promised.' (Quoted in Zelter, *Darstellungen*, p. 265.) Schütz had repeatedly performed for Goethe compositions by J. S. and C. P. E. Bach, and Handel, among others; see *Der Briefwechsel zwischen Goethe und Zelter*, ii. 4 (Goethe's letter of 4 Jan. 1819). According to information kindly supplied by Frau C. Rudnik of the Goethe- und Schiller-Archiv in Weimar, none of the works mentioned in Zelter's letter of 17 Mar. 1822 is present today in Goethe's collections of autographs or of other music.

Facsimile 1. Sonata in A minor H. 143/W. 65, 33, i. D-ddr WRgs, GSA 33/33

past were by no means neglected, and the choral society set high artistic standards with its performance of Mozart's Requiem and of Haydn's oratorios *The Creation* and *The Seasons*.[62] To establish a more or less complete chronology of performances by the Singakademie[63] and the Ripienschule of works by C. P. E. Bach is at present impossible, and so recourse must be had to scattered clues contained in the secondary literature, particularly in the writings of Miesner[64] and Schünemann.[65]

In 1814 the *Passions-Cantate* was added to the repertoire.[66] It will be remembered that Zelter had obtained from Poelchau's library a manuscript score of this work,[67] which remained unpublished during the composer's lifetime. In the same year Bach's *Heilig* was also heard for the first time,[68] and Zelter's arrangement of this work was to become a standard item in the repertoire of the Singakademie. We know from a letter that Zelter wrote to Goethe that this same work was also performed by another choir in April 1828 under Spontini's direction:

In order to sanctify such a day [the Day of Atonement], our *Generalmusikdirektor* Spontini has established a charity for musicians; sacred works for choir and orchestra are performed in the theatre.
Today's selection consisted of choice rarities: two powerful symphonies by Beethoven, half of a Mass setting by the same, half of a Credo by Sebastian Bach, and a German Sanctus by Emanuel Bach.[69]

While the reporter writing for the *Allgemeine Musikalische Zeitung* found words of praise,[70] the review in the *Berliner Allgemeine musikalische Zeitung* signed by

---

[62] The standard texts on the history of the Berlin Singakademie are the following: Martin Blumner, *Geschichte der Singakademie zu Berlin* (Berlin, 1891); Schünemann, *Singakademie* (see n. 1 above); *Sing-Akademie zu Berlin*, ed. Werner Bollert (Berlin, 1966).

[63] Other Berlin choirs besides the Singakademie gave performances of Bach's vocal works. Miesner, in *Bach in Hamburg*, p. 73, assumes that a performance of the oratorio *Die Israeliten in der Wüste* was included in Rellstab's concerts. See also Guttmann, *Rellstab*, p. 33. The *Berlinische Zeitung von Staats- und gelehrten Sachen* of 17 Mar. 1828 gives notice of a concert to be given on 19 Mar. by the singing class of the Gymnasium zum Grauen Kloster with this same work.

[64] Miesner, *Bach in Hamburg*.                        [65] Schünemann, *Singakademie*, pp. 28 ff.

[66] Ibid., p. 45.                                                        [67] See above.

[68] Schünemann, *Singakademie*, p. 45. According to Günter Graulich, preface to C. P. E. Bach, *Heilig*, H. 778/W. 217 (Neuhausen-Stuttgart, 1975), the manuscript in question was probably D-brd B, Mus. ms. Bach P 780.

[69] *Briefwechsel zwischen Goethe und Zelter*, iii. 28–9 (letter of 30 Apr. 1828): 'Solchen Tag [Bußtag] zu heiligen, hat unser Generalmusikdirektor Spontini eine wohltätige Stiftung für Musiker gemacht; da im Theater vom Orchester und den Sängern geistliche Stücke aufgeführt werden.
Die heutige Wahl bestand in auserlesenen Raritäten: zwei starke Sinfonien von Beethoven; eine halbe Messe von ebendiesem; ein halbes Credo von Sebastian Bach und ein deutsches Sanctus von Emanuel Bach.' The concert included Beethoven's Fifth Symphony, *Coriolan* Overture, and the Kyrie and Credo from his *Missa solemnis*, Op. 123; six movements of the Credo from J. S. Bach's B minor mass, BWV 232; and C. P. E. Bach's *Heilig*, H. 778/W. 217.

[70] See *AMZ*, 30 (1828), cols. 365–6.

A. B. Marx was thoroughly scathing about this C. P. E. Bach work. Marx criticized the way that it begins with a trite introductory movement.

It is said that this is by Emanuel Bach. As he himself admitted, he was obliged by the greatness of his father (or rather through the lack of an equally high calling) to pursue a different path,[71] and of this we need hardly remind ourselves; Spontini would surely have been convinced by his artistic sense alone of the inappropriateness of any introduction, to say nothing of the paltry example before us, had he only acquainted himself with the grandeur of the work he was tackling on this occasion. Stranger still, almost comical, was the *direct* juxtaposition of the *Heilig* with this trite *Ariette*, the hollow key-contrast between heaven and earth, and the wooden fugue 'Alle Lande sind . . . ' (sung in German, incidentally, after the Latin text of the Credo), following the enthusiastic shouts of joy in the 'Resurrexit' . . . [72]

In spite of Marx's violent attacks, which must be understood as a polemical expression of the viewpoint of the musical *Fortschrittspartei*[73] in Berlin, Bach's *Heilig*, in Zelter's arrangement for three unaccompanied choirs, was performed regularly by the Singakademie between 1829 and 1834.[74]

An undated essay by Zelter discovered by Heinrich Miesner among a set of parts of the *Heilig* provides information on Zelter's ideas about arrangement.[75]

[71] This statement by Marx is probably derived from Forkel. See Johann Nikolaus Forkel, *Ueber Johann Sebastian Bachs Leben, Kunst und Kunstwerke* (Leipzig, 1802), 44.

[72] *Berliner Allgemeine musikalische Zeitung* of 7 May 1828, 7 (1828), 154: 'eine leiermässige Einleitung vorausgeschickt [worden sei]. Man sagt, sie sei von Emanuel Bach. Wie dieser selbst gestanden hat, von der Grösse seines Vaters (eigentlich von dem Mangel gleich hohen Berufes) in eine andere Bahn gewiesen zu sein, darf nicht einmal erst in das Gedächtniss zurückgerufen werden; Spontini hätte durch Kunstsinn allein schon von der Unangemessenheit jeder, und von der Dürftigkeit dieser Einleitung überzeugt werden müssen, wenn er sich nur mit dem grossen Gegenstand seiner diesmaligen Thätigkeit vertraut gemacht hätte. Noch seltsamer, fast lächerlich war die *unmittelbare* Anknüpfung des *Heilig* mit seiner kleinlichen Ariette und seinem hohlen Modulationswechsel zwischen Himmel und Erde und der ledernen Fuge "Alle Lande sind u.s.w." (übrigens deutsche gesungen, nach dem lateinischen Texte des Credo) nach dem begeisterten Jubelruf des "Resurrexit" . . .'

[73] The term *Fortschrittspartei* indicates that A. B. Marx's principal concern was the promotion of contemporary music, Beethoven's instrumental style representing for him the culmination of all previous historical development. See A. Forschert, 'Adolf Bernhard Marx und seine "Berliner Allgemeine musikalische Zeitung" ', *Studien zur Musikgeschichte Berlins im 19. Jahrhundert*, ed. Carl Dalhaus (Regensburg, 1980), 381–404.

[74] See Blumner, *Singakademie*, pp. 33, 220; see also the reviews in *Berliner Allgemeine musikalische Zeitung*, 6 (1829), 394; and in the periodical *Iris im Gebiete der Tonkunst*, 2 (1831), 72: 'Berlin. On Sunday [26 Oct.] the Singakademie gave a concert in aid of poor cholera victims. Sadly it was poorly attended. The programme consisted of motets by Seb. Bach, the *Heilig* by Phil. E. Bach, several pieces by Fasch, a Sanctus by Spohr, and two motets by Zelter.'

[75] This Zelter manuscript is quoted in Miesner, *Bach in Hamburg*, pp. 95–6, and reproduced here in full: 'The idea which the great composer of the *Heilig* wished to bring directly to our attention lies without any doubt in the contrast of the two choirs with one another, as is sufficiently clear from the names he gave them: angels and peoples.

'The Choir of Angels is intended to represent the heavenly, the supernatural, and the Choir of Peoples the earthly, the natural; the two begin apart from one another, they seek one another, and they are finally united.

'So far everything in the performance and in the effect of the piece is easily explained. But now the question arises: how did the *Ariette* (so labelled by the composer), "Herr, werth daß Schaaren

He did not hold to be sacrilegious even such drastic changes in the dramatic character of a work as are involved here, namely in the re-scoring of orchestrally accompanied choral music in an a cappella style. In the case of certain of J. S. Bach's scores he would sometimes even distort the text by simplifying the melodic line, by omissions, etc.[76]

It has not been possible to ascertain whether the Singakademie performed C. P. E. Bach's oratorio *Auferstehung und Himmelfahrt Jesu* during Zelter's period of office.[77] Zelter certainly knew this work when he in his turn addressed himself to the task of setting Ramler's text to music, and he evidently assumed a high degree of familiarity with Bach's setting both within and outside Berlin. This also explains why Zelter omitted to set the bass aria 'Ihre Tore Gottes'. When questioned about this, he replied that Bach's setting of the aria was so colossal, so great, so divine, that perhaps any composer who tried to follow it

der Engel dir dienen'', attain the honour of being called an introduction to the *Heilig* itself, that is, to the chorus of angels? The diminutive label *Ariette, allegretto* already indicates a lighter, loose style, and the piece itself is somewhere in between something and nothing, the text is flat, the melody thin; suited neither to an alto, nor to a soprano; the expression is meagre, and the accompaniment is cast in an idiom more light-hearted than forceful, considering that it is supposed to depict a world in confusion. Only the bass line strides around with sufficient vigour to reveal something of the seriousness of the intention.

'My theory is as follows: Bach began to work on the *Heilig* thinking of this as the main part, but came to feel that the earthly choir needed to come first, before the choir of angels, if the desired effect was to be achieved. He considered a lively and bustling earthly life expressed in violin figuration to be both necessary and sufficient for this purpose, and since the piece is not an aria, he called it an *Ariette*, and wrote quite innocently against the title of the work: with two choruses *and* an *Ariette*; this alone seems to suggest that the *Ariette* is an appendix placed *at the beginning*, and for that very reason is not a genuine introduction to the *Heilig*.

'In these circumstances, then, lies the proper effect: after the key of G major the *Heilig* of the angelic choir enters in the key of E major with maximum impact, as if from the clouds.

'I arrived at these ideas while I was arranging the *Heilig for three choirs a cappella* for the use of the Singakademie. For there was no way that I could manage to arrange the *Ariette* without instruments: so I found it necessary to add a new chorus to the introductory movement, and I felt obliged to take note of the *key* and the *cadence* used by Bach.

'When it came to an attempt to perform this splendid piece as it appears in Bach's printed score [from the year 1779], a further difficulty emerged involving this very *Ariette*, in that among our best singers there was neither an alto nor a mezzo-soprano who felt able to render this piece comfortably and with the requisite energy, as is often enough the case with Bach's vocal line. Thus it was that the bass part [footnote by H. Miesner: 'by Zelter'], which is supplied in this score directly above the continuo bass line, first arose, and indeed a strong bass voice with a good sound can be heard even better. In the end it seemed to me that a four-part chorus, such as is written above this solo part, possessed greater sonority after all, and that it would have been better to let the chorus remain. Besides the score I also acquired from the estate of the late composer an autograph manuscript in which Bach himself had added a four-part chorus to the *Ariette*, and if we had known of this revision earlier, then we could certainly have saved ourselves ingenuity, but this simply goes to show that we not only pay tribute to our great masters, but that we also take pains to understand them.' The arrangement of the *Ariette* for four-part chorus that Zelter mentions has apparently not survived. See G. Graulich, preface to C. P. E. Bach, *Heilig*.

[76] Schünemann, 'Bachpflege der Berliner Singakademie', pp. 153–4.
[77] I am indebted to Dr Rudolf Elvers for the information that during the period from 1828 to 1832, at least, this work was not publicly performed by the Singakademie.

would be put to shame.[78] When Zelter's oratorio received its first performance in April 1807,[79] the reviewer in the *Allgemeine Musikalische Zeitung* wrote, among other things: 'It was interesting for the connoisseur to compare Zelter's setting with Bach's, and disappointing—if I might after all offer a word of criticism—to be deprived of the three very beautiful arias included in Bach's setting.'[80]

While it must be assumed that the performances of Bach's music which it has been possible to establish here represent only a small proportion of the total, the range of vocal works suitable for performance by the Singakademie seems in any case to have been fairly small. Passion settings, inauguration cantatas, Easter music, funeral music, etc. were all ruled out as possible repertoire on account of their functional character and their stylistic disunity—Zelter described C. P. E. Bach's church music as 'patched together'[81]—and on the other hand such major works as the *Magnificat, Die Israeliten in der Wüste*, and *Klopstocks Morgengesang am Schöpfungsfeste* did not manage to hold their own in the programmes of the Singakademie, perhaps through resistance from the public, but probably also on account of certain reservations felt by Zelter himself.[82]

Rather more evidence is available concerning performances of Bach's instrumental works by the Ripienschule. This group used to meet regularly on Friday evenings for rehearsals; on Thursday lunch-times in conjunction with the Singakademie older music would be given a hearing 'both complete and in extracts'.[83] At the very first meeting on 10 April 1807 works by C. P. E. Bach, Handel, and Hasse were played.[84] Under the date 29 January 1808, the *Journal für die Ripienschule* lists symphonies, keyboard concertos, and cello concertos by Bach.[85] On 25 March in the same year further works by the 'Hamburg Bach' were performed.[86] Schünemann, who has made a critical study of the *Journal*, has been able to ascertain that the incipits of the works performed have been recorded accurately, and that even the years of composition have been given for concertos by C. P. E. Bach.[87] Schünemann has also shown that in August 1813 orchestral pieces by Handel, Hasse, and C. P. E. Bach, 'who appears very frequently in the programme',[88] were performed. And in the

[78] See Miesner, *Bach in Hamburg*, p. 75.

[79] The autograph of Part 1 of Zelter's oratorio *Auferstehung und Himmelfahrt Jesu* is located in D-ddr Bds, Mus. ms. autogr. C. F. Zelter, 1. The work was regularly performed by the Singakademie until 1813. Evidence for this is found in *AMZ*, vols. 9, 10, 12, 15.

[80] *AMZ*, 9 (1806–7), col. 465: 'Interessant war für den Kenner die Vergleichung der Zelterschen Komposition mit der Bachschen, und ungern—um doch etwas zu tadeln—vermisste er die drey sehr schönen, von Bach ebenfalls komponirten Arien.' Besides the bass aria already mentioned, 'Ihre Tore Gottes', there was the bass aria 'Willkommen, Heiland'. A third aria by C. P. E. Bach, 'Mein Geist, voll Furcht und Freuden', was arranged as a duet by Zelter.

[81] See Miesner, *Bach in Hamburg*, p. 62: 'geflickt'.

[82] Zelter's remarks in this connection are discussed below.

[83] Zelter's words: 'im Ganzen und Stückweise'. See Schünemann, *Singakademie*, p. 28.

[84] Ibid.   [85] Ibid.   [86] Ibid., p. 29.   [87] Ibid., p. 28.

[88] Ibid., p. 44: 'der sehr oft im Programme erscheint'.

following years, 1814–16, many of C. P. E. Bach's concertos were heard.[89] On 19 April 1816 the players rehearsed some of Bach's music once again,[90] but after this the records break off.

With regard to the aims and objectives of the Ripienschule, which he had originally intended to operate under the auspices of the university, Zelter had this to say:

I conduct each week . . . a theoretical and practical seminar in the presence of a full orchestra, in which every student who can sing or play an instrument is welcome to take part. The purpose of this seminar is to give to young composers an opportunity to hear their own efforts side by side with those of real masters, and to compare them; for in this way instruction and actual performance go hand in hand in a historical and artistic setting. Only thus can a musical seminar be of value, whereas on the other hand merely lecturing about art and artists would always be a pointless exercise.[91]

Zelter adapted one or two of Bach's symphonies to match the forces of his *Ripienschule* by adding wind parts to the original string versions.[92] The harpsichord concertos from Bach's years in Berlin and Potsdam were particular favourites. It was presumably c. 1807–8 that Sara Levy appeared as a soloist in these works.[93] Many years later, on 2 October 1829, Zelter was to note in his diary: ' . . . 1. Carl Philipp Emanuel Bach: *Concerto 2 D major*, played by the young Eckert. 2. From Bach's 'B minor Mass' No. 2, No. 9 four times, and Nos. 14 and 15.'[94]

Here too the number of Bach's works that were actually performed can safely be assumed to have been much higher. In every case the evidence produced underlines Zelter's enthusiasm for this music. Concerned as he was to provide a theoretical basis for his appreciation of C. P. E. Bach, he could not allow to pass unchallenged comments which indicated a low opinion of Bach's artistic merits. Not least for such a reason as this did Zelter find himself

---

[89] Ibid., pp. 45, 49.       [90] Ibid., p. 49.

[91] Quoted in A. Morgenroth, *C. F. Zelter. Eine musikgeschichtliche Studie*, pt. 1, 'Biographisches', Ph.D. diss., Univ of Berlin, 1922, 66: 'Ich unterhalte . . . ein wöchentliches theoretich-praktisches Collegium im Beisein eines vollständigen Orchesters, woran jeder Studierende singend oder eines Instruments mächtig, frei Anteil nehmen könnte. Der Zweck dieses Collegiums ist, angehenden Komponisten eine Gelegenheit zu geben, ihre eignen Versuche gegen Kunstwerke wirklicher Meister zu hören und zu vergleichen; da denn die Ausübung und Lehre historisch und artistisch Hand in Hand gehen. Nur so kann ein musikalisches Collegium von Nutzen sein, wenn dagegen die blosse Rednerei über Kunst und Künstler überall ohen Frucht sein würde.'

[92] Welter, 'Musikbibliothek', p. 38, mentions unspecified symphonies in G, E flat, D, B minor, B flat, and A, some of them in arrangements by Zelter with additional wind instruments.

[93] In Schünemann, 'Bachpflege', p. 144, it is summarily stated that, 'Frau Levy, whose name often appears as a soloist, performed on 31 December [1807] the D minor Concerto and on 19 February 1808 the 5th Brandenburg Concerto for harpsichord, flute, and violin (D major) [by J. S. Bach].'

[94] Zelter, *Darstellungen*, p. 296: ' . . . 1. Carl Philipp Emanuel Bach: *Concerto 2 D-dur*, gespielt vom kleinen Eckert. 2. Aus Bachs 'H-moll-Missa' No. 2, No. 9 viermal und No. 14 und 15.' K. A. F. Eckert (1820–79) was Zelter's pupil, and he later became a virtuoso pianist, composer, and Kapellmeister.

embroiled in a critical debate over Johann Nikolaus Forkel's book *Ueber Johann Sebastian Bachs Leben, Kunst und Kunstwerke* (Leipzig, 1802).

In the review of Forkel's biography of Bach, which appeared anonymously in the *Allgemeine Musikalische Zeitung* on 23 February 1803, Zelter did, it is true, express broad agreement,[95] although he did not hesitate to point out certain disproportions inherent in Forkel's approach: 'The reviewer would have liked to see a twelfth [chapter], in which it could have been shown how Sebastian Bach was to influence both his own period and the present era'.[96] For Zelter the figure of C. P. E. Bach enters the scene at this point. He continues:

Bach was one of those artists whose style resists all attempts at imitation. All that could take its lead from him was something entirely new, and consequently C. P. E. Bach seems to have emerged with a great genius that bears not the slightest resemblance to that of his father. Through these two heroes of art, who have released genius from the chains of the old order and from the narrow confines of earlier theory with its multiple prohibitions, which imposed bonds and burdens upon every free flight of fancy, instead of allowing it space and sure direction, through these two heroes, then, the music of Germany has been given a momentum which Herr Forkel will not neglect to treat fully in his history of modern music.[97]

Through his intellectual preoccupation with Forkel's Bach book, Zelter seems to have arrived at the idea of writing a rejoinder. As he read it, a growing number of critical questions and comments, corrections, and completions occurred to him.[98] Erwin R. Jacobi[99] has counted 170 manuscript anno-

[95] Zelter's review expressing agreement was written for largely tactical reasons, as he makes clear in an undated letter to Forkel, which he presumably never dispatched: 'But in many places I am not happy with your description, yet I did not want to say so in the review so as not to bewilder the public, preferring to point them towards the works themselves. That is why I would rather enter into correspondence with you personally on the matter. Here and there you have made either too much or too little of the good qualities, and therein lie my objections.' (Quoted in Jacobi, 'Zelters kritische Beleuchtung', p. 464.)

[96] *AMZ*, 5 (1802–3), col. 368: 'Rec.[ensent] hätte noch einen zwölften [Abschnitt] gewünscht, worin gezeigt gewesen wäre, was Sebastian Bach auf sein Zeitalter und das jetzige gewirkt habe?'

[97] Ibid., cols. 368–9: 'Bach war keiner von den Künstlern, deren Manier oder Weise sich nachahmen lässt. Was aus ihm hervorgehen konnte, war wieder neu erschaffen, und so scheint Karl Philipp Em. Bach entstanden zu seyn, dessen hoher Genius auch nicht die entfernteste Aehnlichkeit mit dem seines grossen Vaters hat. Durch diese beyden Helden der Kunst, die das Genie von den Ketten des alten Bundes erlöseten, von den engen Schranken der frühern Theorie, die alles verbot, und jeden freyen Schwung kühner Geistigkeit, statt ihr Raum und sichere Führung zu gewähren, mit Last und Banden belegte, hat die Musik der Deutschen einen Gang bekommen, welchen genau zu bezeichnen, Herr Forkel in seiner Geschichte der neuen Musik nicht verfehlen wird.'

[98] Zelter had written to Georg Poelchau as early as 16 Aug. 1801: 'Concerning his [Forkel's] critical sense, even in historical matters, there are many areas in which I do not share his opinion, nor ever shall.' (D-ddr Bds, Mus. ep. C. F. Zelter, 47.) See also Schulze, *Studien zur Bach-Überlieferung*, pp. 148 ff.

[99] See Jacobi, 'Zelters kritische Beleuchtung'. Unfortunately, I was not able to see Zelter's personal copy, in the collection of the Harvard University Library. The work named in the article 'Jacobi, Erwin R.', *New Grove*, ix. 444, as *C. F. Zelter: Kritik von J. N. Forkels Bachbiographie, mit einem vollständigen Reprint von Forkels Text* (Tutzing, 1974) never appeared.

tations in Zelter's personal copy of Forkel's book, interleaved as it is with blank pages. There are further documents relating to this mass of queries: two essays by Zelter, probably dating from 1802 or 1803, are currently located in the Goethe- und Schiller-Archiv in Weimar.[100] The first manuscript, which is incomplete, consists of three folios written on both sides, and contains a short account of three sons of Bach, Wilhelm Friedemann, Carl Philipp Emanuel, and Johann Christian.[101] The second document was to have been the start of a lengthy monograph on the 'Hamburg Bach', which did not, however, progress beyond the stage of an initial rough outline. Only two out of the eighteen points had Zelter begun to elucidate.

Together with scattered references to C. P. E. Bach by the director of the Singakademie—it is worth mentioning in particular a handwritten essay which H. Miesner discovered inserted within the parts of Bach's 1769 setting of the *St Matthew Passion*[102] and Zelter's contributions to F. Stoepel's history of music (1821)[103]—these two Weimar sources combine to provide an adequate documentary basis for an outline of Zelter's attitude towards the personality and the achievement of this master.[104]

[100] Shelf-mark GSA 95/I, 4. The history of these documents, which formed a part of Zelter's estate, must await subsequent investigation. Not only Morgenroth, *C. F. Zelter*, but also Bitter, *Carl Philipp Emanuel*, ii. 262, quotes from the first of these essays. Bitter, in fact, makes frequent reference to Zelter's writings: see ibid., i. 105; ii. 112, etc.

[101] The transmission of this Zelter essay by Morgenroth, *C. F. Zelter*, and quoted from the latter source in W. Reich, *Karl Friedrich Zelter, Selbstdarstellung* (Zurich, 1955), 335 ff., is careless and inaccurate in places.

[102] Quoted in Miesner, *Bach in Hamburg*, pp. 61–2. It is the *St Matthew Passion* H. 782 (not listed in Wotquenne's catalogue) that is meant here.

[103] F. Stoepel, *Grundzüge der Geschichte der modernen Musik* (Berlin, 1821), 70 f. Zelter's contribution reads as follows: 'C. P. Eman. Bach, the second son of Johann Sebastian. After leaving his father's house he seems to have thrown off his schooling straight away, for from this point onwards he reveals himself to be an original. In respect of his technique, his modulation, and his rhythm he counts as one of the most correct composers of all time, which is all the more to his credit since these qualities are never lost amid the spiritedness and boldness of his ideas. His symphonies, his concertos, and his oratorios contain powerful effects quite unfamiliar in their time, which seem to border on the unattainable. His personal style is the heroic idiom, which he also applies in his keyboard sonatas, thereby frequently lending considerable splendour to this instrument. More recent critics have found his manner of handling the harpsichord or fortepiano hard, even chopped up; yet all those who have heard the master himself agree that his style is vigorous, but cantabile, stirring, and in allegros brilliant. The reason why he has never been universally performed and loved may lie in the strength, profundity, and seriousness of his expression, besides which, although his keyboard pieces are comfortable to play and lie conveniently under the hands, his accompaniments are not, and are sometimes found to be unplayable. His latest works are not his best, for in isolation from Berlin his genius did not flourish at all.'

[104] Further evidence that Zelter took constant pains to enlarge this documentary basis is provided by the fact that he possessed some of C. P. E. Bach's letters in the originals or else took copies of them. Among them were Bach's letters to Forkel, which Zelter had acquired from Forkel's estate, and also the letter sent by Bach's widow to Sara Levy on 5 Sept. 1789. See *Bach-Dokumente*, vol. 3, 'Dokumente zum Nachwirken Johann Sebastian Bachs 1750–1800', ed. Hans-Joachim Schulze (Kassel, 1972), 284 (no. 801), 288 (no. 803), as well as *Suchalla/Briefe*, Letter 184, and Bitter, *Carl Philipp Emanuel*, ii. 307–11. Zelter's copy of a letter from Bach to the Greifswald lawyer J. H. Grave dated 28 Apr. 1784 is owned by D-ddr WRgs, shelf-mark GSA 95/I, 4, and also quoted in Bitter, *Carl Philipp Emanuel*, ii. 303–4.

It was principally the following passage by Forkel which Zelter felt obliged to contradict:

As I have stated earlier, Bach's sons were his most distinguished pupils. The eldest, Wilhelm Friedemann, came closest to his father in the originality of all his ideas. All his melodies are differently shaped from those of other composers, and yet they are not only extremely natural but at the same time extraordinarily fine and delicate. If played sensitively, as they were by the composer, they cannot fail to delight every connoisseur. It is only a pity that he improvised, merely rooting around in his imagination for musical delicacies, more than he composed. Thus it is that the number of fine works by him is not large.

C. P. E. Bach was the first to follow. He went out into the world sufficiently early to discover how to compose for a wide audience. Hence in the clarity and intelligibility of his melodies he approaches the popular style, though he scrupulously avoids the commonplace. Incidentally, the two eldest sons admitted freely that they were driven to adopt a style of their own by the wish to avoid comparison with their incomparable father.[105]

For Zelter the central targets in Forkel's argument were the concepts of originality and popularity. Zelter was prepared neither to accept Forkel's assessment of the relative merits of the two brothers, nor to swallow the notion of originality that he used as a criterion, meaning thereby maximum resemblance of compositional idiom to the style of J. S. Bach. He countered as follows:

History shows that original minds differ from one another precisely by virtue of their originality. Seb. B[ach] was an original, precisely because he was quite unlike anyone else, and if this is correct, then whichever of his two sons came closest to him must have been the less original, in other words the unoriginal one, and this is indeed the case: Friedemann Bach's ideas are strange, but not new; peculiar but not rich [Here Zelter has added: if they sometimes achieve fluency it is only of a limited kind], he searched for everything and Sebastian found everything: that is the difference. His technique is meticulous, clean, full of notes, grace-notes, and close imitations. Kirnberger described this style of composition as *Pritzelwerk*. What is peculiar to him is a strong, inherited

---

[105] Forkel, *Bachs Leben*, p. 44: 'Ich habe oben gesagt, daß Bachs Söhne sich unter seinen Schülern am meisten ausgezeichnet haben. Der älteste, Wilh. Friedemann, kam in der Originalität aller seiner Gedanken seinem Vater am nächsten. Alle seine Melodien sind anders gewendet als die Melodien anderer Componisten, und doch nicht nur äußerst natürlich, sondern zugleich außerordentlich fein und zierlich. Fein vorgetragen, wie er selbst sie vortrug, müssen sie nothwendig jeden Kenner entzücken. Nur Schade, daß er mehr fantasirte und bloß in der Fantasie nach musikalischen Delicatesse grübelte, als schrieb. Die Anzahl seiner schönen Compositionen ist daher nicht groß.

'C. Ph. Emanuel folgt zunächst auf ihn. Dieser kam frühe genug in die große Welt, um noch zu rechter Zeit zu bemerken, wie man für ein ausgebreitetes Publikum componiren müssen. Er nähert sich daher an Deutlichkeit und leichter Faßlichkeit seiner Melodien schon etwas dem Populären, bleibt aber noch vollkommen edel. Beyde älteste Söhne gestanden übrigens offenherzig; sie hätten sich nothwendig eine eigene Art von Styl wählen müssen, weil sie ihren Vater in dem seinigen doch nie erreicht haben würden.'

Facsimile 2. C. F. Zelter, *Charakteristik der Bach-Söhne*, manuscript draft, fo. 1ᵛ. D-ddr WRgs, GSA 95/I, 4

penchant for a small-scale, affected style, twisting and turning so as to avoid the conventional.[106]

It would appear that Zelter's evaluation of the character of W. F. Bach is tinged with a certain dislike, deriving from his knowledge of Friedemann's difficult mental and emotional problems. Later, in a letter to Griepenkerl of 13 March 1829, a copy of which Zelter sent to Goethe, he spells it out clearly.[107] Zelter's attitude to Bach's eldest son remained remarkably tense, critical, and distant. Stoepel's euphoria in claiming that 'Friedemann was the most ingenious and intellectually gifted of Sebastian Bach's sons'[108] was to be dampened by Zelter.[109] The stylistic and aesthetic doubts which plagued Friedemann are summed up in the expression *Pritzelwerk* and in the charge of inaccessibility laid against his music, although it should be admitted that the judgements do less than justice to the historical significance of this composer, and even Zelter was later to modify them in part.[110]

His judgement of C. P. E. Bach was quite different.

---

[106] C. F. Zelter, *Charakteristik der Bach-Söhne*, manuscript draft, fo. 1ʳ: 'So viel die Geschichte bekundet sind Originale eben durch ihre Originalität von einander entfernt. Seb. B.[ach] war eben darum Original weil er keinem nahe war und wenn diese Bemerkungen wahr ist so müßte *der* Sohn welcher ihm am Nächsten kam der weniger originale, d. heißt: der unoriginale seyn und das trift hier zu: Friedemann Bach ist in seinen Gedanken fremd aber nicht neu; sonderlich aber nicht reich [Einschub Zelters: sind sie manchmal fließend so ist doch kein Strohm darinn] er hat alles gesucht und Sebastian hat alles gefunden: das ist der Unterschied. Sein Satz ist gewissenhaft, rein, voll Noten, Nötchen und engen Nachahmungen. Kirnberger nannte diese Art zu komponieren, Pritzelwerk. Das Besondere an ihm aber ist der große und angeerbte Geschmack zu einem kleinen Style der sich künstelt und dreht und windet um dem Bekannten zu entgehn.' For kindly providing assistance in the transcription of this Zelter manuscript I am much indebted to Herr Kirst from the Staatsarchiv Dresden. One or two of the ideas present in the passage quoted here reappear almost verbatim in Zelter's letter to Griepenkerl of 13 Mar. 1829: 'So what does it mean when Forkel says that Friedemann came closest to his father? Is this logical? What is originality? Either Friedemann was original or he was not. If the former, then from the outset he was the artist he was by nature, and he had no one else either above or beside him; for the closer he came to some earlier artist, by so much the less was he an original.' (*Briefwechsel zwischen Goethe und Zelter in den Jahren 1796 bis 1832*, ed. F. W. Riemer, 6 vols. (Berlin, 1833). v. 209.)

[107] Ibid., pp. 209–10. Griepenkerl for his part held in high esteem the music of Bach's eldest son, and registered with regret 'that almost all Berlin musicians, Zelter, Mendelssohn, Meyerbeer, etc. have a low opinion of Friedemann.' See K. Heller, 'Friedrich Konrad Griepenkerl. Aus unveröffentlichten Briefen des Bach-Sammlers und -Editors', *BJ*, 64 (1978), 220.

[108] Stoepel, *Grundzüge*, p. 68: 'Friedemann war unter den Söhnen Sebastian Bach's der genialste und geistig kräftigste'.

[109] Zelter wrote (ibid., pp. 69–70): 'Friedemann Bach, the eldest son of Johann Sebastian. A first-rate harpsichordist and organist, and possibly for that reason his father's favourite. With his great desire in his work to free himself from his time, he never quite threw off his schooling; thus his works, while they are undeniably very correct, and very finely wrought, seldom achieve great fluency. Forkel regards him as an original, but adds that both in his compositions and even in his improvisations he roots around for musical delicacies. He died in Berlin, where his music has been heard often enough to confirm that Forkel was right.'

[110] For example in the letter to Griepenkerl mentioned earlier (see n. 106), and in connection with Zelter's identification of the autograph of BWV 596, falsely claimed as an original composition by W. F. Bach. See Schulze, *Studien zur Bach-Überlieferung*, pp. 148 ff.

This composer is simply a born original. His keyboard concertos, his symphonies, his keyboard sonatas, being the product of a great and marvellous imagination [Here Zelter has added: new, sound, unstudied, melodious, powerful, touching, profound, and filled with imagination.] . . .

He writes with assurance, freedom, steady fluency, and depth, all in a thoroughly different style, so different indeed that one might suppose his father far less pleased by it all than if Emanuel had been less original. Hasse allegedly said of him that he was the greatest composer and musician in the world. It may easily be imagined that Seb. Bach would not have gained Hasse's approval, and Haydn can have known nothing at all of Seb. B[ach], for when he refers to the *old* Bach he means Emanuel.

Let it be made known if any composer before Emanuel Bach has written such spirited symphonies as the four printed ones [H. 663–6/W. 183] or the Berlin symphonies, or the van Swieten set [H. 657–62/W. 182]; such magnificent ritornellos and fine accompaniments as [in the] concertos; such brilliant sonatas; such stirring adagios; such powerful, bold, grand arias and recitatives as in his Passion [H. 776/W. 233]; in the Ascension music [H. 777/W. 240], in the Easter music [H. 803/W. 244] in the *Israeliten* [H. 775/W. 238], or in his other vocal works. In short: C. P. E. Bach was an *Originalgenie* like his great father, precisely because he was so unlike him in every respect save only in the purity and thoroughness and delicacy of his technique; [Here Zelter has added: One might say that] Emanuel, just like Sebastian, was born a whole generation too early.'[111]

Zelter defines originality—much as Forkel had done—as the expression of maximum artistic individuality, and he emphasizes in connection with C. P. E. Bach both the singularity of his musical output and the novelty of the phase in

---

[111] Zelter, *Charakteristik*, fos. 1$^r$–2$^r$: 'Dieser ist ein reines gebornes Original. Seine Clavierconcerte, seine Sinfonien, seine Klaviersonaten welche aus einer schönen großen Phantasie kommen sind [Einschub Zelters: neu, gesund, ungesucht, melodisch, kräftig, rührend, tief und voll Phantasie.] . . .

'An ihm ist Sicherheit, Freiheit, Strom und Tiefe, nur alles anders, ja so anders daß man denken kann, sie haben dem Vater nicht so gefallen als wenn sie weniger original gewesen wären. Hasse soll von ihm gesagt haben: er sey der größte Componist und Musikus in der Welt. Daß Seb. Bach Hassens Beyfall nicht haben konnte läßt sich denken und Haydn muß von Seb. B.[ach] gar nichts gekannt haben denn wenn er von dem *alten* Bach spricht, meint er den Emanuel.

'Man weise nach ob ein Componist vor Em. Bach solche geistvolle Sinfonien wie die 4 gedruckten oder wie die Berliner, oder wie die Suitenschen; Solche prachtvolle Ritornelle und schöne Begleitungen wie [in den] Concerte[n]; solche brillante Sonaten; solche rührende Adagios; solche kräftige, große Arien und Recitative wie in seiner Passion; in der Himmelfahrtsmusik, in der Ostermusik, in den Israeliten und in seinen sonstigen Singmusiken, gemacht habe. Kurz: Carl Philipp Emanuel Bach war ein Originalgenie wie sein großer Vater, eben weil er ihm in Allem unähnlich war nur nicht in der Reinigkeit und Gründlichkeit und Feinheit seines Satzes [Einschub Zelters: Man könnte sagen:] Emanuel, so wie Sebastian sind ein ganzes Seculum zu früh gebohren.'

This idea is obviously derived from Burney. See *Dr. Burney's Musical Tours in Europe*, ed. Percy A. Scholes, 2 vols. (London, 1959), ii. 220, where the following passage occurs (originally published in London in 1773 as *The Present State of Music in Germany* and issued in German translation in Hamburg in the same year): 'however, the great musician appears in every movement [referring to the six *Flügel-Concerte*], and these productions will probably be the better received, for resembling the music of this world more than his former pieces, which seem made for another region, or at least another century, when what is now thought difficult and far-fetched, will, perhaps, be familiar and natural.'

musical history which this output embodied. In putting forward this idea, Zelter aligns himself with a tradition of theoretical and aesthetic thinking which had been substantially shaped several decades earlier by Johann Georg Sulzer. In his *Allgemeine Theorie der Schönen Künste* (1771–4) Sulzer had declared: 'The original [artist] is one who bases his work on his own impressions of the world, and develops it according to his own insights.'[112] C. P. E. Bach's new expressive musical language was seen by many contemporaries as the artistic manifestation of an *Originalgenie*. Johann Friedrich Reichardt stresses Bach's 'originality of ideas', which 'frequently demands original, unusual, or intense expression...'[113] Charles Burney explains further: 'However, each candid observer and hearer, must discover, in the slightest and most trivial productions, of every kind, some mark of originality in the modulation, accompaniment, or melody, which bespeak a great and exalted genius.'[114]

Zelter's judgement was made from an altogether different historical perspective. Works by C. P. E. Bach were not widely cultivated during the first third of the nineteenth century, and the man himself was merely an object of historical interest.[115] The high performance figures mentioned earlier are potentially misleading, since it goes without saying that they would have been much higher in Berlin, a great centre of the Bach cult, than elsewhere, and Zelter's personal enthusiasm for Bach's music must also be taken into account. When Zelter describes Bach as an 'original', he is placing himself in a common stylistic tradition with Bach, but in so doing he is to some extent simply repeating a cliché: throughout his life Zelter felt himself to be rooted in the musical tradition of eighteenth-century Berlin. His musical philosophy was nourished from the same source. 'Under his [Frederick the Great's] reign, music in Berlin achieved a degree of perfection, which clearly indicates how much it mattered to him. The names of Bach, Fasch, Graun, Quantz, Benda ... will never be forgotten, and they alone would be sufficient to immortalize the name of their great patron.'[116]

[112] Johann Georg Sulzer, *Allgemeine Theorie der Schönen Künste*, vol. 2 (Leipzig, 1774), 795: 'Original ist der, dessen Handlungen aus seinen eigenen Vorstellungen entstehen, und der in der Ausführung seinen eigenen Begriffen folgt.'

[113] Johann Friedrich Reichardt, '*Über die deutsche comische Oper* (Hamburg, 1774), 19: 'Originalität der Gedanken, [die] oft nothwendig einen originalen; ungewöhnlichen oder schweren Ausdruck erfordert...'

[114] Quoted from *Dr. Burney's Musical Tours*, ii. 214.

[115] See Ottenberg, *Bach*, p. 198 ff.

[116] From Zelter's first memorial of 28 Sept. 1803. Quoted in C. Schröder, *Carl Friedrich Zelter und die Akademie* (Berlin, 1959), 76: 'Die Musik hat unter seiner Regierung in Berlin einen Grad der Vollkommenheit erreicht, welche ein Beweiß ist, daß es ihm Ernst damit war. Die Namen Bach, Fasch, Graun, Quanz, Benda ... werden leben wie die Zeit und wären allein hinlänglich den Namen ihres großen Beschützers zu verewigen.' In theoretical matters too Zelter takes his lead from the Berlin writers Marpurg and Kirnberger. See *Briefwechsel zwischen Goethe und Zelter*, ii. 13–14 (letter of 2 June 1819).

Inasmuch as Zelter does not judge C. P. E. Bach's achievement by the standards of his father's music, but rather attempts to understand it on its own terms, he advances beyond Forkel, who is much more conservative in this area. For Forkel, J. S. Bach was the *ne plus ultra* in music; by effectively distancing themselves from this paragon, the following generation of composers were taking what he saw as a step in the wrong direction.[117] Zelter was anxious to situate C. P. E. Bach's work historically. He wrote to Goethe on 9 March 1814:

I remember very clearly how at the time the music of the Leipzig Bach, and of his son, the Hamburg Bach, both of them quite new and original, was almost unintelligible to me, even though a strange sense of something of real value attracted me to it. Then came Haydn, whose style was criticized for as it were travestying the bitter seriousness of his predecessors, and so they now came to be held in esteem. Finally Mozart appeared, and through him it became possible to understand all three composers, from whom his own work had taken its lead.[118]

Even if Zelter in this passage has somewhat over-simplified the effect of historical developments in eighteenth-century music on his four leading composers, still he finds embodied in their very example an overarching historical continuity. The implications for C. P. E. Bach were as follows: that he both injected a measure of new life into the technical language and expressive possibilities of the music of his day and at the same time laid important foundations for the emergence of the Viennese Classical style.

Zelter had further occasion to defend the music of C. P. E. Bach against criticism from Forkel, who believed that it showed signs of affinity with the 'popular style'.[119] Zelter retorted:

What is the popular style anyway? He writes more clearly than his predecessors, but that does not make him popular—one searches in vain for jaded expressions and outworn figures in his music. He has written sonatas and easy pieces for children and for ladies, even the so-called *rondeaux*, but let no one be misled by these titles; the pieces are as one would expect, but the forms are so novel and imaginative that they are quite unlike any earlier pieces, compared with let us say the allemandes, courantes, sarabandes, loures, gigues, and mourquies [here Zelter has added: in which there was plenty of fertile soil but no seed]. How different his organ sonatas [H. 84–7, 133–4/W.

[117] See F. Peters-Marquardt and A. Dürr, 'Forkel, Johann Nikolaus', *MGG*, vol. 4, cols. 518–19, and also J. N. Forkel, 'Ueber die Musik des Ritters Christoph von Gluck . . .', *Musikalisch-kritische Bibliothek*, vol. 1 (Gotha, 1778), 53–210.

[118] *Briefwechsel zwischen Goethe und Zelter*, i. 383: 'Sehr deutlich erinnre ich mich, daß die Musik des Leipziger Bach und seines Sohnes, des Hamburger Bach, die beide ganz neu und original sind, zu ihrer Zeit mir fast unverständlich vorkam, wie wohl ein dunkles Gefühl des Echten mich dahin anzog. Da kam Haydn, dessen Art getadelt ward, weil sie den bittern Ernst seiner Vorgänger gleichsam travestierte, wodurch sich die gute Meinung nun auf jene zurückwarf. Endlich erschien Mozart, durch den man alle 3 erklären könnte, aus welchen er herausgearbeitet hat.'

[119] Forkel, *Bachs Leben*, p. 44; see the passage quoted above and n. 105.

70] and keyboard fugues [H. 75.5, 99–102/W. 119, 2–7] are from those of his predecessors, and is this what is meant by 'popularity'?[120]

It is evident that Zelter applies the notion of the 'popular' in a pejorative sense, to refer to a certain eclecticism on the part of the artist. Zelter expresses concern at the great burgeoning of mass-produced art substitutes, and he senses a danger that 'art ... might be suffocated under the pressure of popular sensationalism.'[121] The dichotomy observable here between concessions by the composer to everyday taste on the one hand and extreme individualism on the other had left its mark on the work of C. P. E. Bach. And yet this dichotomy was a fruitful one for Bach, since he composed simultaneously for the *Liebhaber* and for the *Kenner*, and hence took account of that division of musical production into a 'completely accessible' amateur tradition *and* a highly specialized style for the connoisseurs.[122] The former was in Zelter's view somewhat suspect. Although in the passage quoted above he attributed originality to all Bach's works without exception, he was later to modify his position.[123]

In a text dated 14 May 1825, Zelter drew a clear distinction between C. P. E. Bach's Berlin works and those written in Hamburg. In the latter he complains of a grave over-simplification of musical language:

His otherwise vigorous humour, filled with the joys of life, he soon began to indulge, and his music became more lightweight; he adapted his style, and thought to pander to the musical amateur by applying himself to lighter tasks.

In the process he gradually lost more and more of his former admirers, Pr[incess] Amalie, Kirnberger, Marpurg, Krause, etc., without attracting new friends for his new style; his late works may be called his weakest, since they show little trace of Bach's seriousness, or uniquely personal touch, which, however, he was clearly unable to set aside entirely. His Hamburg works, then, are an unhappy compromise, for the composer, perhaps, more unsatisfactory than for anyone else, and thus did he depart this world.[124]

---

[120] Zelter, *Charakteristik*, 2ʳ⁻ᵛ 'Was heißt denn Populär?—Klarer ist er wie seine Vorgänger doch nicht populär, denn abgetriebene Gedanken und abgeriebene Floskeln sucht man vergebens bey ihm. Er hat Sonaten, Handstücke für Kinder und Frauen gemacht ja sogar sogenannte Rondeaux, aber man laße sich nicht durch diese Titel verführen; die Stücke sind was sie seyn sollen aber die Formen sind so neu und geistreich, daß sie anderen Stücken vor ihm durchaus unähnlich sind, wenn man sie mit den Allemanden, Couranten, Sarabanden, Louren, Giguen und Mourquies vergleicht über [Einschub Zelters: die hinaus wohl Acker aber keine Saat war]. Wie unterschiedlich sind seine Orgelsonaten und Klavierfugen von denen seiner Vorgänger und das wäre seine Popularität?'

[121] *Briefwechsel zwischen Goethe und Zelter*, i. 48 (Zelter's letter to Goethe of 15 July 1803); 'Kunst ... unter dem Druck einer populären Sensation erstickt.'

[122] This whole question has been treated in detail by Peter Schleuning, to whom the author is much indebted on several counts. See Peter Schleuning, *Die freie Fantasie. Ein Beitrag zur Erforschung der klassischen Klaviermusik* (Göppingen, 1973), 257 ff.

[123] See in particular Zelter's comments about C. P. E. Bach as a vocal composer, quoted below (n. 144).

[124] Quoted in Miesner, *Bach in Hamburg*, p. 61, 'Bey einem sonst munteren Humor jedoch der das Leben liebt und genießt fing er bald an sich zu gefallen und gefälliger zu werden; so änderte er

This assertion by Zelter can perhaps be justified in the case of such works as the six *Flügel-Concerte*,[125] H. 471–6/W. 43, or the pieces contained in *Musikalisches Vielerley*,[126] but to apply it also to the principal genres—keyboard sonata, symphony, oratorio, etc.—as Zelter does is surely mistaken. Be that as it may, it remains a somewhat paradoxical statement.

In Zelter's eyes, C. P. E. Bach was first and foremost a great instrumental composer, and contemporary keyboard music in particular was to feel his influence profoundly. Most of all it was through the sonatas and concertos of the Berlin period, according to Zelter, that this influence was exercised. 'In 1738 he came to Berlin and in 1740 he entered the service of Frederick the Great. Here his period of real artistry seems to have begun, the years of instruction from his father having of necessity been devoted mainly to student exercises.'[127] In the artistic atmosphere of the Prussian capital, and amid opportunities for intellectually stimulating exchanges with such musicians as Carl Heinrich Graun, Jiří Antonín (Georg) Benda, and Johann Joachim Quantz, Bach forged his personal style, and, as Zelter has also observed, this tended from the outset towards the idiom of the original, the unconventional:

Generally speaking his technique is immaculate. In this piece he had to contend with a formidable rival in Graun, a composer very hard to equal, but at the same time one who never attempted anything really innovative, partly through a natural unadventurousness, and partly through a preference, evident throughout his music, for easily intelligible, gentle cantilena.

Bach's genius was free to blossom here. His spirited performing style at the keyboard, from which he was able to draw a most strong and powerful tone combining brilliance with a singing and 'speaking' manner of execution, was something hitherto quite unknown. His improvisations delighted every heart, spoke to every intellect. Stirring, lively, natural, cheerful, rich in thoughts and ideas, all is new and fresh, and with every repetition offers renewed pleasure as it is further illuminated, clarified, and transfigured.[128]

seine Kunstart, und gedachte der Musikliebhaberey zu fröhnen indem er sich leichterer Arbeiten befliß.
    'Dadurch verlor er sich nach und von seinen alten Verehrern, die Pr.[inzessin] Amalie, Kirnbergern, Marpurg, Krause u. a. ohne seiner neuen Art neue Freunde zu erwecken und man darf seine letzten Compositionen die schwächern nennen indem ihnen die Kraft, der Ernst und das ihm allein eigene abgeht, das er freilich nicht ganz ablegen könne. So bewegen sich seine Hamburgischen Arbeiten in einer Mitte die ihm selber vielleicht am wenigsten gefiel und so ist er aus der Welt gegangen.'

125 Published as *Sei concerti per il cembalo concertato, accompagnato da due violini, violetta e basso* (Hamburg, 1772).
126 Published in Hamburg in 1770.
127 Carl Friedrich Zelter, *Über C. P. E. Bach*, manuscript draft, D-ddr WRgs, GSA 95/I, 4, fo. 1ʳ: 'Im Jahre 1738 kam er nach Berlin und 1740 in den Dienst Friedr. d. Gr. Hier scheint seine wahre Künstler Epoche anzufangen, wenn er sich in der Schule seines Vaters meist mit Schularbeiten beschäftigen müssen.'
128 Ibid., fo. 2ᵛ: 'Sein Satz ist, allgemein genommen, von musterhafter Reinigkeit. In diesem Stücke hatte er an Graun einen ausserordentlichen Rival[en] neben sich, dem gleichzukommen

Facsimile 3. C. F. Zelter, *Über C. P. E. Bach*, manuscript draft, fo. 1^r.
D-ddr WRgs, GSA 95/I, 4

Zelter's comments in the document discovered by Heinrich Miesner were equally appreciative:

Nature seems to have chosen our C. P. E. Bach to be the apostle of his great father, to raise stringed keyboard instruments to the highest level of musical expression after the organ; his many fine and original keyboard pieces and concertos provide eloquent testimony thereto, and will continue to do so.[129]

Zelter's views find echoes in many similar judgements by Burney, Schubart, Reichardt, etc.,[130] and may well be based on these, since in listing the essential qualities of Bach's style he stresses the notion of the 'vocally inspired' composer,[131] underlines the importance of the *redende Prinzip*[132] in his music, and draws attention to his penchant for improvisatory style.[133]

Obviously the works with which Zelter was most familiar were Bach's harpsichord concertos, for he had performed them repeatedly. 'The ritornellos of his Berlin and Potsdam concertos are and will remain the most sublime examples ever written, and yet this is not easily recognized, for they demand a style of execution which is quite unique, and an orchestra which must be fully initiated into his genius.'[134]

Here too Zelter's view of C. P. E. Bach is astonishingly penetrating and

sehr schwer war, der sich aber auch in keine große Wagstücke einließ, theils aus Bequemlichkeit, theils aus Gefälligkeit für eine verständliche ruhige Cantilena, wovon alle seine Werke zeugen.

'Bachs Genie fand hier seine Freiheit. Sein geistvolles Spiel auf dem Klavier, dem er den stärksten kräftigen Ton entlockte und dadurch das Brillante mit sangbaren und sprechenden Vortrag verband, war etwas bis jetzt ganz unerhörtes. Seine Art zu phantasieren entzückte jedes Herz, sprach zu jedem Verstande. Erweckend, belebt, natürlich, heiter und groß von Gedanken und Ideen ist alles neu, frisch, ja es erneuert sich, in dem es sich durch die Wiederholung aufklärt, erklärt und verklärt.'

[129] Quoted in Miesner, *Bach in Hamburg*, p. 61: 'Die Natur scheint unsern C. Ph. E. Bach zum Apostel seines großen Vaters ausersehen zu haben, das Clavierinstrument nach der Orgel auf die höchste Stufe des musikalischen Ausdrucks zu erheben wovon seine vielen schönen originalen Clavierstücke und Concerte ein redendes Zeugniß sind und bleiben werden.'

[130] See the literature listed in n. 138.

[131] This term, 'singend denkend', goes back to C. P. E. Bach, who writes as follows in his *Versuch*, pt. 1, chap. 3, par. 12, 'In paragraph 8 above the practice of listening to accomplished musicians was recommended as a means of acquiring a good style of performance. Here it is more particularly advised that no opportunity should be missed of hearing good singers; in this way one learns to *think vocally* [my italic]. Indeed it is a good idea to sing a melody to oneself, in order to perceive how it should be performed correctly.'

[132] This term goes back to Arnold Schering. See his article 'Carl Philipp Emanuel Bach und das "redende Prinzip" in der Musik', *Jahrbuch der Musikbibliothek Peters*, 45 (1938), 13–29.

[133] C. P. E. Bach's penchant for improvisatory writing has frequently been the subject of investigation, for example in E. Eugene Helm, 'The "Hamlet" Fantasy'; Schleuning, *Die freie Fantasie*, pp. 146 ff; Hans-Günter Ottenberg, 'Zur Fantasieproblematik im Schaffen Carl Philipp Emanuel Bachs', *Studien zur Aufführungspraxis und Interpretation von Instrumentalmusik des 18. Jahrhunderts*, vol. 13 (Blankenburg/Harz, 1980), 74–80.

[134] Quoted in Miesner, *Bach in Hamburg*, pp. 61–2: 'Die Ritornelle seiner Berliner und Potsdamer Concerte sind und bleiben das Erhabenste was jemals in der Art geschrieben worden welche jedoch kaum zu erkennen sind, da sie einen Vortrag erfordern der ganz eigen ist und ein Orchester erfordert daß ganz in seinen Genius eingeweiht seyn muß.'

accurate. He considers appropriate the type of interpretation that aims for authentic re-creation of a Bachian idiom.[135] Unfortunately it cannot be established exactly which concertos Zelter had in mind here. It seems possible, though, that he was referring to such works as the two D minor concertos, H. 425/W. 22 and H. 427/W. 23. For these belong to that category of compositions which Bach—to quote his own words—'wrote in complete freedom'.[136] Here we are dealing with an artist whose aim it is to give musical expression to passionate feelings. In terms of their aesthetic character, the mood of the opening movements of these concertos would be best described with such expressions as 'enraged', 'unbridled', 'thrilling', 'bizarre'. It is precisely on the appearance of specific individual traits in these works—such as thematic formulations in which rhythmic regularity is entirely avoided, tellingly labelled by Besseler as *Individualthemen*,[137] constant changes of direction, abrupt switches in mood, etc.—that C. P. E. Bach's reputation as an *Originalgenie* is to a large extent based. Frequently encountered in contemporary critical writings are such phrases as 'bold style', 'extremely difficult to play', 'utterly individual taste', 'bizarrerie', 'harmonic richness'.[138] Zelter's understanding of Bach's harpsichord concertos is accurately conveyed by language of this kind.

Zelter's estimation of C. P. E. Bach as a composer of vocal music was to change considerably as time went by. The thoroughly positive note sounded in connection with the vocal genres in his reply to Forkel[139] later gave way to a more detached, more critical attitude. In 1825 he wrote concerning C. P. E. Bach:

As a vocal composer he was simply unable to attain the leading position accorded him in the instrumental field by every connoisseur.

His recitative is full of vigour and precision; his arias are more *declamatory!* than cantabile and are unmelodious; his choruses are mostly pitched too high for the voices, and contain a wealth of detail which is unsuited to a choral medium; his vocal fugues are frankly more artificial than fluent—somewhat laboured in fact.

These weaknesses apply only in general terms, for there are individual moments of

---

[135] Here a certain parallel between the thought of Zelter and that of C. F. D. Schubart becomes apparent. The latter writes in his *Ideen zu einer Ästhetik der Tonkunst* (Vienna, 1806), 295, 'If I wish to perform a sonata by Bach, I must immerse myself so thoroughly in the spirit of this great man that I lose my personal identity and express instead a Bachian idiom.'

[136] C. P. E. Bach, 'Selbstbiographie', *Carl Burney's . . . Tagebuch einer musikalischen Reise*, vol. 3, trans. C. D. Ebeling and J. J. C. Bode (Hamburg, 1773), 209 (not present in the original English text *The Present State of Music in Germany*).

[137] See Heinrich Besseler, 'Bach als Wegbereiter', *AfMw*, 12 (1955), 1 ff.

[138] These phrases are almost without exception taken from C. F. D. Schubart, *Ideen*, pp. 177–81. Similar judgements are also found in J. F. Reichardt, *Schreiben über die Berlinische Musik* (Hamburg, 1775), 7, 13, 19–22; the same author's *Briefe eines aufmerksamen Reisenden die Musik betreffend*, pt. 1 (Frankfurt am Main and Leipzig, 1774), 111–12; pt. 2. (Frankfurt am Main and Breslau, 1776), 7–22; and *Dr. Burney's Musical Tours*, ii. 187–215.

[139] See Zelter, *Charakteristik* and *Über C. P. E. Bach*.

great beauty and inspiration, such as the deeply moving tenor aria 'Wende dich zu meinem Schmerze'.[140]

Otherwise his pieces taken together are always sublime in style and not ponderous if well performed.

In his declamation, on the other hand, he stands out from among his contemporaries once again; not one of them could have produced anything to match the tenor aria 'Verstockte Sünder'.[141]

That Bach may not have felt at liberty to follow his own ideas in composing the vocal works may be deduced from the fact that the music which he provided for the churches in Hamburg was frequently patched together, with new texts supplied for new occasions, and often it was even interwoven with music by other composers. Such plagiarism is particularly evident in this manuscript,[142] where entire choruses and *turba* choruses from J. S. Bach's *St Matthew Passion* are copied directly.

It may well be imagined that Bach had little desire to set to music biblical stories and pious bleating merely to supply the needs of regular observance, but I possess many items of his church music in which choruses or arias by Homilius, G. Benda,[143] and the like are included, and simply because Bach wanted to perform appropriate music for a particular Sunday without too much effort!

The wealth of detail and the preciousness of the melodic line seems to have remained with him from his father's schooling, for to his solid German taste, Italian music can have had little appeal. . . .'[144]

---

[140] From C. P. E. Bach, *Passions-Cantate* (1769–70), H. 776/W. 233.          [141] Ibid.

[142] C. P. E. Bach's *St Matthew Passion* of 1769, H. 782 (not in Wotquenne's catalogue).

[143] Miesner, *Bach in Hamburg*, p. 62, laments in a footnote that no critical literature is available on either of these composers. Individual details of borrowings from Homilius are provided ibid., p. 77, and in Clark, 'Occasional Choral Works', pp. 180–1. *NV*, 85–9, 91, lists several sacred works by G. Benda and G. A. Homilius.

[144] Quoted in Miesner, *Bach in Hamburg*, p. 62, 'Als Singkomonist hat er nun nicht zur Wirkung gelangen können, die ihm als Instrumentalkomponist jeder Kenner zugestand.

'Sein Rezitativ ist springend und wörtlich; seine Arie mehr *deklamierend*! als kantabel und nicht melodisch; seine Chöre liegen den Singstimmen meist zu hoch und haben ein Mikrologisches das dem Chore nicht zusteht; seine Singfugen sind redlich mehr gekünstelt als fließend ja sie zerren sich wohl.

'Diese Mängel sind nur im allgemeinen anzunehmen und man findet im Einzelnen das Schönste und Beste ja wohl das Rührende wie die Tenorarie: "Wende dich zu meinem Schmerze" in dieser Musik zu nennen ist.

'Außerdem sind seine Stücke im Ganzen immer erhaben im Styl und nicht schwerfällig, wenn sie gut ausgeführt werden.

'In der Deklamation ragt er dagegen wieder unter seinen Zeitgenossen hervor und keiner von ihnen dürfte etwas aufzuweisen haben das der Tenorarie: "Verstockte Sünder" beykäme.

'Daß er sich selber in seinen Singkompositionen nicht geistig frey gefühlt habe ließe sich dadurch errathen indem die für die Hamburger Kirchen von ihm betstimmten Musiken gar oft geflickt, andere Texte für neue Gelegenheiten unterlegt ja mit fremden Compositionen durchflochten sind. Das Letztere wird an diesem Manuscript besonders fühlbar indem sämtliche Chöre und Volkschöre aus der Passion dem Seb. Bach secundum Matthaeum abgeschrieben sind.

'Daß er nun, der Observanz zu fröhnen wenige Lust gehabt habe, biblische Relationen oder Volksgebell in Töne zu bringen ist wohl anzunehmen, aber ich besitze viele Kirchenmusiken von ihm worin sich Chöre oder Arien von Homilius, G. Benda und dergleichen befinden um nur für den bestimmten Sonntag ohne viel Mühe eine bestimmte Musik aufzuführen!

'Das Mikrologische, Prizzelhafte der Cantilene scheint ihm aus der Schule seines Vaters anzukleben, dem als kräftig Deutschen die italienische Musik nicht zusagen wollen. . . .'

No doubt it was as a result of becoming acquainted in the mean time with a great deal of the 'vocal music for liturgical and other festivities'[145] written in Hamburg—that is to say Passion settings, cantatas, choruses, etc.—that Zelter was now able to judge Bach's vocal music more critically and with more discrimination. Above all, though, it would have been his daily encounter with the medium of song that helped Zelter to form a definite ideal of vocal style; this was only partly realized in Bach's vocal music, although fully satisfied by Haydn's. Finally mention should be made of the fact that in due course Zelter wrote in similar terms about the vocal works of W. F. Bach.[146]

More than any other it was Zelter who helped to endow the fate of musical life in Berlin with the aim of thoroughly reassessing the directions in which it was moving. His judgement in matters musical carried weight and brought him, a friend and musical adviser of Goethe, the reputation of a recognized authority. At the same time his interpretation of the processes of musical history was not without its contradictions:

In fact for Zelter, setting aside his respect for J. S. Bach, the key composers in the Classical period were C. P. E. Bach and J. Haydn; he spoke warmly of the *Creation*, and Haydn replied in person. Yet even Mozart he did not always understand, and of Beethoven he actually made the extraordinary though well-intentioned request for an a cappella arrangement of the *Missa solemnis* to suit the requirements of his Singakademie.[147]

C. P. E. Bach's artistic distinction, emphasized once again in this quotation, was as we have seen to have far-reaching consequences both for Zelter's practical music-making and for his musical outlook. As a practical musician, in his earlier years mainly as a violinist in various amateur groupings, and later on as director of the Singakademie and the Ripienschule, Zelter had performed an impressive number of works by C. P. E. Bach; not least among the consequences of this was that it helped give rise to a certain continuity in the reception of Bach's music in Berlin at least until 1832.

This concern with actual performance went hand in hand with Zelter's constant efforts to enlarge his personal music library and that of the Singakademie, particular attention being paid to the collection of Bachiana. Zelter took great care of this treasure, which included many of Bach's original manuscripts, so that it survived almost intact into the present century, only to be lost in the course of the Second World War.

To Zelter the theorist we owe some remarkable insights into, among other things, the aesthetic, stylistic, technical, and practical performing aspects of Bach's music. His accounts of major areas of the work of this composer

[145] C. P. E. Bach, 'Selbstbiographie', p. 207: 'Singstücke für die Kirche und unterschiedliche Feyerlichkeiten'.
[146] Zelter, *Charakteristik*, fo. 1ᵛ.
[147] Martin Geck, 'Zelter, Karl Friedrich', *MGG*, vol. 14, col. 1212.

constitute some of the most penetrating writing about C. P. E. Bach from the first half of the nineteenth century; at times he could be called upon as an expert in this field.[148]

A worthwhile topic for future research would be the extent to which Zelter through his activity as a teacher passed on his knowledge of Bach's music to others.[149] When Felix Mendelssohn Bartholdy performed for Goethe works 'by all different great composers in chronological order'[150] it is reasonable to suppose that this would have included works by the 'Hamburg Bach' as a direct consequence of Zelter's teaching, and when in later years Mendelssohn displayed an interest in the F major symphony H. 656/W. 181,[151] it may be that this was awakened as far back as the time when he was still a performer in the Ripienschule.

If one final proof of Zelter's affinity to the person and to the work of C. P. E. Bach were needed, it would be this: when the general director of the royal theatres and museums in Berlin, Count Karl Friedrich Moritz Paul von Brühl, enquired of Zelter which busts of famous musicians ought to be exhibited in one of the rooms of the theatre that was soon to be opened, Zelter replied as follows in a letter dated 28 August 1819: 'J. S. Bach, Handel, *C. P. E. Bach* [my italic], J. G. Graun, Haydn, Gluck, and Mozart.'[152]

[148] See for example Zelter's contribution to Stoepel, *Grundzüge*, pp. 70–1.

[149] As a music professor at the Berlin Akademie der schönen Künste from 1809 onwards, Zelter had to hold public seminars each year on the history of music, and on the rudiments of music, composition, style, etc. See C. Schröder, *Carl Friedrich Zelter und die Akademie* (Berlin, 1959), 116. See also the announcement of lectures on figured bass in *AMZ*, 15 (1813), col. 758.

[150] Quoted in F. F. von Biedermann, *Goethes Gespräche*, vol. 4 (Leipzig, 1909), 274: 'von allen verschiedenen großen Komponisten nach der Zeitfolge'.

[151] He wrote on 12 Feb. 1847 to the director of the Leipzig Ratsbibliothek, Robert Naumann: 'Do you possess in your library any symphonies by C. P. E. Bach in score or in parts? I should particularly like to have another look through the one in F major [there follows the incipit of H. 656/W. 181] or another of the larger works, and would therefore entreat you, should you have any of these items, to allow me to see it for a few days.' Quoted in *Felix Mendelssohn Bartholdy, Briefe aus Leipziger Archiven*, ed. H.-J. Rothe and R. Szeskus (Leipzig, 1972), 232.

[152] D-ddr Bds, Mus. ep. C. F. Zelter, p. 3.

# C. P. E. Bach through the 1740s: The Growth of a Style

## David Schulenberg

IT is the fate of all but the best-known composers to be remembered chiefly for a few remarkable idiosyncracies, even if these are absent from many of their works, or are the superficial products of just one stage of a stylistic development such as can be discerned in the music of more closely studied figures. With C. P. E. Bach, discussion of his stylistic development has taken a second place to descriptions of his style in general, and especially to attempts to account for those aspects of his music that most obviously distinguish it from that of his contemporaries. But as his music has become more widely accessible and more frequently studied, it has become clear that Bach's style underwent changes of the magnitude that one would expect to find with a composer whose fifty-year career spanned what we now regard as an important transition in music history. While it would be a mistake to suppose that Bach's own development reflected that of European musical style in general, one can nevertheless point to certain transitions in Bach's own music—above all, the transition from Bach's youthful style to one that is for the first time truly distinctive and fully mature.

The years 1742 to 1748 saw, among other things, C. P. E. Bach's first significant publications, his marriage (in 1744), and the second and more famous of his father's visits to Berlin. It was also during these years that his music took on many of the qualities for which we continue to value it, particularly in the Württemberg sonatas, a number of other sonatas for solo keyboard, and a dozen or so harpsichord concertos. These were new genres; while he no doubt had access to models by other composers (including his father), through his almost exclusive concentration on these genres of composition Emanuel in effect invented his own distinctive types of keyboard sonata and concerto during the 1730s and 1740s. Moreover, in a few concertos and sonatas from the late 1740s one finds direct presentiments of the extraordinary solo and ensemble works of Bach's Hamburg period.

The most important accomplishment of the 1740s was the perfection of Bach's unique expressive language, now known for its intense rhetoric founded upon sudden pauses, shifts in surface motion, harmonic shocks, and occasional formal experimentation. But Bach's mature style is equally characterized by carefully notated melodic embellishment and, though it may seem paradoxical, a fairly rigid formal design in most movements (despite the often elaborate, seemingly arbitrary detail).[1] Indeed, Bach's adoption by the mid-forties of an essentially unvarying type of sonata form for most instrumental movements made possible some experimental designs that appear to depart entirely from the usual ones. In fact they do not, and the presence of a solid underlying structure distinguishes them from equally radical but less cogent works by his brother Wilhelm Friedemann, who in his free fantasias and sonatas sometimes seems to string sections and modulations arbitrarily together. Friedemann perhaps sought to retain the freedom enjoyed by J. S. Bach in what are often designated his 'architectonic' forms, which actually leave great leeway for free extension or interpolation; Sebastian doubled the length of several movements in *Das wohltemperirte Clavier*, for example, by adding new sections after the original final cadence. But such freedom was dangerous for members of the next generation, whose style depended increasingly on the balancing of phrases within more or less symmetrical closed tonal designs. Thus the most successful works of C. P. E. Bach often possess a more rigid architecture than do those of his father.

Nevertheless, in addition to concerns with chromatic harmony and written-out embellishment, C. P. E. Bach shared with his father a zeal for editing his own keyboard works as part of a deliberately organized *oeuvre*. Just as Sebastian had devoted much effort relatively late in his career to the revision of his earlier keyboard music, Emanuel, once called to Berlin, seems to have felt compelled to bring up to date works that he had written as a student at Leipzig and during several years in Frankfurt an der Oder. According to the estate catalogue (*NV*) issued by Bach's widow, the years that saw the emergence of Emanuel's style were also ones in which he revised most of the surviving earlier works, including the first seventeen keyboard sonatas and the first three harpsichord concertos.[2] Less far-reaching revisions of these and later works continued to take place thereafter, but evidently Bach did not feel that these involved a sufficiently great alteration to be described as renewals (*Erneuerungen*).

Although many uncertainties surround the dating and identification of the earliest versions of the works that Bach first wrote at Leipzig or Frankfurt, it is possible to reach a few tentative conclusions about Bach's stylistic development prior to the 1740s.[3] He seems never to have systematically emulated his

---

[1] Darrell Berg seems to have been the first to point out the 'inflexibility' of Bach's formal procedure, in 'The Keyboard Sonatas of C. P. E. Bach: An Expression of the Mannerist Principle', Ph.D. diss., State University of New York at Buffalo, 1975, 96.

[2] *NV* describes these works as 'erneuert'. The dates of composition that I give here come from *NV*, although those for early works rarely have independent confirmation.

[3] I discuss the dating of early versions of certain sonatas in my review of *The Collected Works for Solo Keyboard by Carl Philipp Emanuel Bach*, ed. Darrell Berg (New York, 1985), in *JAMS*, 40 (1987), 14–21.

father's fugal counterpoint except in a few rather weak works composed around 1752, about the time he helped get Sebastian's *Kunst der Fuge* into print. Still, sonatas as late as the first of the Württemberg set, composed in 1742, contain movements whose imitative counterpoint is modelled on that of Sebastian's two-part inventions. The earliest example is the opening Presto of the first work listed in *NV*, a sonata in B flat published in 1761 but originally composed in 1731 (H. 2/W. 62, 1). The opening subject is a quotation from the invention in F BWV 779, and the movement as a whole is a thoroughgoing parody of this piece, reworking it into a variant of the sonata form that Emanuel would adopt as his norm. Another frequent borrowing from Sebastian is the arpeggiando figuration employed in a great many of Emanuel's early sonatas (notably that in D minor H. 5/W. 65, 3) to compose out progressions that would not be out of place in a work of the elder Bach. Such arpeggiation can be traced to some of the preludes that probably constituted Emanuel's first keyboard lessons. Likewise borrowed from works of Sebastian, but ultimately stemming from the Italian concerto rather than the French unmeasured prelude, are the arpeggiated figures that comprise much of the solo passage-work in Emanuel's own first concerto H. 403/W. 1, composed in 1733.[4]

Of greater interest than the obvious borrowings from Sebastian, however, are the formal designs into which they are incorporated and the occasional presence, even in apparently early versions of these works, of those hallmarks of Emanuel's own style mentioned above. While many early sonata movements, such as the one parodying the invention, use rounded binary designs, others are formally indistinguishable from the ternary type that Bach preferred from the 1740s onwards.[5] Bach knew comparable ternary forms in some of his father's dance movements and preludes, but for the somewhat more extensive type used in a sonata his models are likely to have been chamber works by a fashionable composer like Telemann, whom Emanuel seems to have imitated in his own flute sonatas, composed mostly in the late thirties and early forties. The allegros in a few of Bach's early keyboard works are quite close in style to those in his flute sonatas, particularly in the use of modulating passage-work after the statement of the initial theme; see, for instance, the first movement of the 1739 sonata in G (H. 20/W. 62, 2).[6]

But even this modest work contains a hint of the sort of device that Bach had

---

[4] Sebastian's autograph of his own harpsichord concertos, D-ddr Bds, Mus. ms. P 234, probably dates from the late 1730s; hence the actual models for Emanuel's first keyboard concertos may have been those violin concerto movements which Sebastian had arranged for organ in a number of cantatas from 1726 onwards.

[5] By 'rounded binary' I mean a form that never restates the opening theme in the tonic, unlike a ternary sonata form. The latter may or may not contain a double bar after the first section; it is distinct from da capo form, in which the first section ends in the tonic.

[6] This and other solo keyboard works referred to can be consulted in the facsimile edition by Darrell Berg; see n. 3.

already been cultivating more profusely in other pieces. A pause in the second bar, answered in conventional *galant* manner on its initial appearance, receives a surprising reply when it recurs in the third section: an unprompted cadence to the subdominant leading into a sequential passage that at first contradicts, then confirms, the tonic key. What is crucial is that the pause— the musical equivalent of a rhetorical question—prepares a harmonic surprise whose rightness is revealed only gradually. Earlier as well as later works offer analogous passages, often far more extreme than this one. Frequently one finds a pause followed by a parenthetical phrase that touches on the minor mode or some other foreign tonal area before finally cadencing in the proper key. Of course, excursions to the minor are common in eighteenth-century music, usually in quiet passages akin to echoes.[7] But with Bach the preceding pause makes the parenthesis in the minor appear to be much more than the temporary digression it is, particularly when chromatic harmony makes the passage the most intense of a given section.[8]

In 1738, at the end of what might be considered his years of apprenticeship, Bach produced the first of three sonatas in which his genius becomes fully apparent, particularly in stunning harmonic surprises that often occur within brief outbursts of virtuoso figuration—the sort of arpeggiation previously found only in the solo passages of the concertos. The most brilliant of these sonatas—the one in G minor composed in 1739 (H. 21/W. 65, 11)—is far more radical than the concerto in the same key written in the following year. The two other sonatas also introduce ideas that were to be important in later works. The slow movement of the sonata in A H. 19/W. 65, 10, though later replaced by a longer movement, ends in a half-cadence and thus links two of the movements in an unbroken sequence. The first movement of the sonata in G H. 23/W. 65, 12, includes the written-out embellishment of a fermata, while its second movement is of a new type, an evocation of *stile antico* in even quarter-notes whose strict voice-leading does not preclude some sharp dissonances. Bach returned to this texture three years later in the opening movement of the sonata in B minor H. 32/W. 65, 13. None of these ideas is really new; Sebastian wrote out cadenzas in his harpsichord concertos, and innumerable Baroque slow movements end in half-cadences. But Emanuel had not previously used such devices in his keyboard sonatas; by doing so he was expanding the vocabulary of the new genre that he was rapidly making his own.

In these works, and in the revisions that he perhaps was already carrying out, the superficial aspects of Bach's mature style—those involving the surface of the music, such as the florid written-out melodic embellishment in the slow

---

[7] The expressive significance of such passages might be suggested by the double meaning of the term *mollis*.

[8] For a relatively early example of such a passage, see the third movement of the revised version of H. 4/W. 65, 2 (1744).

movements and the disruptions of the ongoing pulse in the allegros—are largely established. But the description of the revised versions as *erneuert* (in *NV*) suggests that Bach regarded them as involving a profound refashioning. To be sure, melodic embellishment must be regarded as a significant change of style when it alters the expressive import of the music as radically as it does in cases such as the slow movement of the sonata in B flat H. 18/W. 65, 9. Extensive interpolations of material, changing the formal proportions if not the fundamental design, occurred in the first two movements of the sonata in E flat H. 16/W. 65, 7, and perhaps in other works whose earliest versions do not survive. Yet many of the *erneuert* works betray an uneasy tension between the simple, relatively untouched quick movements and the heavily altered slow ones. In the first suite (H. 6/W. 65, 4) the final Gigue seems impossibly short in relation to the Adagio, which must have been considerably altered. (The early version apparently no longer exists.) Even newly composed works, especially the sonata in G minor H. 21, possess a slightly manic quality as a result of the packing of so many surprises and shocks within too compact a sonata form, though this remains true of many later compositions as well and is a source of much of their peculiar charm.

That Bach was capable of sustaining his style to considerably greater breadth, even if withholding his most audacious touches, is clear from his concertos of the same period. But the style continued to mature at levels deeper than the surface. This becomes apparent when the G minor concerto of 1740, H. 409/W. 6, is compared with the masterpieces of a few years later. The concerto is no student exercise, and shows none of the dependence on outside models—chiefly those furnished by Sebastian's works—evident in the first concerto. The ritornellos are now written in the *galant* three-part texture that places most of the interest on an upper part laden with melodic embellishment and rhetorical pauses.[9] More importantly, all three movements can be best understood as sonata forms whose essential structure is articulated by the solo entrances, not the ritornellos.[10]

But although each movement of the concerto follows the same essential plan, the piece is weakened by some oddities in the design of the first movement—despite its impressive opening tutti, which is longer and contains more extreme expressive contrasts than any previously written by Bach.[11] Within the initial tutti the contrasting phrases—mostly quiet, parenthetical passages—are successfully subordinated to a self-contained ternary design.

[9] Passages in the ritornellos of the first concerto were revised to reduce the texture to three voices; see Rachel Wade, *The Keyboard Concertos of Carl Philipp Emanuel Bach* (Ann Arbor, 1981), 89.

[10] I discuss this crucial aspect of Bach's mature concertos in *The Instrumental Music of Carl Philipp Emanuel Bach* (Ann Arbor, 1984), 28–9 and 130–7.

[11] Until it appears in the Carl Philipp Emanuel Bach Edition, the concerto can be examined in the edition by Fritz Oberdörffer (Kassel, 1952), which is adequate for study although based on a faulty source which gives an early version of the piece.

Yet a work of a few years later, the E minor concerto H. 428/W. 24, reveals a more refined formal sense as well as greater sophistication in the treatment of detail.

The opening tutti of the earlier concerto moves quickly to a rhetorical pause on the dominant; only after a dramatic series of parenthetical phrases does the section conclude in the tonic. But in only one other part of the movement does Bach succeed in generating an equally compelling sense of dramatic tension—in the retransition, the passage that prepares the return of the opening material in the original key.[12] The sequential dialogue between harpsichord and strings—which grows out of a similar alternation within the initial tutti—is rendered especially urgent by the increasing brevity of each statement, or, to put it another way, the acceleration of the exchanges. A comparable series of sequences built out of increasingly short units occurs at an analogous point in several sonatas from roughly the same time, notably the first Württemberg sonata (last movement). Indeed, the use of this device to prepare the most crucial articulation in the concerto shows that by now Bach understood his concertos as employing a variant of sonata form.

In fact the conception of the concerto movement as a sonata, its three main sections framed by ritornellos, is perhaps clearer in the concertos of around 1740 than in many later ones. Apart from the ritornellos, the tutti entries in the first movement of H. 409 are in most cases little more than interjections punctuating what is essentially a passage for solo harpsichord. True, Bach aims at a more complex syntax in the second solo section, but the result is only a diffusion of the dramatic impulse; the strongly articulated tutti and solo entries, each one perhaps dramatic in itself, neutralize one another. In this example, at least, one could understand one writer's reference to a 'loose alternation of solos and ritornellos' as constituting the 'middle sections' of Bach's concerto movements.[13] Bach's later concertos are both more cogent and more flexible in structure, as the E minor concerto of 1748 demonstrates. A simple but previously unknown type of dialogue between soloist and tutti in the third movement grows out of an almost Haydnesque passage in the opening ritornello[14] (see Example 1). This later provokes a series of interruptions of one party in the dialogue by the other; more than a series of punctuation marks, the exchange between soloist and tutti is essential to the rhetoric of the section (see Example 2).

The reinforcement by the tutti of the deceptive cadence in measures 108–9 was a late alteration; it represents a relatively superficial addition to the series

---

[12] The retransition is the most variable part in Bach's concerto designs; here its function is taken by a brief solo section falling between the third and fourth ritornellos (measures 212–55). See Shelley Davis, 'H. C. Koch, the Classic Concerto, and the Sonata-form Retransition', *JM*, 2 (1983), 45–61, and the article by Shelley Davis in this volume.

[13] Daniel E. Freeman, 'The Earliest Italian Keyboard Concertos', *JM*, 4 (1985–6), 137.

[14] Pippa Drummond is thus mistaken in seeing 'intimations of Haydn's infuence' in a similar passage in Bach's last concerto; see *The German Concerto* (Oxford, 1980), 342.

Example 1. Concerto in E minor H. 428/W. 24, iii, late version, mm. 15–24. D-brd B St 263 (An 303 and an additional unidentified copyist)

of exchanges that disrupt, and thus dramatize, the drive to the soloist's final cadence.[15] Comparable revisions of uncertain date occur in the G minor concerto and probably others as well; they demonstrate that Bach aimed at loosening the relationship between soloist and tutti in the solo sections. But such revisions could only underline whatever was already implicit in the phrasing of the original.

By 1748 such revisions were unnecessary to reveal Bach's mastery of concerto syntax, which allowed him on occasion to play with what had become the basic conventions of the form. The entrance of the tutti after a modulating solo passage is a chief dramatic *locus* in any concerto movement; normally an anticipation of that entrance, especially an anticipation in the same key as the eventual tutti, weakens the form as seriously as a premature arrival on the tonic in the development section of a Classical sonata.[16] Yet the false reprise of the Classical style manages to be both witty and dramatic. Bach achieves a more or less equivalent effect in the first movement of the E minor concerto—not, to be sure, at the return, but in the second solo section (see Example 3). The tutti breaks in with the ritornello theme at the conclusion of the soloist's passage-work (measure 117). But the real ritornello follows only after a rapid exchange between soloist and tutti (measures 124–9), which

---

[15] The tutti entry in measure 109 is found only in sources giving a version of the work which dates probably from no earlier than the 1750s; details will be given in my critical report for the concerto in the Carl Philipp Emanuel Bach Edition.

[16] This was one of the mistakes Bach had made in the first movement of the G minor concerto, in which a solo statement of the main theme in D minor anticipates the ritornello in that tonality.

Example 2. Concerto in E minor H. 428/W. 24, iii, late version, mm. 96–111.
D-brd B St 263 (An 303 and an additional unidentified copyist)

prepares the unusually urgent unaccompanied cadential phrase marking the
end of the solo section (measures 130–7).[17]

The E minor concerto shows how conventional signs, like the apparent
preparation for a ritornello in measures 115–16, can afterwards be contra-

---

[17] Early copies of the work contain variants suggesting that here too the division of the melodic
line between solo and tutti, beginning in measure 124, could have been a second thought, though
one that led to an immediate change while Bach was still composing. The earliest preserved
version of the passage is illustrated as being closer to the state of the work in 1748.

Example 3. Concerto in E minor H. 428/W. 24, i, early version, mm. 115–38.
D-brd B P 709 (unidentified copyist, owned by Müthel)

dicted to acheive effects of wit or drama much more sustained than those achieved by the rhetorical pauses in Bach's earlier works. By the time of the E minor concerto Bach also had lost any qualms he might have had earlier about adopting effects borrowed from or inspired by Italian opera. H. 428 immediately followed the work that is arguably Bach's best concerto of the 1740s—perhaps of them all. The concerto in D minor H. 427/W. 23 represents in many respects a heightened and more successful version of what Bach had attempted eight years earlier in the G minor work.[18] Its opening ritornello again starts with a fiery dotted motif and is interrupted early on by a rhetorical pause, this time preceded by an even more grating dissonance than in H. 409. But the drum-bass in eighth-notes and the more virtuosic treatment of both strings and soloist—the latter is provided with two written-out

    [18] Of various existing editions, the best is that by Arnold Schering from the revised autograph score, D-brd B, Mus. ms. P 354 (Denkmäler deutscher Tonkunst, vols. 29–30; Leipzig, 1904–8).

cadenzas in the first movement—suggest Bach's free borrowing from the vocabulary of contemporary dramatic music.

A more subtle sort of drama occurs in the slow movement, which opens on the dissonance V–6/5 in C major.[19] Although the dissonance is soon resolved, and F established as the tonic, the dissonant opening gesture of each tutti undermines the structural function of the ritornello, which is to establish tonal stability while constituting an unambiguous formal articulation. Instead the tonality is suspended while the break between two formal divisions is obscured. The breaks involved are not only between solo and tutti sections, but between whole movements, for the dissonance at the opening of the slow movement joins with the closing D minor sonority of the preceding Allegro to form a continuous harmonic progression. The harmonic juxtaposition was Bach's first thought; as the autograph shows, the opening of the slow movement underwent considerable melodic *Veränderung*, but originated probably as a succession of two ungarnished chords.[20] The progression recurs, in different melodic realizations, throughout the tutti statements and in the written-out cadenza.

Despite the clear advance in compositional craft and sophistication in Bach's concertos through the 1740s, there is no reason to suppose that he was moving in the direction of the Viennese Classical language. Even in the D minor concerto (as in other concertos of the decade) the essence of the form is unchanged, and Bach maintains a tendency to recapitulate long stretches of passage-work in the final solo section, giving the music a formal, schematic quality quite different from that of Classical works. Although several short, unchallenging keyboard works of the later 1740s employ the regular phrasing and conventional harmony that seem to predominate in Bach's works of the next decade, a group of extraordinary keyboard sonatas written at about the same time goes far beyond the concertos in their employment of devices that can be regarded as manneristic, even anti-Classical. The harmonic shocks, rhetorical pauses, and radical changes of texture and pacing for which Bach is famous appear here in concentrations that Bach was to employ in ensemble works only in the concertos and symphonies of the Hamburg period. At least five sonatas—H. 37/W. 52, 4; H. 46/W. 65, 16; H. 47/W. 65, 17; H. 51/W. 65, 20; and H. 60/W. 65, 24—can be counted in this group, which must be judged a series of brilliant experiments; for they are not always entirely successful.[21]

---

[19] A dominant seventh is a dissonance in Bach's vocabulary, particularly when the bass is the raised fourth degree; the fifth in the 6/5 chord 'is treated as a dissonance' (*Essay*, p. 244).

[20] On the reconstruction of the original version, see Wade, *Keyboard Concertos*, p. 99, and Schulenberg, *Instrumental Music*, pp. 50–1.

[21] Berg previously referred to some of the same sonatas as having a 'serious or experimental character' (The Keyboard Sonatas, p. 96). The phenomenon was not confined to C. P. E. Bach; several sonatas by W. F. Bach from the same decade can be described in similar terms.

Like the concertos, these sonatas contain devices that seem to contradict the customary structural formulas; most striking is the sonata in G minor (H. 47/W. 65, 17), whose first movement combines fantasia style with what at first appears to be ritornello form. The absence of a central double bar and the alternation between measured and unmeasured notation distinguish this first movement from those of most other sonatas. Yet the cadences and tonal plateaux of the movement articulate Bach's usual (that is, ternary) sonata form, even though there is no head-theme of the regular sort. A passage in octaves resembles a unison ritornello theme, but the movement opens with an unmeasured passage in fantasia style. The latter recurs at the close of the second section, where a cadence is expected; but instead of a D minor cadence, unmeasured arpeggiation commences a modulating passage functioning as retransition. The original cadenza-like passage returns shortly afterwards, marking the return, and the movement closes with an unmeasured transition to the second movement.

The sonata thus combines ideas from two quite different genres: the improvised fantasia (cadenza, prelude); and the three-movement operatic overture or sinfonia, from which come both the suggestion of a ritornello theme and the linking of the first two movements. As in the sonatas composed at the beginning of the decade, Bach continues to expand the vocabulary of sonata style. But now the changes extend to the very structure of the piece, or at least disguise it, as in the first movement. Actually, this is an exceptional case; Bach would never again closely combine fantasia style with that of the sinfonia, although he had done so to a limited degree in H. 46 in C, the only previous sonata in which the first two movements are joined. There, as in most of Bach's Hamburg sinfonias, the juncture is intentionally jarring, less a transition than a dramatic collision of tempos and keys. The use of fantasia style for the transition in the G minor sonata is a particularly graceful solution to the problem of unifying the cycle. The unmeasured writing recalls the initial idea of the first movement, and mediates between the impetuous closing theme of the latter and the gentle opening of the Adagio.

The emergence of this slow movement in a limpid G major is one of the most perfectly conceived moments in any of Bach's works. As in a number of the Württemberg sonatas, the Adagio is in a sort of rondo form. Its contrast with the first movement is heightened by the remote tonality, B minor, to which it moves in the course of its first section. Yet the Adagio is sufficently concise that it can be heard as a long digression between the two outer movements; the return of G minor in the last movement comes soon enough that the entire sonata can be heard as an unbroken three-part fantasia, even in the absence of a connecting passage between the last two movements.

Thus in one of his earliest cyclic works Bach achieves as convincing a unity as in any of his later compositions. If the sonata gives any disappointment it is because the monophonic statements of the chromatic subject of the last movement may suggest to some hearers the opening of a fugue, and of course the subject receives no imitative development (nor any development at all). In fact much of the movement consists of virtuoso figuration not unlike that employed in Bach's contemporary concertos, and the movement reaches a climax in a powerful series of broken chords in the second ('development') section. The flaw, if it is one, stems from Bach's challenging the basic design of the mid-eighteenth-century sonata, for the movement seems intended to complement and balance the opening one, not merely to round out the cycle in an agreeable manner.

The other 'experimental' sonatas are outwardly less radical, but perhaps have more direct parallels in later works. The sonata in F sharp minor, H. 37 of 1744, was the only one of the five that Bach eventually published. It is notable for the alternating rhythmic styles in the first movement, whose opening arpeggiation in unbroken sixteenth triplets gives way several times to a quieter, more cantabile texture moving with an eighth-note pulse. An antecedent might be found in the alternating forte and piano (or tutti and solo) passages in parts of the first movement of the G minor concerto H. 409/W. 6. But now Bach juxtaposes radically different rhythmic types within a solo movement, a procedure more akin to the combination of measured and unmeasured notation in the G minor Sonata. An even closer parallel, however, can be found in the alternating tempos in the first movement of Bach's so-called *Programm-Trio* of 1749 (H. 579/W. 161, 1), the most radical example of a dialoguing type of trio sonata cultivated at Berlin, and one of Bach's few chamber works in which the innovations of the keyboard music are applied.[22]

Although it is not yet apparent in H. 37, in several of these works Bach was concerned not only with the form of individual movements, but with that of the cycle as a whole. This is obvious with the connected movements of H. 46 and H. 47, but it is also clear in those individual movements which, like the last of H. 47, avoid conventional types and thus give the work as a whole a distinctive shape. Both H. 46 and H. 51, employing a strategy opposite that used in H. 47, conclude in unexpectedly restrained movements. These are substantial movements, but lyrical and retrospective in character, not challenging the first for the dramatic centre—probably because in both sonatas it is the second movement that carries the greatest weight. In H. 46 the slow movement—really the extended coda of the opening Allegro—is a sort of measured fantasia incorporating fragments from the first movement as well as passages of quasi-recitative. While H. 51 contains no such innovations, it is in some respects a more mature and sophisticated work. The Adagio is in D minor, the mediant—more distant than the customary relative minor—and this, together with the unusual intensity of the movement, makes the gentle opening of the final Allegro particularly poignant.

[22] On such works, see David Fuller, 'Accompanied Keyboard Music', *MQ*, 60 (1976), 228, and Schulenberg, *Instrumental Music*, pp. 79–84.

The first movement, whose orchestral textures, shifting rhythmic pacing, and lurches in tonal direction bring it remarkably close to the Hamburg symphonies of thirty years later, significantly embellishes the ternary sonata structure, though not as radically as in the G minor sonata. The most surprising feature is a quiet digression in the second section, a sequence that might have been scored for two flutes and bassoon. The passage, which springs unexpected from a series of fiery tremolos in D minor, deflects the movement to E flat and ultimately to G minor. Such a digression might seem a rather clumsy way of getting from one key to another. But the very function of the passage seems to be that of an incursion from outside Bach's customary closed structure. As such it looks forward to the insertion of a complete Adagio and a Minuet into the sonata form of the one-movement concerto of 1771 (H. 475/ W. 43, 5). The sonata's orchestral textures suggest that as early as the 1740s Bach would have liked to extend the types of writing found in these sonatas to ensemble music, but not until receiving van Swieten's commission for unrestrained orchestral writing (which led to the six string symphonies of 1773) would he realize the musical vision glimpsed here.

Nevertheless, the first movement cedes to the second the position of greatest import in H. 51. The Adagio is unique in Bach's keyboard sonatas for its florid two-part counterpoint, both parts being as heavily embellished as anything in the North German repertory (including the astonishingly ornate works of Müthel). The movement is in full-fledged ternary sonata form, and the equality of the parts extends to the placement of the statements of the main theme in the bass. The Adagio ends with a passage in orchestral style that seems to prepare a cadenza, though no source gives the customary fermata. Even so, a real allargando seems necessary here if the passage is to provide a sufficiently firm conclusion to one of Bach's most ambitious slow movements. The movement, incidentally, poses a seemingly insoluble problem of performing medium; as in the other experimental sonatas, the style and the dynamic markings demand the expressivity of the clavichord, but on a single keyboard the crossing melodic lines can be executed only imperfectly.[23]

The difficulty in determining the optimal medium for this and other works is not insignificant. While every movement demands the types of freedom available only to a solo keyboard player, many passages derive from orchestral or vocal writing. As early as the first Prussian sonata of 1740 Bach had followed his father in writing secco recitative for the keyboard. In the odd little D-minor sonata of 1749 (H. 60/W. 65, 24) he extended his reach toward organ style and *stile antico*, although the autograph indicates 'Sonata per il Cembalo'.[24] No doubt the greatest number of new ideas imitated in the

---

[23] Many of the dynamic markings in the edition in *Le trésor des pianistes* (Paris, 1863) stem from an unauthorized posthumous print (Leipzig, *c.*1802); of those that are authentic, many were late additions by Bach. But even some of those in the earliest dependable sources cannot be played on the harpsichord.                         [24] Reproduced in Berg's facsimile edition.

keyboard works of this period came from Italian opera; as E. Eugene Helm suggests, the opening of the Berlin Royal Opera in 1742 may have encouraged Bach's 'dramatic impulse, which was to take many forms'.[25] Indeed, real drama, whether in the momentary heightened rhetoric of an unexpected pause or in the long-range tensions generated by a concerto movement, is more likely to be found in Bach's instrumental works than in the musical dramas of the Berlin stage, if the customary view of C. H. Graun's operas can be accepted. The virtuosity and rhetoric of *opera seria*, like the formal conventions of the aria and concerto, are increasingly put to unconventional use or placed in unconventional contexts in Bach's keyboard works of the 1740s. Yet perhaps his most important discovery was that the simple, rational sonata form employed in countless blander works by his contemporaries could be a stage for rhetoric, wit, and drama extending deep beneath the musical surface.

[25] *Helm/Grove*, p. 846.

# C. P. E. Bach, J. C. F. Rellstab, and the Sonatas with Varied Reprises

## Howard Serwer

IN 1758–9 C. P. E. Bach composed a set of *Sechs Sonaten fürs Clavier mit veränderten Reprisen* ('Six Sonatas For Keyboard with Varied Reprises'; H. 126, 136–140/W. 50) and, in partnership with the publisher Georg Ludwig Winter of Berlin, he published them in 1760.[1] The original print of this set appeared, as did many Berlin music prints of the day, in two forms: one with German front matter and another with French.[2] Only recently has this very interesting set of sonatas become available in modern editions, one by Etienne Darbellay and another by Eiji Hashimoto,[3] and even so, it is still almost unknown except to specialists. In his preface Bach explained the meaning of the phrsae 'varied reprises':

These days it is absolutely necessary that one varies repetitions; it is expected of every performer . . .. In the composition of these sonatas, I have in mind especially beginners and also those amateurs who, on account of their age or for other reasons, no longer have the patience or the time to practise very much. Apart from something easy, I have wanted to provide them with the pleasure of having variations without being required to invent them themselves or have someone else compose them and then with much effort, learn them by heart.[4]

---

[1] Arrangements in which the composer shared in the cost of publication (and in the profits, if any) were not at all unusual at this time.

[2] The title of the German issue is 'Sechs Sonaten fürs Clavier/mit veränderten Reprisen/—/Ihro Königlichen Hoheit/der Prinzeßin Amalia von Preußen/unterthänigt zugeignet/und verfertiget/von/ . . . /—/Berlin, 1760./Gedruckt und zu finden bey Georg Ludwig Winter.' The French title is 'VI. SONATES/POUR LE CLAVECIN/AVEC DES REPRISES VARIÉES./DEDIÉES/A SON ALTESSE ROYALE/ MADAME LA PRINCESSE AMELIE/PRINCESSE DE PRUSSE/PAR/CHARL/PHIL. EMAN. BACH./—/à BERLIN. 1760./CHEZ GEORGE LOUIS WINTER.'

[3] *C. P. E. Bach, Sechs Sonaten mit veränderten Reprisen*, ed. Etienne Darbellay (Winterthur, 1976); *Sechs Sonaten mit veränderten Reprisen*, ed. Eiji Hashimoto (Tokyo, 1984).

[4] *Sechs Sonaten*, preface: 'Das Verändern beym Wiederholen ist heut zu Tage unentbehrlich. Man erwartet solches von jedem Ausführer. . . . Bey Verfertigung dieser Sonaten habe ich vornehmlich an Anfänger und solche Liebhaber gedacht, die wegen gewisser Jahre oder anderer Verrichtungen nicht mehr Gedult und Zeit genug haben, sich besonders stark zu üben. Ich haben ihnen bey der Leichtigkeit zugleich auf eine bequeme Art das Vergnügen verschaffen wollen, sich mit Veränderungen hören zu lassen, ohne das sie nöthig haben, solche entweder selbst zu erfinden, oder sich von andern vorschreiben zu lassen, and sie mit vieler mühe auswendig zu lernen'.

No autograph is known to exist for these sonatas, the earliest sources being the surviving exemplars of the Winter's 1760 print. None the less, as will be described below, there are autographic materials that I hope to show were written out a quarter-century after the works were composed.

The other known eighteenth-century prints of this collection include an edition by John Walsh (London, 1762—doubtless pirated), later reissued by John Randall in the 1770s, and editions by J. G. I. Breitkopf and J. C. F. Rellstab, both of the latter appearing curiously close together in time: late 1785 and early 1786 respectively. At least forty exemplars of Winter's 1760 print exist today along with eleven of the Walsh and Randall, eleven of Rellstab's, and two of the Breitkopf.[5] This essay will relate the surviving autographic materials to the Breitkopf and Rellstab prints, thereby suggesting an answer to the question of why Rellstab and Breitkopf, both active in Germany, reissued the sonatas within six months of one another—while Bach himself was still living.

Georg Ludwig Winter was a music publisher active in Berlin from 1750 until his death in the late 1760s or early 1770s.[6] Thereafter, his widow continued the business until 1785, when she sold it to J. C. F. Rellstab, of whom more later. One of the exemplars of the Winter print with French front matter, now in the British Library has an inscription in Bach's hand that reads 'First Part of my Reprisen Sonaten with some variations'.[7] Indeed seven movements of the fifteen that make up the first five sonatas have variations in the hand of the composer written, crammed, even scrawled in the margins and in between the staves of the print (see Facsimile 1). A copy of the print with German front matter now in the Bibliothèque Nationale (Paris) has all the autograph variants except one for the third movement of the fifth sonata. It is from this copy that we have dates of composition of the pieces in the set.[8]

Though there is no autograph for this collection, there are extant a number of manuscript copies. According to E. Eugene Helm, most seem to have been taken from one or another of the prints and, for present purposes, are of little interest.[9] My own examination of some of these copies confirms this impression. Three of the manuscripts, however, are of great interest.

[5] RISM A/1, B70.

[6] Rudolph Elvers, 'Winter, Johann Ludwig', *New Grove*, xx. 455. Elvers reports that Rellstab took over Winter's business in 1787, but Bach's letter to Breitkopf of 23 July 1785 makes it clear that Rellstab owned the business by 1785.

[7] GB Lbm K.10.a.28.: 'Erster Theil/meiner/Reprisen Sonaten/mit/einigen Veränderungen'. Darbellay (*Sechs Sonaten*, xx, n. 14) suggests the possibility that because Bach used the phrase 'erster Theil meiner Reprisen Sonaten' he may not have referred to the two *Fortsetzungen* but to the two sets of *Kurze und leichte Clavierstücke mit veränderten Reprisen* . . . (H. 193–203/W. 113 and H. 228–38/W. 114) of 1766 and 1768 respectively.

[8] Darbellay, *Sechs Sonaten*, xvi–xvii.

[9] Hashimoto reports on p. 21 of his edition that the copy of the Winter print in the Germanisches Nationalmuseum in Nuremberg differs from the copies in London and Vienna, suggesting the possibility of 'stop-press' corrections.

both instances it would appear that the variations were already in place. Bach's rewriting of these pieces seems then, to have concentrated on those movements not in binary or variation form.

Bach composed and, with Winter, published two other sets of sonatas whose titles indicate that Bach or Winter intended that they be perceived as continuations of the first set. These are *Fortsetzung von Sechs Sonaten fürs Clavier* (1761) and *Zweyte Fortsetzung von Sechs Sonaten fürs Clavier* (1763). As the absence of the phrase *veränderten Reprisen* in their titles suggests, the latter sets do not contain the written-out varied reprises characteristic of the first. However, they figure in our story because manuscripts P 1135 and Bc 5885 contain variations on some of the pieces in these collections.

I have already pointed out the curious fact that Breitkopf and Rellstab issued separate reprints of the first set in 1785 and 1786. It might also be noted that though Bach engaged in constant revision and polishing of many of his works,[10] the massive and systematic nature of the revisions of the *Reprisen Sonaten*, suggests something beyond the mere urge to polish. Indeed it seems strange that Bach would go to so much trouble over works designed, as he said, for 'beginners and also those amateurs who . . . no longer have the patience or the time to practise very much.' Could it be that the competing prints of 1785–6 and the composer's variants to the sonatas are related in some way?

In 1911, Hermann von Hase published a description of the correspondence between J. G. I. Breitkopf and Carl Philipp Emanuel Bach.[11] In fact, von Hase was able only to describe the letters from Bach to Breitkopf from 1766 to 1787 because regrettably neither Breitkopf's letters nor the Breitkopf copy-books from this period have survived. All we have of Breitkopf's responses are occasional memoranda or cost calculations jotted on the backs of the letters. None the less, it is possible to reconstruct much of the relationship between the two, who clearly held each other in the highest regard—though, as we will see, on occasion Bach must have tried Breitkopf's patience more than a little.[12]

In his account of Bach's correspondence with Breitkopf, von Hase took note of a letter from the summer of 1785 in which the composer complained about the conduct of the Berlin publisher J. C. F. Rellstab. Von Hase explained that Bach's displeasure with Rellstab arose from the fact that the latter wished to reissue the *Reprisen Sonaten* even though Bach still had some copies of his own to sell. Von Hase also reported that Bach asked Breitkopf to help him punish Rellstab. More recently, Rachel Wade in her book on C. P. E. Bach's concertos

[10] For example, Bach's own copy of his *Passions-Cantate* (H. 776/W. 233) shows literally scores of corrections and changes made over almost two decades.

[11] Hermann von Hase, 'Carl Philipp Emanuel Bach und Joh. Gottl. Im. Breitkopf', *BJ*, 8 (1911), 86–104.

[12] Von Hase was able to only scratch the surface of the Bach–Breitkopf correspondence; for one thing there were dozens of letters, and for another, the Breitkopf archives contained letters from many other eminent musicians; von Hase published summaries of these in a series of articles in the years following 1911.

has also taken note of Bach's antipathy to Rellstab and his desire to punish him.[13] How was Bach going to punish Rellstab?

Because Bach was very angry, and because he was corresponding at this time with Breitkopf about other matters, his letters are often a bit disorganized. Accordingly it is necessary to rearrange their contents now and again to present the events more or less in chronological order. We already know the beginning: Bach and Winter published three sets of sonatas in 1760, 1761, and 1763.

The relevant portion of the correspondence begins with the long letter mentioned by von Hase and Wade from Bach to Breitkopf dated 23 July 1785 (S. 153).[14] At the beginning of the letter, Bach gives the impression that the principal matter of business at hand was the ongoing negotiations for the publication of the fifth 'Kenner und Liebhaber' collection; (H. 281, 268, 282–3, 279, 284/W. 59). Bach begins with a report to Breitkopf that he, Bach, has hopes of rounding up more subscriptions for the cantata *Die Auferstehung und Himmelfahrt Jesu* than he had previously estimated.[15] After a few more lines of small talk, Bach gets to what is really on his mind: a problem with J. C. F. Rellstab. He writes, 'At the moment I am engaged in a nasty correspondence with a young smart alec and insolent boor by the name of Rellstab in Berlin who is starting up a music printing business.'[16]

Johann Carl Friedrich Rellstab (1759–1813) had studied keyboard and composition in Berlin until 1779 when, on the death of his father, he assumed control of the latter's printing business. He enlarged the operation, turned to publishing, and, it would appear from Bach's remarks, entered the music printing business shortly before the summer of 1785. Indeed, in 1787 he applied for a monopoly in Prussia for printing music with movable type in a manner that he claimed was superior to that of Breitkopf of Leipzig.[17] From remarks that Bach makes in the letter of 23 July, it seems clear that Rellstab had been experimenting with music printing as early as 1785.

Bach reported to Breitkopf that Rellstab had written to him to tell him that he, Rellstab, had purchased the entire remaining stock of the *Reprisen Sonaten* from the widow of Georg Ludwig Winter, the original publisher. According to Bach, Rellstab said that there were no more copies of the first part in Berlin.

---

[13] Rachel Wade, *The Keyboard Concertos of Carl Philipp Emanuel Bach* (Ann Arbor, 1981), 31–2.

[14] *Suchalla/Briefe*, pp. 180–5. "S." refers to the number assigned to the letter by Suchalla in his edition; "l". refers to the line number in the letter. I extend my sincere thanks to Dr Suchalla for his willingness, in advance of the publication of his edition of the letters, to help me with the reading of a number of very difficult places. In a very few instances I disagree with his rendering, but in no case is the meaning affected significantly. The translations are mine.

[15] See the article by Stephen Clark in this volume.

[16] *Suchalla/Briefe* S. 153, l. 13: 'Ich habe jetzt eine häßliche Correspondenz mit einem jungen Naseweiß u. groben Flegel, Nahmens Rellstab in Berlin, der mit einen neuen Notedruckerey anfängt.'

[17] See Wilhelm Hitzig, 'Ein berliner Aktenstück zur Geschichte des Notendruckverfahrens', *Festschrift Peter Wagner zum 60. Geburtstag*, ed. Karl Weinmann (Leipzig, 1926), 81–6.

(Bach observed bluntly at this point, 'This I do not believe.')[18] In this letter Bach explained to Breitkopf that the publication had been a joint venture with the late Winter in which Bach put up some of the money in the expectation of making a profit from the sale of the sonatas. Bach went on to report that after Winter's demise, he had difficulty getting an accounting or payment from Winter's widow for the copies sold, so that 'I was compelled to agree that we divide the copies between us because otherwise I would have had to wait for an eternity for an accounting.'[19] This must have taken place at some point after June 1772, the time when Winter's widow is known to have taken over the business. Bach said that at that time he gave Frau Winter a receipt indicating that their account was settled. We do not know how many copies Bach received from Frau Winter in settlement of the account, but in the present letter, which could have been written a decade after the event, he told Breitkopf that he still had on hand forty-two copies of the first part, two of the second, and 260 of the third.

In this same 1785 letter, Bach implied that Rellstab had misrepresented the situation to him by claiming that Bach's settlement with Frau Winter meant that neither side had any rights as against the other with respect to these sonatas. Rellstab claimed that Frau Winter could therefore do what she wished with the sonatas, including republish them, and that he, Rellstab, had simply acquired whatever rights she had. Bach disagreed, claiming that the dividing of the copies was simply a form of payment, that nothing was said about the rights to the sonatas, and that he continued to have whatever rights to the sonatas that he had in the past. Because Bach had put up his own money, he held that he would decide when and if the sonatas should be reissued.

Rellstab had other ideas. He proposed to print 300 copies to be sold at the coming *Michaelsmesse* (September) and offered to take Bach in as a partner if he would advance 1 louis d'or per gathering as a printing fee.[20] Bach said that he answered Rellstab courteously, offering him all of his remaining stock of the three series of sonatas at a cheap price, either all at once or little by little. Bach also told Rellstab he could not assent to a new printing of the first part while he still had copies because a new issue under such circumstances would amount to piracy. The word Bach used was *Nachdruck*, which still carries 'piracy' as one of its meanings. Moreover, he said that he checked with the book-dealers in Hamburg before he used the word 'piracy' in his letter to Rellstab, and that they agreed that such an action by Rellstab would indeed be piracy. It would appear that Bach did not have a copy of the receipt he had given Frau Winter, for he told Breitkopf that he asked a friend in Berlin who knew his hand to

---

[18] *Suchalla/Briefe*, S. 153, l. 20: 'dies glaub ich nicht.'

[19] *Suchalla/Briefe*, 5.153, ll. 51–3: 'dadurch wurde ich gezwungen, dass wir die Sonatenexemplare theilten (weil ich sonst hätte ewig auf eine Berechnung warten müßen.)'

[20] This seems to have been the normal price for printing one gathering of four sides. See the letter of February 1786 (S. 161a, esp. l. 3) containing Breitkopf's calculations of costs and revenue for editions of 300, 400, and 500 copies of Bach's *Auferstehung und Himmelfahrt Jesu*.

examine the receipt he had given Frau Winter that was now in Rellstab's possession and make a copy of it for him.

According to Bach, Rellstab wrote a reply in which he threatened to publish the receipt, but Bach told Breitkopf that he suspected that Rellstab would invent a receipt to suit his own purposes. Bach enclosed, in his letter to Breitkopf, the threatening letter from Rellstab, but the whereabouts of this letter is unknown today. Because it seemed to Bach that, notwithstanding his objections, the "young smart alec" was going to reissue the sonatas, he asked Breitkop for help.

Inasmuch as Bach was unwilling to go into business with Rellstab, there were, as Bach saw it, two possibilities. As a first suggestion, Bach proposed that 'If a buyer could be found, and he wished, I would compose variations and elaborations on the first collection (without the least fee), merely so that the pirate will be stuck. Perhaps we could do something.'[21] Later in the letter Bach even offered to send along an entirely new sonata, gratis. This proposal seems to imply that the purchaser would reissue the first set of sonatas with the new variations, and if that is true, it leaves unanswered the question of what the purchaser would do with the copies of the obsolete version. The phrase 'Perhaps we could do something' seems to be more than a hint that Bach wanted Breitkopf to intervene.

Alternatively, if no one would buy them, then Bach proposed to dump his remaining stock of the first set so cheaply that Rellstab would not be able to compete. Whether he was the seller or the dumper ('Verkaufer oder Verschleuderer') of these sonatas, he begged Breitkopf to keep the source of them to himself.

In a long postscript, Bach explained to Breitkopf in great detail that he not only offered Rellstab his three sets of sonatas cheaply, but offered to throw in 'eine Kleinigkeit' for his press. Bach noted in passing that he also proposed to let Rellstab have his Prussian and Württemburg sonatas to practise on in his new music printing operation. At the end of the postscript Bach observed, almost as an afterthought, that he would be content to take 50 Rthl. for the 300 copies in his possession. This would amount to 4 gr. each, or an eighth of the normal price of 1 Rthl 8 gr.

Breitkopf apparently either did not answer Bach's letter of 23 July or was evasive in his reply, for on 26 August Bach wrote again saying, 'inasmuch as you have not given me any counsel in this nasty matter, even though I begged you for it, I will have to do what I think is best because the Fair is at hand.'[22] None the less, Rellstab must be punished. Bach pointed out that he, Bach, was

---

[21] S. 153, ll. 93–7: 'Findet sich ein Käufer, u. hat er Lust, so will ich mich dem ersten Theile, Veränderungen oder Vermehrung (ohne die geringste Bezahlung) vornehmen, blos, daß der Nachdruck erstickt wird. Vielleicht könnten wir etwas machen.'

[22] S. 154, ll. 1–2: 'Da Sie mir in dem so Verdrießlichen Sache keinen Rath geben, so sehr ich Sie auch bat: so muß ich mir nun selbst rathen, da die Meße vor der Thüre ist.'

not in a good position to sell them, that Breitkopf had many more contacts, etc. Therefore Bach announced that in a few days he was sending the sonatas to Breitkopf asking Breitkopf to give him whatever he would, even it were to be less than 50 Rthl, and he gave several reasons why Breitkopf should take them, stating that they were easy, good, popular, etc.

On 14 September 1785, not long before the *Michaelsmesse*, Bach wrote that the previous Saturday he had sent the sonatas to Breitkopf, keeping only one copy of each for himself. Once again he asked Breitkopf to 'give me what you will for all these sonatas'[23] and once again, he asked Breitkopf not to disclose where he, Breitkopf, obtained them.

On 20 September Bach wrote to thank Breitkopf for accepting the sonatas. He enclosed a formal release to Breitkopf, a copy of the receipt he had given to Frau Winter, and a copy of her receipt issued to Rellstab, and he promised to send Breitkopf the new sonata very soon. In this letter, Bach now told Breitkopf that he need not keep silent about the matter explaining that 'just as Frau Winter sold her rights to Rellstab, I have sold mine to you.'[24]

On the back of the letter Bach wrote suggestions about the publication of the new sonata. Because it is unlike the other sonatas, it should be published separately, with an Italian title, and with some copies using the C clef and others using the G clef, 'otherwise this evil fellow will claim it is part of the others and will pirate it.'[25] On 23 September Bach wrote that the new sonata was on the way. 'It is short, easy, and almost without an adagio because such things are no longer stylish.'[26]

On 19 October Bach wished Breitkopf luck with the 'Reprisen Sonaten and the new sonata', and on 30 November he wrote thanking Breitkopf for a statement of his account and assuring him that he need not worry about an accounting for the *Reprisen Sonaten*.

All who have studied the works of C. P. E. Bach are aware that he retouched and revised his works constantly throughout his long life. To the extent that he did this because he was dissatisfied with this or that aspect of a piece, he was rather unusual for his era. If the typical eighteenth-century composer revised a work, such revision often arose from a revival under new circumstances of performance or because the composer decided to reuse all or part of one of his works for a new purpose. A revised edition of a work, particularly a small-scale instrumental piece or collection, was quite uncommon. In the case of the *Reprisen Sonaten* and its two *Fortsetzungen*, the large number of variants written out is so anomalous as to require an explanation that goes beyond the

---

[23] S. 155, ll. 10–11: 'geben Sir mir für alle diese Sonate, so was Sie wollen.'

[24] S. 156, ll. 22–4: 'Was die Wintern Rellstaben abgetreten hat, das habe auch ich Ihnen abgetreten.'

[25] S. 156, ll. 43–4: 'sonst druckt der böse Mensch sie Ihnen nach u. wendet vor, sie gehöre zu den andern.'

[26] S. 157, ll. 5–7: 'Sie ist ganz neu, leicht, kurz u. beynahe ohen Adagio, weil dies Ding nicht mehr Mode ist.'

composer's well-known tendency to polish.[27] Not only is the number of changes in relation to the scale of the movements changed very large, but the apparently systematic preference to vary non-sonata forms, and the selection of the collections that Rellstab wanted to publish, mark this as something unusual.

It could be argued that the extensive and systematic variations and elaborations written into P 1135 and into the French copy of the first set, and the fair copy that Bach made of the revised version of the third movement of the third sonata, were intended to create a new version of the piece in order to spoil Rellstab's sale. It seems possible (and perhaps even likely) that at about the time Bach wrote the letter of 23 July 1785 to Breitkopf, he began by writing variants on the first two sonatas in what is today P 1135, but decided soon after that it would be easier to insert variants into his own copy of the first set. However, the number of changes to the last movement of the third sonata was so large that Bach decided to write out the revised form of that movement in fair copy (D-ddr LEm R. 12). He then turned to the second set, recording the variants for five of the slow movements on the separate sheets (P 1135), and started on the third set.[28] Michel thereafter copied from P 1135 and from Bach's exemplar of the print the variants and the new version of the third movement of the third sonata into B Bc 5885.[29]

Could it be that either Bach or Breitkopf soon realized that to make the old text of the sonatas obsolete while there were still some 300 copies in hand would not make very much sense? That Breitkopf bought Bach's stock and also produced a new printing of the sonatas—unchanged—suggests firstly that Breitkopf recognized that Bach was being a bit foolish and made him aware of it, and secondly that Breitkopf was not afraid to compete directly with Rellstab. Indeed, in spite of Rellstab's claims two years later that his type was better than Breitkopf's, his work never measured up to Breitkopf's standard.

And what of Rellstab? In the preface to his edition he explained that

I purchased the right to publish the three parts of C. P. E. Bach's sonatas from Winter's heirs. The first set was sold out so I had to publish it; the other two parts are still

---

[27] Philip Barford, 'Some Afterthoughts by C. P. E. Bach', *MMR*, 90 (1960), 96, describes the variants in P. 1135 and concludes 'that the revisions are all in favour of a more subtle interpretation and a more advanced clavier technique than Bach had in mind when he first composed the sonatas.'

[28] That Bach titled P. 1135 'Einige Veränderungen . . .' and Michel headed Bc 5885 'Veränderungen . . . für Scholaren . . .' may perhaps be explained by Bach's insistence on secrecy in the matter. The presence of variants on one of the Württemburg sonatas and two of the *Leichte Sonaten* is less amenable to explanation.

[29] Bach's variants to the *Reprisen Sonaten* begin on fo. 2 of P 1135. Fo. 1 and part of fo. 6 contain variants for the sixth Württemburg sonata (H. 36/W. 49, 6). Variants to the *Reprisen Sonaten* and the first *Fortsetzung* follow on fo. 2–5, those of the second *Fortsetzung* on fo. 11ᵛ. In addition, both P 1135 and Bc 5885 contain variants for *Leichte Sonaten* of 1766 and for a sonata (H. 116) that had been published in 1755. B Bc 5883 contains two further versions of the first sonata of the first *Fortsetzung*, the one sonata from the set not varied in P 1135 and Bc 5885.

available [in the original edition]. Because it is my purpose to sell my own publications more cheaply than they could be copied, I have reduced the price of this fourteen-sheet [i.e. fifty-six-page] part from the usual 1 Thlr. 8 Gr. to 1 Thlr. and have extended the reduction of a quarter to the other two [parts].[30]

Winter's original edition (and Breitkopf's 'official' reprint) were printed at six systems to the page and took up forty pages, or ten sheets. Rellstab's edition had only five systems to a page and for that reason had to run longer than Winter's. That Bach's machinations had their effect is evident from the fact that Rellstab had to sell an edition that was more costly to produce than Breitkopf's for a price twenty-five per cent lower than the norm.

[30] *Sechs Sonaten mit veränderten Reprisen* . . . (Berlin, Rellstabschen Musikhandlung und Musikdruck, [1786]: 'Den Verlag der drey Theile von C. P. E. Bachs Sechs Sonaten habe ich von der Winterschen Erben an mich gekauft. Dieser erste Theil fehlte, ich habe ihn also neu auflegen lassen. Die beyden andern Theile sind noch voräthig. Da meine Hauptabsicht bey Anlegung meiner neuen Noten Officin ist, die Sachen meines eigenen Verlags wohlfeiler, als sie je können abgeschrieben werden, zu liefern, so habe ich diesen 14 Bogen starken Theil der sonst 1 Thlr. 8 Gr. kostete auf 1 Thlr. huruntergesetzt, und eben diese Verminderung um ein Viertel habe ich auch mit den andern beyden vorgenommen.'

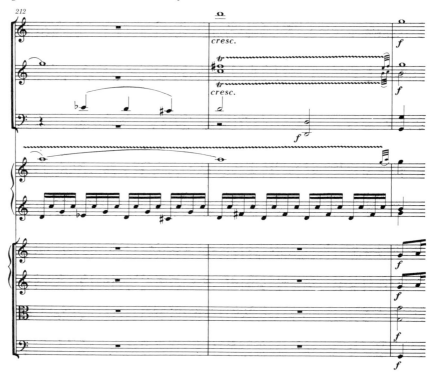

phrase establishing and closing in the dominant ends inconclusively on the third of the new scale (measure 41), preparing for its immediate repetition (to new text). This time the cadential resolution marks the onset of a repeated tonic pedal, supporting a breathlessly rising vocal line. The harmony moves once more towards a cadence, as the singer repeats his last line of text in a broadened cadential line. But now the resolution is only to a first-inversion tonic chord (measure 52), and the singer embarks on a six-measure phrase extension, emphatically virtuoso in effect by reason of its huge leaps and high notes, leading finally to his final trill and the re-entry of the orchestra.[3]

Although Forman never clearly defines the individual elements that make up the 'piano climax', it is possible from his several descriptions to derive its essential characteristics. First and most important is its virtuoso quality: the

---

[3] Note that in the plan of this aria, which corresponds in many ways to the earlier da capo arias discussed below, the double statement of the first stanza of text (A) is disposed in a single modulating section comparable to (if longer than) the $A_1$ of earlier models. A close similar to this one, but even more flamboyant, occurs as the second part of the Countess's 'Dove sono' in *Le nozze di Figaro* (1786), Act III; the gesture is brilliantly parodied in Donna Elvira's entrance aria in *Don Giovanni* of the following year.

Example 2. W. A. Mozart, *Idomeneo*, Act II, scene 1, 'Se il tuo duol', mm. 42–58. Ed. Daniel Heartz, *NMA*, II/5, vol. 11 (1972)

whole point, as he sees it, is to spotlight the solo virtuoso, whether pianist or singer. In the aria (as in the example from *Idomeneo*) this effect can be achieved by a variety of means, including wide leaps and a high register; but in the concerto it nearly always must result from fast notes, that is, figuration with a rapid surface rhythm. These persistently fast notes help support the second characteristic of Forman's 'piano climax', its sense of driving toward the cadence that will finally bring the entrance of the orchestra. As he explains, '[the 'piano climax'] is designed so that the piano can generate pace and tension with varied rhythms, but always with increasing vigour and urgency until, with the speed of a runner breasting the tape, it arrives at the final trill.'[4] And that cadential drive is intensified, finally, by a succession of cadential delays that increase the tension of the passage and intensify the effect of the final resolution.[5] Arbace's aria and K. 503 both include such delays, effected both by slowing down preparatory progressions and by overlapping phrase endings with beginnings of new, virtuoso cadential phrases; and in both cases the delays help to create a rise in tension towards the final cadence that is also aided by melodic ascents and by manipulations of harmonic rhythm.

Thus the closing solo passages of Mozart's operatic arias and of his piano concertos show clear correspondences of both effect and devices. Mozart's piano soloist (often Mozart himself) projects a persona, or a character, by

---

[4] Forman, *Mozart's Concerto Form*, p. 42.          [5] Ibid., p. 55.

means of a non-verbal, purely musical text. And just as Mozart uses much the same musical grammar and vocabulary in all his works, he employs similar devices for related musical purposes. In the view of Forman and of many others, however, these musical devices are particular to opera: they were conceived and developed there, and only then consciously transferred to the concerto as a way of imparting more 'drama' to that instrumental genre.[6] Forman believes that this transfer was first made by Johann Christian Bach, in two of the six concertos he published in 1763, soon after his arrival in London. 'It was Christian Bach', he states, 'who first saw the logic of appropriating an Italian operatic convention and of popping it in, duly recast for the piano, at this point.'[7] It is the intent of the following pages to question both of these assertions, first that the Mozartean 'piano climax' originated as an established operatic convention that was 'popped in' to the concerto, and second that it was Johann Christian Bach who was chiefly responsible for the use of such a device in the concerto. Put another way, the question is whether the 'piano climax' is derived from a gesture peculiar to opera, or whether it is as indigenous to a show-piece for a virtuoso instrumentalist as to one for a virtuoso singer.

The two ritornello-form movements of J. C. Bach's Op. 1 in which Forman perceived a 'piano climax' are presumably the first movements of nos. 1 and 2. It is in these two movements that the closing measures of the first solo section maintain the persistently rapid surface rhythm that appears to have most impressed Forman about Bach's 'piano climax'.[8] Most striking is the close in the first movement of Op. 1 no. 1 (see Example 3). The solo's cadence in the dominant key (F major) has been extended by a repeated tonic pedal, supporting two nearly identical four-measure cadential phrases. At measure 93 there begins a passage of rising figuration, still over an implied tonic pedal and accompanied increasingly strongly by the orchestra.[9] At the highest melodic point the orchestra drops out and the line descends in a two-measure cadential phrase; but the cadence resolves only to a first-inversion chord, and the phrase begins to repeat. This time, however, the harmonic rhythm of the second measure of the phrase is slowed so that one measure becomes two, the rhythmic continuity now being provided by left-hand figuration together with the closing right-hand trill, which resolves (as usual) simultaneously with the orchestral entrance. The propulsion of the rapid figuration is made much more effective here by the emphatically slowed harmonic rhythm; the sense of

---

[6] Ibid., p. 28; see also Reinhard Strohm, 'Merkmale italienischer Versvertonung in Mozarts Klavierkonzerten', *Analecta musicologica*, 18 (1978), esp 220.

[7] Forman, *Mozart's Concerto Form*, pp. 42–3.

[8] Ibid., p. 42.

[9] In its earlier partial appearance in the ritornello (measures 38–41), this passage has alternating *f* and *p* markings; here the absence of such dynamics, together with the gradual thickening of the texture, suggests the possibility of an implied crescendo.

Example 3. J. C. Bach, Op. 1 No. 1, i, mm. 92–104. Ed. Richard Maunder, The Collected Works of Johann Christian Bach 1735–1782, vol. 33 (New York, 1985)

Example 4. J. C. Bach, *Allesandro nell'Indie*, Act III, scene 9, 'Trafiggero quel core', fac. ed., The Collected Works of Johann Christian Bach, vol. 32 (New York, 1985)

*a* mm. 18–22

*b* mm. 42–48

Whatever the source of the incipient 'piano climax', then, it cannot be uncritically assumed to be the operatic aria. And this conclusion carries the further implication that the larger impulse to which Forman attributes this gesture, the desire to 'make a curtain', that is, to make an effective exit from the stage, is not necessarily the operative one in the concerto.[14] For the origins of J. C. Bach's 'piano climax' we must in fact look not to his operas but to his earlier keyboard concertos, composed between 1750 and 1753 while he was living with his elder brother Carl Philipp Emanuel in Berlin. These five concertos have the appearance of emulations—by a young composer, and one who eventually showed himself to belong to a radically new stylistic generation—of the concertos then being written by composers in Berlin, and particularly by the most innovative of them, Carl Philipp Emanuel Bach. Although there are many instances of extended solo cadential passages in these adolescent works, perhaps the most striking occurs in the first movement of the second concerto, in F minor, at the close of the first solo section (see Example 5). After a succession of phrases cadencing in the new key of A flat

Example 5. J. C. Bach, Concerto in F minor, i, mm. 63–84. Ed. Richard Maunder, The Collected Works of Johann Christian Bach, vol. 32

tonic resolution (measure 50) overlaps with a repetition of the previous two measures (figuration and final cadence), which this time concludes decisively as the orchestral ritornello begins. Thus as in the typical aria of 1762, the solo's close is postponed by the simple repetition of a partial phrase without any new harmonic manipulation.

[14] Note also that although the 'piano climaxes' of the first two concertos of Op. 1 are repeated verbatim (in the tonic) at the end of the last solo section (i.e. just before the closing ritornello), the initial statement, which occurs less than half-way through the movement, is surely perceived as the primary one. Furthermore, as the aria cadenza at the close of $A_2$ is increasingly emphasized and conventionalized in the 1760s, the preparation for it has the effect of weakening and sometimes even shortening the cadential 'climax' of $A_1$, which thus never recurs just before the actor-singer's exit. See, for instance, Cleofide's aria from *Alessandro*, cited in n. 12 above.

major or its dominant, the solo begins its cadential phrase, moving first to a very weak full cadence and then through a more decisive cadential preparation. The diversion of the expected full close by the deceptive cadence in measure 69 generates a repetition of the second part of the phrase, its tonic resolution overlapped with the entrance of the orchestra as if to begin the second ritornello (measure 72). That entrance is abortive, however, and after stating the first two measures of the ritornello the orchestra drops out. The solo now embarks on a ten-measure passage of figuration, always moving toward its final cadence but reaching it only with the true entrance of the ritornello. The figuration pattern of the first six measures is more rapid than any so far in the movement; moving in a regular harmonic rhythm (one chord per measure), first in another confirmation of the new tonic (measures 74–5) and then in a cadential progression interrupted by the submediant chord in measure 78, the passage finally reaches the tonic in measure 80. Here the even more rapid descending scale avoids a rhythmic break and leads to yet another cadence, to a first-inversion chord, which is bridged once more by scale figuration that persists until the very last two cadential eighth-notes of the solo section.

In this passage the teenaged Bach seems to have used all the means at his disposal to delay the close of the solo section, increasing our anticipation of that close and thereby making it more important. The only element of Forman's 'piano climax' that is missing here is the continuation of rapid left-hand figuration through those last two cadential eighth-notes, that is, the very element that he seems to have found the most obvious. It is possible, though, that that figuration was employed by Bach in his first two published concertos as a subsidiary device, to maintain rhythmic tension through the sudden deceleration of harmonic movement that in both cases accompanies it. In any case, the solo cadential passages in these two concertos, like the one in the earlier Berlin concerto, are too different from typical aria cadences to support a theory of simple transfer from one to the other. Forman's uncritical assumption that such a transfer took place arose from his belief in the initial and continuing derivation of the solo concerto from the aria, a derivation that has never been established and seldom even seriously investigated. At least within this decade or so for Johann Christian Bach, however, all that can be concluded is that structurally important cadential passages receive compar-able emphasis—if not necessarily identical treatment—in both aria and concerto.

It should not be surprising, in fact, that the specific techniques used by the youngest Bach in his earliest concertos to provide this emphasis have their source in the concertos of his elder brother and apparent mentor at the time, Carl Philipp Emanuel. As we shall see, C. P. E. Bach's works of the 1730s already focus particular attention on solo cadential passages. This cadential stress can be traced in turn to two parallel stylistic circumstances, one—presumably originating in opera—Italian, and the other within a German instrumental tradition. The cadential repetitions that appear so regularly in Johann Christian Bach's *Alessandro nell'Indie*, first of all, can be traced to the arias of Vinci and Hasse in the new Neapolitan style of the 1720s. Instead of emphasizing an approaching cadence by means of a full break (usually after a high pitch) followed by a slow syllabic descent to the cadence, as is common for instance in Handel, Vinci more often prolongs the cadential approach without interrupting the forward movement. In Hasse's *Siroe* of 1733, an expected harmonic resolution is often undercut by an unstable chord position or deceptive progression that leads directly to a repetition of that phrase, which may itself be extended in the same way again before finally resolving in the expected way.[15] Since no element of virtuosity is present here, it seems unlikely that a 'storming virtuoso exit' is the goal of this procedure. The most obvious effect is the emphatic stress given to the last line of text, a line which in a good Metastasian libretto is eminently worth stressing. This is perhaps reason enough for a musical procedure in a style in which the clear projection of the text seems to be of paramount importance. It is also true, however, that this style is characterized by a new clarity and simplicity of harmony and especially of harmonic structure, so that the cadential emphasis at a definitive place in the harmonic plan might have served purposes of structural definition as well. At any rate, this device which is already common in Hasse's *Siroe* is an expected convention in J. C. Bach's Italian operas.

As has already been suggested, however, this typical aria convention has very little of the harmonic and rhythmic propulsion associated with the solo cadences in even the earliest of J. C. Bach's concertos: its aim seems to be one of emphasis, whether of text or harmonic event, not one of driving anticipation. That propulsive quality first appears in the concerto itself, and perhaps most clearly in the concertos of Johann Sebastian Bach. His solo concertos include many examples of extended solo passages that build harmonic tension and escalate the level of virtuoso activity as they approach a tutti return—an unusually flamboyant example can be seen in the solo passage immediately preceding the final ritornello in the first movement of the D minor harpsichord concerto (BWV 1052). It is particularly instructive to compare Bach's concertos for unaccompanied harpsichord with their original models. Example 6*b* shows the end of the first solo section of the opening movement of BWV 975, in G minor, in comparison with the passage from Vivaldi's Op. 4 no. 6, Ryom 316a (Example 6*a*) upon which it is based. Vivaldi's closing section in this case resembles—rather atypically for his concertos—an aria cadence typical of Handel's generation. A rapid virtuoso phrase, beginning as a sequential repetition of the preceding phrase, is extended to prolong the dominant of the new key (D minor), to which it finally resolves with a rise to the upper octave and a full break in the melodic line (measure 50). The slower stepwise descending cadence moves twice to a deceptive cadence that necessitates a repetition, each time in more decisive fashion. Bach first accelerates the figuration on the prolonged dominant, and then undercuts the

---

[15] See, for example, in Vinci's *Didone abbandonata* of 1726, Selene's aria in Act I, Scene 3 (fo. 14ᵛ), and Araspe's in Act I, Scene 8 (fo. 39); and in Hasse's *Siroe*, Ladice's aria in Act II, Scene 1; fac. edns. of both works by Howard M. Brown in *Italian Opera 1640–1770* (New York, 1977).

break at the melodic climax both harmonically, by implying at first a first inversion and then a deceptive cadence, and rhythmically, by maintaining the sixteenth-note motion in the bass, a device he repeats at each cadential repetition. The declamatory effect that is so strong in Vivaldi's version is thus virtually lost; but in its place is a sense of propelling movement towards the re-entry of the orchestra with its ritornello affirming the new key.[16]

Although it has always seemed reasonable to suppose that Carl Philipp Emanuel Bach's harpsichord concertos owed much to those of his father, which he must at the very least have heard during his teens in Leipzig, the pieces themselves seem very different. Their formal plan follows that of a younger Italianate generation, and their style is often taken to have been modelled on the fashionable Italian opera of the 1720s and 1730s. At least in the cadential passages that end the solo sections, however, C. P. E. Bach's concertos show the influence of the elder Bach as much as that of more modern Italian opera composers. His second keyboard concerto, H. 404/W. 2, written

Example 6. *a* Antonio Vivaldi, Concerto in G minor Op. 4 no. 6, (Ryom 316a) i, mm. 44–57. Ed. Angelo Ephrikian (Milan, 1965). *b* J. S. Bach, Concerto in G minor BWV 975, i, mm. 44–57. Ed. Ernest Naumann, Johann Sebastian Bachs Werke, vol. 42 (Leipzig, 1894)

---

[16] Bach's treatment of a more typical Vivaldi solo cadence may be seen in the G major concerto BWV 973, based on Vivaldi's violin concerto Op. 7 no. 8 (Ryom 299). In the last part of the third solo section, which leads to the orchestral return of the tonic, Bach uses the soloist's left hand to provide increasing rhythmic intensification and cadential harmonic direction, and in the last four measures intensifies the harmonies as well. Note that here, as in later keyboard concertos, the sense of rhythmic acceleration and intensification is dependent on the multiple lines and varied textures available to a keyboard solo part.

in 1734 while he was probably still in Leipzig, exhibits the clear four-ritornello form already established in Italianate North Germany,[17] and a modern *galant* melodic style characterized by long sighing appoggiaturas and an avoidance of decisive downbeats. Yet the close of the first solo section in the first movement (see Example 7) has obvious parallels with the comparable passage by J. S. Bach shown in Example 6. After an extended passage of solo figuration establishing the new key (B flat major), the orchestra has entered as if for the second ritornello, but has in fact made only a brief interjection leading into the final solo cadential phrase. The unaccompanied harpsichord proceeds first through an extremely weak full cadence to a first-inversion chord (measure

[17] See the article by Shelley Davis in this volume.

Example 7. Concerto in E flat major H. 404/W. 2, i, mm. 50–9. D-brd B, Mus
ms. Bach P 354

51), then through another full cadence, this time with the third in the melody
and with an immediate melodic extension (measure 52), and then to a
deceptive cadence (measure 53) extended to a half-cadence at the beginning of
measure 54. A sudden digression to the subdominant requires two measures
to reach a resolution to yet another cadence, which is avoided by another
deceptive progression, this time to the lowered sixth. Another half-cadence
and a very brief tutti interjection lead at last to the conclusive cadence that
coincides with the beginning of the second ritornello in measure 59.[18] It is
revealing to compare this passage with the vocal cadences of Hasse's *Siroe*,
written just one year earlier, when the phrase repetition at the end of the $A_1$
section had not yet become a rigid convention: whereas Hasse often builds
tension (usually by a rise in register) in the phrases just *before* the cadence,
emphasis on the cadence itself is limited to extending repetitions.[19]

By 1742, when he was nearing 30, Bach had worked out a variety of ways
to enhance the effect of the cadences that brought a solo section to a close and
simultaneously introduced a ritornello. At the end of the first solo of his
eleventh keyboard concerto (H. 413/W. 10, in B flat major), for instance, he
has manipulated an aria-derived phraseology to enhance anticipation of the
cadence and intensify its effect. The new key (F major) is established barely
more than half-way through the solo section by an orchestral interjection of
the opening motif of the ritornello, which is followed by a long passage of solo
figuration leading towards a cadence that coincides with another orchestral
interjection, once again affirming the new key. Example 8 begins at the end of
these four orchestral measures, as the solo begins its final cadential passage. In
aria-like fashion, a four-measure cadential phrase is diverted to a deceptive
cadence, and a brief bridge leads to its repetition an octave lower. The
recurrence of the deceptive cadence in the repetition, however, is embedded in
ornamental figuration which transforms measure 100 into an extension of the
phrase, an effect supported by the subsequent bass motion *upward* through the
dominant chord.

This close can usefully be compared to the comparable one in an aria from
Hasse's *Arminio*, written in 1745, three years later than this concerto (see
Example 9). Although this aria, Varo's 'Corre al cimento ardita' in Act III,
Scene 9, is relatively atypical of the opera as a whole by reason of the unusually
extended preparation for the solo cadence, the extension devices are not
fundamentally different from those found in operas from a decade earlier. The
first word of the last line of text ('l'audace') has been set to a melismatic phrase

---

[18]  Although Bach revised this work in 1742, the autograph shows no signs of any reworking of
this passage; see Rachel W. Wade, *The Keyboard Concertos of Carl Philipp Emanuel Bach* (Ann Arbor,
1981), 90 and illus. 14, concerning some of the changes that do appear.

[19]  A notable exception to this generalization is Arasse's aria 'L'onda che mormora' (*Siroe*, Act I,
Scene 9); here the $A_2$ section adds an extra restatement of the text to provide for a long tonic
extension, which is cadential throughout and incorporates some of the virtuoso melismas of the
penultimate phrases of $A_1$ and $A_2$.

Example 8. Concerto in B flat major H. 413/W. 10, i, mm. 91–103. B Bc, 5887

Example 9. J. A. Hasse, *Armino*, Act III, scene 9, 'Corre al cimento ardita', mm. 42–8. Ed. Rudolf Gerber, *Das Erbe deutscher Musik*, vol. 28 (Mainz, 1966)

of quite heroic proportions. In measure 42 the text phrase begins once more, in what will be the final cadence of the $A_1$ section. The deceptive cadence ending this first statement generates its repetition, beginning as usual with its initial tonic harmony, the vocal line varied so as to lie a third higher. The full cadence that closes the phrase this time is bridged now by the vocal line, which rises to the upper octave to begin its final stepwise cadential descent. This passage builds to an impressive level of excitement, but one that depends heavily on the increasing tension in vocal timbre attendant upon the rise in register. Moreover, the dynamic gradations that the singer is surely intended to provide, combined with the possibilities of articulation and emphasis inherent in the declamation of the text and its repetition, provide the possibility of supporting that tension to produce a truly climactic moment on a stage. Some of these effects are available to some melody instruments as well, the violin probably chief among them. But these devices cannot have the same effect on the harpsichord, or even on the eighteenth-century piano. The composer who wishes to impart dramatic emphasis to cadential—or any other—points in a piece (a goal common in one way or another to most eighteenth-century music) will use all the means at his disposal, but cannot succeed merely by transferring musical devices from one genre to another.[20]

In the first movement of the A major concerto H. 411/W. 8, written a year earlier than H. 413/W. 10, Bach ended the first solo section with a cadential passage that owes little to the devices or phraseology of the aria (see Example 10). After a passage of figuration (accompanied by the orchestra) that firmly establishes E major as the new key, the solo continues alone in a brief cadential phrase. Its conclusion in measure 84 coincides with the beginning of another cadential preparation using a progression of which Bach was particularly fond during this period: a tonic pedal under which a descending diminished fifth unfolds, leading forcefully to a dominant chord. At this point the solo is interrupted, however, by the orchestra breaking in to complete the cadence. Its resolution is weakened by the solo continuation, in a more rapid rhythm than has so far appeared in the movement, with yet another cadential phrase, its precipitous descent leading at last to the ritornello. The devices of cadential extension used here, all common ones in Bach's concertos of the early 1740s, differ in essential ways from the devices used in the aria to emphasize the close of vocal sections. Most important here are harmonic devices and the intervention of the orchestra to interrupt the solo cadence. The large melodic shape—a slow rise during the figuration passage, stabilized at the high point during the first cadence, and then a threefold descent—has affinities to an aria closing passage, as to passages in many if not all other eighteenth-century genres. But the most basic element of the aria cadence, the emphatic repetition of text and music, plays no real part here.

A related but not identical group of devices serves to delay the close of the second solo section of the same movement (see Example 11). A long approach to the relative minor (F sharp minor), in which the section will close, is concluded by a standard cadential phrase. The expected tonic is replaced by the submediant, and this deception is given further emphasis by the simultaneous entrance of an orchestral interjection in a four-measure chromatic turn around the new dominant. That dominant is then prolonged by the solo's virtuoso movement outward to another dominant harmony, which leads only then to the final cadence of the section. The harmonic goal in this instance turns out not to depend on the entrance of a ritornello; a conventional descending bass makes a perfunctory transition to the tonic

---

[20] Opera composers who also wrote concertos often used similar techniques of solo cadential emphasis in both genres. At least in the works of Hasse, however, concerto cadences sometimes appear to be more extended, and to utilize more devices of harmony and rapid rhythm, than is usual in arias; see esp. the penultimate solo section of the first movement of the flute concerto in F major (ed. Zoltan Jeney and Jean Pierre Müller; Budapest, 1972), a work that was published for keyboard alone by Walsh in 1742. Cadential techniques familiar from Hasse's arias and concertos also appear frequently in fast binary movements of his solo sonatas, emphasizing the cadences that close each part.

Example 10. Concerto in A major H. 411/W. 8, i, mm. 81–92. D-ddr Bds, Mus. ms. Bach P 352

Example 11. Concerto in A major H. 411/W. 8, i, mm. 185–96. D-ddr Bds, Mus. ms. Bach P 352

entrance of the tutti, which begins a co-operative solo–tutti recapitulatory return.

In these early concertos, C. P. E. Bach worked out a variety of means of extending a cadence after it had been essentially completed, with the apparent aim of creating a dramatic tension in which the frustration of our expectations merely strengthens their force, thereby lending excitement to the eventual conclusion. He soon began to extend the cadence backwards as well—that is, to expand the preparation for the cadence. A good example of this technique can be seen in the first solo section of the first movement of H. 427/W. 23 in D minor, written in 1748.[21] The four-measure excerpt from the ritornello in measure 79 (performed now in alternating measures by tutti and solo) serves to confirm the new key (G minor) and set up the expectation of a cadence. Instead of that cadence, however, we hear a repetition of the same measures in the orchestra as an accompaniment to very rapid solo figuration. This time the awaited cadence is forestalled once more, by a full-voiced, forte blocked chord on V of V. The chord reverberates in a brief rising and then falling solo passage of figuration, changing into a diminished seventh as it goes. The ensuing cadence is immediately stalled by a fermata (an occasion for a brief solo ornamental phrase, not a cadenza) and then diverted in a sequential rise settling finally at its peak into a cadence once more. Only now does the cadence get as far as a dominant chord, which is extended for one final measure by a deceptive cadence that spawns a rapid descent to the final resolution.

A somewhat similar cadential passage is shown in Example 12, taken from the first solo section of the first movement of H. 441/W. 31 in C minor. G minor, the key of the second ritornello, is stabilized at the outset of the last third of the solo section by a varied version of the opening theme, stated by solo and tutti in alternation. Example 12 begins with the ensuing phrase, in a now rather intricate continuation of the solo–tutti alternation, serving to prolong an augmented sixth chord. The dominant harmony to which that chord resolves in measure 97 erupts in rapid descending figuration leading to the low dominant pedal. The rhythmic acceleration begun in the lower register continues in the nearly two-octave melodic ascent that culminates in the middle of measure 106, nearly at the point at which the line had begun its descent, the repetition from measure 97 making it clear that the intervening passage is in effect an interpolated delay. The final cadence itself is peremptory, with a rapid harmonic rhythm, and effectively destroys the momentum built up over the previous eight measures. Bach's intent is nevertheless clear: to emphasize the heroic efforts of the solo part to bring its section to a final close.

These examples from C. P. E. Bach's concertos provide a historical context for the cadential passages in the concertos written by his younger brother between 1750 and 1753 (the year of composition of H. 441/W. 31). One of

---

[21] Ed. Arnold Schering, Denkmäler deutscher Tonkunst, vols. 29–30 (Leipzig, 1907), 62–102.

*Jane R. Stevens*

Example 12. Concerto in C minor H. 441/W. 31, i, mm. 93–108. Ed. György Balla, Nagels Musik-Archiv, 253 (Kassel, 1976)

many striking characteristics of the concertos published by J. C. Bach in London ten years later is in fact the relative absence of cadential delay and emphasis. There are many possible reasons for this, not least among them the modern clarity and simplicity of their harmonic style. But the new device that he used there for the first time arose out of that new harmonic style, and it is therefore not surprising that both he and still younger composers continued to find it useful. That new device, the slowing of harmonic motion on the dominant and the pre-dominant chord, with a concomitant rapid surface rhythm, altered what was perhaps the only place that C. P. E. Bach had accepted as inviolate in its essential harmonic and rhythmic framework. The other techniques used in Op. 1 and in J. C. Bach's later concertos are all familiar from Emanuel's cadential passages; and the underlying goal of these passages, to build tension and increase the impact of a solo close, is probably as old as the keyboard concerto itself.

It thus seems unlikely that J. C. Bach discovered the 'piano climax' in the aria and simply transferred it to an instrumental genre. Even the notion that it was essentially a stage exit gesture is dubious, since in both aria and concerto its first appearance is followed by a great deal more music; the exit, then, can only be a temporary musical one. It is much easier to agree with Forman's less explicitly stated conviction that the 'piano climax' represents one of several 'moments of supremacy' for the solo piano, one which extends the 'dramatic moment' in a 'tension towards finality'.[22] But the means available to this end for an instrument, which has neither the text nor the subtle timbre variations available to a singer, are not the same as for a voice (which for its part does not have the figuration capabilities of a keyboard instrument). This is perhaps one reason why at least for German composers, devices of harmony and rhythm play a more important role in the concerto than in the aria, where the declamation of the text is a dominant structural element. Eighteenth-century composers may be expected to use similar musical devices to serve similar

---

[22] Forman, *Mozart's Concerto Form*, pp. 54–5.

musical purposes, as for instance the clarification or emphasis of an important structural point in a piece. It is much less likely, in the absence of an intent to set up a specific association for the purposes of a single piece, that devices particular to one genre would be simply transferred to another.

Furthermore, there is no reason to assume that the underlying purpose of these cadential passages, whether in arias or concertos, remained unchanged over half a century, much less that it was precisely the same in both genres. The issue of the historical and structural relationships of aria and concerto is much too broad to be addressed here. It seems self-evident, however, that a concert is not a staged drama, and that no instrument can stand in for a singing actor. The interactions between these two genres are complex, and cannot be forced into simplistic models in which one merely appropriates from the other. If we are to believe eighteenth-century writers on music, including Carl Philipp Emanuel Bach himself, all instrumental music draws its expressive content and effect from the feelings and actions of men. This is not at all the same thing, however, as asserting that sonatas, symphonies, and concertos are merely instrumental settings, or even analogues, of particular vocal-dramatic models. If we are ever to understand the 'content' of eighteenth-century instrumental music, we must study its interrelationships with opera with the same degree of care and sophistication manifested so impressively by the composers themselves.

# Filiation and the Editing of Revised and Alternate Versions: Implications for the C. P. E. Bach Edition

## Rachel W. Wade

EDITING is a process of constant decisions, and one of the most vexing decisions to be made concerns the presentation of a work existing in more than one authentic version. In particular the critical report, which is a hefty volume even under normal circumstances, swells immensely as the editor attempts to cope with the seeming fickleness of the composer. In the past a prevalent methodology reduced the editor's anxiety somewhat by requiring him only to find the last version of the composer, the 'Fassung letzter Hand' discussed by Georg von Dadelsen in an article of 1961.[1] This approach gave the creators of literary or musical works total power over the definition of their output. Carried to an extreme, it means that a composer might write a sonata at the age of 20, see it disseminated, performed, and studied by the musical public, and then, at the age of 70, completely rewrite the sonata, implicitly removing his approval of its earlier form.

The untenableness of this approach is most apparent when one considers the separate question of authenticity. It is possible that a composer whose tastes have changed drastically might find his early work so repulsive that he denies ever having written it. This denial need not take the form of an outright lie. Simply by not including the odious early works in a list of his compositions, the composer can cast doubt on their authenticity and have a reasonable chance of success in convincing scholars, who generally find so little evidence for determining authenticity that they would even be interested in the opinion of the composer's maid. But if some clever detective work by twentieth-century scholars should uncover the deception, it would be normal to expect these early pieces to be restored immediately to the list of authentic works, and to take their place in the complete edition of that composer's works. If so, why should not the early versions of a work be given the same respect?

It is as if each musical work or version of a work has a *lifetime* which begins at the moment it is disseminated to the public and ends when the work is no longer performed or studied enough to have an impact. Historians in effect recognize this when they speak of the resurrection of a work that has faded into

---

[1] 'Die "Fassung letzter Hand" in der Musik', *AM*, 33 (1961), 1–14.

obscurity. With this approach the creator retains the right to sketch, refine, and revise in privacy, but as soon as he presents his sonata to others, he has given it life, for it is at this point that his work becomes a part of the general heritage, influencing other composers and contributing to the vitality of a society's musical culture.

The editors of the great complete editions that began around the middle of this century acknowledged this state of affairs by including the early versions, but they initially paid homage to the notion of the 'Fassung letzter Hand' by printing the early versions in an appendix, or by describing them in prose in the critical report. Implicit in this treatment is a second-class citizenship for the early versions. For editors respectful of the composer's final preference, the appendix and the critical report offered an acceptable way to present early versions without giving them an equal share of the limelight.

In recent years there has been an increasing tendency for complete editions to present various versions of a work within the body of a volume, arranged chronologically. This method has been adopted by the members of the C. P. E. Bach Edition, which is among the most recent of the many complete editions. In light of this decision, we in the C. P. E. Bach Edition next find ourselves confronted with the challenging task of determining the relationships between the sources of a work revised perhaps several times, and then presenting that information in the critical reports.

# Who Reads the Critical Report?

It is commonly assumed by members of the musical public that the critical report is there for the benefit of the performer. They conclude that the extensive lists of variant readings provided by the editor will allow a performer to look up additional information about any questionable passages. When performers do not actually use the critical report in this way very often, the cry is heard, 'Who reads the critical report? Why must we all pay for these long sections of prose when it is the music that we want?'

On the basis of two or three decades of experience with the great editions of the works of Bach, Haydn, Mozart, and other composers, we can answer the first question: it is primarily musicologists who read the critical report. And, in answer to the second question about the value of the report, it is necessary to adopt a slightly different view of its function: rather than being a resource for the performer, the critical report has actually been much more valuable as a repository of information, gathered by the editor but used by subsequent scholars. This view of the function of the critical report might be termed the 'telephone directory' approach, after some comments made by Arthur Mendel in 1978:

But is the fact that even professional musicologists do not actually read long lists of variants really an argument against completeness? Doubtless 99 per cent of the details heaped up in the telephone directory are inconsequential to each one of us; but no two of us make the same selection of those we hold consequential. . . . The significance of a variant may very well escape me and be apparent to you, but it cannot be apparent to anyone if it is not in the list. . . . The computer makes it possible to state in the critical report that all variants have been noted, and if they are presented in tables or other concise and logical form they are as easily found (and can be as easily ignored) as Arthur Mendel in the Princeton telephone directory.[2]

The validity of Mendel's view of the function of the critical report can be demonstrated in two recent developments in Bach research, both occurring after Mendel's article was published. The first example is found in the work of Yoshitake Kobayashi. In his article 'Neuerkenntnisse zu einigen Bach-Quellen an Handschriftkundlicher Untersuchungen' in the *Bach-Jahrbuch* of 1978, Kobayashi argued that the sonata in G minor for violin and harpsichord, BWV 1020, is actually a work of C. P. E. Bach. He was able to make this argument on the basis of an editor's preface by Alfred Dürr, who reported that one nineteenth-century copy of the work was copied from an eighteenth-century manuscript owned by Johann Gottfried Schicht. The nineteenth-century copy attributes the work to Johann Sebastian Bach, while the Schicht copy merely states the work to be by 'Bach', with no Christian name. Therefore it is possible that the mistaken attribution resulted from a false assumption on the part of the nineteenth-century copyist, namely that 'Bach' always meant Johann Sebastian Bach. Then Kobayashi contributed the information that Schicht acquired his music collection largely from the firm of Breitkopf. In Breitkopf's catalogue this sonata appears attributed unambiguously to Carl Philipp Emanuel. Therefore it is likely that the Breitkopf firm created Schicht's copy at a time when the name Bach alone could easily mean Carl Philipp Emanuel Bach, who was, after all, the Bach that this firm dealt with most often. Then later, when J. S. Bach had become more famous than his son, this copy with the attribution merely to Bach led to a false assumption and consequently a false attribution to J. S. Bach. The conclusion could only be reached with evidence from studies of provenance and filiation, the latter being normally reported in the critical report even if the filiation has not affected the actual editing of the musical text significantly.

The field of Bach scholarship provides a second example of the way in which critical reports have served as a repository of information. In questions of authenticity, the investigation of manuscript provenance assumes a central role. If one can demonstrate that the manuscript in question was owned by the composer's brother, that manuscript is obviously much more reliable than one belonging to persons outside the composer's circle. Just such a demonstration

---

[2] Arthur Mendel, 'The Purposes and Desirable Characteristics of Text-Critical Editions', *Modern Musical Scholarship*, ed. Edward Olleson (Stocksfield, 1978), 25–6.

was provided by Hans-Joachim Schulze recently.[3] By a long and complex argument, Schulze traced back the ownership of two large sources of German keyboard music, the Andreas-Bach-Buch and the Möllersche Handschrift, through many nineteenth and eighteenth-century owners and finally to Johann Christoph Bach, the eldest brother of Johann Sebastian. Schulze was able to do this in part because he made use of no less than eight critical reports published in the *Neue Bach-Ausgabe*. These reports provided raw data on the identity of copyists, the dating of single works in the manuscripts, and, most importantly, the analysis of the dependence of various sources. Analysis of dependence became significant because, when Schulze could identify who had access to the two manuscripts and copied from them, he was able to substantiate his suppositions regarding the ownership of the manuscripts at various times. Thanks to Schulze's work, the authenticity of various attributions in these sources seems assured.

In order to use an editor's conclusions effectively in scholarship, it is necessary to understand what the editor must do in order to write his critical report. Regarding filiation, one must become aware of both the possibilities and the limitations of various techniques, particularly with regard to music, for which no general guide to filiation yet exists. Consequently it is not surprising that up to now the best use of raw data in critical reports has been made by scholars who have themselves written critical reports.

## Filiation

Thinking of filiation as an action performed by an editor underscores the essential nature of the process: that it involves judgement and that two editors presented with the same data may come to different conclusions. For this reason, it is imperative for the editor to present the evidence showing why he believes one source to be dependent on another, not just the bare summary of his work in the form of the stemmatic diagram. Most commonly, the evidence is presented in the notorious lists of variant readings so odious to non-scholars.

Of the meagre literature available on filiation in music, two recent articles by Margaret Bent and Stanley Boorman offer a starting-point for discussion of problems encountered in the eighteenth-century repertoire, even though their remarks were made in regard to Medieval and Renaissance music,[4]

Margaret Bent began by observing that parallels exist between the task of establishing relationships between sources in literary texts and in music.

---

[3] Hans-Joachim Schulze, *Studien zur Bach-Überlieferung im 18. Jahrhundert* (Leipzig and Dresden, 1984), 30–55.

[4] Margaret Bent, 'Some Criteria for Establishing Relationships between Sources of Late-Medieval Polyphony', and Stanley Boorman, 'Limitations and Extensions of Filiation Technique', both in *Music in Medieval and Early Modern Europe*, ed. Iain Fenlon (Cambridge, 1981), 295–317, 319–46.

However, she noted, the classical text is more nearly the literary work than the musical notation is the music, since the musical notation is incomplete and depends more on the performer's knowledge of the tradition. Bent then listed several possible situations that may occur when a scribe copies a piece, some of which will be illustrated here from the works of Carl Philipp Emanuel Bach. First, the copy may be a faithful interpretation of the exemplar. This is obvious and needs no illustration. Second, according to Bent, the copyist may improve upon his exemplar by correctly resolving certain kinds of ambiguities and self-evident errors. An illustration of such a self-evident error is found in a manuscript copy of C. P. E. Bach's concerto in G major, H. 405/W. 3, the composer's third work in the genre (1737).[5] In this copy, St 496, the scribe miscopied one note of the tutti theme, which is quite memorable since it plays on the contrast between scalar runs and large leaps. Furthermore, following the concerto tradition, the tutti theme is heard many times during the course of the movement, and of course the copyist must also copy this theme many times. If a musically aware copyist were using St 496 as his exemplar, it is not unreasonable to suppose that he would recognize this error as such and quietly emend it while preparing his copy. The significance of this for filiation is that any lack of correspondence between two sources in such cases does not establish the independence of these sources, and often it is necessary to eliminate situations of obvious error from consideration while attempting filiation, as long as the sources disagree. Of course, it is always possible that a given scribe was not very sophisticated, or that he did not hear in his mind the notes he was copying, in which case he would preserve the error of the exemplar.

The third instance described by Bent is one in which the scribe may be copying a piece which he knows from performance to be corrupt, so that he emends it from his memory of a performance. Fourth, the scribe or editor of a manuscript may introduce deliberate and unnecessary changes of a more or less radical nature. Among the works of C. P. E. Bach, such radical changes were introduced by the publisher Johann Carl Friedrich Rellstab, with whom C. P. E. Bach clashed bitterly, as his correspondence with Breitkopf shows.[6] Another example in the 'deliberate and unnecessary' category is a manuscript copy of Bach's first concerto, H. 403/W. 1, in which the copyist apparently did not have quite enough space at the end of the first movement, so he rewrote two measures of four beats each as one measure of six beats as he approached the bottom of the page.[7] In studying the work of copyists closely the editor can

---

[5] D-brd B, Mus. ms. Bach St 496, Cembalo, i, measure 182.

[6] Rachel W. Wade, *The Keyboard Concertos of Carl Philipp Emanuel Bach* (Ann Arbor, 1981), 31–2. See also the contribution of Howard Serwer in this volume and *Suchalla/Briefe*, pp. 181–3, 184, 186, 189–91, 263, 499–501, 509–10, 540, 561.

[7] D-ddr LEm, Poel. mus. Ms. 41, i, measure 86.

identify both the conscientious and the irresponsible, the lazy and the absent-minded, until an entire repertoire of human foibles has been assembled.

The mistakes and habits of the scribe account for other possible occurrences mentioned by Bent. For the filiation of musical sources the mistakes of the copyist may signal whether he was working from a score or a set of parts. For example, Elias Kulukundis has analysed a crossed-out section in a source for the flute version of Bach's concerto in D minor H. 425/W. 22:

> The copyist was writing out one line at a time, starting at the top of the system. In the middle of copying out the flute part, he discovered that he had left a bar out of the first violin part. He stopped immediately, leaving the flute part unfinished and the bass not yet copied, crossed out three bars, filled in the bass up to that point, and then resumed copying at the top of the next page from the point of the error. Working from parts, the error would have been apparent during the scoring of the second violin part and required insertion of an extra bar.[8]

Stanley Boorman has reviewed the problems of stemmatic study and concluded that the key to expanding our knowledge in this area lies in an analysis of the working habits and characteristics of the scribe.[9] In this regard, he stressed that the so-called 'accidentals' or 'non-substantives' in the readings are just as important as changes in the text.[10] Here it may be best to restrict the discussion to the term 'non-substantive', to avoid confusion; to musicians, an accidental is a flat or a sharp, but to a textual critic, it is a detail of spelling, punctuation, and so forth that could be altered in literary texts by the printer without ruffling the feathers of the author. According to Philip Gaskell,

> It is a commonplace that the spelling of English authors in the sixteenth and early seventeenth centuries was very varied. . . . Compositors considered some spellings to be acceptable and others not, and they regularly brought their author's spellings into line with what they thought was right (unless, as happened occasionally, the author insisted upon the retention of his own spelling). This is not to say that there was a codified or even a standardized printers' orthography—there is no evidence of anything of the kind—but compositors did learn their trade from each other and they did change their jobs, so that it is not surprising to find a greater uniformity of spelling within the printing trade than outside it.[11]

In keeping with these circumstances of book production the copy-text method of editing literary texts developed.[12] Under this system the author's final intention is considered to be a combination of his preference in choice of

---

[8] Elias N. Kulukundis, 'Thoughts on the Origin, Authenticity and Evolution of C. P. E. Bach's D Minor Concerto (W. 22)', *Festschrift Albi Rosenthal* (Tutzing, 1985), 201.

[9] Boorman, 'Limitations', p. 323.

[10] Ibid., p. 324.

[11] Philip Gaskell, *A New Introduction to Bibliography* (Oxford, 1972), 344–5.

[12] Ibid., pp. 338–360. An overview of recent writings on copy-text is provided in Gaskell's bibliography, pp. 411–3.

words, sentence structure, and other 'substantives', along with the compositor's preference in spelling, punctuation, and other 'non-substantives'.

The applicability of copy-text theory to the editing of music depends on establishing that a composer did expect his publisher to follow notational conventions of the time rather than the peculiarities of his manuscript, and also on determining what constituted a non-substantive in music publishing during a given era. For editing the works of a composer like C. P. E. Bach, who had only a fraction of his works published, it would also be desirable to establish that the music copyists of the time resembled compositors in their consistency of treating various notational idiosyncrasies of a composer's manuscript, and also to show that the composer was not surprised when a copyist altered his notation.

Attention to non-substantives is all the more important when editing a work in several versions, since the methodology developed for the emendation of ancient Greek and Latin texts cannot always be employed successfully for music. Music survives in a form fundamentally different from the ancient texts for which the rules of classical philology were developed: namely, any musical source is likely to have been continually altered from its origin to the present, particularly with regard to slurs, ornaments, dynamics, and other performance indications that performers have felt free to add. Consequently, it is extremely difficult to determine, for example, why a given slur has been omitted from a manuscript copy. The copyist may have overlooked the slur while copying from source A, or the slur may not have been in source A when he copied from it, or he might have used source B as his exemplar, since B also lacks the slur. In spite of these limitations, however, the method still may be employed successfully by an editor fully aware of its historical development,[13] as is demonstrable after a consideration of the usual sources and documents available to an editor of music.

The original sources preserving the music of Carl Philipp Emanuel Bach exemplify the types usually encountered in the editing of music, and these sources furthermore reveal the composer's penchant for revision and preparation of alternate versions and arrangements. Until recently the true extent of his habits remained unknown, since only half of his music has been available in modern edition, and since the secondary literature consisted primarily of biographies and stylistic studies of the separate genres. In 1980 our knowledge of C. P. E. Bach's music took a quantum step forward with the publication of Eugene Helm's biography and work-list for C. P. E. Bach in *The New Grove Dictionary of Music and Musicians*.[14] Here Helm has identified many works of doubtful authenticity, and he has detailed the revision and reuse of

---

[13]  An extensive discussion of the applicability of philological methods to the filiation of musical sources has been provided by Georg Feder in 'Textkritische Methoden: Versuch eines Überblicks mit Bezug auf die Hadyn-Gesamtausgabe', *Haydn-Studien*, 5 (1983), 77–109.

[14]  *Helm/Grove.*

material by C. P. E. Bach to an extent never before discussed. For example, Helm identified many sonatina movements as arrangements of little character pieces or of the pieces for flute or violin and clavier, while only a few of these correspondences had been previously identified, notably by Hans Uldall and Ernst Schmid.[15] Helm's *Grove* article, together with Hans-Günter Ottenberg's recent biography of C. P. E. Bach,[16] provides the most up-to-date information on the composer in print. Another quantum leap forward will undoubtedly occur when Helm's thematic catalogue is published.[17]

## Documents to be Consulted in Editing Works of C. P. E. Bach

In editing music by C. P. E. Bach there are generally many different source materials available that shed light on the genesis and revision of a work. First, sketches may provide important clues to the process or they may confirm or deny a reading about which an editor would remain in doubt if only later sources could be consulted. (Unfortunately not very many sketches for C. P. E. Bach's music have survived.) Next, the composer may have penned a score and subsequently continued to revise. The easiest revision to recognize is a section crossed out in the autograph score, such as that in C. P. E. Bach's concerto in A major H. 410/W. 7.[18] In this passage, which exhibits the usual score order of violino primo, violino secondo, viola, cembalo, and basso, the original keyboard part has been crossed out and a new one entered on the staves for the second violin and the viola immediately above, which happened to have been blank at that point. For corrections of single notes, which after all could have resulted from error in writing as well as changes in the text, C. P. E. Bach normally wrote the name of the intended pitch above the note.

Another revision that might be made in an autograph score is less obvious, since the composer may have decided to get rid of an early version by snipping out a leaf, and the only clue to this is an irregularity in the gathering structure of the source, or the presence of a stub where there was once a whole leaf. These stubs, as well as changes in paper type and gathering structure, can almost never be seen on microfilm. Even though one may no longer be able to see the early version, the fact that it existed at one time may eventually have important consequences for the editing of the work. An example illustrating this point is found in the autograph score of the concerto in E flat major H. 404/

[15] Hans Uldall, *Das Klavierkonzert der Berliner Schule* (Leipzig, 1928), 59–66; Ernst Fritz Schmid, *Carl Philipp Emanuel Bach und seine Kammermusik* (Kassel, 1931), 15–54.

[16] *Carl Philipp Emanuel Bach* (Leipzig, 1982).

[17] *Thematic Catalogue of the Works of Carl Philipp Emanuel Bach.* I am very grateful to Professor Helm for sharing his catalogue with me over the last few years.

[18] D-ddr Bds, Mus. ms. autogr. Bach P 352, i, measures 98–101.

W. 2.[19] Portions of this score have been erased, and some of it has been obscured by a piece of paper pasted onto the original leaf. The erasures are easy to see when viewed directly, and even on film the presence of erasure is apparent from the redrawn staff lines, which are slightly crooked. The erasure comes as no surprise, since the catalogue of Bach's estate published two years after his death listed this concerto as his second one, composed in Leipzig in 1734 and revised in Berlin in 1743.[20] Furthermore, the concerto was published in an unauthorized edition by Antoine Huberty. Huberty's edition differs significantly from that of the autograph score, but since the edition was not authorized by the composer, its version cannot be judged authentic without further information. On the basis of catalogues issued by the publishing firm, Huberty's print probably dates from *c.*1762, or about twenty-eight years after the concerto was composed. It is significant, however, that the Huberty print labels the concerto 'No. 2', the same number eventually given this concerto in the catalogue of the composer's estate (*NV*). The decisive evidence in this matter is provided by a look at the autograph manuscript under ultraviolet light, which reveals in a striking manner the original notes Bach wrote before his erasure. These notes correspond to the readings in the Huberty print. Consequently, even though the print was not authorized, it reflects a source copied from the autograph score before 1743. The editor of this work can justifiably use the Huberty print as an authentic source of the early version for those passages that are obscured by pasted-on bits of paper in the autograph score.

There is a great deal of evidence that Bach resented the exploitation of his works by unscrupulous publishers. In addition to many remarks he made in letters and in the *Versuch*, he appears to have kept a tight rein on some of his works, so that they did not fall into the hands of a publisher like Huberty. There are often notes in the composer's hand on title-pages of manuscript copies, stating that nobody has that work yet, or that only this or that acquaintance has it. These notes presumably were for the benefit of his wife and unmarried daughter, who were likely to survive him, and who could expect a higher fee from a publisher for the works that had never been circulated. These notes might have also identified pieces the composer intended to revise further before disseminating them. As he must have noticed with his second concerto, it is not easy to suppress an early version once it has been published.

Another kind of revision, the interpolation of new material into an existing work, probably occurred more often than one would guess from the surviving sources. For many works no autograph survives. At the same time fragments of identifiable compositions appear in the composer's hand on the reverse of other totally unrelated works. For example, Bach wrote some revisions for his fourth concerto, H. 406/W. 4, on the reverse of a bifolio containing a copy of

---

[19] D-brd B, Mus. ms. autogr. Bach P 354, i, measures 103–7.   [20] *NV*, 26.

the prelude in G major from his father's *Wohltemperierte Clavier*, Book 2 (BWV 884), also in his hand.[21] And, on the reverse of a manuscript copy of the last two pages of J. S. Bach's toccata in E minor BWV 830, i, he penned a different version of the last movement of his sonata with varied reprises H. 138/W. 50, 3.[22] Likewise, he wrote horn parts for his symphony in E flat H. 654/W. 179 on the reverse of leaves containing sections of his rondo in C major H. 260/W. 56, 1, and his sonata in F major H. 269/W. 56, 4.[23] In this last case, it is quite plausible that the bars of the keyboard rondo mixed in with the symphony parts were a later addition to the rondo, as Richard Kramer has suggested.[24] The flags at the beginning of this section in the autograph, as well as the mark at the end resembling a sideways 'B', are typical symbols indicating insertion in Bach's autographs.[25] Typically, it is difficult to date such revisions, which makes all the more important a study of Bach's handwriting as it changed in the course of time.[26]

Once Bach did release a work for authorized publication, a whole new set of documents was created. Among these are the galley proofs of the printer, on which corrections were entered in the margin. Such galley proofs once existed for Johann Sebastian Bach's canonic variations on 'Von Himmel hoch da komm ich her', BWV 769/769a.[27] Only recently we in the C. P. E. Bach Edition have learned that a complete set of corrected galley proofs exists for the composer's oratorio *Die Israeliten in der Wüste*, H. 775/W. 238. These proofs, which are preserved in an American private collection, contain many corrections on each page, including changes of pitches, addition of omitted dynamics, and corrections of alignment and other mechanical details (see Facsimile 1). While the corrections do not seem to be in the hand of the composer, they undoubtedly represent his intention, since he acted as the publisher of this edition, which was printed in 1775.

In spite of the paucity of corrected proofs, the knowledge that these once existed gives additional authority to the authorized prints. Such knowledge can be extracted from Bach's correspondence with publishers, which contain sentences such as 'Enclosed are my remarks about sheet H.'[28] As Ernst Suchalla has established, this sentence from a letter of 12 October 1765 refers to Bach's *Sechs Leichte Clavier-Sonaten*, H. 162–3, 180–3/W. 53, published in

---

[21] D-ddr Bds M. Thul. 18 Beilage.          [22] D-ddr LEm, Ms. R 12.

[23] D-brd B, Mus. ms. Bach St 236.

[24] Richard Kramer, 'The New Modulation of the 1770s: C. P. E. Bach in Theory, Criticism, and Practice', *JAMS*, 38 (1985), 585–9.

[25] See the facsimile of the autograph leaf for the rondo in Kramer, 'The New Modulation', p. 585. The flags are at the beginning of the 10th and 11th staves, and the sideways 'B' is at the end of the 15th stave.

[26] Such a study is being undertaken by Professor Pamela Fox of Miami University, Oxford, Ohio.

[27] Hans Klotz, *NBA*, IV/2 *Kritischer Bericht* (Kassel, 1957), 87. The corrected proofs have been missing since the end of World War II.

[28] *Suchalla/Briefe*, p. 258: 'Hierbey kommen meine Anmerkungen über den H Bogen.'

Facsimile 1. *Die Israeliten in der Wüste* (Hamburg, 1775), corrected galley proof page

1766 by Breitkopf.[29] Suchalla's commentary to the letters also explains the term 'sheet H'. Each sheet of paper used for the edition was assigned a letter of the alphabet. This large sheet was then folded to form a bifolio, labelled at the bottom edge of the two recto sides in the form 'A' and 'A2'. 'sheet H' accordingly refers to pages 29–32 of the edition and contains the end of H. 181/W. 53, 3 and the beginning of H. 182/W. 53, 4.

Even after Bach released his work to a publisher, he might change his mind, as is evident in a letter he wrote to Johann Heinrich Voss, who published his song 'Lyda', H. 737/W. 202G2:

If it is not yet too late, dear Herr Voss, please change the following in my 'Lyda', namely [two bars of music] instead of [same two bars, different version]. The f[orte] and the starch must go. The phrase 'o Lyda' is better if it is softer. I remain as ever E. Bach. Hamburg, 9 September 74.[30]

Even after the publication of his music Bach continued to revise, or at least to write new versions that he considered equally good as the printed one.[31] It is also clear that important 'stop-press' corrections were made in the authentic prints, as Eiji Hashimoto has already established.[32] The significance of this for future editing activity is very great, for it means that each copy of the authentic prints must be examined for possible variants.

The unpublished works can present even greater problems than the published ones, since the circulation of a large number of manuscript copies more or less guarantees that a certain number of unauthentic versions will be created at the same time the composer is tinkering with his own scores. Probably the most monumental case of this is C. P. E. Bach's *Passions-Cantate* (Passion Cantata), H. 776/W. 233, which he composed in 1769 and continued to revise from then on. He even was so careful as to mail his revisions to owners of manuscript copies, of which there are nineteen or twenty still extant. The Passion Cantata was a very popular work, as Stephen Clark has demonstrated by a thorough analysis of the payment records for performances as well as other documents in his recent dissertation.[33] Bach made many revisions in the work. It was not published during his lifetime—a curious anomaly, considering its obvious marketability. In this regard Clark

[29] Ibid., pp. 258–9.

[30] Published in facsimile in *Carl Philipp Emanuel Bach's Autobiography*, ed. William S. Newman (Hilversum, 1967), following p. 201. The original reads: 'Weñ es noch nicht zu spät ist, liebster Herr Voss, so belieben Sie folgendes in meiner Lÿda zu ändern, nehm[lich] [two bars of music] statt [same two bars, different version]. Das F[orte] u[nd] die Steife muss weg. Der Ausdruck, o *Lyda*, ist besser weñ er sanfter ist. Ich bin wie allezeit E. Bach. Hamburg, d[en] 9 Sept[ember] 74.'

[31] Such recompositions of sonata movements have been discussed by Darrell Berg in 'C. P. E. Bach's "Variations" and "Embellishments" for his Keyboard Sonatas', *JM*, 2 (1983), 151–73.

[32] Carl Philipp Emanuel Bach, *Sechs Sonaten fürs Clavier mit veränderten Reprisen*, ed. Eiji Hashimoto (Tokyo, 1984), 21, 23, 100–1; Carl Philipp Emanuel Bach, *Fortsetzung von Sechs Sonaten fur Clavier*, ed. Eiji Hashimoto (Tokyo, 1984), 113–14.

[33] 'The Occasional Choral Works of C. P. E. Bach' (Ph.D. diss., Princeton, 1984), 44–50.

develops the interesting theory that perhaps Bach did not publish the cantata because he considered it a more personal piece than those he sent out for publication.[34] While no autograph exists for this work, there is a copy[35] identified by the composer as one he had frequently used and which he judged best. This copy, known in abbreviated form as P 337, contains the composer's stamp of approval on its title-page:

Passion cantata, set to music in the year 1769 in Hamburg by me, C. P. E. Bach. NB this score is by no means in the handwriting of the author (for there is no original of this cantata in this version, since the author has changed it a great deal). It is, however, as correct as possible and certainly more correct than all other copies, since the owner, namely the author, has read through it quite often.[36]

In spite of the composer's guarantee, this source does contain one impossible requirement: because of a 'colla parte' indication in the fugue 'Auf daß wir der Sünde' (no. 18b) the second oboe is called on to play notes not available on the instrument, including the C sharp directly above middle C.[37] In several other copies of this cantata different copyists solved this problem differently, leading to significant variants among the sources. An alert scribe copying from a playable exemplar could nevertheless have realized why the oboe part differed from the strings in only one bar, and substituted his own solution to the problem, rendering this passage of litt'* use for decisions about filiation.

## Evaluation of Various Techniques for Editing Multiple Versions

In spite of the reservations expressed earlier, the traditional methodology developed for the emendation of ancient Greek and Latin texts does have its place in editing the music of C. P. E. Bach. This methodology, involving a patient and detail-conscious comparison of known exemplars, was designed for the reconstruction of a lost original not subject to revision by the author in the span of time when copies were prepared. An editor of music may have a revised autograph score, parts reviewed by the composer, letters, corrected page proofs, and every other imaginable authentic document, and yet that editor may still be dealing with a lost original. The composer may have discarded his first score, or he may have erased the extant autograph score so thoroughly that he obliterated the first version in the score. Here the many

---

[34] Ibid., pp. 61–2.          [35] D-brd B, Mus. ms. autogr. Bach P 337.

[36] As translated by Clark, 'Occasional Choral Works', p. 51. Clark's transcription of the original is: 'Passion-Cantate, von mir, C. P. E. Bach, anno 1769 in Hamburg in Musik gesetzt. NB diese Partitur ist zwar nicht von der Handschrift des Autors, (denn von dieser Cantate in dieser Einrichtung existiert kein Original, weil der Autor hernach vieles geändert hat); sie ist aber so correkt wie möglich und ganz gewiss correkter, als alle übrigen Exemplare, weil sie der Besitzer, nemlich der Autor sehr oft durchgesehen hat.'

[37] I am grateful to Charles Gallagher for bringing this instance to my attention.

manuscript copies of admittedly uncertain origin may still act as witnesses to that original version, if the editor can identify which of these sources is likely to reflect the early version, which the later, and which some sort of hybrid between the two. For this the study of copyists and provenance of a source can be profitably employed.

The task of editing Bach's first concerto, H. 403/W.1 illustrates well the problem of dealing with a lost original. It has been established that there are two extant versions of this concerto, for which a set of parts in the hand of the composer was missing from the Berlin Staatsbibliothek after World War II.[38] Recently Darrell Berg located the autograph parts in the Biblioteka Jagiellońska, Kraków.[39] The autograph parts preserve the later version, that of all the manuscript copies except one in Berlin.[40] As comforting as it is to have an autograph at last, it is also likely, considering Bach's usual working habits, that an autograph score for his first concerto once existed and may still come to light. Such a score might preserve the early version, or a hybrid of the two versions, or predominately the later version with erasures at the measures differing from the early version. Accordingly, in approaching the many manuscript copies, it would be helpful to ascertain which of these might have been copied from an autograph score and which were copied from other secondary sources.

If there are enough sources and enough variant passages, the relative dating of the sources may even be implied by the readings each preserves, as, for example, with the concerto in A major H. 422/W. 19. Claudia Widgery, editor of this concerto for the C. P. E. Bach Edition, has been able to identify which manuscript copies are early ones or have descended from early ones, based on the readings for measures 75 and 153 in the first movement. Bach erased and rewrote these measures extensively,[41] but only after allowing various copies of the original version to be prepared.

The copy-text method offers great potential in editing music, as long as the non-substantive or accidental elements can be satisfactorily identified. For eighteenth-century music the non-substantive elements might include various notational conventions, stem direction in certain cases, and the layout of the page. Occasionally eighteenth-century composers desired a sound that might be simple to produce but difficult to notate in the standard way. In such cases many copyists might try to refine the unconventionality of the autograph notation, and thus signal what they were using as their exemplar. This occurred with the concerto in D major H. 414/W. 11 (see Facsimile 2). Bach required the keyboard player to strike a single note on each successive

[38] Wade, *Keyboard Concertos*, pp. 86–9, 235.

[39] I am grateful to Professor Berg for inventorying the sources now in Poland and acquiring a microfilm copy for the use of the C. P. E. Bach Edition. A detailed account of the circumstances that led to the removal of a large group of music manuscripts from Berlin to Poland is given by Nigel Lewis in *Paperchase: Mozart, Beethoven, Bach . . . The Search for their Lost Music* (London, 1981).

[40] D-brd B, Mus. ms. Bach P 239.          [41] D-ddr Bds, Mus. ms. autogr. Bach P 352.

least in string parts, can be viewed as a feature of the text that the copyist was permitted to change.

Becoming familiar with a composer's usual habits of writing offers an extremely valuable tool for the editor of multiple versions. Its disadvantage is primarily a practical one, in that an editor may not be in a position to study composers' autographs for hours on end in order to develop the requisite expertise. In this situation, as in many others, the team approach of complete editions enjoys a clear advantage over solitary editing projects, in that at least one person reviewing any editor's manuscript, such as the general editor, should be able to raise possibilities to the volume editor that are based on knowledge of the composer's general habits.

In editing music there are two special circumstances that make attention to methodology especially important: the tendency mentioned earlier for performers or other musicians to alter various details, such as slurring and ornaments, and the long tradition of 'normalizing' or making consistent any small discrepancies in phrasing, dynamics, and so on that may occur between the various parts or in subsequent passages.

A very simple tactic can make all the difference: the direct examination of the musical sources, rather than reliance on microfilm or photocopies. On direct examination erasures can be seen, and not only is the correct reading made clear, but also new data concerning the filiation of the sources becomes available. For example, in Bach's concerto in C minor H. 448/W. 37, a seeming inconsistency in slurring occurs in the autograph score (see Example 1).[47] Since most of the manuscript copies present the slur in the first violin part, measure 200, the same way that is found in the bass, viola, and second violin parts in the two measures immediately preceding, the traditional approach of normalization presses the editor to make all the string parts consistent by writing the slur in measure 200 over all three notes (in round brackets, of course). But when one examines closely the sets of parts corrected by the composer, an erasure in the first violin part marks the time when a slur originally over all three notes was changed to affect only the first two notes, just as in the autograph score.[48] Bach probably had to go to some effort to preserve the subtle idiosyncrasies of slurring, dynamics, and other elements, idiosyncrasies that are such a trademark of his style. We are fortunate that he did make this effort, and that study of erasures can give editors the impetus to follow the autograph, no matter how many manuscript copies exist with a conveniently 'consistent' text.

For editing music the utility of the various approaches to editing literary texts varies with the composer and the situation. Ideally, the method chosen

---

[47] D-ddr Bds, Mus. ms. autogr. Bach P 356, i, measures 198–201. The filiation of the sources is discussed by Elias N. Kulukundis in his edition of this concerto for the C. P. E. Bach Edition (Oxford, in preparation).

[48] D-brd B, Mus. ms. Bach St 526, i, measure 200.

Example 1. Concerto in C minor H. 448/W. 37, i, mm. 198–201. D-ddr
Bds, Mus. ms. autogr. Bach P 356 (autograph)

should allow the editor a certain confidence in making decisions, so that the
editor is able to avoid what Alfred Dürr found not uncommon in critical
editions: a tendency to avoid conclusions, amass data, and be cowardly in
general by placing slurs in the music exactly as ambiguously as the slurs
appear in the source, by positioning a 'pianissimo' sign under as many notes as
possible to obscure the time it takes effect, and by adding over each sharp in the
new edition a natural in brackets above the staff and a flat in parentheses
below, each accompanied by a question mark.[49] Particularly with regard to
the difficult task of filiation, if the evidence for a conclusion can be presented
clearly and precisely, the critical reports of the C. P. E. Bach Edition might also
function as a reservoir of information for subsequent generations of scholars in
the way envisaged by Arthur Mendel.

[49] 'Editionsprobleme bei Gesamtausgaben', *Musik und Verlag: Karl Vötterle zum 65. Geburtstag*,
ed. Richard Baum and Wolfgang Rehm (Kassel, 1968), 237.

# A new look at C. P. E. Bach's Musical Jokes*

## Susan Wollenberg

IN writings from his day to the present, the highly personal and characteristic effect of C. P. E. Bach's instrumental works has been generally acknowledged. Reichardt, commenting retrospectively on a first hearing of the symphonies H. 657–62/W. 182 (1773), evoked concepts of boldness, originality, and novelty, as well as humour; Geiringer in the 1950s, synthesizing an account of Bach's character and work, expressed notions of 'ingenuity', 'virtuosity' (in composition) and—in connection with the rondos—the idea of a musical counterpart to Bach's 'witty and spirited conversations', this music revealing 'an exquisite sense of humour'.[1] Such descriptions rightly promote an appreciation of the spirit underlying Bach's compositional processes, rather than a sterile analysis of form. The outmoded 'search for the evolution of sonata form' in his works has been supplanted in recent analytical studies by a readiness to evaluate his personal style on its own terms.[2] Geiringer's choice of the word 'exquisite' provided a significant pointer, suggesting a sense of that attention to precise detail which was essential to Bach's compositional thought.[3] His musical

* I should like to thank Dr F. W. Sternfeld (Exeter College, Oxford) and Bernard Harrison (Keble College, Oxford) for some useful discussions; and Susan Orchard (Christ Church, Oxford) for her help with Daniel Weber's treatise, and for providing the reference to Lessing.

[1] J. F. Reichardt, 'Noch ein Bruchstück aus J. F. Reichardts Autobiographie; sein erster Aufenthalt in Hamburg', AMZ, 16 (1814), col. 29, quoted in Karl Geiringer, The Bach Family. Seven Generations of Creative Genius (London, 1954), 368; see also pp. 358–9.

[2] Pamela Fox, 'Melodic Nonconstancy in the Keyboard Sonatas of C. P. E. Bach', Ph.D. diss., University of Cincinnati, 1983, 8, n. 12. See Fox, 'Melodic Nonconstancy', passim; and Darrell Berg, 'The Keyboard Sonatas of C. P. E. Bach: An Expression of the Mannerist Principle' (diss., Ph.D. State University of New York at Buffalo, 1975); Hans-Günter Ottenberg, Carl Philipp Emanuel Bach (Leipzig, 1982), trans. Philip Whitmore (Oxford, 1987); David Schulenberg, The Instrumental Music of Carl Philipp Emanuel Bach (Ann Arbor, 1984); Rachel Wade, The Keyboard Concertos of Carl Philipp Emanuel Bach (Ann Arbor, 1981). Schulenberg, for example, states that his analyses 'might be understood as defining the standards which the works set for themselves' rather than positing absolutes (see Schulenberg, Instrumental Music, p. 145).

[3] This, like many of Bach's personal traits, has been seen by some critics as a weakness in relation to the overall structure: see William S. Newman, 'The Keyboard Sonatas of Bach's Sons and their Relationship to the Classic Sonata Concept', Proceedings for 1949 of the Music Teachers' National Association, 236–48 (referring to the 'inordinate attention' paid to 'minutiae'; quoted in Fox, Melodic Nonconstancy, p. 225, n. 18). Schulenberg (Instrumental Music, p. 78) perceives that '. . . the care with which "capricious" details were frequently added to works undergoing revision testifies to planning and calculation at the local level'.

humour often depends for its effect on a single exquisite detail, cleverly manipulated; the possibilities of analysing this manipulation of detail have not yet been exhausted, and indeed may be inexhaustible.

Another important element in the literature has been a recognition of the part played by the listener in the realization of certain compositional effects. Barford has written that 'Composers are not always writing consciously for posterity',[4] but a more pertinent question is whether the composer is writing consciously for the listener, a listener who is expected to be engaged with what is happening in the music from moment to moment. When Barford states that closer examination of the music suggests the importance of the relationship between composer and performer ('. . . performer and composer are to be considered a closely integrated pair')[5] this might valuably be extended to the notion of an intimate triangle of composer, performer, and listener.[6] The effecting of 'musical jokes' in particular exploits such a relationship. Fox has convincingly assumed (and, following Hosler, has documented, for example from C. P. E. Bach, Quantz, and Scheibe) the eighteenth-century composer's wish to maintain the listener in a state of alertness: 'he [C. P. E. Bach] utilized defeat of expectation to arouse the listener's attentiveness'.[7] Marpurg noted that a friend of his, a mere musical amateur, had been gripped by steadily fixed attention in listening to Bach's sonata H. 29/W. 48, 6.[8] Complementary to the idea that Bach's music 'demands attentive listening'[9] is the perception by various writers on Bach of compositional procedures deliberately designed to leave the listener 'in a state of confusion'. Particularly significant for the present paper is Fox's commentary on those movement-openings where 'Bach seems determined to command the listener's immediate attention' by disorientating means or 'expectational defeat'.[10] In Bach's instrumental works (especially those for solo keyboard, and the orchestral symphonies) the listener's attentiveness is heightened not by creating a constant flow of smooth-running ideas but by the use of unexpected or disruptive (Fox's 'non-

[4] Philip Barford, *The Keyboard Music of C. P. E. Bach* (London, 1965), 105.

[5] Ibid., p. 100.

[6] This also ties up with ideas of author, text, and reader relationships expounded in modern literary theory.

[7] Fox, 'Melodic Nonconstancy', p. 128. Hosler notes that C. P. E. Bach, Mattheson, L. Mozart, Quantz, and Scheibe 'all point out the pleasurable benefits of playing with the listener's expectations.'; see Bellamy Hosler, *Changing Aesthetic Views of Instrumental Music in 18th-century Germany* (Ann Arbor, 1981), 20; and further, pp. 29, 58 ff.

[8] See Ottenberg, *Bach*, p. 61; Hosler, *Changing Views*, p. 61, quotes Scheibe on the importance of 'uninterrupted . . . attentiveness ' ('ununterbrochene Aufmerksamkeit').

[9] Ottenberg, *Bach*, p. 184 ('Bachs Sinfonien wollen mit wachen Sinnen gehört werden').

[10] Fox, 'Melodic Nonconstancy', pp. 143 and 136 (supported by a quotation from Scheibe, with reference to Hosler, *Changing Views*, p. 58). See also Ottenberg, *Bach*, p. 61, describing the opening of H. 25/W. 48, 2.

constant') procedures: '. . . it is in this very discontinuity that his [Bach's] individuality is manifested'.[11]

A third important element noted by writers on C. P. E. Bach is the marked stylistic diversity found within his works, indeed often within a single work or movement.[12] What is particularly important here is that this should not be seen as the uncertain vacillation of a composer caught in a 'difficult', 'transitional' period between two distinct style-epochs (another outmoded view), nor, clearly, can it be seen as a personal process of evolution following a neat chronological pattern within his work as a whole, each style supplanting its predecessor. Rather it provides evidence of Bach's stylistic eclecticism and compositional virtuosity, in that he was able to reproduce with facility a wide range of styles (including Baroque motivic-contrapuntal, lightweight *galant* and tear-jerking *empfindsam*, as well as a more regulated 'high Classical' manner); in this respect (as in other respects), like his father, Bach had a lively interest in the diversity of current styles and was able to adopt them as and when he wished, for a few bars or an entire piece.[13] The three, interrelated, elements discussed above: humour, linked with ingenuity and novelty (as manifested in what in Haydn's work we appreciate as 'surprises');[14] the listener's engagement with the work at a detailed level; and stylistic incongruity deriving from the deliberate manipulation of different idioms; all these are further related to the phenomenon which forms one of the central concerns of this paper, the parodistic treatment of material, seen particularly in Bach's solo keyboard sonatas and symphonies.[15]

First I would suggest that in general many of Bach's effects are intended by the composer (and are to be perceived by the performer and the listener—and

---

[11] Ottenberg, *Bach*, p. 61: '. . . gerade in dieser Diskontinuität liegt das Individuelle begründet'. Hosler discusses with particular reference to Baumgarten and Meier the phenomenon of *Verwunderung*, 'a kind of heightened attentiveness brought on by the perception of "the unexpected, the wonderful, and the pleasantly surprising" ' ('Das Unerwartete, das Wunderbare, und das auf angenehme Art Überraschende'). See Hosler, *Changing Views*, p. 96.

[12] For an extended treatment of Bach's 'Stylistic Mixture of Melodic Procedures' see Fox, 'Melodic Nonconstancy', pp. 184–211.

[13] See Wade, *Keyboard Concertos*, pp. 59 ff.

[14] For a specialized investigation of this topic see Steven Paul, 'Wit, Comedy and Humour in the Instrumental Music of Franz Joseph Haydn' (Ph.D. diss., University of Cambridge, 1981), and 'Comedy, Wit and Humor in Haydn's Instrumental Music', *Haydn Studies: Proceedings of the International Haydn Conference, Washington, DC, 1975* (New York and London, 1981), 450–6. Paul's remark that 'no thorough study of this important aspect of his style' had previously been made with regard to Haydn (*Haydn Studies*, p. 450) applies equally to C. P. E. Bach (whom surprisingly he does not once mention in his article). In his dissertation Paul argues for a view of Haydn as 'the "inventor" of pure, intrinsic musical humour' ('Wit, Comedy and Humour', p. 359) and mentions C. P. E. Bach only *en passant*.

[15] At this point it should be stressed that references to 'parody' here use the term in its humorous sense (cf. Leonard Ratner, *Classic Music: Expression, Form, and Style* (New York and London, 1980), 387–9 and *passim*).

conveyed by the performer to the listener) as 'musical jokes' or 'tricks'.[16] This is not to imply that his work is shallow or trivial; rather, his use of procedures creating such 'jokes' adds depth and meaning to an already intense and intellectually lively manner of expression.[17] The selection of examples that follows can be assigned to certain discernible categories.[18] Example 1*a* shows (at measure 16) a typical ploy: a stock cadential phrase with one essential factor omitted. (A useful method of demonstrating the precise unexpected qualities of the originals is to recast passages in a hypothetically 'expected' format. Thus Example 1*b* shows the same phrase in its hypothetical form.) This whole movement is in a musically playful, or 'ludic' style.[19] The B natural at the beginning of measure 16 is clearly an appoggiatura, but by leaving it suddenly and totally unaccompanied at this point the composer thwarts expectations and allows the knowing listener—the *Kenner*—the satisfaction of recognizing and savouring the implications of the moment. It is worth pointing out that the bisectional structures with repeats (whose very repetitiveness has seemed to some writers to be at odds with the essential discontinuity of Bach's thought) give opportunities of intensifying the effect of such 'jokes'. (Because the receptive listener is prepared after a first hearing of a passage, its repetition

---

[16] Ratner, *Classic Music*, p. 387, comments percipiently on the humour underlying much Classical music: 'Much of the instrumental music of the Classic masters is saturated with comic rhetoric which may be vaguely sensed but is not often fully savoured'. A stimulating treatment of the subject was given in Alfred Brendel's lecture 'Does Classical Music have to be entirely serious?' (8th Darwin Lecture, delivered in the Concert Hall of the Music Faculty, University of Cambridge, 20 Nov. 1984, first broadcast on BBC Radio 3 on 8 Apr. 1985). Quotations from this (as yet unpublished) lecture are taken from the broadcast version.

[17] Hosler, *Changing Views*, in particular pp. 2 and 16–17, usefully draws attention to 18th-century aesthetic problems in accepting the creation of comic effects as an artistically serious endeavour, and to the equating of comic art with triviality and inferiority, and shows that it was with the Romantics that 'music's Tändelei alone was somehow capable of expressing profound and wonderful things' (*Changing Views*, p. 190).

[18] Brendel's examples were taken mainly from Haydn and Beethoven, and he seemed to take C. P. E. Bach's generation as representing utter seriousness: 'For C. P. E. Bach's contemporaries, elevated affections . . . had to be suggested by certain devices of musical style. Haydn applied such devices to the lowest category of poetics [the comic]', and Brendel further adduced Zelter's opinion that Haydn was criticized by his contemporaries because he burlesqued the 'deadly seriousness of his predecessors, J. S. Bach and C. P. E. Bach'. Ottenberg by contrast recognizes throughout his sympathetic discussions of C. P. E. Bach's work the crucial element of 'Spaßlichkeit' (see for example Ottenberg, *Bach*, p. 223, for his comments on the fantasia in C H. 291/W. 61, 6): 'Das Hauptthema ist so recht geeignet, die Dimension des musikalischen Spaßes in ihren mannigfachen Spielarten auszukosten'.

[19] At each stage in the movement, what is 'given' suggests (to the reasonably initiated observer) a particular consequence; an unexpected consequence is then substituted, and this in turn suggests a particular expectation that too is thwarted, and so on. (For example, given the 'Italian sixth' chord at measure 14, itself an unexpected and unexpectedly prolonged event in this harmonic context, the F sharp in the bass at measure 15, intervening (again with some unexpectedness) between the A flat and G, posits the appearance of the diminished seventh often used as intermediary between augmented sixth and Ic or V at the cadence, but an unexpected chromatic chord ($\#IV_7$) is substituted, and other factors add to the effect, such as the melodic leap in the right hand to an unsupported high E in place of the expected G. Dynamics and articulation at the cadence add to the playful effect). On the value of hypothetical recasting see *Essay*, p. 441 n. 8.

Example 1. Sonata in F major H. 243/W. 55, 5, iii. 'Kenner und Liebhaber',
vol. 1 (Leipzig, 1779)

*a* mm. 11–16
*b* 'Expected' format, mm. 15–16

or parallel restatement—and the subsequent repetition of the parallel restatement—offers the chance to enjoy the joke in a more intensely knowing state.)[20]

Another ploy is to omit some crucial factor at the expected moment and then to insert it at the 'wrong' moment as if in (somewhat mocking) compensation for its original omission (see Example 2: Fox has described this passage in terms of its discontinuity.)[21] Here (Example 2, measure 12) Bach typically leaves the

[20] There is an element here of Brendel's *faux pas* theory; in Example 1*a*, the first time it occurs, the listener might think the performer has accidentally omitted to sound the accompanying notes to this appoggiatura, but subsequent recurrences confirm that this was no *faux pas* but a correct rendering of a 'joke'.

[21] Fox, 'Melodic Nonconstancy', p. 84 ('The melodic line resolves down to $g^1$ in measure 12. The bass, however, does not provide a strong reinforcement to the resolution. No left hand support is provided on the downbeat of measure 12, and only a single accompanying note—the thirty-second note $b$—sounds with the $g^1$ (of equally short duration) in the right hand. This understated cadence is immediately followed by a unison outburst which arpeggiates the chord of resolution in rapid thirty-seconds. The melodic line expires *pianissimo*, making the *forte* unison interruption even more disruptive.')

Example 2. Sonatina in G major H. 8/W. 64, 2, ii, mm. 11–13. Pamela Fox,
'Melodic Nonconstancy' p. 85, Example 27

double appoggiatura unsupported, but then following the cadence phrase he
introduces a rush of triadic figures in octaves, emphasizing the G which should
have been sounded (and whose omission 'disturbs' the listener) in the bass at
the beginning of the measure: seemingly a compensatory gesture (understate-
ment followed by overstatement), and one with considerable dramatic impact.
Example 3a illustrates the trick of bringing in what would be expected in one
context, in another quite incongruous context (the 'right' thing in the 'wrong'
place). In this example the harmonic progression (over a Baroque chaconne
bass of a type particularly favoured by C. P. E. Bach for movement-openings)
spanning measures 1–4 is apparently established at the outset and at its close
as a straightforward prolongation of the tonic (cf. Handel: Example 3c). But by
introducing the irritant A flat in the fourth chordal component of this phrase,
Bach disturbs the original impression and creates from this point on a
harmonic progression belonging more naturally with a conventional move-
ment-ending, where the subdominant is first approached through its dominant seventh before reasserting its function as IV (enhanced as (II₇b) in the
progression IV (II₇b)–V–I. The irritant effect of the A flat (exacerbated,
typically for this composer, by an ornament on the offending note)[22] is then
intensified by a repetition (in measure 4) of the effect, preceded by a
preposterous leap of a thirteenth. As with other 'eccentric' passages, it is
possible to recompose this extract in an inoffensive manner (see Example 3b).[23]
This passage could almost be interpreted as a brief parodistic portrayal of those
codas where a cadential progression is reiterated, as if the composer were
reluctant to close off the movement.[24] Because the gesture occurs here at the

[22] See Ottenberg, Bach, p. 61: 'Wenn Bach die Septime zusätzlich mit einem Triller versieht,
dazu noch auf unbetonter Zählzeit, dann ist der Eindruck musikalischer Irregularität offenbar.'
[23] Again Brendel's faux pas theory might be relevant here. A good example, in the category of
'false start', is H. 32/W. 49, 4, iii. The music recommences (measure 5) differently, as though now
correcting what was a false start (the use of pauses and irregular phrasing adds to the uncertainty,
while the open-endedness proves useful later).
[24] An example of 'delaying action' at the final cadence occurs at the end of the symphony H.
651/W. 176, iii where it belongs in spirit with the vivacity of the 'hunting-style' finale.

Example 3. Sonata in B flat major H. 25/W. 48, 2, i. 'Prussian Sonatas'
(Nuremberg, 1742/3)

*a* mm. 1–6.
*b* 'Hypothetical' version of H. 25/W. 48, 2, i, mm. 1–4.
*c* G. F. Handel, 'Arrival of the Queen of Sheba' Sinfonia, *Solomon*, pt. III,
harmonic reduction

very opening of a movement, it has an added degree of eccentricity. Arguably Bach's musical tricks are carefully planned and executed, with all possible levels of the music involved; it is not irrelevant that in his personal life he was known as a 'wit' and a 'practical joker'.[25] In the *Versuch* he recommended the use of 'rational deceptions' when creating an improvised compositional structure:[26] although there the phrase referred specifically to modulatory playfulness, it is a term that serves to evoke the spirit of Bach's musical jokes in general.

The 'rational deceptions' categorized and illustrated in the examples above belong with what Brendel has described as the 'stock-in-trade of the comic': 'breaches of convention, appearance of ambiguity, proceedings that masquerade as something they are not'. And, as Brendel has further noted, 'breaches of order' clearly need a 'framework of order' to be effective. An established musical logic, 'available to the musical layman', creates this framework for musical jokes. In the commentary above on some examples of Bach's jokes, such phrases as 'stock cadential phrase' and 'expected moment' obviously relate to the question of the listener's preparedness. For an ideal listener is not simply required to be alert to the particular piece; he must also possess some preconception of what is 'expected' behaviour in such a piece as a whole, and in individual contexts such as movement-openings and endings. The jokes discussed so far thus make their effect largely by twisting the expected to become the unexpected. It seems a small step from there to the parodistic process referred to earlier, wherein the element of mockery is paramount. A composer so easily able to reproduce the features of various styles could also choose to imitate them 'tongue-in-cheek'. Again, a series of musical examples with commentary will illustrate the point.[27] As a preliminary it is interesting to consider briefly some eighteenth-century ideas of musical humour as set out by Daniel Weber in a short but significant treatise to which Ratner has drawn attention.[28] This document apparently represents a rare (if not ideally lucid) attempt to formulate for music similar theories of comedy to those evolved by literary analysts, in particular C. P. E. Bach's friend Lessing,[29] and it thus helps to set the scene for the present enquiry.

[25]  See *Helm/Grove*, p. 845; Geiringer, *The Bach Family*, p. 339; and Reichardt, loc. cit. (n. 1).

[26]  *Essay*, p. 434: 'This and other rational deceptions make a fantasia attractive.'

[27]  This suggestion of parody (see also n. 15 above) seems new in relation to specific passages and procedures, although Ottenberg has pointed out (in relation to the 'Kenner und Liebhaber' sets generally) that 'Humour is combined with irony.' ('Humor verbindet sich mit ironischem Zungenschlag'; *Bach*, p. 222.)

[28]  Weber expressed as his aim 'to fill a gap in the aesthetics of music, which have not yet been systematically treated' ('eine Lücke in der noch nicht systematisch bearbeiteten musikalischen Aesthetik auszufüllen'). See D. Weber, 'Abhandlung: Ueber komische Charakteristik und Karrikatur in praktischen Musikwerken', *AMZ*, 9 (1800), cols. 137–43, 157–62. The quotation above is from col. 138. The treatise was originally written in 1792, with supplementary material added in 1800. See also Ratner, *Classic Music*, pp. 387 ff.

[29]  See for example G. E. Lessing, 'Vom Wesen der Komödie. Aus dem 28. und 29. Stück der Hamburgischen Dramaturgie', in *Kritik und Dramaturgie, ausgewählte Prosa*, ed. K. H. Bühner (Stuttgart, 1967), 59–63.

In spite of his belief that music with text can more easily convey humour, and the fact that his treatise is mainly concerned with music for theatrical comedy, Weber recognizes the possibility of creating 'comic caricature' in working out 'purely instrumental musical humour, without singing or speaking'.[30] Much of his attempt to define and classify comic species is based on his concept of the 'rules'; and the special ways in which the composer may apply or deviate from these rules are essential to Weber's perception of the comic in music.[31] He states that, just as in the visual arts, so also in music, not every comic piece is 'marked with the stamp of caricature'.[32] The comic composer who does not intend to 'descend to the level of caricature, allows himself only cautious deviations from the general rules' (which suggests that the composer who wishes to create caricature may depart more radically from the rules).[33] Weber takes as an example of 'musical depiction, mimicry and caricature' the coachman's aria 'Brillant dans mon emploi' (Philidor). Here the singer strikes up 'a theme which suggests the expectation of a serious bravura aria. A practised ear soon notices in the meantime that it is not meant to be too serious, and the hoped-for bravura aria is not going to turn out as one is accustomed to in grand opera.'[34] Thus besides the idea of bending the rules for comic effect, Weber acknowledges the role of 'defeat of expectation'. Musical reference to the conventions of serious opera, introduced into comic opera in a spirit of caricature (and quite apart from the intrinsic comedy of situation and character contained within the libretto) is a well-recognized feature of eighteenth-century style. The notion of setting up what is apparently a serious piece along conventional lines in order to distort it (to the delight of the knowing listener) into caricature can be shown to be valid also for purely instrumental music.

Weber also uses the term 'parody' and suggests that 'just as poets sometimes parody one another in order to exhibit one another to public ridicule, so too composers often do this',[35] though the parody may not have a specific object; the example Weber offers (from Hiller) parodies in general the style of 'the old-

---

[30] ' . . . und die Bearbeitung des Stoffes der lyrischen sowohl als der blos instrumentalen, ohne Gesang und Rede spielenden Farçe, [heisse ich] *komische Karrikatur*.' ('Abhandlung' col. 138; see also col. 140.)

[31] '[Der komische Styl in praktischen Musikwerken] besteht . . . in einer speciellen Anwendung der Regeln der Harmonik und Melodik, wodurch bey dem Zuhörer, dessen Gehör dazu gestimmt ist, ein Gefühl des Lächerlichen erweckt wird.' (Ibid., col. 139.)

[32] ' . . . so ist auch nicht jedes lächerliche Tongemählde mit dem Stempel der Karrikatur bezeichnet.' (Ibid., col. 139.)

[33] ' . . . so vergönnt sich der komische Tonsetzer, der nicht bis zur Karrikatur herabsinken will, oder muss, nur mässige Abweichungen von der allgemeinen Regel . . . ' (Ibid., cols. 139–40.)

[34] ' . . . ein Thema . . . , welches eine ernsthafte Bravourarie erwarten lässt. Ein geübter Hörer merkt inzwischen bald, dass es damit so ernstlich nicht gemeynt sey, und die gehoffte Bravourarie nicht so ausfällen werde, wie man's in der hohen Oper gewöhnt ist.' (Ibid., cols. 140–1.)

[35] 'So wie übrigens Dichter einander zuweilen parodiren, um einander im Publikum zum Gelachter auszustellen, so thun es auch manchmal die Tonsetzer.' (Ibid., col. 143.) It is a practice of which Weber evidently disapproves.

fashioned ['altmodisch'] opera arias'. I would suggest that when C. P. E. Bach uses 'old-fashioned' styles (which in fact may mean the idioms of his father) he does so in entire seriousness, and that in his work it is the 'modish' which is parodied. Various writers have suggested that C. P. E. Bach avoids the merely fashionable ('What was criticized in his pieces was their capricious style, often *bizarrerie*, their affected difficulty, eccentric arrangement of notes . . . and their intransigent opposition to the fashion of the moment.')[36] Leaving aside those pieces where Bach adopts a lightly fashionable manner or some conventional formula (such as the 'hunting-style' finale in the symphony H. 654/W. 179) without undue complication,[37] it can be claimed that there are cases where he makes more sophisticated reference to fashionable ideas in order to mock them, and to mock the listener's expectations (in ways which the knowing listener will appreciate). Those same gestures and levels of the music in which, for utterly serious expressive purposes, Bach characteristically invests so much significance (dynamic contrasts, syncopated repetitions, sudden pauses) may elsewhere be exploited for parodistic effect. For example, what Fox describes as 'A full range of dynamic indications, notated with growing exactitude throughout his career, intended to shade subtly the many changes of mood'[38] does indeed serve serious *empfindsam* purposes; but Bach's dynamic indications could also be designed to ridicule such modern conventions as 'symphonic' crescendos and *f–p–f–p* contrast phrases.

Example 4*a* (from the first movement of H. 243/W. 55, 5) demonstrates a play on the use of detailed dynamic indications. This passage could be interpreted as a parody of the stereotyped sequential statement of a motif with progressive dynamics (crescendo effect), often used as a symphonic starting-device.[39] Where the stereotyped version would normally stress the tonic (commonly with a pedal bass underpinning the sequence), Bach's distorted version aims conversely to obscure the tonic (a favourite ploy in his work).[40] Example 4*b* shows the progression in skeleton form, clambering uncertainly up into the tonic key of F,[41] while Example 4*c* gives a hypothetical

[36] 'Unbeugsamkeit gegen den Modegeschmack': C. F. D. Schubart, *Ideen zu einer Ästhetik der Tonkunst*, 1784–5 (Vienna, 1806), 179, translated in Berg, *Keyboard Sonatas*, p. 53.

[37] As in some of the Prussian sonata finales, with their good-natured espousal of a vivacious *buffo* style, using aspects such as register and dynamics entertainingly and carrying off some light-hearted jokes (see especially the finales of sonatas 1, 2, and 5, H. 24, 25, and 28/W. 48, 1, 2, and 5; the finale of sonata 6 (H. 29/W. 48, 6) is perhaps the most unpredictable and imaginative of the set, possibly containing some element of mockery, especially in its opening procedures).

[38] 'Melodic Nonconstancy', p. 5.

[39] For an interesting later manifestation of parody based on sequential presentation of an opening motif with *f–p–f–p* contrasts, see Beethoven, Op. 90, i (also tonally misleading); and compare C. P. E. Bach, H. 142/W. 52, 2, iii).

[40] See Fox, 'Melodic Nonconstancy', pp. 133–4, on the discontinuity of this passage.

[41] In movements subsequent to the first, this kind of opening may relate to—and be explained by—the close of the previous movement (as with the finale of the sonata H. 243/W. 55, 5 or some of the symphonies with linked movements, such as H. 664/W. 183, 2, H. 661/W. 182, 5 and H. 662/W. 182, 6).

Example 4. Sonata in F major H. 243/W. 55, 5, i. 'Kenner und Liebhaber', vol.
1 (Leipzig, 1779)

*a* mm. 1–3
*b* Harmonic reduction extracting the basic sequential progression
*c* 'Hypothetical' version

[outline bass only]

reconstruction possessing the stability and continuity so lacking in Example
4*a*. C. P. E. Bach was perhaps one of the first composers to endow the opening
of an instrumental movement with more than a purely annunciatory
significance. Aspects of his technique such as the impression of 'beginning in
the middle' and the 'non-tonic opening' evoke a sense of subtlety and mystery
more typical of nineteenth-century compositional procedures. The importance
of these enigmatic beginnings relates to the whole movement, not in terms of
establishing the *Affekt* but in terms of the relationship that is established

Example 5. Sonata in B minor H. 245/W. 55, 3, i, mm. 1–4. 'Kenner und Liebhaber', vol. 1 (Leipzig, 1779)

between composer, performer, and listener, and between the composer and his material.

By definition, the use of another common opening device, the forceful theme outlining the tonic triad, would seem to be precluded in Bach's 'non-tonic openings'; but Example 5 shows how in one case a 'non-tonic opening' (H. 245/W. 55, 3, i) contains the three notes of the tonic triad at the start, in an unaccompanied upbeat scramble—thus tentatively rather than forcefully—followed by a phrase harmonized in D major, though offering little tonal stability.[42] Those three introductory notes could be seen as a *reductio ad absurdum* of the triadic theme, calculated with ironic intent. Straightforward triadic themes are apparently quite rare in Bach's work. In connection with the symphonies, Gallagher and Helm have suggested that 'Formula avoidance is so much in evidence in these works that it seems to be Bach's motto, in the first movements above all. At the start of a first movement he avoids that triad in three hammerstrokes that predictably begins many an early Classic symphony.'[43] This is true to a certain extent. Bach does use formulas (it would be difficult to evade them entirely) but uses them, not unthinkingly or mechanically, but with characteristic twists (sometimes a slight detail, sometimes a more extended treatment), developing various comic usages that give the standard formulas a remarkable freshness. For example in the opening of the symphony H. 648/W. 173, which is based, conventionally, on a rising triad outline, the sixteenth-note scale motif reappears turned upside-down at measure 5.[44] In Bach's symphonic output as a whole, a humorous context is

[42] For commentary on this passage see Fox, 'Melodic Nonconstancy', pp. 135–6, and, on this and H. 243/W. 55, 5, i, Charles Rosen, *The Classical Style: Haydn, Mozart, Beethoven* (London, 1971), 112–15, partly reviewed and quoted in Fox, 'Melodic Nonconstancy', pp. 134–6. Interestingly, a full version of the formula, properly establishing the tonic, occurs in Beethoven, Op. 132 (finale).

[43] See Charles C. Gallagher and E. Eugene Helm, eds., *C. P. E. Bach: Six Symphonies*, The Symphony, 1720–1840, Series C, vol. 8 (New York and London, 1982), xiii. See also *Helm/Grove*, p. 853.

[44] Compare the use of the cadential formulas in the sonata H. 136/W. 50, 1, iii—humorously placed at each of three different registers—where in the varied reprise the third statement turns the

often established for the simplest of materials, thus transforming them (as with Haydn). To discuss the ramifications of Bach's 'musical jokes' in the symphonies would require a monograph in itself. Here, some selected passages must suffice as examples.

At the opposite extreme to the technique of *reductio ad absurdum* mentioned is the opening of the symphony H. 663/W. 183, 1, where a deceptive and parodistic portrayal of the triadic formula is spread over eighteen measures. The three statements of the arpeggio theme, topped first with repeated Ds, then with F sharps, and then with Bs (separated by pauses to confound the listener),[45] create an extended triadic outline—almost the conventional 'hammerstroke' but altered to outline the 'wrong' triad[46]—drawn out to absurd lengths (see Example 6). That the next event is a diminished-seventh chord mocks the listener's hope of any establishing of a clear key-centre. Only from measure 27 onwards does the arpeggio idea behave with more normal effect in a more continuous and coherent repetition structure and clearly laid-out orchestral texture. It is the juxtaposition of such normal behaviour and the abnormal contexts in which the same material appears initially, that emphasizes the element of parody in the tonally playful opening, in which a variety of musical jokes (such as the false start and restart) is contained. In another case, the first movement of H. 654/W. 179 (see Example 7a), the 'wrong'-note and 'wrong'-triad techniques are applied to a three-note 'hammerstroke' appearing in the wrong place. Further confusion, or enigma, is created by the altered echo of the phrase and by the already unexpected proceedings in measures 3–4 (Example 7b demonstrates the expected progression). The effect of these various proceedings is that by the time the music begins to depart from the tonic it has scarcely been in it, although here again (as in H. 245, first movement) the 'right' notes of the 'right' triad are in fact contained in diminution at the outset of the movement. It is this, taken together with the parodistic form of the 'hammerstroke' in measures 5–6, that constitutes one of the tonal and motivic jokes in the opening bars.

As with the triadic formulas, so with certain conventional textural patterns it is Bach's rejection of the obvious, *per se*, that has attracted comment; Fox refers to the enrichment of his texture by 'the avoidance of stereotypical chord

formula upside-down (nicely leading towards the next section as well as providing a little local surprise); and with longer-range repercussions when the inverted version (i.e. the leading-on rather than the closing-off form of the cadence) appears at the corresponding end of the varied reprise of the second section, creating some uncertainty as to whether this is in fact the end of the whole movement.

[45] Note the use of progressive dynamics (*mf, f, ff*), and reservation of the tutti until measure 19. Most pertinently on Bach's symphonic dynamics see E. Suchalla, *Die Orchestersinfonien Carl Philipp Emanuel Bachs* (Augsburg, 1968), 115 ff.

[46] The 'right' triad contained in diminution beneath the Ds is of course turned into $V_7$ of G major, replacing the possible tonic implications of D by explicit dominant function.

Example 6. Sinfonia in D major H. 663/W. 183, 1, i, mm. 1–19. *Vier Orchester-Sinfonien* (Leipzig, 1780); Ed. Steglich (Leipzig, 1942)

and Alberti-bass patterns'.[47] A textural rarity in Bach is the Alberti bass, as Fox suggests, but again the familiarity of the device offers possibilities of parody. Example 8 presents a passage remarked on by numerous writers; in choosing to employ the conventional pattern here Bach typically adds a 'twist'. The whole appears as a 'joke' Alberti bass, with its doubling of treble and bass (outlining the characteristic falling chromatic fourth), set rhythmically against the beat in an eccentric and ungainly manner quite alien to the facile elegance of the genuine article.[48]

Such passages as these seem to fulfil the criteria for an interpretation of parodistic intent. For some element of parody to exist, an identifiable original form must be suggested, a degree of distortion must be present, and the original must constitute a recognized device or style-trait. Regarded in this way, the *brisé* textures of, for example, the first movement of H. 59/W. 62, 10 appear as

---

[47] 'Melodic Nonconstancy', p. 5.

[48] Equally Bach could use a similar bass 'straight', with elegant expressive melody above it, as in the symphony H. 650/W. 175, iii, measures 49 ff.

parody. It should be stressed that this is only one possible interpretation, and
that it has only limited application; it can be argued for certain (in fact quite
numerous) passages but not at all for others. The richness of reference in
C. P. E. Bach's work makes it impossible to uphold any one analysis as the
prime one. (At the same time it makes it important to consider all possibly valid
ways of looking at his music.) Nor, of course, does the particular meaning that
may be assigned to a passage at its first appearance necessarily hold in exactly
the same way for subsequent appearances. To take one example: in the first
movement of H. 243/W. 55, 5 (see Example 4a), the apparent arbitrariness of
the key chosen for the opening phrase (C minor) is significantly modified when
it returns at the beginning of the repeat of the first section, thus immediately
following the C major cadence which closes off the second main key area
(strongly established, unlike the first), and forming with it a major–minor
contrast. The reappearance of the opening gesture at the head of the second

Example 7. Sinfonia in E flat major H. 654/W. 179, i. Ed. Gallagher and Helm
(New York and London, 1982), 145

*a* mm. 1–8
*b* 'Expected' progression

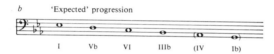

**Example 8. Sonata in G major H. 119/W. 62, 19, iii, mm. 1–6. *Musikalisches Mancherley* (Berlin, 1762), 26**

section is used to create further 'surprise' and tonal uncertainty in relation to what preceded it; and to the listener who had (after two hearings) retained in his memory the outline of the original progression, what follows is unexpected in that it remains in the key of the second phrase (see measures 15–17 ff.). These changes of meaning in different contexts ensure that the reuse of a particular gesture does not dull the listener's interest and attentiveness (apart from the fact that the gesture is striking enough, as here, to warrant rehearing). It may also be pointed out that the essence of this kind of opening can have implications beyond the movement where it is introduced. In H. 243/ W. 55, 5, the second (Adagio maestoso) and third (Allegretto) movements pick up the tonal ambiguity associated with the first movement (Allegro), as well as being linked together by a unifying long-range progression (see Example 9). Bach's 'eccentricities' are not (*pace* Rosen) isolated events.[49]

There are passages, or whole sections, in C. P. E. Bach's music which if analysed in all seriousness could be regarded as illogical, ill-balanced, even incompetent. But, as Schulenberg has observed in rejecting Rosen's view that Bach's 'passion lacked wit', it is important not to take 'some of Bach's more extreme passages too seriously'.[50] This stricture would apply to a movement such as the first (Allegro) of the sonata H. 29/W. 48, 6. As often in Bach, a promising initial phrase is cut short and never receives the regular continuation that might have been expected (see Example 10a, with hypothetical reconstruction in Example 10b). And when some continuity is restored to the music, it is in such an extreme form as to seem almost to be mocking the use of the conventional materials (scales, arpeggios) with which the keyboard sonata composer might fill out his structure. From measures 6 to 14 there might appear to be some difficulty in departing from the tonic key. But this is surely, like the other irregular and unpredictable aspects of much of Bach's instrumental music, not incompetence but wit, exercised together with a

Example 9. Sonata in F major H. 243/W. 55, 5, reduction to basic progression. 'Kenner und Liebhaber', vol. 1 (Leipzig, 1779)

---

[49] See Rosen, *The Classical Style, passim*, particularly pp. 48 and 79. Commentators on H. 663/ W. 183, 1, i, for example, have noted how the eccentric opening progression is developed, not isolated, in the movement.

[50] Schulenberg, *Instrumental Music*, p. 135.

Example 10. Sonata in A major, H. 29/W. 48, 6, i. 'Prussian Sonatas'
(Nuremberg, 1742/3)

*a* measures 1–5
*b* 'Hypothetical' version

feeling for the long-range effect of passages and proceedings. (The dogged emphasis on the tonic key in measures 6–14 adds all the more freshness to the subsequent adventurous approach to the dominant through its dominant minor (measures 15–23), and there are further repercussions of the passage later in the section, as well as some intriguing connections of events and ideas between the first and second sections.) An appreciation of the cleverness and originality manifest in such music is enhanced by an alertness to its humour.[51] While inevitably the 'irritants', the apparently arbitrary elements, the capriciousness and mockery present in Bach's work, are indeed bound simply to irritate and alienate some listeners, for others they will exert the exquisite and witty effects that the composer surely intended: ' . . . whereby a sense of the comic is aroused in the listener whose hearing is attuned to it.'[52]

[51] Sometimes the joke resides in one particular passage (like the punch line of a verbal joke), or there may be a whole series of antics (like a clown's act) filled with octave displacements, rhythmic displacements, and a variety of surprises; good examples of such sophisticated musical clowning are the finale of the sonata H. 59/W. 62, 10 and the first movement of the sonata H. 286/W. 61, 2. The listener can not afford to let his attention stray in such movements (nor indeed can the performer), nor can assumptions be too readily made (for example at cadence points).

[52] Original given in n. 31.

# C. P. E. Bach in Literature: A Bibliography

## Stephen L. Clark

THE following bibliography is a survey of the secondary literature about C. P. E. Bach, intended for the specialist and non-specialist alike. It lists printed books and articles, as well as dissertations and masters' theses, that deal significantly with C. P. E. Bach and his music. Items are numbered to facilitate cross-referencing (particularly of reviews) and to allow for an index, which is located at the end of the bibliography.

General studies of eighteenth-century music or culture are included only if they contain a chapter or section specifically devoted to C. P. E. Bach. General anthologies of letters with entries by C. P. E. Bach are included since bibliographic control of his correspondence is a continuing problem, although Ernst Suchalla's edition of the letters to Breitkopf and Forkel (item 334) is a valuable new resource. Music and musical editions are not listed; much of that information will be included in E. Eugene Helm's forthcoming *Thematic Catalogue of the Works of Carl Philipp Emanuel Bach* (item 151).

Standard indexes (including *Bibliographie des Musikschrifttums*, *The Music Index*, and *RILM*) and dissertation bibliographies were the main sources of citations. The numerous recent dissertations about C. P. E. Bach (especially items 25, 121, 305, 315, 328, and 354) were a particularly rich source and I acknowledge my debt to the authors of those works. In addition, I thank Rachel W. Wade and Pamela Fox for their assistance with the project, and Deborah Polley of the Lilly Library at Wabash College for her patience with a flood of inter-library loan requests.

1. Agay, Denes, 'The Search for Authenticity', *Clavier*, 14/8 (1975), 29–31.
2. Altmann, Wilhelm, 'Karl Philipp Emanuel Bach als Kunstfreund. Ein Autograph des Komponisten', *Der Kunstwanderer*, 1 (1919), 36–7.
3. Arnold, Frank Thomas, *The Art of Accompaniment from a Thorough-bass, as Practised in the XVIIth and XVIIIth Centuries*, (London: Oxford University Press, 1931; repr., London: Holland Press, 1961).
4. Auerbach, Cornelia, *Die deutsche Clavichordkunst des 18. Jahrhunderts*, Ph.D. diss., University of Freiburg, 1928 (3rd edn., Kassel: Bärenreiter, 1959).
5. Babitz, Sol, 'A Problem of Rhythm in Baroque Music', *MQ*, 38 (1952), 533–65.
6. —— 'Concerning the Length of Time that Every Note must be Held', *MR*, 28/1 (1967), 21–37.
7. Bach, Carl Philipp Emanuel, *Versuch über die wahre Art das Clavier zu spielen*, vol. 1

(Berlin: Henning, 1753), vol. 2, (Berlin: Winter, 1762). Rev. edns., vol. 1 (Leipzig: Schwickert, 1787), vol. 2 (Leipzig: Schwickert, 1797). Fac. repr., ed. Lothar Hoffmann-Erbrecht (Leipzig: Breitkopf & Härtel, 1957, 1969, 1976). English trans. as *Essay on the True Art of Playing Keyboard Instruments* by William J. Mitchell (New York: Norton, 1949); reviews, items 74, 215, 288. French trans. as *Essai sur la vraie manière de jouer des instruments à clavier* by Dennis Collins (Editions Jean-Claude Lattes, collection Musique et musiciens); review, item 23. Partial French trans. in item 236. Italian trans. as *L'interpretazione della musica barocca: Saggio di metodo per la tastiera* by Gabriella Gentili Verona (Milan: Curci, 1973); review, item 274.

8. —— 'Einfall einen doppelten Contrapunct in der Octave von sechs Tacten zu machen, ohne die Regeln davon zu wissen', *Historisch-kritische Beiträge zur Aufnahme der Musik*, ed. Friedrich Wilhelm Marpurg, vol. 3/1 (Berlin, 1757), 167–81. English trans. in item 146.

9. —— *Selbstbiographie*, in *Carl Burney's . . . Tagebuch seiner musikalischen Reisen*, vol. 3, Hamburg, 1773 (see item 50). Fac. repr., *Carl Philipp Emanuel Bach's Autobiography*, ed. William S. Newman, Facsimiles of Early Biographies, vol. 4 (Hilversum: Knuf, 1967); reviews, items 125, 133, 154. Repr., *Selbstbiographer deutscher Musiker des XVIII. Jahrhunderts*, ed. Willi Kahl (Cologne: Stufen Verlag, 1948). English trans. in item 247, and Hermand, Jost and Steakly, James, eds., *Writings of German Composers* (New York: Continuum, 1984), 34–9.

10. Bach-Dokumente, vol. 1, *Schriftstücke von der Hand Johann Sebastian Bachs*, ed. Werner Neumann and Hans-Joachim Schulze. Supplement to *Johann Sebastian Bach: Neue Ausgabe sämtlicher Werke* (Kassel: Bärenreiter, 1963).

11. Bach-Dokumente, vol. 2, *Fremdschriftliche und Gedruckte Dokumente zur Lebensgeschichte Johann Sebastian Bachs 1685–1750*, ed. Werner Neumann and Hans-Joachim Schulze. Supplement to *Johann Sebastian Bach: Neue Ausgabe sämtlicher Werke* (Kassel: Bärenreiter, 1969).

12. Bach-Dokumente, vol. 3, *Dokumente zum Nachwirken Johann Sebastian Bachs 1750–1800*, ed. Werner Neumann and Hans-Joachim Schulze. Supplement to *Johann Sebastian Bach: Neue Ausgabe sämtlicher Werke* (Kassel: Bärenreiter, 1972).

13. *The Bach Reader*, ed. Hans T. David and Arthur Mendel, rev. edn. (New York: Norton, 1966).

14. *Bach-Urkunden: Ursprung der musikalischen Bachischen Familie: Nachrichten über Johann Sebastian Bach von Carl Philipp Emanuel Bach*, ed. Max Schneider, Veröffentlichungen der Neuen Bach-Gesellschaft, XVII, vol. 3 (Leipzig: Breitkopf & Härtel, 1917).

15. Baldwyn, Rodney, 'Two Notes on C. P. E. Bach: "The Organ Sonatas" ', *MT*, 105 (1964), 839.

16. Barford, Philip Trevelyan, 'The Sonata Principle: A Study of Musical Thought in the Eighteenth Century', *MR*, 13 (1952), 255–63.

17. —— 'C. P. E. Bach: A Master of the Clavichord', *MO*, 76 (1953), 601–3.

18. —— 'A Fantasia by C. P. E. Bach', *MMR*, 85 (1955), 144–50.

19. —— 'Some Afterthoughts by C. P. E. Bach', *MMR*, 90 (1960), 94–8.

20. —— *The Keyboard Music of C. P. E. Bach Considered in Relation to his Musical Aesthetic and the Rise of the Sonata Principle* (New York and London: Barrie and Rockliffe, 1965). Reviews, items 54, 81, 94, 124, 159, 227, 249, 286, 337.

20a. Baruch, Gerth-Wolfgang, 'Stuttgart: Eine Markuspassion Sucht ihren Autor', *Musica*, 40 (1986), 454–5.

21. Bashaw, Donna Ruth, 'The Evolution of Philosophies and Techniques of Piano Pedagogy from 1750 to 1900 Traced through the Teachings of C. P. E. Bach, Clementi, Czerny, Chopin, and Leschetizky', MA thesis, California State University, Fullerton, 1980.

22. Baumgart, Ernst Friedrich, 'Über harmonische Ausfüllung älterer Claviermusik, hauptsächlich bei Ph. Em. Bach', *AMZ*, 5 (1870), 185–9, 193–5, 201–2, 209–10.

23. Beaussant, Philippe, review of item 7, *Harmonie*, 152 (1979), 128.

23a. Bellermann, H. 'Nachtrag zu Kirnberger's Briefen', *AMZ*, 7 (1872), cols. 441–4.

24. Berens, Kathleen Mary, 'Selected Sonatas of Carl Philipp Emanuel Bach', DMA diss., The Catholic University of America, 1976.

25. Berg, Darrell Matthews, 'The Keyboard Sonatas of C. P. E. Bach: An Expression of the Mannerist Principle', Ph.D. diss., State University of New York at Buffalo, 1975.

26. —— 'Towards a Catalogue of the Keyboard Sonatas of C. P. E. Bach', *JAMS*, 32 (1979), 276–303.

27. —— 'C. P. E. Bach's "Harp Sonata" ', *American Harp Journal*, 7 (1980), 8–16.

28. —— review of item 355, *Notes*, 39/1 (September 1982), 100–1.

29. —— 'C. P. E. Bach's "Variations" and "Embellishments" for his Keyboard Sonatas', *JM*, 2 (1983), 151–73.

30. Bernhardt, Reinhold, 'Aus der Umwelt der Wiener Klassiker, Freiherr Gottfried van Swieten (1734–1803)', *Der Bär*, (1929–1930), 74–166.

31. Beurmann, Erich, 'Die Klaviersonaten Carl Philipp Emanuel Bachs', Ph.D. diss., Georg-August-Universität, 1952.

32. —— 'Die Reprisensonaten Carl Philipp Emanuel Bachs', *AfMw*, 13 (1956), 168–79.

33. Bitter, Carl Hermann, *Carl Philipp Emanuel und Wilhelm Friedemann Bach und deren Bruder*, 2 vols. (Berlin: Wilhelm Müller, 1868; repr., Leipzig and Kassel: Bärenreiter, 1973).

34. —— 'Die Söhne Sebastian Bachs', *Sammlung Musikalischer Vorträge*, ed. Paul Graf Waldersee, Series 5 (Leipzig: Breitkopf & Härtel, 1884; repr., Wiesbaden: Breitkopf & Härtel, 1976), 1–40.

35. Bittner, Carl, 'Was Bedeutet Phil. Em. Bachs "Versuch" für die Gegenwart?', *Deutsche Tonkunstler Zeitung*, 33/6 (March 1937), 154–5.

36. Blom, Eric, review of item 52, *ML*, 39 (1958), 192.

37. Branscombe, Peter, review of item 332, *ML*, 67 (1986), 205.

38. Brauß, Martin, 'Manierismus: Ästhetische und didaktische Aspekte einer

Compositionstechnik am Beispiel des Instrumentalen Rezitativs bei C. Ph. E. Bach', *Musik und Bildung*, 17 (1985), 416–22.

39. Brewer, Richard Harding, 'The Two Oratorios of Carl Philipp Emanuel Bach in Relation to Performance', DMA diss., University of Southern California, 1965.

40. —— 'C. P. E. Bach and His Oratorios', *CJ*, 21 (1981), 34–40.

41. Brothier, Jean Jacques, 'Carl Philipp Emmanuel, le Bach de Berlin', *Revue internationale de musique*, 8 (autumn 1950), 123–32.

42. Brown, A. Peter, 'The Earliest English Biography of Haydn', *MQ*, 59 (1973), 339–54.

43. —— 'Approaching Musical Classicism: Understanding Styles and Style Change in Eighteenth-century Instrumental Music', *CMS*, 20/1 (spring 1980), 7–48.

43a. —— 'Joseph Haydn and C. P. E. Bach: The Question of Influence', *Haydn Studies: Proceedings of the International Haydn Conference, Washington, DC, 1975*, ed. Jens Peter Larsen, Howard Serwer, and James Webster (New York: Norton, 1981) 158–64.

44. —— *Joseph Haydn's Keyboard Music: Sources and Styles* (Bloomington: Indiana University Press, 1986).

45. Broyles, Michael, 'The Two Instrumental Styles of Classicism', *JAMS*, 36 (1983), 210–42.

46. Buck, Charles H., 'Revisions in Early Classical Concertos of C. P. E. Bach: Revelations from a New Source', *JAMS*, 29 (1976), 127–32.

47. Bücken, Ernst, 'Der galante Stil', *ZfMw*, 6 (1923–4), 418–30.

48. —— *Die Musik des Rokokos und der Klassik* (Wildpark-Potsdam: Athenaion, 1928), 161–73.

49. —— ed., *Musiker-Briefe* (Wiesbaden: Dieterich, 1940), 3–13.

50. Burney, Charles, *Carl Burney's . . . Tagebuch seiner musikalischen Reisen*, vol. 3: *Durch Böhmen, Sachsen, Bradenburg, Hamburg und Holland* [trans. J. J. C. Bode] (Hamburg, 1773). Fac. repr., ed. Richard Schaal, Documenta Musicologica, Series 1, vol. 19 (Kassel: Bärenreiter, 1959).

51. —— *Dr Burney's Musical Tours in Europe*, ed. Percy A. Scholes, 2 vols. (London: Oxford University Press, 1959), 211–22.

52. Busch, Gudrun, *C. Ph. E. Bach und seine Lieder*, Kölner Beiträge zur Musikforschung, ed. Karl Gustav Fellerer, vol. 12 (Regensburg: Gustav Bosse Verlag, 1957). Reviews, items 36, 158, 228, 239.

53. Butler, Douglas L., 'After J. S. Bach, Decadence?', *Music*, 8/3 (1974), 34–5, 42–3.

54. Byrt, John Clare, review of item 20, *ML*, 47 (1966), 66–7.

55. —— 'Form and Style in the Works of Sebastian and Emanuel Bach', Ph.D. diss., Oxford University, 1970.

56. Canave, Pas Corazon G., *A Re-evaluation of the Role Played by Carl Philipp Emanuel Bach in the Development of the Clavier Sonata*, Ph.D. diss., Catholic University of America, 1956 (Washington, DC: Catholic University Press, 1956). Review, item 246.

57. Chamblee, James Monroe, 'The Oratorios and Cantatas of Carl Philipp Emanuel Bach', Ph.D diss., University of North Carolina, 1973.

58. —— 'The Vocal Music of Carl Philipp Emanuel Bach', *American Music Teacher*, 28/5 (1979), 24–7.

59. Cherbuliez, Antoine Elisée, *Carl Philipp Emanuel Bach, 1714–1788*, Neujahrsblatt der Allgemeinen Musikgesellschaft in Zürich, 128 (Zurich and Leipzig: von Hug, [1940]).

60. Chiba, Junnoske, 'A Study of 18th-Century Performance Practice: Comparisons of the Writings of J. J. Quantz, C. P. E. Bach, and Leopold Mozart', MA thesis, Musashino Academy of Music, 1976.

61. Chrysander, Friedrich, ed., 'Briefe von Karl Philipp Emanuel Bach und G. M. Telemann', *AMZ*, 4 (1869), 177–81, 185–7.

62. —— 'Matthias Claudius, der Wandsbeker Bote, über Philipp Emanuel Bach', *AMZ*, 16 (1881), cols. 577–83.

63. —— 'Eine Klavier-Phantasie von Karl Philipp Emanuel Bach mit nachträglich von Gerstenberg eingefügten Gesangsmelodien zu zwei verschiedenen Texten', *Vierteljahrsschrift für Musikwissenschaft*, 7 (1891), 1–25.

64. Clark, Stephen L., 'The Occasional Choral Works of C. P. E. Bach', Ph.D. diss., Princeton University, 1984.

65. —— 'The Letters from Carl Philipp Emanuel Bach to Georg Michael Telemann', *JM*, 3 (1984), 177–95.

66. Clercx, Suzanne, 'La Forme du Rondo chez Carl Philipp Emanuel Bach', *RdM*, 16 (1935), 148–67.

67. —— 'Carl Philipp Emanuel Bach', *La revue musicale*, 16 (1935), 245–55.

68. Cohen, Peter, *Theorie und Praxis der Clavierästhetik Carl Philipp Emanuel Bachs*, Ph.D. diss., University of Hamburg, 1973; Hamburger Beiträge zur Musikwissenschaft, vol. 13 (Hamburg: K. D. Wagner, 1974). Review, item 196.

69. —— 'Diskussionen' (response to item 196), *Mf*, 32 (1979), 249–50.

70. Cole, Malcolm Stanley, 'The Vogue of the Instrumental Rondo in the Late Eighteenth Century', *JAMS*, 22 (1969), 427–32.

71. —— 'Rondos, Proper and Improper', *ML*, 51 (1970), 388–99.

72. Collins, Michael, 'A Reconsideration of French Over-dotting', *ML*, 50 (1969), 111–23.

73. Cooper, Kenneth, 'The Clavichord in the Eighteenth Century', Ph.D. diss., Columbia University, 1971.

74. Craddock, Peter, review of item 7, *Music in Education*, 39 (1975), 29.

75. Cramer, Hermann, 'Die Violincell-Kompositionen Philipp Emanuel Bachs', *AlMz*, 57 (1930) 316–9.

76. —— 'Einiges zu Ph. E. Bachs Kammermusik', *AlMz*, 57 (1930), 519–20.

77. Crickmore, Leon, 'C. P. E. Bach: Six Harpsichord Concertos', MA thesis, University of Birmingham, 1956. Review, item 322.

78. —— 'C. P. E. Bach's Harpsichord Concertos', *ML*, 39 (1958), 227–41.

79. —— 'Two Sons of Music', *Music and Musicians*, 13 (November 1964), 14–15, 45.

80. Daffner, Hugo, *Die Entwicklung des Klavierkonzerts bis Mozart* (Leipzig: Breitkopf & Härtel, 1906).

81. Dahlhaus, Carl, review of item 20, *Neue Zeitschrift für Musik*, 127 (July–August 1966), 307–8.

82. —— 'Si vis me flere . . .', *Mf*, 25 (1972), 51–2.

83. Dale, Kathleen, 'C. P. E. Bach and the Keyboard', *MMR*, 76 (1946), 187–92.

84. Davis, Patricia, 'The Significance of the Piano Fantasies among the Works of Mozart and Phillip [sic] Emanuel Bach', MA. thesis, American University, 1964.

85. Davis, Shelley, review of item 96, *MT*, 123 (April 1982), 261–2.

86. Daymond, Emily R., 'Carl Philipp Emanuel Bach', *PRMA*, 33 (1906–7), 45–52.

87. DeCola, Felix, 'A Lagniappe from Felix DeCola', *Clavier*, 13/1 (1974), 27–9.

88. Dekker, W. H. J., 'Enkele Merkwaardige Voorslagen', *MM*, 25/7 (July 1970), 209–11.

89. Derr, Ellwood R., 'Exemplia Gratia: CPE recycled; or, the Bach–Beethoven Connection', *In Theory Only*, 2/9 (December 1976), 28–30.

90. —— 'Beethoven's Long-term Memory of C. P. E. Bach's "Rondo in E-Flat," W. 61/1 (1787), manifest in the "Variations in E-Flat for Piano," Opus 35 (1802)', *MQ*, 70 (1984), 45–76.

91. Dietrich, Fritz, 'Matthias Claudius und C. P. E. Bach', *ZH*, 9 (1940), 73–5.

92. Doflein, Erich, 'Carl Philipp Emanuel Bach', *Der Musikerzieher*, 35/1 (October 1938), 62–3.

93. —— 'Neues von und über Ph. E. Bach', *ZH*, 9 (1940), 109–14.

94. Donington, Robert, review of item 20, *Tempo*, 77 (Summer 1966), 26.

95. O'Douwes, Henk, 'Carl Philipp Emanuel Bach Als Koorkomponist', *MM*, 13/4 (April 1958), 115–17.

96. Drummond, Pippa, *The German Concerto: Five Eighteenth-Century Studies*, Oxford Monographs on Music, vol. 9 (New York: Oxford University Press, 1980). Reviews, items 85, 142, 284.

97. Dumm, Robert, 'Piano Footnotes: An Analytic-interpretive Lesson on C. P. E. Bach's "Solfeggietto" ', *Clavier*, 2/3 (1963), 21–3.

98. Edler, Arnfried, 'Zwischen Handel und Carl Philipp Emanuel Bach: Zur Situation des Klavierkonzerts im mittleren 18. Jahrhunderts', *AM*, 58 (1986), 180–221.

98a. —— 'Das Charakterstück Carl Philipp Emanuel Bachs und die französische Tradition', *Aufklärungen: Studien zur deutsch-französischen Musikgeschichte im 18. Jahrhundert: Einflüsse und Wirkungen, ii*, ed. Wolfgang Birtel and Christoph-Hellmut Mahling, 'Annales Universitatis Saraviensis: Reihe Philosophische Fakultät', vol. 20 (Heidelberg: Winter, 1986), 219–35.

99. Eggebrecht, Hans Heinrich, 'Der Begriff des Komischen in der Musikästhetik des 18. Jahrhunderts', *Mf*, 4 (1951), 144–52.

100. —— 'Das Ausdrucks-Prinzip im musikalischen "Sturm und Drang" ', *Deutsche Vierteljahrschrift für Litteraturwissenschaft und Geistesgeschichte*, 29 (1955), 323–49.

101. Eibner, Franz, 'Zum Rhythmus der klassischen Musik', *Musikerziehung*, 21/2 (November 1967), 67–72.

101a. Eitner, Robert, 'Quantz und Emanuel Bach', *Monatshefte für Musik-Geschichte*, 34 (1902), 39–46, 55–63.

102. Elder, Elinor Goertz, 'Carl Philipp Emanuel Bach's Concept of the Free Fantasia', MA thesis, Eastman School of Music, 1980.

103. Engberg, Eileen Martine, 'The Sons of Johann Sebastian Bach', SMM thesis, Union Theological Seminary, 1945.

104. Engel, Hans, review of item 343, *ZfMw*, 12 (1929–30), 240–6.

105. —— *Das Solokonzert*. Das Musikwerk, vol. 25 (Cologne: Arno Volk Verlag, 1964). English edn., *The Solo Concerto*, Anthology of Music, ed. Karl Gustav Fellerer, vol. 25 (Cologne: Arno Volk Verlag, 1974).

106. —— 'Carl Philipp Emanuel Bach', *Chigiana*, 1 (1964), 77–90.

107. —— *Das Instrumentalkonzert*, I: *Von Den Anfangen bis gegen 1800* (Wiesbaden: Breitkopf & Härtel, 1971).

108. Engelke, Bernhard, 'Neues zur Geschichte der Berliner Liederschule', *Riemann-Festschrift* (Leipzig: Max Hesse, 1909), 456–72.

109. —— 'Gerstenberg und die Musik seiner Zeit', *Zeitschrift der Gesellschaft für Schleswig-Holsteinische Geschichte*, 56 (1927), 417–48.

110. Ernest, Wayne, 'The Organ Sonatas of C. P. E. Bach: A Comparison of Three Modern Editions with Selected Extant Manuscripts', DMA diss., University of Cincinnati, 1979.

111. Essner, Walter, Über die Kunst Carl Philipp Emanuel Bachs', *ZfM*, 103 (1936), 922–7.

112. Faisst, Imanuel, 'Beiträge zur Geschichte der Claviersonate von ihrem ersten Auftreten bis auf C. P. Emanuel Bach', repr. (from *Caecilia*, 25 (1846), 129–58, 201–31; 26 (1847), 1–28, 73–83) in *Neues Beethoven-Jahrbuch*, 1 (1924), 7–85.

113. Finscher, Ludwig, 'Das Originalgenie und die Tradition. Zur Rolle der Tradition in der Entstehungsgeschichte des Wiener klassischen Stils', in *Studien zur Tradition in der Musik: Kurt von Fischer zum 60. Geburtstag*, ed. Hans Heinrich Eggebrecht und Max Lütolf (Munich: Katzbichler, 1973), 165–75.

114. Fischer, Kurt von, 'C. Ph. E. Bachs Variationwerke', *RBM*, 6 (1952), 190–218.

115. —— 'C. P. E. Bachs Variationenwerke (Zusammenfassung)', *Kongressbericht Internationale Gesellschaft für Musikwissenschaft 5. Kongress Utrecht 1952* (Amsterdam: Alsbach, 1953), 189–90.

116. —— 'Arietta variata', *Geiringer Festschrift*, 224–35.

117. Fischer, Oskar, 'Zum musikalischen Standpunkte des Nordischen Dichterkreises', *SIMG*, 5 (1903–4), 245–52, 475.

118. Fischman, N., 'Estetika F. E. Bacha', *Sovetskaya muzika* 28/8 (1964), 59–65.

119. Flinsch, Erich, 'Philipp Emanuel Bachs Einfluss auf Beethovens Schaffen', *MU*, 50 (1959), 368–71.

120. Flueler, Max, *Die Norddeutsche Symphonie zur Zeit Friedrichs d. Gr. und besonders die*

*Werke Ph. Em. Bachs*, Ph.D. diss., Friedich-Wilhelms-Universität zu Berlin, 1908 (Berlin: Ebering, 1908).

121. Fox, Pamela Mollard, 'Melodic Nonconstancy in the Keyboard Sonatas of C. P. E. Bach', Ph.D. diss., University of Cincinnati, 1983.

122. Freyse, Conrad, 'Unbekannte Jugendbildnisse Friedemann und Emanuel Bachs', *Bericht über die wissenschaftliche Bachtagung der Gesellschaft für Musikforschung* (Leipzig: Peters, 1950), 349–54.

123. Friedlander, Max, 'Ein ungedrucktes Lied Philipp Emanuel Bachs', *Peters-Jahrbuch*, 6 (1899), 65–7.

124. Fuller, David R., review of item 20, *Notes*, 23/4 (June 1967), 726–7.

125. —— review of item 9, *Notes*, 25/1 (September 1968), 42–3.

126. —— 'Harpsichord Registration', *Diapason*, 69/8 (July 1978), 1, 6–7.

127. Gantz, Beatrice, 'Problems of Articulation in Baroque Keyboard Music (at the Piano or the Organ)', *Bach*, 7/2 (1976), 3–13.

128. Gat, Jozsef, 'Néhány megjegyzés Ph. E. Bach Díszítéseinek Jatékához (Zur Ornamentik bei C. Ph. E. Bach)', *Magyar zene*, 3 (1962), 143–6.

129. Geiringer, Karl, 'Artistic interrelations of the Bachs', *MQ*, 36 (1950), 363–74.

130. —— *The Bach Family: Seven Generations of Creative Genius* (New York: Oxford University Press; London: Allen and Unwin, 1954).

131. Gerlach, Sonja, 'Gedanken zu den "veränderten" Violinstimmen der Solosonaten von Franz Benda in der Staatsbibliothek Preussischer Kulturbesitz, Berlin', *Musik. Edition. Interpretation. Gedankschrift Günter Henle*, ed. Martin Bente (Munich: Henle, 1980), 199–212.

132. Godt, Irving, 'C. P. E. Bach—His Mark: Historical and Fresh Approaches to Analysis', *CMS*, 19/2 (fall 1979), 154–61.

133. Godwin, E. J., review of item 9, *Consort*, 29 (1973), 47.

134. Gonnerman, Wilhelm, ' "Magnificat" von Carl Philipp Emanuel Bach in Potsdam', *MG*, 32 (February 1982), 110–11.

134a. Grimm, Hartmut, 'Freie und gezügelte Phantasie: Zur Ästhetik einer Gattung des 18. Jahrhunderts und ihre Zurücknahme', *MG*, 35 (1985), 592–7.

135. Grosse, Hans and Jung, Hans Rudolf, eds., *Georg Philipp Telemann. Briefwechsel* (Leipzig: VEB, 1972), 372–3.

136. Grossmann, Ferdinand, review of item 372, *Österreichische Musikzeitschrift*, 24 (1969), 110.

137. Haacke, Walter, *Die Söhne Bachs* (Königstein im Taunus: Hans Köster, 1962). Review, *Musikhandel*, 13/1 (1962), 11.

138. Haag, Charles Robert, *The Keyboard Concertos of Carl Philipp Emanuel Bach*, Ph.D. diss., University of California at Los Angeles, 1956 (Rochester, NY: University of Rochester Press, 1960).

139. Hager, Nancy Barnes, 'Rhythm and Voice-Leading as a Facet of Style: Keyboard Works of J. S. Bach, C. P. E. Bach, and Mozart', Ph.D. diss., City University of New York, 1978.

140. Hammitt, Jackson Lewis III, 'Sacred Music in Berlin, 1740–1786', Ph.D. diss., University of Michigan, 1970.

141. Harnoncourt, Nikolaus, 'Zu Problemen der Wiedergabe von Bachs Chor-Orchester-Werken', *Österreichische Musikzeitschrift*, 24 (1969), 76–80.

142. Harris, Ellen T., review of item 96, *Notes*, 37/4 (June 1981), 858–9.

143. Hase, Hermann von, 'Carl Philipp Emanuel Bach und Joh. Gottl. Im. Breitkopf', *BJ*, 8 (1911), 86–104.

144. Hein, Robert G., ' "Die Israeliten in der Wüste", An Oratorio by C. P. E. Bach', *American Choral Review*, 21/2 (July 1979), 3–8.

145. Helm, Ernest Eugene, *Music at the Court of Frederick the Great* (Norman: University of Oklahoma Press, 1960).

146. —— 'Six Random Measures of C. P. E. Bach', *JMT*, 10 (1966), 19–51.

147. —— 'The "Hamlet" Fantasy and the Literary Element in C. P. E. Bach's Music', *MQ*, 58 (1972), 277–96.

148. —— 'To Haydn from C. P. E. Bach: Non-tunes', *Haydn Studies: Proceedings of the International Haydn Conference, Washington, DC, 1975*, ed. Jens Peter Larsen, Howard Serwer, and James Webster (New York: Norton, 1981), 382–5.

149. —— 'Bach, Carl Philipp Emanuel', *New Grove*, vol. 1, 844–63; repr. in *The New Grove Bach Family* (London: Macmillan, 1983), 251–306.

150. —— 'An Honorable Shortcut to the Works of C. P. E. Bach', *Music in the Classic Period: Essays in Honor of Barry S. Brook*, ed. Allan W. Atlas (New York: Pendragon, 1985), 85–98.

151. —— *Thematic Catalogue of the Works of Carl Philipp Emanuel Bach* (New Haven: Yale University Press [in preparation]).

152. Hesford, Bryan, 'The Organ Sonatas of Carl Philipp Emanuel Bach', *MO*, 89 (1966), 487.

153. Heuschneider, Karin, *The Piano Sonata of the Eighteenth Century in Germany* (Cape Town, Amsterdam: A. A. Balkema, 1970), 30–56.

154. Higbee, Dale, review of item 9, *American Recorder*, 11/1 (winter 1970), 25.

155. Hoffmann, Hans, *Die norddeutsche Triosonate des Kreises um J. G. Graun und C. Ph. E. Bach*, Ph.D. diss., Christian-Albrechts-Universität, Kiel, 1924 (Kiel: Walter G. Mühlau, 1927).

156. Hoffmann-Erbrecht, Lothar, *Deutsche und italienische Klaviermusi, zur Bachzeit*, Ph.D. diss., Leipzig, 1954. Jenaer Beiträge zur Musikforschung, vol. 1 (Leipzig: Breitkopf & Härtel, 1954).

157. —— 'Sturm und Drang in der deutschen Klaviermusik von 1753–1763', *Mf*, 10 (1957), 466–79.

158. —— review of item 52, *Musica*, 12 (March 1958), 181–2.

159. —— review of item 20, *Mf*, 22 (1969), 120–2.

160. —— 'Klavierkonzert und Affektsgestaltung. Bemerkungen zu einigen d-Moll-Klavierkonzerten des 18. Jahrhunderts', *Deutsches Jahrbuch der Musikwissenschaft für 1971* (Leipzig: Peters, 1973), 86–110.

161. —— 'Johann Sebastian und Carl Philipp Emanuel Bachs Nürnberger Verleger', *Die Nürnberger Musikverleger und die Familie Bach*, ed. Willi Wörthmüller (Nurnberg: Bollman, 1973), 5–10.

162. ——— review of item 258, *Mf*, 9 (1986), 72–3.

163. Holschneider, Andreas, 'C. Ph. E. Bachs Kantate "Auferstehung und Himmel-
     fahrt Jesu" und Mozarts Aufführung des Jahres 1788', *MJ*, 1968/70, 264–80.

164. ——— 'Die musikalische Bibliothek Gottfried van Swietens', *Bericht über den
     Internationalen Musikwissenschaftlichen Kongress Kassel 1962*, ed. Georg
     Reichert and Martin Just (Kassel: Bärenreiter, 1963), 174–8.

165. Hörner, Hans, *G. Ph. Telemanns Passionsmusiken*, Ph.D. diss., Christian-Albrecht-
     Universität zu Kiel, 1930 (Borna-Leipzig: Universitätsverlag von Robert Noske,
     1933) 134–5.

166. Jaacks, Gisela, 'Musikleben in Hamburg zur Barokzeit', *Hamburg Porträt*
     (Hamburg: Museum für Hamburgische Geschichte, 1978).

167. Jacobi, Erwin R., 'Das Autograph C. Ph. E. Bachs Doppelkonzert in Es-dur für
     Cembalo, Fortepiano, und Orchester (Wq. 47, Hamburg 1786)', *Mf*, 12
     (1959), 488–9.

168. ——— 'Five Hitherto Unknown Letters From C. P. E. Bach to J. J. H. Westphal',
     *JAMS*, 23 (1970), 119–27.

169. ——— 'Communication', *JAMS*, 23 (1970), 545.

170. ——— 'Three Additional Letters from C. P. E. Bach to J. J. H. Westphal', *JAMS*, 27
     (1974), 119–25.

171. Jacobs, Richard M., 'The Chamber Ensembles of C. P. E. Bach using Two or More
     Wind Instruments', Ph.D. diss., Iowa State University, 1964.

172. Jalowetz, Heinrich, 'Beethovens Jugendwerke in ihren melodischen Beziehungen
     zu Mozart, Haydn, und Ph. E. Bach', *SIMG*, 12 (1910/11), 417–74.

173. Jeans, Susi, 'An unknown 'Minuetto con trio' by J. S. Bach?', *MT*, 96 (1955),
     259–61.

174. Johnson, Lilla Joyce Finch, 'I. The "Kenner und Liebhaber" Fantasias of Carl
     Philipp Emanuel Bach and Selected Fantasias of Wolfgang Amadeus Mozart: A
     Comparative Study. II. Franz Liszt's Piano Style as reflected in the "B Minor
     Sonata" and the Fantasia Quasi Sonata "Apres une Lecture Du Dante". III.
     Rhythmic Techniques in Twentieth Century Music Including Those Employed
     in the Piano Sonatas of Elliot Carter and Leon Kirchner', Ph.D. diss.,
     Northwestern University, 1972.

175. Johnson, Steven Philip, 'Thematic and Tonal Structures in the First Movements
     of the "Württemburg" Sonatas of C. P. E. Bach', MA thesis, California State
     University, Fullerton, 1979.

176. Jones, Gregory Paul, 'Heinrich Christoph Koch's Description of the Symphony
     and a Comparison with Selected Symphonies of C. P. E. Bach and Haydn', MA
     thesis, University of California at Los Angeles, 1973.

177. Jurisch, Herta, 'Prinzipien der Dynamik im Klavierwerk Philipp Emanuel Bachs',
     Ph.D. diss., Universität Tübingen, 1959.

178. ——— 'Zur Dynamik im Klavierwerk Ph. E. Bachs', *Bericht über den Internationalen
     Musikwissenschaftlichen Kongress Kassel 1962*, ed. Georg Reichert and Martin
     Just (Kassel: Bärenreiter, 1963), 178–81.

179. Kada, Mariko, 'C. P. E. Bach's Concertos for Cembalo', *Ongaku-gaku*, 14 (1968), 65–75.

180. Kahl, Willi, 'Geschichte, Kritik, und Aufgaben der K. Ph. E. Bach-Forschung', *Beethoven Zentenarfeier: Internationaler Musikhistorischer Kongress* (Vienna: Universal-Edition, 1927), 211–16.

181. Kardos, Cornelie, 'Die Barbarina und Philipp Emanuel Bach', *Neue Musikzeitung*, 28 (1908), 193–5.

182. Kast, Paul, *Die Bach-Handschriften der Berliner Staatsbibliothek*, Tübinger Bach-Studien, vols. 2/3, ed. Walter Gerstenberg (Trossingen: Hohner, 1958).

183. Kellar, Allan, 'The Hamburg Bach: Carl Philipp Emanuel Bach as Choral Composer', Ph.D. diss., University of Iowa, 1970.

184. Kenyon, Nicholas, 'A C. P. E. Bach Oratorio', *MT*, 118 (1977), 197–8.

185. Kinsky, Georg, 'Zur Echtheitsfrage des Berliner Bach-Flügels', *BJ*, 21 (1924), 128–38.

186. —— 'Zwei Stammbuchblätter von W. Friedeman und C. Phil. Em. Bach', *BJ*, 21 (1924), 139.

187. Kirkpatrick, Ralph, 'C. P. E. Bach's "Versuch" Reconsidered', *Early Music*, 4/4 (October 1976), 384–92.

188. Knödt, Heinrich, 'Zur Entwicklungsgeschichte der Kadenzen im Instrumental-konzert', *SIMG*, 15 (1914), 375–419.

189. Kobayashi, Yoshitake, 'Neuerkenntnisse zu einigen Bach-Quellen an Handsch-riftkundlicher Untersuchungen', *BJ*, 64 (1978), 43–60.

190. Kochevitsky, George A., 'Letters', *PQ*, 113 (spring 1981), 2.

191. —— and Uzler, Marienne, 'Letters', *PQ*, 122 (summer 1983), 2–3.

192. Köhler, Karl-Heinz, 'Carl Philipp Emanuel Bach', 49. *Bachfest der Neuen Bachgesellschaft Frankfurt an der Oder 1974* (Leipzig: Meesedruck, 1974), 103–7.

193. —— 'Die Bach-Sammlung der Deutschen Staatsbibliothek—Überlieferug und Bedeutung', *Bach-Studien*, 5 (1975), 139–46.

194. Konecne, Steven Craig, 'A Comprehensive Performance Project in Saxophone Literature and an Essay consisting of Three Trio Sonatas by C. P. E. Bach, J. P. Schiffelholz and G. P. Telemann Transcribed, Realized and Edited for Saxophones and Piano', DMA diss., University of Iowa, 1984.

195. Kramer, Richard, 'The New Modulation of the 1770s: C. P. E. Bach in Theory, Criticism, and Practice', *JAMS*, 38 (1985), 551–92.

196. Kross, Siegfried, review of item 68, *Mf*, 31 (1978), 221–4.

196a. Kubota, Keiichi, 'Über die musikalische "Empfindsamkeit" ', *Mf*, 39 (1986), 139–48.

197. Kulukundis, Elias N., 'Thoughts on the Origin, Authenticity and Evolution of C. P. E. Bach's D Minor Concerto (W. 22)', *Festschrift Albi Rosenthal*, ed. Rudolf Elvers (Tutzing: Schneider, 1985), 199–215.

198. Kurzwelly, Albrecht, 'Neues über das Bachbildnis der Thomasschule und andere Bildnisse Johann Sebastian Bachs', *BJ*, 11 (1914), 1–37.

199. Laaff, Ernst, 'Carl Philipp Emanuel Bach. Lebenslauf und Kunstlerpersönlichkeit', *MU*, 50 (1959), 364–8.

200. —— 'Carl Philipp Emanuel Bach. Der Klavierspieler und Komponist', *MU*, 51 (1960), 1–6.

201. La Mara [Ida Marie Lipsius], ed., *Musikerbriefe aus fünf Jahrhunderten*, vol. 1 (Leipzig: Breitkopf & Härtel, 1886), 207–12.

202. Lasocki, David, and O'Loughlin, Niall, 'Letters to the Editor: Editing C. P. E. Bach', *MT*, 117 (1976), 825.

202a. Lenneberg, Hans, review of item 334, *Journal of Musicological Research*, 7 (1987), 294–302.

203. Lisco, John D., 'C. P. E. Bach and the Fantasia', MA thesis, University of Kentucky, 1978.

204. Longyear, Rey M., 'Binary Variants of Early Classic Sonata Form', *JMT*, 8 (1969), 162–85.

205. Lorince, Frank E., 'A Study of Musical Texture in Relation to Sonata-Form As Evidenced in Selected Keyboard Sonatas from C. P. E. Bach through Beethoven', Ph.D. diss., University of Rochester, 1966.

206. Maack, Rudolf, 'Report from Germany', *American Choral Review*, 20/1 (January 1978), 20–3.

207. MacArdle, Donald W., 'Beethoven and the Bach Family', *ML*, 38 (1957), 356–7.

208. Maier, Guy, 'A "Conversation" with Carl Philipp Emanuel Bach', *Etude*, 73/1 (January 1955), 21, 56.

209. Mandelli, Alfredo, 'Lettura, sempre lettura (gradita)', *Rassegna Musicale Curci*, 30 (1977), 35–7.

210. Marks, Paul F., 'The Rhetorical Element in Musical "Sturm und Drang": Christian Gottfried Krause's "Von der musikalischen Poesie" ', *MR*, 33 (1972), 93–107.

211. —— 'Aesthetics of Music in the Philosophy of "Sturm und Drang": Gerstenberg, Hamann, and Herder', *MR*, 35 (1974), 247–59.

212. Marshall, Robert L., 'J. S. Bach's Compositions for Solo Flute', *JAMS*, 32 (1979), 463–98.

213. Meer, John Henry van der, *Die klangfarbliche Identität der Klavierwerke Carl Philipp Emanuel Bachs* (New York, London, and Amsterdam: New Holland, 1978). Review, item 304.

214. —— 'Die klangfarbliche Identität der Klavierwerke Carl Philipp Emanuel Bachs', *Medelingen der Koninklijke Nederlandse Akademie van Wetenschappen*, 41/6 (1978), 129–76.

215. Mendel, Arthur, review of item 7, *MQ*, 35 (1949), 323–8.

216. —— 'More for the Bach Reader', *MQ*, 36 (1950), 485–510.

217. Mersmann, Hans, 'Ein Programmtrio Karl Philipp Emanuel Bachs', *BJ*, 14 (1917), 137–70.

218. Miesner, Heinrich, *Philipp Emanuel Bach in Hamburg*, Ph.D. diss, Berlin, 1928 (Leipzig: Dr Martin Sädig oHG, 1929; repr., Weisbaden: Breitkopf & Härtel, 1969).

219. —— 'Ungedruckte Briefe von Philipp Emanuel Bach', *ZfMw*, 14 (1931/32), 224–6.

220. —— 'Urkundliche Nachrichten über die Familie Bach in Berlin', *BJ*, 29 (1932), 157–63.

221. —— 'Die Grabstätte Emanuel Bachs', *BJ*, 29 (1932), 164–5.

222. —— 'Beziehungen zwischen den Familien Stahl und Bach', *BJ*, 30 (1933), 71–6.

223. —— 'Aus der Umwelt Philipp Emanuel Bachs', *BJ*, 34 (1937), 132–43.

224. —— 'Porträts aus dem Kreise Philipp Emanuel und Wilhelm Friedemann Bachs', *Musik und Bild: Festschrift Max Seiffert zum siebzigsten Geburtstag*, ed. Heinrich Besseler (Kassel: Bärenreiter, 1938), 101–12.

225. —— 'Philipp Emanuel Bachs musikalischer Nachlass', *BJ*, 35 (1938), 103–36; 36 (1939), 81–112; 37 (1940–8), 161–81.

226. Milliot, Sylvette, *La Sonate* (Paris: Presses Universitaires de France, 1978), 27–33, 35–7.

227. Milner, Anthony, review of item 20, *Composer*, 18 (1966), 19.

228. Mintz, Donald, review of item 52, *Notes*, 16/1 (December 1958), 63–4.

229. Mitchell, William J., 'C. P. E. Bach's "Essay": An Introduction', *MQ*, (1947), 460–80.

230. —— 'Modulation in C. P. E. Bach's "Versuch" ', *Geiringer Festschrift*, 333–42.

230a. Mittmann, Paul, 'Carl Philipp Emanuel Bachs Flötenmusik', *Die Musik-Woche*, 6 (1938), 773–4.

231. Moldenhauer, Hans, 'From my Autograph Collection: C. Ph. E. Bach—Dittersdorf—Mozart', *Bericht über den internationalen musikwissenschaftlichen Kongress Wien: Mozartjahr 1956*, ed. Erich Schenk (Graz/Cologne: Hermann Böhlhaus Nachf., 1958), 412–5.

232. Mölln, Hans von, 'C. P. E. Bach, ein Hamburger Musikdirektor', *Schleswig-Holstein-Hansische Monatshefte*, 2 (1927), 299–300.

233. Moser, Hans-Joachim, 'Philipp Emanuel Bach und die Hausmusik', *ZH*, 7 (1938), 177–80.

234. Müller, Fritz, 'Carl Philipp Emanuel Bach', *ZfM*, 105 (1938), 1323–5.

235. —— 'Ph. E. Bach als Klavierkomponist', *AlMz*, 65 (1938), 746–7.

236. Muller, Jean-Pierre, 'La technique de l'accompagnement dans la musique de XVIIIe siècle tirée du traité de C. P. E. Bach "Versuch über die wahre Art das Clavier zu spielen" (Berlin 1762)', *RBM*, 23 (1969), 5–121; 26–7 (1972–3), 159–236.

237. Müller, Werner, 'Das Ausdrucksproblem in der Klaviermusik C. Ph. E. Bachs', Ph.D. diss., Universität des Saarlandes, 1959.

238. —— 'Die Artikulation im Klavierwerk C. Ph. E. Bachs', *Festgabe für Joseph Müller-Blattau, zum 65. Geburtstag*, ed. Walter Salmen, *Annales Universitatis Saraviensis, Philosophische Facultat* 9/1 (Saarbrücken: Universitäts- und Schulbuchverlag, 1960), 51–63; (2nd edn., 1962), 55–67.

239. Müller-Blattau, Joseph, review of item 52, *Mf*, 11 (1958), 366–7.

*Nachlass-Verzeichniß*, see *Verzeichniß . . .*, item 345.

240. Nastasi, Mirjam, 'Rhetorik in der Musik. Dargestellt am Beispiel C. Ph. E. Bachs und seiner Sonate in A-moll für Flote allein', *Tibia*, 1 (1976), 213–20; 2 (1977), 281–7.

241. Nelson, Richard Bruce, 'Theories of Harmonic Modulation in Selected German Treatises of the Eighteenth Century', Ph.D. diss., University of Rochester, Eastman School of Music, 1984.

242. Neumann, Frederick, 'La Note Pointée', *RdM*, 51 (1965), 66–92. Trans. as 'The Dotted Note and the So-called French Style', *Early Music*, 5/3 (July 1977), 30–24.

243. —— and Babitz, Sol, 'Correspondence: French Over-dotting', *ML*, 50 (1969), 430–2.

244. Newlin, Dika, 'C. P. E. Bach and Arnold Schoenberg: A Comparison', *The Commonwealth of Music, in Honor of Curt Sachs* (New York: The Free Press, 1965), 300–6.

245. Newman, William S., 'The Keyboard Sonatas of Bach's Sons and their Relationship to the Classic Sonata Concept', *Proceedings for 1949 of the Music Teachers' National Association* (Pittsburgh, Pennsylvania, 1951), 236–48.

246. —— review of item 56, *Notes*, 14/3 (June 1957), 363–4.

247. —— 'Emanuel Bach's Autobiography', *MQ*, 51 (1965), 363–72.

248. —— *The Sonata in the Classic Era*, 3rd edn. (New York: Norton, 1983).

249. Noble, Richard D. C., review of item 20, in *Consort*, 23 (1966), 189–91.

250. Nohl, Ludwig, *Musiker-Briefe* (Leipzig: Duncker und Humblot, 1867; 2nd edn., 1873). English trans. by Lady Wallace as *Letters of Distinguished Musicians: Gluck, Haydn, P. E. Bach, Weber, Mendelssohn* (London: Longmans, Green, 1867).

251. Norman, Gertrude, and Schrifte, Miriam Lubell, eds., *Letters of Composers: An Anthology 1603–1945* (New York: Knopf, 1946), 41–2.

252. Norton, Michael Lee, 'The Sacred Song Arrangements of C. P. E. Bach', MA thesis, Ohio State University, 1976.

253. Oppel, Reinhard, 'Über Beziehungen Beethovens zu Mozart und zu Ph. E. Bach', *ZfM*, 5 (1922/23), 30–9.

254. Ord-Hume, Arthur W. J. G., 'Ornamentation in Mechanical Music', *Early Music*, 11/2 (April 1983), 185–93.

255. Ottenberg, Hans-Günter, 'Carl Philipp Emanuel Bach—Komponist im Umfeld Lessings. Erforschung und Pflege eines wenig bekannten Erbes in der DDR', *MG*, 29 (1979), 144–8.

256. —— 'Zur Fantasieproblematik im Schaffen Carl Philipp Emanuel Bachs', *Studien zu Aufführunggspraxis und Interpretation von Instrumentalmusik des 18. Jahrhunderts—Die Einflüsse einzelner Interpreten und Komponisten des 18. Jahrhunderts auf die Musik ihrer Zeit*, vol. 13 (Blankenburg/Harz, 1980), 74–80.

257. —— 'Annotationen zu einem Konzertsatz von Carl Philipp Emanuel Bach', *Studien zu Aufführunggspraxis und Interpretation von Instrumentalmusik des 18. Jahrhunderts—Die Entwicklung des Solokonzerts im 18. Jahrhundert*, vol. 20 (Blankenburg/Harz, 1982), 16–23.

258. —— *Carl Philipp Emanuel Bach* (Leipzig: Verlag Philipp Reclam jun., 1982). Reviews, items 162, 307, 311, 346, 370. English trans. by Philip Whitmore (Oxford: Oxford University Press, 1987).

258a. —— 'Zur Frage der Authentizität der Choralbearbeitung "Aus der Tiefe rufe ich" (BWV 745)', *BJ*, 72 (1986), 127–30.

259. Otterbach, Friedemann, ed., *Bach. Briefe der Musikerfamilie* (Frankfurt: Fischer, 1985), 95–122.

260. Otto, Hans-Gerald., 'Zwischen Bach und Mozart: zum 250. Geburtstag Carl Philipp Emanuel Bachs', *MG*, 14 (May 1964), 147–8.

261. Paap, Wouter, 'Carl Philipp Emanuel Bach, De Meester Van Het Clavichord', *MM*, 19/4 (April 1964), 98–103.

262. Parkinson, John A., 'Two Notes on C. P. E. Bach: The "Solfeggietto" ', *MT*, 105 (1964), 89.

263. Petsch, Christoph, 'Ein unbekannter Brief von Carl Philipp Emanuel Bach an Ch. G. von Murr in Nurnberg', *AfMw*, 22 (1965), 208–13.

264. Picken, Laurence E. R., 'A Keyboard Fugue by "Bach" ', *PRMA*, 76 (1949–50), 47–57.

265. Pilková, Zdeňka, 'Die Familien Bach und Benda', *Bericht über die Wissenschaftlichen Konferenz zum III. Internationalen Bach-Fest der DDR 1975*, ed. Werner Felix (Leipzig: VEB Deutscher Verlag fur Musik, 1977), 215–21.

266. —— 'Die Cembalosonaten Jiří Bendas und ihre Beziehung zu den Kompositionen C. Ph. E. Bachs Tasteninstrumente', *Cembalo, Clavichord, Orgel: Konferenzbericht der 5. Wissenschaftlichen Arbeitstagung, Blankenburg/Harz, 1. bis 3. Juli 1977*, ed. Eitelfriedrich Thon and Renate Bormann, Studien zur Aufführungspraxis und Interpretation von Instrumentalmusik des 18. Jahrhunderts, 6/1 (Magdeburg: Rat des Bezirkes; Leipzig: Zentralhaus für Kulturarbeit der DDR, 1978), 67–72.

267. Plamenac, Dragan, 'New Light on the Last Years of Carl Philipp Emanuel Bach', *MQ*, 35 (1949), 565–87.

268. Poos, Heinrich, 'Harmoniestruktur und Hermeneutik in C. P. E. Bachs fis-moll-Fantasie', *Bericht über den Internationalen Musikwissenschaftlichen Kongress Berlin 1974*, ed. Hellmut Kühn und Peter Nitsche (Kassel: Bärenreiter, 1980) 319–23.

269. Randebrock, Ekkehard, 'Studien der Klaviersonate Carl Philipp Emanuel Bachs', Ph.D. diss., Westfalische Wilhelms-Universität, 1953.

270. Ratner, Leonard G., 'Ars combinatoria. Chance and Choice in Eighteenth Century Music', *Geiringer Festschrift*, 343–63.

271. Reeser, Eduard, *The Sons of Bach* (Stockholm: Continental Book Company, 1949).

272. Reichardt, Johann Friedrich, 'Noch ein Bruchstück aus J. F. Recihardt's Autobiographie; sein erster Aufenthalt in Hamburg', *AMZ*, 16 (1814), cols. 21–34.

273. Reijen, Paul van, 'De Muziek Aan Het Hof Van Frederick De Grote', *MM*, 21/12 (December 1966), 376–80.

330                    *Bibliography*

274. Répaci, Francesco A., review of item 7, *NRMI*, 8/3 (1974), 462–6.

275. Riefling, Reimar, 'Om Johan Sebastian Bachs aetlinger', *Norsk musiktidsskrift*, 12/4 (December 1975), 137–46.

276. Riemann, Hugo, 'Die Söhne Bachs', *Blätter für Haus- und Kirchenmusik*, 1 (1897), 28–30.

277. —— 'Die Söhne Bachs', *Präludien und Studien*, vol. 3 (Leipzig: H. Seemann, 1901; repr. Hildesheim, G. Olms, 1967), 173–84.

278. Riemer, Otto, Johann Sebastian II: Ein Gedenkblatt für den jüngsten Sohn Philipp Emanuels', *Musica*, 4 (July–August 1950), 270–3.

279. Rifkin, Joshua, ' ''. . . wobey aber die Singstimmen hinlänglich besetzt seyn müssen . . .'': Zum Credo der h-Moll-Messe in der Aufführung Carl Philipp Emanuel Bachs', *Baseler Jahrbuch für Historische Musikpraxis*, 9 (1985), 157–72.

280. Rixman, Eunice Elizabeth, 'The Sacred Cantata ''God hath awakened the Lord'' (''Gott hat den Herrn aufgeweckt'') by Carl Philipp Emanuel Bach, in Relation to its Performance', DMA diss., University of Southern California, 1969.

281. Rochlitz, Friedrich, 'Karl Philipp Emanuel Bach', *Für Freunde der Tonkunst*, vol. 4 (Leipzig: Carl Cnobloch, 1832), 271–316.

282. Rose, Gloria, 'Father and Son: Some Attributions to J. S. Bach by C. P. E. Bach', *Geiringer Festschrift*, 364–9.

283. Rose, Juanelva M., 'The Harmonic Idiom of the Keyboard Works of Carl Philipp Emanuel Bach', Ph.D. diss., University of California at Santa Barbara, 1970.

284. Ruile-Dronke, Jutta, review of item 96, *Mf*, 35 (1982), 93–4.

285. Sachs, Arjeh, 'C. P. E. Bach and his Book (250th Anniversary of his Birth)', (in Hebrew, with English abstract), *Tatzlil: Forum for Music Research and Bibliography* 5 (1965), 93–5, 157.

286. Sadie, Stanley, review of item 20, *MT*, 107 (1966), 35–7.

287. Saint-Foix, Georges de, 'A Propositio della scritto: Torrefranca, La fortuna di Ph. E. Bach nell'ottocento', *RMI*, 26 (1919), 332–7.

288. Salter, Lionel, review of item 7, *Music Teacher*, 54/5 (May 1975), 27.

288a. ——'Which Bach', *Consort*, 42 (1986), 50.

289. Salzer, Felix, 'Über die Bedeutung der Ornamente in Philipp Emanuel Bachs Klavierwerken', *ZfMw*, 12 (1929/30), 398–418.

290. Sams, Eric, review of item 332, *MT*, 127 (1986), 50.

291. Schaal, Richard, review of item 355, *Mf*, 7 (1984), 26–7.

292. Schenker, Heinrich, *Ein Beitrag Zur Ornamentik. Als Einführung zu C. Ph. E. Bachs Klavierwerke* (Vienna: Universal, 1908; repr. Vienna: Universal-Edition, 1954). Trans. as 'A Contribution to the Study of Ornamentation', by Hedi Siegal (''based on a preliminary draft by Carl Parrish''), in *The Music Forum*, 4 (1967), 1–139.

293. —— 'Ph. Em. Bach: Kurze und leichte Klavierstücke mit veränderten Reprisen, (1766), Nr. 1, *Allegro* [H. 193/W. 113, 1]' and 'Ph. Em. Bach: Sonate C-dur (1779) [H. 244/W. 55, 1]. Erster Satz', *Der Tonwille*, 4 (1923), 10–14.

294. Schenkman, Walter, 'Three Representative Collections of Keyboard Works by Carl Philipp Emanuel Bach', DMA diss., Indiana University, 1963.

295. —— 'Three Collections of Keyboard Works by C. P. E. Bach', *Bach* 8/4 (1977), 23–36; 9/1 (1978), 141–50.

296. Schering, Arnold, 'Joh. Phil. Kirnberger als Herausgeber Bachscher Chorale', *BJ*, 15 (1918), 1–14.

297. —— 'C. Ph. E. Bach und das redende Prinzip in der Musik', *Jahrbuch der Musikbibliothek Peters*, 45 (1938), 13–29; also in Schering's *Vom musikalischen Kunstwerk*, ed. F. Blume (Leipzig: Koehler & Amelang, 1949).

298. Schicke, Thorsten P., 'Zum 270. Geburtstag des "Hamburger Bach": Erinnerung an einen vergessenen "Clavier-Ästheten"', *Musik und Kirche*, 54 (1984), 289–90.

299. Schleuning, Peter, *Die Freie Fantasie. Ein Beitrag zur Erforschung der Klaviermusik des 18. Jahrhunderts*, Ph.D. diss., University of Freiburg, 1970; Göppinger Akademische Beiträge, 76 (Göppingen: Kümmerle, 1973).

300. Schmid, Ernst Fritz, *Carl Philipp Emanuel Bach und seine Kammermusik* (Kassel: Bärenreiter, 1931).

301. —— 'Joseph Haydn und Carl Philipp Emanuel Bach', *ZfM*, 14 (1931–2), 299–312.

302. —— 'Carl Philipp Emanuel Bach', *MGG*, vol. 1 (Kassel: Bärenreiter, 1949–51), cols. 924–42.

303. Schmidt, Christopher, 'Philipp Emanuel Bach und das Clavichord', *Schweizerische Musikzeitung*, 92 (1952), 441–6.

304. Schott, Howard, review of item 213, *Galpin Society Journal*, 34 (March 1981), 162–4.

305. Schulenberg, David, *The Instrumental Music of Carl Philipp Emanuel Bach*, Ph.D. diss., State University of New York at Stony Brook, 1982 (Ann Abor: UMI Research Press, 1984). Reviews, items 329, 357.

306. —— 'Composition as Variation: Inquiries into the Compositional Procedures of the Bach Circle of Composers', *CM*, 33 (1982), 57–87.

307. Schulz, Margit, 'Kolloquium zu Carl Philipp Emanuel Bach', *Musikforum*, 29/4 (1984), 29–30; review of item 258, *Musikforum*, 29/2 (1984), 29.

308. —— 'Frankfurt/Oder: Oratorium von Carl Philipp Emanuel Bach erstaufgeführt', *MG*, 35 (1985), 54.

309. Schulze, Hans-Joachim, 'Marginalien zu einigen Bach-Dokumenten', *BJ*, 48 (1961), 79–99.

310. —— review of item 355, *BJ*, 69 (1983), 125–7.

311. —— review of item 258, *BJ*, 70 (1984), 177–8.

312. —— review of item 354, *BJ*, 70 (1984), 181–3.

313. Schünemann, Georg, 'Friedrich Bachs Briefwechsel mit Gerstenberg und Breitkopf', *BJ*, 1 (1916), 20–35.

314. —— *Die Singakademie zu Berlin 1791–1941* (Regensberg: Gustav́ Bosse Verlag, 1941).

315. Selinger-Barber, Renate, 'Die Klavierfantasien Carl Philipp Emanuel Bachs. Studien zur Uberlieferung und Stilistik', MA thesis, Universität Hamburg, 1984.

316. Serbin, Max, 'A. C. P. E. Bach Mystery Story', *American Record Guide*, 24 (September 1957), 7, 33.

317. Sherwood, Anne Kathryn, 'Two Keyboard Sonatas of Johann Christian Bach and Carl Philipp Emanuel Bach: A Historical Perspective', DMA diss., North Texas State University, 1979.

318. Sietz, Reinhold, 'Die Orgelkompositionen des Schulerkreises um Johann Sebastian Bach', *BJ*, 32 (1935), 33–96.

319. Simon, Ernst, *Mechanische Musikinstrumente früherer Zeiten und ihre Musik* (Wiesbaden: Breitkopf & Härtel, 1960), 51–5.

320. Sincero, Dino, 'La "Sonata" di Filippo Emanuele Bach', *RMI*, 5 (1898), 677–9.

321. Sittard, Josef, *Geschichte des Musik- und Konzertwesens in Hamburg* (Altona und Leipzig: Verlag von A. C. Reher 1890; repr. Hildesheim: Olms, 1971), 41–52, 102–13.

322. Smith, Chester Fanning, review of items 77 and 328, *CM*, 9 (1969), 197–200.

323. Sonneck, Oscar Georg, 'Zwei Briefe C. Ph. Em. Bachs an Alexander Reinagle', *SIMG*, 7 (1906/07), 112–14.

324. Stangeland, Robert A., 'Dimensions in Piano Technique', *PQ*, 110 (summer 1980), 40–3; 111 (fall 1980), 32–7.

325. ——, 'Letters', *PQ*, 114 (summer 1981), 4.

326. Steglich, Rudolph, 'Karl Philipp Emanuel Bach und der Dresdner Kreuzkantor Gottfried August Homilius im Musikleben ihrer Zeit', *BJ*, 12 (1915), 39–145.

327. Steiner, Carol, 'Empfindsamkeit', *CM*, 9 (1969), 13–14.

328. Stevens, Jane R., 'The Keyboard Concertos of C. P. E. Bach', Ph.D. diss., Yale University, 1965. Review, item 322.

329. —— review of item 305, *Notes*, 42/1 (September 1985), 55–6.

329a.——'Formal Design in C.P.E. Bach's Harpsichord Concertos', *Studi Musicali*, 15 (1986), 257–97.

330. Stilz, Ernst, 'Über harmonische Ausfüllung in der Klaviermusik des Rokoko', *ZfM*, 13 (1930–1), 11–20.

331. Stockhammer, Robert, 'Philipp Emanuel Bach, Wegbereiter der Wiener Klassik', *Musica*, 18/2 (1964), 83–4.

332. Stoljar, Margaret Mahony, *Poetry and Song in Late Eighteenth Century Germany: A Study in the Musical 'Sturm und Drang'* (London: Croom Helm, 1985). Reviews, items 37, 290.

333. Suchalla, Ernst, *Die Orchestersinfonien Carl Philipp Emanuel Bachs nebst einem thematischen Verzeichnis seiner Orchesterwerke*, Ph.D. diss. Johannes-Gutenberg Universität zu Mainz, 1968 (Augsburg: Blasaditsch, 1968).

334. —— ed., *Briefe von Carl Philipp Emanuel Bach an Johann Gottlob Immanuel Breitkopf und Johann Nikolaus Forkel*, Mainzer Studien zur Musikwissenschaft, vol. 19 (Tutzing: Hans Schneider 1985). Reviews, items 202a, 370.

335. Tegtmeier, Konrad, 'Carl Philipp Emanuel Bachs letzte Ruhestätte', *Deutsche Rundschau*, 249 (October–December 1936), 45–8.

336. Terry, Miriam, 'C. P. E. Bach and J. J. H. Westphal—A Clarification', *JAMS*, 22 (spring, 1969), 106–15.

337. Tetley-Kardos, Richard, review of item 20, *Music Journal*, 25/2 (February 1967), 72.

338. Tishkoff, Doris Patricia, 'Sensibility in the Eighteenth Century as Seen in the Fantasies from the "Für Kenner und Liebhaber" of Carl Philipp Emanuel Bach', Ph.D. diss., Michigan State University, 1983.

339. Todd, R. Larry, 'Joseph Haydn and the Sturm und Drang: A Revaluation', *MR*, 41 (1980), 172–96.

340. Torrefranca, Fausto, 'La fortuna di Ph. E. Bach nellottocento', *RMI*, 25 (1918), 402–47.

341. Town, Stephen, 'Sechs Lieder von Christian Furchtegott Gellert (1715–1769) as set by Carl Philipp Emanuel Bach and Ludwig van Beethoven: A Comparative Analysis', *National Association of Teachers of Singing Bulletin*, 36/5 (1980), 30–6.

342. Uldall, Hans, 'Beiträge zur Frühgeschichte des Klavierkonzerts', *ZfMw*, 10 (1927–8), 139–52.

343. —— *Das Klavierkonzert der Berliner Schule*, Ph.D. diss., Marpurg, 1927; Sammlung musikwissenschaftlicher Einzeldarstellung, 10 (Leipzig: Breitkopf & Härtel, 1928). Review, item 104.

344. Vanhulst, Henri, 'La pratique de l'improvisation d'aprés les traites de clavier de l'empfindsamer Stil', *RBM*, 25 (1971), 108–53.

345. *Verzeichniß des musikalischen Nachlasses des verstorbenen Capellmeisters Carl Philipp Emanuel Bach* (Hamburg: Schniebes, 1790). Repr. in item 225. Fac. edn., item 355.

346. Viertel, Karl-Heinz, review of item 258, *MG*, 34 (November 1984), 609–10.

347. Virga, Patricia Helen, 'Eight Manuscript Sonatas by Carl Philipp Emanuel Bach: A Bibliographic and Stylistic Study', MM thesis, Syracuse University, 1970.

348. Vriesländer, Otto, 'Carl Philipp Emanuel Bach als Klavierkomponist', *Ganymed Jahrbuch*, 4 (1923), 174–91.

349. —— *Carl Philipp Emanuel Bach* (Munich: R. Piper, 1923).

350. —— 'Carl Philipp Emanuel Bach als Theoretiker', *Von Neuer Musik*, 1 (1925), 222–79.

351. Wachs, Morris, 'Diderot's Letters to Carl Philipp Emanuel Bach', *Romanische Forschungen*, 77 (1965), 359–62.

352. Wackernagel, Bettina, *Joseph Haydns frühe Klaviersonaten. Ihre Beziehungen zur Klaviermusik um die Mitte des 18. Jahrhunderts*, Ph.D. diss., Universität Würzburg, 1973 (Würzburger Musikhistorische Beiträge 2, Tutzing: Hans Schneider, 1975).

353. Wade, Rachel W., 'Communication', *JAMS*, 30 (1977), 162–4.

354. —— The Keyboard Concertos of Carl Philipp Emanuel Bach, Ph.D. diss., New York University, 1979 (Ann Arbor: UMI Research Press, 1981). Review, item 312.

355. —— ed., The Catalog of Carl Philipp Emanuel Bach's Estate (New York: Garland, 1981). Reviews, items 28, 291, 310.

356. Wagner, Günter, 'Motivgruppierung in der Expositionsgestaltung bei C. Ph. E. Bach und Beethoven. Zur kompositionsgeschichtlichen Kontinuität im 18. Jahrhundert', Jahrbuch des Staatlichen Instituts für Musikforschung Preußischer Kulturbesitz, (1978), 43–71.

357. —— review of item 305, Mf, 39 (1986), 73–4.

358. Waterman, Muriel Moore, 'The Double Keyboard Concertos of Carl Philipp Emanuel Bach', MM thesis, University of Arizona, 1970.

359. Weiss, Piero, ed., Letters of Composers through Six Centuries (Philadelphia: Chilton, 1967), 104–8, 142–3.

360. Welter, Friedrich, 'Die Musikbibliothek der Sing-Akademie zu Berlin', Sing-Akademie zu Berlin, ed. Werner Bollert (Berlin: Rembrandt Verlag, 1966), 33–47.

361. Werner, Richard Maria, 'Gerstenbergs Briefe an Nicolai nebst einer Antwort Nicolais', Zeitschrift für deutsche Philologie, 23 (1891), 43–67.

362. Westrup, J. A., 'C. P. E. Bach—A Touchstone to Taste', The Listener, 19 (1938), 488–9.

363. Whipple, Weldon Lavon, 'Beethoven's Organ Trios: Authentic or Spurious?' Diapason, 68/8 (July 1977), 1, 8–10.

364. Whitwell, David, 'Bach's Sons—Their Music for Winds', Instrumentalist, 21/8 (March 1967), 53–6.

365. Wien-Claudi, Hertha, Zum Liedschaffen Carl Philipp Emanuel Bachs (Reichenberg: Gebrüder Stiepel, 1928).

366. Wiese, Klaus Martin, 'Oratorium von C. P. E. Bach für die Praxis wiedergewonnen', Musik und Kirche, 44 (1974), 253–4.

367. —— 'Ein neuer Ton im Osterjubel', Gottesdienst und Kirchenmusik, 4 (1974), 130.

368. Wilhelm, Friedrich, 'Briefe an Karl Wilhelm Ramler nebst einem Briefe an Lessing', Vierteljahrschrift für Litteraturgeschichte 4 (1891), 254, 256–7.

369. Williams, Peter, 'The Harpsichord Acciaccatura: Theory and Practice in Harmony, 1650–1750', MQ, 54 (1968), 503–23.

370. Wollenberg, Susan, review of item 258, ML, 65 (1984), 373–6; review of item 334, ML, 69 (1988).

371. Woods, William C., 'The Sounding Board: Variant Versions', Clavier, 13/7 (1974), 4, 26–7.

372. Wotquenne, Alfred, Catalogue thématique des oeuvres de Charles Philippe Emmanuel Bach (1714–1788) (Leipzig: Breitkopf & Härtel, 1905). Repr. as Thematisches Verzeichnis der Werke von C. Ph. E. Bach (Wiesbaden: Breitkopf & Härtel, 1964, 1972, 1980). Review, item 136.

373. Wustmann, Gustav, 'Ein Brief Carl Philipp Emanuel Bach's', ZIMG, 10 (1908), 1–4.

374. Wyler, Robert, *Form- und Stiluntersuchungen zur ersten Satz der Klaviersonaten Carl Philipp Emanuel Bachs*, Ph.D. diss., Universität Zürich, 1960 (Biel: Graphische Anstalt Schüler, 1960).

375. Yeston, Maury, 'Rubato and the Middleground', *JMT*, 19/2 (1975), 286–301.

376. Yoshida, Miwako, 'A Revision of the Score of the Clavier Concertos Wq. 43 by C. P. E. Bach', MA thesis, Ochanomizu University, 1976.

377. Youngman, Hilary P., 'Heirs to Bach's Genius', *Etude*, 68/7 (July 1950), 20, 51.

378. Zeraschi, Helmut, 'Carl Philipp Emanuel Bachs Komposition "für eine Drehorgel" ', *Beiträge zur Musikwissenschaft*, 3/2 (1961), 61–6.

379. Zuber, Barbara, 'Witz und Genialität:Ein Versuch über Carl Philipp Emanuel Bachs Sinfonien', *Neue Zeitschrift für Musik*, 148/3 (March 1987), 4–9.

# Index to Bibliography

# Index of Names

*(Facsimiles and Examples indicated in italic)*

# Index of Works by C. P. E. Bach

*(Facsimiles and Examples indicated in italic)*

## *Concertos and Sonatinas*